SANSKRIT DRAMA
AND
DRAMATURGY

SANSKRIT DRAMA AND DRAMATURGY

Biswanath Bhattacharya

Foreword
Prof. Ramaranjan Mukherji

1994
Sharada Publishing House
DELHI–110052

First Published 1974
Second edition 1994

ISBN : 81–85616–30–2

Published by :
B.L. Bansal
for SHARADA PUBLISHING HOUSE
(Publishers on India's Past and Present)
E–239, Shastri Nagar, Delhi-110052
Phone: 7516539

Printed at:
Garg Offset Works
B–76, Naraina Ind. Area, New Delhi

In the sacred memory of

my parents,

Pandit Taracharan Bhattacharya

and

Shrimati Sumati Devi

FOREWORD

Indian Dramaturgy has a long history of its own: it begins from the speculations of Bharata, the author of the great Natyasastra and winding its course though the thought-currents of many exponents of Dramaturgy finally receives a beautiful treatment at the hands of Visvanatha, the author of the most popular treatise on Poetics, entitled 'Sahityadarpana'. Since Indian literary theory considers Emotion as the centre of gravity of all literary arts, and believes in the principle that, for the presentation of Emotion the literary artists are required to take care of the excitant and the ensuent, the permanent feeling and the accessories, without the assistance of which the central feeling cannot be communicated and a platform for the grand confrontation between the universalised subject and the generalised object of experience cannot be constructed. The duty of the literary artists, therefore, is to construct poetical paintings, competent to introduce to the connoisseur the generalised excitant and ensuent, as also the universalised permanent and transient moods. It is to signify these factors, that are responsible for attainment of Aesthetic Experience that the expression "Objective Co-relative" has been employed by no less a critic than T.S. Eliot, the most profound literary artist-cum-critic of the twentieth century.

All along Sanskrit Dramaturgy has been considered as an essential component of Sanskrit Poetics, because, while Sanskrit Poetics in general has tried to emphasise the process of Aesthetic Experience presented through the medium of Poetry in general, Sanskrit Dramaturgy has attemped to expound the process when presented through the medium of

Drama, where, apart from the music of sound and sense, the visual effect makes itself felt to a great extent.

The traditional division of Poetry into two types,—that which is capable of being presented on board and that which is capable of being read out and heard springs from the role played by visual effect in appreciation of a specimen of Poetic Art. While Sanskrit Poetics in general can fulfil its obligations by analysing the process of Aesthetic Experience and expounding the three-tier functions of expression through which the primary, the figurative and the implicit contents are raised into comprehension, as also by identifying the literary excellence and the poetic embellishments, that are employed by literary artists to impart charmingness to the poetic texture, Sanskrit Dramaturgy is required to analyse in details the plot and its divisions, the different stages in its development, moving through which the main incident in the plot reaches denouement starting from an embryonic state,—that is to say, a state which is referred to as the seed or the germ of the plot. It is required also to expend its energy in analysing the different techniques of acting, that are to be employed for presentation of different types of Plays, projecting diverse predominent emotional moods. The task of an exponent of Sanskrit Dramaturgy, therefore, is more difficult than that of an expounder of Sanskrit Poetics.

Though much has been said of Sanskrit Poetics through the medium of English and the concepts projected by Sanskrit Poetics have been made known to the Western World through the efforts of Dr. P.V. Kane, Dr. S.K. De, Dr. V. Raghavan, and such other stalwarts, the area of Sanskrit Dramaturgy has remained in the cool shade of neglect for a pretty long time and large number of serious attempts have not been made to project these concepts and to trace the similarity and distinction between the concepts presented by Indian Dramaturgy and those presented by Western Dramaturgy, available in the works of Aristotle and Butcher. It is refreshing to note that Professor Biswanath Bhattacharya of Banaras Hindu University has chosen a comprehensive analysis of Sanskrit Dramaturgy as the subject matter of his magnum opus entitled "Sanskrit Drama and Dramaturgy" and has presented all the concepts tackled by numerous writers on Indian Dramaturgy through the medium of English. Dr. Bhattacharya has also tried to make a comparative estimate of the thought-currents introduced by Indian Dramaturgy and those projected by Western Dramaturgy with reference to the original texts belonging to both these disciplines. The deep penetration of Dr. Bhattacharya into all the original texts dealing with Indian Dramaturgy and Western Dramaturgy has helped him in making this comparative analysis as clear as possible: it has also been successful in presenting to the critical world the fact that Sanskrit Dramaturgy could reach a height, that eluded tight grasp of Western Dramaturgy.

The book 'Sanskrit Drama and Dramaturgy' has another great value also. The analysis of the characteristic features of the successful specimens of Dramatic Art, as presented by Dr. Bhattacharya through the medium of English is likely to give a clue to the searching students to adjudicate the dramatic value of the Western Dramas through application of Indian yard-sticks, and similarly to evaluate Sanskrit Dramas through application of Western principles of evaluation. The book, therefore, is going to be acclaimed by the critical world as a significant source book, competent to open a new arena of knowledge namely the arena of Comparative Dramaturgy. An analysis of this work is also likely to develop a new principle of dramatic evaluation by dove-tailing the principles of Indian criticism and Western criticism. I congratulate Dr. Bisvanath Bhattacharya for this magnificent work which has not only enriched the stock of human knowledge, but has tremendous potentialities of opening new chambers of knowledge, and welcome the new edition of "Sanskrit Drama and Dramaturgy" to the area of Indological studies.

Calcutta

Ramaranjan Mukherji
20. 8. 93

(Prof. Ramaranjan Mukherji)

PREFACE

The present work embodies, in the main, the author's research on the evolution of dramatic technique, on the basis of works on dramaturgy in Sanskrit and its application by the playwrights. The period covered stretches from the antiquity and ends with *circa* thirteenth century A. D. which may conclusively be taken as the period marked by decadence, the process of which had already set in.

Beginning from Bharata down to Viśvanātha, there are many remarkable treatises on the dramatic art that present interesting and varied viewpoints, in spite of their general adherence to Bharatan tenets. It is this divergence that requires greater attention than the uniformity of ideas, as it proves beyond doubt the urge to solve the problems that any living tradition of drama has to face. A critical and comparative study of all these reveals the position of dramatic art in different ages, and is useful in appreciating the development of the technical aspect of Sanskrit drama.

Dramaturgy as such rests entirely on the drama and so a study of one is incomplete without that of the other. Dramatic principles, however perfect and well-expounded they may be, are bound to remain hypothetical if not applied in actual practice by the playwrights. Keeping this in view, the present work has been divided into two parts. The first part deals with the theoretical viewpoints of the codifiers on the nature of drama, the structure, the Preliminaries and the dramatic style. The whole gamut of dramatic theory up to the 13th century has been subjected to a critical assessment and the approach has been new in so far as the focus has been consistently upon the requirements of the practising playwright. Drama being a performing art, its norms and conventions need an evaluation on the basis of their practicality.

The second part deals with technique and its application and comprises an assessment of all the major varieties of drama right from Aśvaghoṣa to Murāri, with whom decadence sets in. Kṛṣṇa Miśra has been taken up, although he belongs to the period of decadence, only because he ushers in or, to be more accurate, revives the symbolic trend.

Prakaraṇa, Nāṭikā, Bhāṇa, Prahasana, Vyāyoga, the other neglected varieties and also the additional varieties, known as Upa-rūpakas, have also been treated in separate sections under the study of technique and its application. The last chapter presents a comparative study of the dramatic practice in Greece and India. On the basis of *Oedipus the King* of Sophocles and *Ūrubhaṅga* of Bhāsa, the two methods have been compared and conclusions deduced therefrom on the basis of accepted canons of comparative criticism.

The goal of the present work is attained, it can be said, in this respect that it presents all the extant views regarding the drama and attemps to point out the factors that led to their formation. Drama as it was viewed by the different critics in different ages has been shown in great detail. How the living tradition of dramatic art conditioned certain later formulations is also pointed out. Thus the work traces the development of dramaturgy simultaneously with drama, presenting at the same time a critical estimation of the dramatic technique as formulated by different Codifiers.

It is hoped that the present work will open up the way for newer and more intensive study of dramatic technique in Sanskrit. The work is expected to pave the path for a more detailed study of all the various varieties of Sanskrit drama *vis-a-vis* the development of technique. The classical Sanskrit drama has its *forte* in its technical excellence and the problem of appreciation is inseparably linked with a proper knowledge of the technique. Only a poetic appreciation of the Sanskrit drama, as has been done so far, is bound to be unscientific and lop-sided. It is felt that the present approach will make the problem of appreciation smoother and more fruitful.

ACKNOWLEDGEMENTS

The author likes to put on record his heartfelt gratitude to Dr. Suryakant, formerly Muyurbhanj Professor of Sanskrit at the Banaras Hindu University under whose guidance the work was prepared. The author is highly grateful to Dr. Ramaranjan Mukherji, former Vice-Chancellor, Universities of Burdwan and Rabindra Bharati and presently Chancellor, Rashtriya Sanskrit Vidyapeeth (Deemed University), Tirupati for kindly writing a foreword to this edition.

The author is under a deep debt of gratefulness to all the scholars in general, whose ideas inspired him and in particular to *Mahamahopadhyaya* Gopinath Kaviraj, Prof. K.P. Mukherji, Ex-Reader in English, B.H.U., Dr. Ramji Upadhyaya, Ex-Professor of Sanskrit, and Prof. S. Mallikarjunan, ex-Reader in English, Dr. Harisingh Gaur Vishwavidyalaya, Sagar. Guidance, encouragement and assistance received from these scholars provided the chief sustenance to the author at all the stages of writing. The author is thankful to Madhubala Trivedi, who prepared the index.

Lastly the author is thankful to Sh. B.L. Bansal proprietor M/s Sharada Publishing House, Delhi who agreed to publish this edition.

BISWANATH BHATTACHARYA

CONTENTS

PART I
THEORETICAL VIEWPOINTS OF CODIFIERS

PART II
TECHNIQUE AND ITS APPLICATION

ABBREVIATIONS

AP.	Agnipurāṇa.
AS.	Abhijñāna Śākuntala.
BP.	Bhāvaprakāśana, Baroda, 1929.
Dhv.	Dhvanyāloka, Chowkhamba, Varanasi, 1940.
DR.	Daśarūpaka.
HIL.	History of Indian Literature, M. Winternitz, Calcutta.
HSL.	History of Sanskrit Literature, Dasgupta & De, Calcutta.
IA.	Indian Antiquary.
IHQ.	Indian Historical Quarterly.
JAOS. JOAOS.	Journal of the American Oriental Society.
JGJRI.	Journal of Ganganath Jha Research Institute.
JOR.	Journal of Oriental Research, Madras.
MR.	Mudrārākṣasa.
ND.	Nāṭyadarpaṇa, Baroda, 1929.
NLRK.	Nāṭakalakṣaṇaratnakośa.
NŚ.	Nāṭyaśāstra, Chowkhamba, Varanasi, 1929.
Rat.	Ratnāvalī.
SD.	Sāhityadarpaṇa, Bombay.
UR.	Uttararāmacarita.
VS.	Veṇīsaṃhāra.

PART I

CHAPTER I

THE FUNDAMENTALS

Drama as a Form of Literature

Dramatic literature occupies a significant place in the domain of literary output. Not only does it occupy a large space in the libraries, but has also its deep and sacred station in the hearts of millions. Even in modern days, on looking at the thronging crowds at the theatre, we realise the truth of Bharata's saying that drama arose out of the desire of the gods who prayed to Brahman in these terms 'we want an object of diversion which must be audible as well as visible.' The prophecy regarding drama by the Creator receives confirmation from this fact as well. In appeasing the angry demons Brahman stated that drama was not a monopoly of the gods alone, that all the ideas could be presented through it, and that everyone, whether in sorrow, weariness or bereavement, or even a sage who has transcended such mortal afflictions would find solace and rest in the drama.[1]

This vast scope has made the drama what it is. In it we find royal personalities like Duṣyanta and Rāmabhadra, noble characters like Cārudatta, great sages like Kaṇva and Durvāsas, illustrious ladies like Śakuntalā and Sītā as well as innumerable types of the common folk. In fact, drama includes in its sphere so easily and charmingly the utmost sublimity and the commonest trivialities; so easily does it

---

1. NŚ. I. 111–112

दुःखार्तानां श्रमार्तानां शोकार्तानां तपस्विनाम् ।
विश्रामजननं लोके नाट्यमेतद्भविष्यति ॥

rise to the highest peak of human grandeur, and descend to the pit of buffoonery; it is so closely associated with the consciousness of the society that in the words of Allardyce Nicoll, the drama is 'at once the most peculiar, the most elusive, and the most enthralling of all types of literature.'[2]

This unique and all-influencing character of drama did not escape the notice of the Indian mind and we have evidence of the great regard it enjoyed as an art-form. Drama claims its origin in the oldest book of the Indo-Aryans, the Vedas. Bharata says[3]—'Brahman took the Recitative from the Ṛgveda, the Song from the Sāman, the Histrionic Representation from the Yajus and the Sentiments from the Atharvan.' All the four sacred Vedas were churned, so to say, by Brahman to create this new art-form. The Indian mind has always been religious without being dogmatic, and so Aesthetics and Poeties had no quarrel with Ethics and Philosophy in ancient India. Drama, like the other arts, accepted its relationship to, and its duty towards religion and morality. It aimed at removing evil and vindicating truth, goodness and beauty. And in this task, it was more effective than the other art-forms insofar as it was the only audio-visual art (dṛśyaṃ śravyaṃ ca), and its representation of life, therefore, the more immediate and persuasive.

Theories on drama began as early as the first or

---

2. Theory of Drama, Allardyce Nicoll, p.7.
3. NS. I. 17

जग्राह पाठ्यमृग्वेदात् सामभ्यो गीतमेव च ।
यजुर्वेदादभिनयान् रसानाथर्वणादपि ॥

second century B. C. Unfortunately the dramatic compositions on which the generalisations rested could not escape the ravages of time. The theories, however, prove their definite existence. The first and the greatest of the theorists, Bharata, and his commentators provide us with a valuable study of the development of drama and dramatic theory; and the increasing importance given to drama is felt from the fact that critics like Sāgaranandin (early 10th century), Dhanañjaya (10th century), Rāmacandra and Guṇacandra (12th century) and Śāradātanaya (1175–1200 A.D.), besides many others, carried on the discussion of the various theories and wrote criticism of the extant drama. It was natural, therefore, that following the lead of Abhinava gupta, to whom goes chiefly the credit of establishing the Rasa theory of the Dramaturgic school in relation to general literature, Viśvanātha (1300–84 A.D.) included drma for the first time in his treatise on poetics, the Sāhityadarpaṇa.

Imitation and Drama

Modern Psychology allots an important place to imitation as is obvious from the observations of William James and others.[4] Apart from the important part it plays

---

4. 'And from this time (i. e. infancy) onward man is essentially the imitative animal. His whole educability and in fact the whole history of civilisation depend on this trait, which his strong tendencies to rivalry, jealousy and acquisitiveness reinforce.' The Principles of Psychology, Vol. II, p. 408.

'Imitation, at first biological, then reflective, is in fact but the first stage in the creation of individuality, and the richer the scope for imitation the richer the developed individuality will be.' —Sir T. P. Nunn, Education, its——and first Principles (3rd. Edition 1945) p. 157.

in the execution of the individual's social and mental uplift-ment, imitation is and has always been the basis of literature in general. The poet and the novelist both imitate the actions of men and the incidents in which they are involved in terms of words, rhythmical or prosaic. The dramatist also depicts life in action, which he selects from the world and as such his art is also imitative in essence. The relation of imitation with drama has been recognised both in the east and the west. We have the definition of tragedy by Aristotle, to whom it was the only dramatic form of worth, as the 'imitation of an action that is serious.'

The sage Bharata defines drama as an imitation of action in these words—[5]

> 'The drama is an imitation of the Emotions (bhāva) of the three worlds.'
>
> 'The drama has been devised by me as an imitation of actions and conducts of people.'
>
> 'An imitation of the world with its seven divisions has been made the basis of drama.'

Later critics also define drama as 'the imitation of situations.'[6] From these observations it becomes clear that drama as a distinct form of literature is one with the other forms of literature as far as imitation is concerned. What, then, are the special features of a drama which distinguish

---

5. NŚ. I. 103, 109, 118.

त्रैलोक्यस्यास्य सर्वस्य नाट्यं भावानुकीर्तनम् ।
लोकवृत्तानुकरणं नाट्यमेतन् मया कृतम् ।।
सप्तद्वीपानुकरणं नाट्ये ह्यस्मिन् प्रतिष्ठितम् ।

6. DR. I.7. अवस्थानुकृतिर्नाट्यम् ।

it from other literary forms ? In short, the question resolves itself into 'What is drama?

"Lokavṛttānukaraṇa", mere imitation of people's actions and conducts serves the purpose, though the definition seems too wide. To make it precise we must hit upon some other characteristic features of the drama as a form of literature. Bharata gives us a clue. It is the fact of 'prayoga', presentation. The first play that was performed by Bharata and his sons in heaven in the presence of the gods was one depicting the defeat of the demons by the gods.[7] This with its corollary of an audience before which it is presented, defines the special nature of dramatic 'imitation.' We may conclude that 'drama is an imitation of action which is meant for presentation before an audience. This presentation must not be narrative but should be capable of interpretation. A drama as a distinct literary form must then have these features. There should be imitation of life and action, capable of being interpreted by the actors through acting (abhinaya) in order to please an audience.

Difference of the drama from other literary forms

From the discussion above we can distinguish drama from other literary types : Mahākāvya, Kathā, Ākhyāyikā, etc., though all these are one so far Rasa is concerned. The drama as a form of literature, on the other hand, presupposes 'abhinaya', acting which is typical to it. The dramatist will take his characters from the world (Nāṭakaṃ

---

7. Vide NŚ. 1. 58

तदन्तेऽनुकृतिर्बद्धा यथा दैत्याः सुरैर्जिताः ।

khyātavṛttaṃ syāt) but the exact presentation of the scenes of life would be disliked by the audience. To copy is not the function of the dramatist, he is to imitate. The dramatist is at liberty to take any natural scene or episode of daily life, but in order to make it drama, he must employ devices to endow a significance to the ordinary episodes so that it may transport the Real (laukika) into the Ideal calaukika). The devices, which a playright makes use of, are called dramatic conventions. These conventions, when related to plot, may be named technique and all these depend upon the stage, the play, and the audience.

We have seen that an additional charm in the drama is due to its 'visibility'. The Kāvyas, Kathās, etc. please the reader but only through the ear. There is a marked difference between them and the drama in this respect. The actors through their acting make drama more appealing. Being at the same time both 'audible' and 'visible', drama has of necessity a difference in its plot as well. A Mahākāvya can never be transformed into a drama only by assigning some portions to certain characters. The story to be told in a drama must be '*dramatic*' in nature. The word '*dramatic*' is popular and the meaning of it is 'something striking'. We often read in newspapers of many dramatic episodes as of a man, for long away from his own brother, meeting him in a distant part of the country suddenly, and their recognition and union. Drama also provides such striking coincidences, and there is the strong convention that at the end Marvellous Sentiment (adbhuta rasa) should find a place to arouse a feeling of wonder in the spectators.

The object of dramatic representation

The drama thus aims at presenting the illustrious

lives of remarkable men through the display of various Sentiments. Mention has already been made of the fact that drama shares the same ideal with the other forms of literature in general i.e. instructing some moral truth that may ennoble the life and character of its votaries. This instruction (upadeśa) of moral truth or useful knowledge, however, must be indirect in literature. All the theorists and literary critics observe that the instruction of the poets must not be plain or direct as that of a teacher or of the Scriptures. The poet is not to state but to suggest the cherished moral values. This difference between the method of teaching of the poet and that of the teacher underlines the importance of the Sentiments in literature. The poet appeals to, and arouses the Sentiments of men who, through a relish of their own Sentiments, reach at the truth suggested by the poet, imagining it their own. The ironical comment of Dhañanjaya[8] on the advocate of knowledge in drama is nicely expressed—'Homage to him, for he has averted his face from what is delightful !'

It may be noted, however, that the joy offered by the drama to the audience, must be moral in essenee; otherwise it would fail in its mission of entertaining people. Immorality can never entertain the mind permamently even if it may succeed in pleasing a limited number for a limited period. The faculties of the mind being inter-related, it is not possible to enjoy anything without satisfying the cognitive faculty which chooses between the good and evil.

Thus drama aims at entertaining the mind and,

---

8. DR. I. 6.

through that, imparts some moral lesson, the effect of which ennobles life and character. This is done by arousing the Sentiments in the spectators, leading to Rasa-realisation. The question of Rasa is fundamental in drama, and so its relation and importance should be investigated.

Rasa and the Drama.

Admittedly the theory of Rasa is the unique contribution of what may be called the Nāṭaka School, foundtd chiefly by Bharata and his followers. Abhinavagupta and Śāradātanaya refer, in their works, to the Dvādasa-sāhasrī, the Nāṭyaveda, and to Sadāśiva, Brahman and some other theorists; however, we have no information about these books and authors except for these references. Whatever may have been the theory of Rasa before the advent of Bharata about the first century B. C., it received a definite and logical shape in the Nāṭyaśāstra in the form of a Sūtra—[9]

'Vibhāvānubhāvavyabhicārisamyogād rasaniṣpattiḥ. The Senctiment is evolved by the combination of the Determinants (vibhāva), the Consequents (anubhāva) and the Transitory Feelings (vyabhicāribhāva).'

That a school of dramaturgy had existed long before the Alaṃkāra school, is clear from the fact that Pāṇini mentions some of the Sūtrakāras, viz. Śilālin and Kṛśāśva in his Aṣṭādhyāyī,[10] while no such mention of schools of Pocties is found. From this we may perhaps infer that the Dramaturgic school is older than the Poetic school. Even as early as Bharata's time there existed the idea of Rasa; and along with it may have existed the idea that Rasa is

---

9. N S VI. p.71.
10. 4. 3. 110–111.

to be sought chiefly in literary products. But Bharata was the first to establish Rasa as the essence of drama with theoretical exactitude. The later rhetoricians took the clue from him and assigned vital importance to it. Rasa came to be treated as the soul (ātman) of all poetic creations. Moreover, Bharata made the excellences (guṇas) and the figures of speech (alaṃkāras) subservient to Rasa, and was perhaps the first to enumerate poetic excellences in a list that has not since been improved upon.

This relation of Rasa with drama has been discussed elaborately by the commentators of Bharata—Lollaṭa, Śaṅkuka, Bhaṭṭa Nāyaka and Abhinavagupta. Of these the earlier three constitute what is called the Rasa School. Although their works are no more extant, their views, preserved in the later treatises, show the gradual growth of the concept of Rasa. Abhinavagupta, the most important commentator of the Nāṭyaśāstra was at the same time the greatest exponent of the Dhvani–theory. As the commentator of both the Nāṭyaśāstra and the Dhvanyāloka, Adhinavagupta served as a bridge, as it were, and established convincingly the view of Dhvanikāra that since Sentiment is the soul of poetry, the suggestion of Sentiment is the highest poetic art. As a result Dramaturgy, though formulat edseparately, got incorporated into Poetics in the course of time.

The credit for this must obviously be given to the Dramaturgic school (Bharata and his followers) and not to the earlier rhetoricians, Bhāmaha, Daṇḍin and others, to whom Rasa was not so important. These chose to treat Rasa only as one of the figures of speech (alaṃkāra) while the dramaturgists gave it a central place as the very soul of poetry and the very object of the poet's art, and the end towards which all figures of speech were to minister.

From the discussion above it is clear that the idea of Rasa was first conceived of by the dramaturgists and it was they who considered Nāṭaka or drama as the fittest vehicle of Rasa. The supernormal (alaukika) and unique character of Rasa, and the psychology working behind the realisation of it were discussed clearly by the followers of Bharata. The *Utpattivāda* of Lollaṭa, the *Anumitivāda* of Śaṅkuka and the *Bhuktivāda* of Bhaṭṭa Nāyaka present the gradual evolution of ideas regarding the realisation of Rasa. These scholars use the drama to illustrate the function of Rasa and even Abhinava, the great master of the Dhvani school, uses drama to illustrate his theory of suggestion (vyañjanā) in the realisation of Rasa. Thus Rasa was first conceived of as belonging to drama, and it was only much later that Rasa came to be included by the Dhvanivādins in their *'dhvani'* which according to them constituted the soul of poetry.[11]

We may now discuss how the dramaturgists came to accept the awakening of Rase as the principal function and how they applied it to drama.

Nāṭyaśāstra says—[12]

"As from the seed comes out the tree, from the tree come the flowers and fruits, so all the Sentiments (rasas) are the seed and the Emotions (bhāvas) dwell in them."

This simile of a tree and the consummation of it into flowers and fruits explains the process and function of Rasa

---

11. Cf. काव्यस्यात्मा ध्वनिः--- Dhv.; वाक्यं रसात्मकं काव्यम्—SD.

12. NŚ. VI. 308 यथा बीजाद् भवेद् वृक्षो वृक्षात् पुष्पं फलं यथा
तथा मूलं रसा सर्वे तेषु भावा व्यवस्थिताः ।

in the domain of drama. The simile is apt inasmuch as we cannot give preference to either the seed or the tree over the other. Both are equally important, and so both the Sentiments (rasa) and the Emotions (bhāva) together effect the Rasa-realisation. The Dominant Emotions (sthāyi) the Transitory feelings (vyabhicārin) and the Temperamental States (sāttvika) are as indispensable as are the Sentiments, the Erotic, the Comic, etc. resulting from them. With these are related the four kinds of histrionic representation—Words (vācika), Gestures (aṅgika), Representation of the Temperament (sāttvika) and Costume and Make-up (āhārya).

Bharata clearly points out that Rasa is a concept of the dramaturgic school exclusively. Not merely does he state[13] that 'these eight are the Sentiments recognised in drama' and 'these are the eight Sentiments spoken by Brahman, the great' but further adds, in the course of explaining the tasteability (āsvādyatā) of Rasa, that as the 'well-disposed persons while eating food cooked with many kinds of spices enjoy its taste (rasa) and attain pleasure and satisfaction so do the cultured spectators taste the Domimant Emotions (sthāyi-bhāvas) histrionically represented by Words, Gestures and Temperament. That is why these are called the dramatic Rasas.'[14]

---

13. Ibid. VI. 15–16.........अष्टौ नाट्ये रसा स्मृयाः।
एते ह्यष्टौ रसाः प्रोक्ता द्रुहिणेन महात्मना।

14. Ibid. VI. 13

यथा हि नानाव्यञ्जनसंस्कृतमन्नं भुञ्जाना रसानास्वादयन्ति सुमनसः पुरुषाः हर्षादींश्चाधिगच्छन्ति तथा नानाभावाभिनयव्यञ्जितान् वागङ्गसत्त्वोपेतान् स्थायिभावानास्वादयन्ति सुमनसः प्रेक्षकाः । तस्मान् नाट्यरसा इति व्याख्याताः।

The process of Rasa-realisation may be summed up here. It is the Emotions that are basic in Rasa. There are eight Dominant Emotions (sthāyi-bhāva)—Love (rati), Mirth (hāsa), Sorrow (śoka), Anger (krodha), Energy (utsāha), Terror (bhaya), Disgust (jugupsā) and Astonishment (vismaya). When these are stimulated in the cultured spectators through the representation of the Determinants (vibhāva), the Consequents (anubhāva), the Transitory feelings (vyabhicārin) and the Temperamental states (sāttvika-bhāva) typical to them by means of the four-fold histrionic device they are relished as the Sentiments (rasa). Thus the eight Dominant Emotions result in eight Sentiments—the Erotic (śṛṅgāra) from Love, the Comic (hāsya) from Mirth, the Pathetic (karuṇa) from Sorrow, the Furious (raudra) from Anger, the Heroic (vīra) from Energy, the Terrible (bhayānaka) from Terror, the Odious (bībhatsa) from Disgust and the Marvellous (adbhuta) from Astonishment.

The Determinants, the Consequents, including those relating to Temperament, and the Transitory feelings typical to each of the Emotions, are enumerated in detail in the *Nāṭyaśāstra* along with the appropriate mode of their representation. The total number of the Transitory feelings is thirty-three, and that of the Temperamental States, eight.

The Determinants are of two kinds—Fundamental (ālambana) and Excitant (uddīpana). The Fundamental Determinants are the Hero, the Heroine and other characters without whom the Sentiment would not be aroused at all. The Excitant Determinants, on the other hand, are the circumstances of time and place that foster the Sentiment aroused. The Consequents are external manifestations of feeling through which the actors exhibit the minds and hearts of the persons of the drama. The eight Temperamental states are, strictly speaking, a separate class of the Consequents—that aim at showing the impact of the feeling on the character.

How the simile of seed, tree, flower and fruit has been used to exemplify the fulfilment of the dramatic plot, and how it has given rise to the five Junctures (sandhis) and other technicalities will be considerded later.

CHAPTER II
DRAMA AND THE DRAMATIST

A Definition of Drama

Dramatic technique is an implement in the hands of the dramatist to execute his artistic function. A correct knowledge and the right use of technique contribute to the success of the playwright. Excepting the infusion of Rasa into the drama, the technique gives to the drama everything else. In other words, technique prepares the body but it cannot give life to it. Rasa, the life of drama, is the creation of genius, which is innate. So in discussing the method of the dramatic artist, we can only judge the technique, and see how and where it helps him.

From the foregoing discussion of the nature of drama a definition can be formulated. By saying, 'Drama is the imitation of actions and conduct of people' (lokavṛttānu-karaṇaṃ nāṭyam), all is not said. Mere imitation cannot give any pleasure—this fact is already accepted and moreover, mere imitation alone cannot distinguish drama as a special form of literature. We may devise a definition of drama by taking up its features point by point. These are—

1. Drama, unlike the Kathā, the Ākhyāyikā, etc., operates in a limited space.
2. All the events have a practical (demonstrational) value.
3. The events are to be distributed among the Acts so as to secure suspense and a continuity of interest.
4. Everything—even sentiments and emotions—is to be displayed by the actions and speech of the

characters in drama.

5. Nowhere should the dramatist come forward to speak out anything as may be done in the Kathā, the Ākhyāyikā, etc.
6. The dramatist should be very careful in suggesting the proper Sentiment throughout the play.
7. The chief plot must not get eclipsed by subsidiary plots or characters.
8. The number of characters is also limited with definite functions—to help develop the play or embellish certain parts of it.
9. The dramatist has to deal carefully with the unsavoury (nīrasa) matter, which nevertheless may be useful.
10. The dramatist must not impose his self in an obtrusive manner.

These are the limitations under which a dramatist has to work. His is the most difficult task of complete self-effacement. Whatever he wishes to say, he must make his characters speak it out. He must avoid the limelight and explain all points, otherwise obscure, through mouthpieces. Moreover, he must be careful about the stageability of the piece (abhineyatva).

Keeping in view all these points, we can define a drama in the following words—'Drama is that form of literature which can be staged by the actors; which is divided into Acts that are neither too long nor too short; the action of which has to undergo several stages to reach the climax; which must not show anything unpleasant; which is free from all comments of the author, the plot of which depicts the nobility of a particular type of character leading to Rasa–realization, by the Spectators.' Such a descriptive definition will remove those difficulties which crop up from the preliminary definition 'Avasthānukṛtir nāṭyam' and such others. Imitation there is, no doubt, but it is no crude imitation. The crudity vanishes by the act of selecting the subject matter. Whenever a dramatist selects a certain event from life, the event thus separated from its context, ceases to be matter of fact. It enters into the ideal world of the poet.

The three prime factors in the composition of Drama :

Apparently in the composition of a drama the dramatist is of the highest importance. Next are the actors who infuse life into the play and work out the Rasa–realization with its useful effect of vindicating the victory of the righteous, as says Bharata, the Ādiguru[1]—'the drama, will educate people.' The last but not the least important factor is the audience, the 'Sahṛdayas' without whom the playwright's skill and the actors' histrionic acumen must go in vain. Without them the dramatist must get ridicule and shame by presenting his piece to 'arasikas' the usual consequence of 'casting pearls before swine.' They are so important that Bharata describes the qualities of the 'prekṣaka' (audience) at length in the twenty seventh chapter.

The Dramatist

From the very definition of drama, it becomes clear that the dramatist has no scope to parade his personal learning or likes or dislikes in his composition. In consequence, even the direction of the movement of the different characters is to be done by the words of the characters

---

1. NŚ. I. 111 हितोपदेशजननं नाट्यमेतद् भविष्यति ।

themselves. So we find no directions in the Sanskrit drama excepting very short sentences as 'Enter Sūtradhāra after the benediction,' 'Enter King as indicated,' 'Going out, enter again,' 'Aside' or the like. Very long and minute stage directions as is seen in the dramas of George Bernard Shaw or modern English plays are undramatic according to Indian thinkers. The dramatist must be so very skilful as to denote the entire background through the very words of the characters themselves. If he takes the help of any other means outside the field of his plot, even from himself, he is to be considered as a teller of stories. The very statements of the men in action in the drama must be so formed that these may abolish the necessity of speaking or explaining on the part of the Dramatist who himself is an outsider. In fact, it is the consummation of the dramatist's skill that he never speaks but whatever he wishes to speak or suggest is done by his characters. This skill of the dramatist we have denoted as the effacement of his individuality. A dramatist must be a non-entity in the drama. This quality of the dramatic artist differentiates him from the writer of a novel. To clear up any obscure point in a novel, the novelist can enter into the field easily to clear it up but the dramatist cannot. This singularity and the total unobtrusiveness of the dramatist are the distinguished features of the great dramatic artists like Bhāsa, Kālidāsa, Śūdraka, etc.

With this quality of self-effacement the dramatist must possess another quality which is restraint of speech. He must not use the drama as a means to parade his poetic power. The plot of the drama being all important, this tendency must be deprecated. Rightly do Rāmacandra and Guṇacandra criticise this, saying : 'Futile description of the sea, etc. should not be resorted to, in order to satisfy mere

2

poetic fancy.'[2] The description of nature in feeling phrases is not prohibited but whenever this takes the upper hand over the plot and checks the advance of the action it is ridiculed as 'kāvya-kaṇḍū', the itching of poetry. So the dramatist must have this restraint or in other words, he must have a good sense of proportion (aucityajñāna). In order to give free scope for Rasa-realisation in the drama, he must not forget the secret (upaniṣat) of Rasa which is 'aucitya.' As Ācārya Ānandavardhana says[3]—'Save impropriety, nothing can spoil the relish. Conformity to well-established propriety is the greatest secret of Rasa.' Whatever a dramatist puts in the mouth of his characters, or makes him do, should satisfy the sense of propriety. This sense of propriety, of course, is not an absolute one but depends on the events displayed and the characters introduced. If, for example, the dramatist presents Rāma as the ideal man, he cannot assign to him abusive speech even under provocation, and has to obliterate the killing of Vālin by him stealthily, a mean act as has been done by Bhavabhūti. In doing so, the dramatist does not follow the source but maintains propriety. From this, it follows that the dramatist must be very careful in presenting even the famous legends, and in order to suggest the proper Sentiment present his characters so skilfully that they fit in well with the circumstances. The suggestion of Sentiment being his chief aim, he is to be guided by the sense of

2. ND. I. p. 32

सिन्ध्वादिकं हि काव्यकण्डूवशात् निष्फलं न वर्णनीयम् ।

3. Dhv. III. p. 330

अनौचित्यादृते नान्यद् रसभङ्गस्य कारणम् ।
प्रसिद्धौचित्यबन्धस्तु रसस्योपनिषत् परा ॥

proportion proper to the suggestion. His characters should act and speak in conformity with the suggested Sentiment.

The dramatist must, of necessity, be a lover of life and this world. An ascetic (Saṃnyāsin), engaged as he always is in seeking the Reality (Tattvajñāna) behind this vast universe, can never depict life in its fulness. The charming love-sports of Duṣyanta and Śakuntalā are meaningless to the heart which contemplates the final truth of 'Brahma satyaṃ jagan mithyā.' This love of human life with its successes and failures, hopes and despairs-yearnings and achievements is the basis of all poetic enter, prise, and this the dramatist shares in common with the poet. This makes the dramatist a Prajāpati, a Creator, as is the poet. This love of human life has been described in a sublime verse by Ācārya Ānandavardhana. He says–[4] 'In the endless world of poetry, the poet only is the Creator. This world changes according to his wishes. If the poet is a lover of the world (Śṛṅgārin), the world of poesy is also permeated with Rasa; on the other hand, if he is an ascetic, everything is tasteless.'

The poet as well as the dramatist must be Śṛṅgārin. This Śṛṅgāra is not the Rasa of that name. It is a general term meaning 'bright'. As says Bharata—[5] 'For example,

---

4. Dhv. III. p. 498

अपारे काव्यसंसारे कविरेव प्रजापतिः ।
यथास्मै रोचते विश्वं तथेदं परिवर्तते ॥
शृङ्गारी चेत् कविः काव्ये जातं रसमयं जगत् ।
स एव वीतरागश्चेन् नीरसं सर्वमेव तत् ॥

5. NŚ. VI. p. 73

यथा यत्किञ्चिल्लोके शुचि मेध्यं दर्शनीयं वा तच्छृङ्गारेणोपमीयते ।
यस्तावदुज्ज्वलवेषः स शृङ्गारवानित्युच्यते ।

whatever in the world is shining, pure or beautiful is compared with Śṛṅgāra. He who is brightly apparelled is said to be invested with Śṛṅgāra.' Until and unless, the dramatist becomes a lover of life he cannot present life so as to make it spectacular and effective. If the dramatist be not in direct touch with this world he cannot bring within his compass the entire world. Only if he is so, can the saying of Bharata,[6] come true :

> 'There is nothing—no knowledge, no skill, no science, no art, no yoga, no activity—that is not seen in the Drama.'

With a very wide and deep knowledge and with these qualities of self-effacement, restraint of speech and humanitarian sentiments, the dramatist handles his theme. The relation of the dramatist with the actors and the audience in respect of the success of his plays will be taken up later. Let us consider here the mission of the dramatist and how the technique helps him in fulfilling it.

Bharata says—[7]

'The poet should write plays that are well-knit through the Junctures (sandhi), easily stageable, delight-

---

6. Ibid. I. 113

न तज्ज्ञानं न तच्छिल्पं न सा विद्या न सा कला।
न स योगो न तत्कर्म नाट्येऽस्मिन् यन्न दृश्यते ॥

7. Ibid. XXI. 120–123

सुश्लिष्टसंधियोगं च सुप्रयोगं सुखाश्रयम्।
मृदुशब्दाभिधानं च कविः कुर्यात् तु नाटकम् ॥
अवस्था या तु लोकस्य सुखदुःखसमुद्भवा।
नानापुरुषसंचारा नाटके सम्भवेदिह ॥
यो यः स्वभावो लोकस्य नानावस्थान्तरात्मकः।
साङ्गाभिनयसंयुक्तो नाट्यमित्यभिधीयते ॥

ful, and full of mild words. The situations of man, arising out of pleasure and pain and related to many persons should be there in the drama.' and again, 'The presentation of human nature in its various conditions through histrionic devices is called drama.'

These statements support the revised definition of drama, suggested earlier and describe the function of the dramatist. In order to compose a play, the dramatist has to acquire the knowledge of the right use of the Junctures, diction, etc. and keep in mind the stageability (prayoga) of the piece, and he must be conversant with the varying natures of people at large in their different stages and circumstances of pleasure and pain—of which the drama is to be a mirror. The mission of the dramatist, we can now say, is to represent the actions of either gods, sages, kings or ordinary human beings for the enjoyment of society.[8] For this, the necessary equipments of the dramatist are also enlisted by Bharata[9]—

'Having observed the nature of the world, the strong and weak points of man, the enjoyment and the logic, then the dramatist should write a play.'

But what should be the aim of such a presentation ? To this question, answers vary. The preceptor Bharata opines that with the advent of Tretāyuga, the entire universe became infested with immoral practices—sexual

---

8. Ibid. 124

देवतानामृषीणां च राज्ञां लोकस्य चैव हि ।
पूर्ववृत्तानुचरितं नाटकं नाम तद् भवेत् ॥

9. Ibid. 128

लोकस्वभावं संप्रेक्ष्य नराणां च बलाबलम् ।
सम्भोगं चैव युक्तिं च ततः कुर्यात् तु नाटकम् ॥

vulgarity (grāmya-dharma), lust and greed, jealousy and anger, and in order to free the world of these, Brahman, the Creator, fashioned the Nāṭyaveda. According to Bharata[10] the drama will be—'Ethical, glorifying, vitalising, beneficial, promoter of intellect and educator of people; It seems that in the beginning this utilitarian purpose was considered to be the foremost. Drama was to be a cathartic agent though with a thick coating of sugar. The first formulators were not bold enough to say that Ānanda, bliss is the *summun bonum* of Drama. But, though they did not accept bliss to be the sole aim of drama formally, the importance Bharata attached to Rasa-realisation in the drama made the point clear.

Dhanañjaya, in the tenth century, actually ridicules in the very beginning of his treatise, those who hold that knowledge is the only gain of dramatic literature, saying 'homage to him for he has averted his face from what is delightful.'[11] To him Rūpaka or Drama 'distil joy'. Commenting on it, Dhanika says : 'Holding that 'the enjoyment of good poetry bestows proficiency in Dharma, Artha, Kāma, Mokṣa and the Arts, and grants fame and pleasure,' ete. some desire to have a knowledge of the *trivarga* (Dharma, Artha and Kāma) as the end of poetic creation. Refuting them it is shown that the end of the ten forms of drama is the tasting of Rasa, realised in one's *own* self n the form of supreme bliss and not merely a knowledgei of the *trivarga* as is derived from History, etc. The paying of homage is sarcastic.'

---

10. Ibid I. 112.

धर्म्यं यशस्यमायुष्यं हितं बुद्धिविवर्धनम् ।
लोकोपदेशजननम्·················· ॥

11. DR. I. 6 तस्मै नमः स्वादुपराङ्मुखाय ।

Rāmacandra and Guṇacandra, the joint authors of Nāṭyadarpaṇa (12th century) employ the word *rañjanā*, relish, and explain Nāṭaka in these words: [12] 'Nāṭaka is so called as it makes the hearts of the spectators dance (nāṭayati) by putting in them a relish in a wonderful manner, and consider 'the attainment of an end that is supernormal and (apparently) improbable' or 'the achievement of a remarkable object' as the end of drama.

It can therefore be said that the conception of Bharata of removing the evil through Rasa-realisation has undergone no real change throughout the ages. Although prominence is given to bliss (ānanda) by the followers, removal of sin, the social utility is nowhere forgotten.

The removal of sin through Rasa-realisation is a typically aesthetic concept. In it the realisation of Rasa is primary and leads to a state of bliss. In this state man sympathises with the sympathies of others without being actually involved. The widening and deepening of man's feeling automatically clears the heart of all meanness and fills it, though temporarily, with the quality of goodness (sattva-guṇa), the highest of the three constituent qualities. Thus in this state without any conscions effort sin is removed. Hence the mission of the dramatist is to transport the audience to that blissful state, reaching where sin and evil are automatically annihilated through the representation of characters in different situations of pleasure and pain.

Such a mission can be fulfilled only when the dramatist is equipped with all the qualities enumerated so

---

12. ND. I. 5

नाटयति--विचित्रं रञ्जनाप्रवेशेन सभ्यानां हृदयं नर्तयति इति नाटकम्
······लोकोत्तरासम्भाव्यफलप्राप्तिः, असाधारणवस्तुलाभः ।

far. Restraint of speech and lucidity of style are the most valuable qualifications of the dramatist, as Bharata[13] says—'The poet should compose the Nāṭaka with pleasant and easily intelligible words' and warns that 'the use of such forms as *Cekrīḍita*, etc. in the drama is as incompatible as are harlots (associated) with a Brāhmaṇa carrying a Kamaṇḍalu.' The emphasis on the use of mild and easily intelligible words and the prohibition of harsh words like *Cekrīḍita*, etc. clearly show that the dramatist should always remember that he is to be understood by even the laymen assembled to witness the play. The authors of the Nāṭyadarpaṇa also say—[14] 'Only such paronomasia and similes are to be employed as may be devised easily while suggesting the Rasa.'

Equipped with these qualities and keeping in view his mission, the dramatist should proceed to handle *Itivṛtta*, the body of Nāṭaka.

---

13. NS XXI. 131–132

मृदुशब्दं सुखार्थं च कविः कुर्यात् तु नाटकम् ।
चेक्रीडिताद्यैः शब्दैस्तु काव्यबन्धा भवन्ति ये ।
वेश्या इव न शोभन्ते कमण्डलुधरैर्द्विजैः ॥

14. ND. I. 15

त एव श्लेषोपमादयो विधेया ये रसनिष्पत्तिप्रयत्नेनैव निष्पद्यन्ते ।

CHAPTER III

STRUCTURE OF THE DRAMA (1)

Itivṛtta or the Plot

The next function of a dramatist, equipped with the qualities stated before, is to find out a theme, conceive the characters and construct the dialogues. In drama, the theme is of prime importance. Bharata observes—'The theme or the plot is the bulk of '*nāṭya*'.[1] A dramatist should, in order to make his creation a success, search out a theme, the 'body' of drama. Though the soul is all-important, the Vedāntin Gītā calls it the *dehin*. So a deserving body should be given importance primarily.

Prof. Allardyce Nicoll enumerates the factors of prime importance in his Theory of Drama—"When, therefore, any dramatist sets to work he will have, at the outset, three things to determine—the theme which is to be dealt with, the characters by means of which that theme is to be displayed, and the medium (the actual dialogue) through which both are to be given expression."[2] He then quotes Aristotle to whom "the elements going to the make-up of a play consisted of the Fable, the characters, the Diction, the Thought, the Decoration, the Music,"[3] and declares—"Tragedy, therefore, does not imitate action for the sake of imitating character, but in the imitation of action that of character is of course involved; so that the action and the plot are the end of tragedy; and the end is of principal interest."[4]

1. NŚ. XXI. 1 इतिवृत्तं तु नाट्यस्य शरीरं परिकीर्तितम् ।
2. Theory of Drama, Allardyce Nicoll, p. 71.
3. Poetics, Ch. VI.
4. Theory of Drama, Allardyce Nicoll, p. 71.

With regard to drama this importance accorded to the Fable by Aristotle and to the Itivṛtta by Bharata is recognised even today. Anyone desirous of composing a drama must have a theme in the first instance. But where does one find a theme? Bharata does not answer the question directly but clarifies the point in the respective definitions of the ten forms of drama. The *Nāṭaka*, he says, must have a theme that is famous, and the actions to be imitated in it must be those of Kings well-noted and dignified.[5] In addition to this famous or legendary theme (prakhyāta), there is another, the invented one (autpattika) which has its scope in the Prakaraṇa and some other forms wherein the action of such characters like the Brāhmaṇas, traders, ministers, priests, counsellors, merchants, etc. is to be displayed.[6] The dramatist is at liberty to select a legendary theme or to devise one by his imagination but he has to display the theme through appropriate characters prescribed for it. On the basis of the nature of the theme and the characters, the drama has been divided into ten different forms. Thus in the drama the theme and the action of appropriate characters are important. Before considering the division of the drama into ten kinds according to the nature of the theme, it would be useful to consult the view of Dhanañjāya, the most important later authority.

Dhanañjaya clearly takes the hint from Bharata and adds a third variety, the Mixed one which is a combination of the legendary and the invented themes. He says that the theme 'is also threefold, owing to a threefold

5. NŚ. XX. 10.

6. Ibid. XX. 52.

classification into legendary, invented and mixed subjects;[7] These are explained as follows—

"The legendary (variety of subject matter is derived) from legends of the past and the like; the invented is devised by the poet; the mixed (arises) from a combination of these two in accordance with a classification into Gods, mortals and the like."[8]

The source of all the themes thus is either the recorded legends, that is, the Rāmāyaṇa, the Mahābhārata, the other Purāṇas, the Kathāsaritsāgara and the like, or the invention of the poet himself. But in the composition of the 'Nāṭaka' variety, invention has no place. It must of necessity have a legendary theme.

Then comes the question of selection. The legends are full of anecdotes. What should then be the special feature by which a particular anecdote is to be selected as the subject matter ? There are enumerated no less than sixty-four specialities, the 'aṅgas', in the Nāṭyaśāstra, but Bharata himself says that to get all these in a theme is almost impossible. The chief feature, we can say, is the 'turns of surprise and the unexpected.' This quality of constant shock and surprise is what makes the theme dramatic. Bharata says[9]—'The Marvellous Sentiment is to be regularly employed in the Conclusion.' About this employment of the Marvellous, Dhanañjaya and Rāmacandra-Guṇacandra also follow suit. The Daśarūpaka declares[10]—'The Marvellous should be employed in the

---

7. DR. I. 15–16 (Tr. C.O. Haas, p. 7).
8. Ibid. p. 7-8.
9. NŚ. XX. 47 निर्वहणे कर्तव्यो नित्यं हि रसोऽद्भुतस्तज्ज्ञैः ।
10. DR. III. 34 कुर्यान् निर्वहणेऽद्भुतम् ।

Conclusion.' The Nāṭyadarpaṇa while explaining the term 'adbhutāntam'—ending in the Marvellous—in the definition of Nāṭaka, observes[11]—'(In it) the Marvellous Sentiment is placed at the end, that is in the Juncture of Conclusion. As the Erotic, the Heroic and the Furious Sentiments lead respectively to the attainment of a beautiful damsel, sovereignty over the world and destruction of foes; so do the Pathetic, the Terrible and the Odious Sentiments counteract the former, and in this way, in order to effect the attainment of a unique and wonderful result, the Marvellous Sentiment must be placed at the end.' A Nāṭaka may have all the Sentiments but one among them must dominate, the others being subordinate. All the Sentiments, except the Marvellous, serve either to attain the desirable end or to make the attainment attractive by putting obstacles before it. The employment of the Marvellous Sentiment is recommended so strongly in order to get 'the unexpected' at the end. Such a theme should therefore be taken up by the dramatist, as is permeated throughout with the possibilities of shock and surprise, and provides scope for the use of the Marvellous Sentiment at the end.

Let us take an example which will make clear the process of selection. Consider, for instance, the case of the greatest Sanskrit dramatist, Kālidāsa. Kālidāsa being possessed of the desire to compose a drama, comes acros the story of Śakuntalā, while reading thc Mahābhārata personally or hearing it in the literary assembly of Vikramāditya,

---

11. ND. I, 15

अद्भुत एव रसोऽन्ते निर्वहणे यत्र । यतः शृङ्गार-वीर-रौद्रैः स्त्रीरत्न-पृथ्वीलाभ-शत्रुक्षयसम्पत्तिः, करुण-भयानक-बीभत्सैस्तन्निवृत्तिरितीयता क्रमेण लोकोत्तरासम्भाव्यफल-प्राप्तौ भवितव्यमन्तेऽद्भुतेनैव ।

the king. The storyof a handsome maiden, secretly wooed in the hermitage of a sage during a single meeting by a Cakravartin King, with a promise to carry her to the Capital as early as possible; the renunciation of her at the court; the condemnation of the king by the forlorn woman; the augury from Heaven and the final union of the lovers, the girl now mother of a lovely child—immediately impresses itself upon the mind of the poet and he contemplates the possibility of putting the actions (carita) of the king and the maiden into a dramatic form. The story, as it is in the Mahābhārata, is itself interesting, and anyone hearing it must call the incidents 'dramatic.' But to give the story a full-fledged dramatic form, the services of a skilful dramatist are needed. To gather more information, we may guess, Kālidāsa searched among the other Purāṇas and perhaps came across the same story in the Padma-Purāṇa. The remarkable possibility of its dramatic success was clearly realised by the dramatist and, as a result, the immortal drama Abhijñāna Śākuntala came into existence.

Thus it is prescribed that the theme is to be taken from the legends. The hero must belong to antiquity and not to the contemporary period. The theorists appear to be very particular in curbing the freedom of the dramatists. To quote Rāmacandra and Guṇacandra–[12] 'If the hero is contemporary, current notions would impair the Rasa of the piece and it would also show want of respect to great men of the past and again 'carita' means

12. Ibid. I, 5
वर्तमाने च नेतरि तत्कालप्रसिद्धिबाधया रसहानिः स्यात्, पूर्वमहापुरुषचरितेषु च अश्रद्धानं स्यात्·········चरितमित्याचरितं न तु कविबुद्धिकल्पितम्······ बाहुल्यापेक्षं चैतत्, तेनाल्पं किमपि रञ्जकम् कल्पितमपि न दोषायेति ।

what has actually taken place and not what is imagined by the poets.' This statement, it seems, entirely drives out the scope of poetic fancy. But it is not exactly so. The same authors clarify their point further—'This refers to an excess, and so the introduction of a little of imaginary incidents that are relishable, is not to be censured.' The Daśarūpuka also says–[13]

"Whatever in it (i.e. in the original story) is at all unsuited to the hero or inconsistent with the Sentiment, is to be omitted or arranged in some other way."

With this limited freedom, the dramatist then proceeds to prepare a full sketch of the plot, divides it into sections, and gives it the final shape.

The Plot and its Subdivisions

Having made the selection of plot from either a legendary source or his own imagination, the dramatist has to consider many other things. His chief end is to present the theme through fitting characters so as to bring about the Rasa–realisation of the audience. Bharata says—and he is echoed by all the later formulators, Dhanañjaya, Śāradātanaya and others, that six factors are to be kept always in mind. These are—[14]

---

13. DR. III. 24-25 (Tr. C.O. Hass, p. 89).

14. NŚ XXI. 53–54

इष्टस्यार्थस्य रचना वृत्तान्तस्यानुपक्षयः ।
रागप्राप्तिः प्रयोगस्य गुह्यानां चैव गूहनम् ।
आश्चर्यवदभिख्यातं प्रकाश्यानां प्रकाशनम् ।
अङ्गानां षड्विधं ह्येतदुक्तं शास्त्रे प्रयोजनम् ।

Also compare DR. I. 15; BPI VII. p. 513; SD. VI. 116-17.

"The arranging of the subject chosen, sustaining interest in the story, infusing of emotion, concealing what is to be concealed, introducing the element of surprise in the representation and disclosing what is to be disclosed."

And to accomplish these, five Junctures (sandhis)–subdivived into sixty-four parts are conceived. We will come later to a discussion of these.

Collocation oj incidents

Keeping these factors in view the dramatist should handle his subject-matter and first of all arrange the incidents. He gets the theme, of course, from the legends, but the treatment of the theme undergoes a 'sea-change' in the hands of the dramatist. In the legends the story is no less dramatically striking, it is however, inadequate in its original form to the dramatist. An instance of this is the subject-matter of *Śakuntalā* as it is found in the *Mahābhārata*. Undoubtedly, the tale there is strikingly dramatic and the personages—Duṣyanta, Śakuntalā, the sage Kaṇva, impress the readers' minds greatly by their bearings and actions. But when the same Śakuntalopākhyāna of the Mahābhārata appears as Abhijñāna Śākuntala of Kālidāsa, it is hundred times more appealing, interesting and marvellous. Here a fine distinction can be made between an ordinary narrative and a dramatic exposition. Allardyce Nicoll rightly observes—"A novel or a tale may be inherently 'dramatic,' but there is no real need for it to be so. The novelist does not have imposed upon him the constant demand for surprise and shock."[15]

This leads to another consideration. It has already been observed that the canvas in other forms of literature,

15. Theory of Drama, Allardyce Nicoll, p. 74.

especially in Kathā, Ākhyāyikā and Mahākāvya may be too elastic. A novelist or a poet may leave no words unused to present his hero or other characters, and is at liberty to go on writing even to a length of a thousand pages. Bāṇabhaṭṭa's 'Kādambarī' may be cited as an example. The great novelist does not hesitate to colour even the minor characters of his story, with his imagination. Māgha is grandiloquent in describing the 'Raivataka' mountain and the six seasons, and devotes to each of them two entire cantos containing 68 and 79 verses respectively.[16] Kālidāsa also describes Pārvatī lavishly in the Kumārasambhava. For the dramatist there is no such freedom. He has, all along, to remember that a multiplicity of characters will not only confuse his limited canvas but will injure the possibility of its being presented on the stage. The canon goes—[17] 'Neither the Nāṭaka, nor the Prakaraṇa should consist of a big horde of men. The chief characters should number either four or five ?

This saying of Bharata finds full support in later treatises on dramaturgy.

On the question of whether only the lives of the illustrious kings of the past are to be displayed in the Nāṭaka variety, there are different views. Bharata merely says that the theme in the Nāṭaka should be well-known and legendary. The later thinkers have widened the scope. According to Sāgara Nandin, well-known contemporary themes can profitably be displayed in the Nāṭaka. He

---

16. शिशुपाल वध. अध्याय 4–5

17. NŚ. XX. 40.

न महाजनपरिवारं कर्तव्यं नाटकं प्रकरणं वा।
ये तत्र कार्याः पुरुषाश्चत्वारः पञ्च वा ते स्युः ।

Also compare, NLRK. p. 71. DR. III 36 SD. VI, 11,

holds—[18] 'The life and action of a great contemporary king may also serve as a theme if the poet can skilfully render it presentable by inventing the five Elements of the Plot, viz. the Germ, the Prominent Point, etc. According to this view, the objection raised by Rāmacandra and Guṇacandra that presentation of the lives of contemporary kings involves disrespect to legendary heroes, is not tenable. Śāradātanaya, although prefers the purely legendary themes, is not totally against the contemporary ones. He leaves the choice to the playwright saying that these may be utilised 'if necessary.'[19] Dhanañjaya is silent on this point. His followers, Viśvanātha and others maintain a similar silence. The comparative priority of Sāgara Nandin in point of date may probably mean that he was the first to suggest the introduction of current themes in the Nāṭaka variety.[20]

It may be said that Kālidāsa was the first to use a comparatively modern theme in his Mālavikāgnimitra, and that its success induced the codifiers to adopt the modification. But later dramatists excepting a few, perhaps dared not follow the new way.

The source of the theme thus may be ancient legends or modern history or a wise combination of the two. But in all cases the subject-matter must be well-known

---

18. NLRK. p. 3

    वर्तमानमपि नृपतेर्महाद्भुतस्य कविबुद्धिप्रकर्षादासादितबीजबिन्द्वादिकं यदि भवति भवत्येव नाटकविषयम् ।

19. BP. p. 200

    चरितं नायकादीनामितिवृत्तमिति स्मृतम् ।
    प्रयोजनवशात् तत्तु वर्तमानमपि क्वचित् ।।

20. For the date of Sāgara Nandin see The Date of Sāgara Nandin, M. R. Kavi, IA. 1937, p. 412.

(khyāta) so that the theatre-goers may easily, without the help of any other agents but the dramatis personae, realise the purport of the drama.

The choice of the subject matter is only the first step towards a play. In the original, the tale had a context and a sequel. In putting it into a dramatic composition, the context is lost. The dramatist takes upon himself the presentation not of the whole life of anybody but of a few days of his life, which are interesting and striking. So, he should pay his full attention first to the entire story as it is found in the source and then decide upon how best the theme can be employed as a Plot in his play. He has to hit upon those incidents only which serve his purpose, i.e. presentation of a noble character and his actions leading to Rasa-realisation. In making a plot out of the theme, he has to remember the limitations as well, under which he has to work. He has to avoid multiplicity of characters, confusing incidents and every other thing that goes against his mission. Although the theme is legendary, the dramatist is granted freedom to make additions and alterations in it for presenting it in the best manner possible. Dhanañjaya observes[21]—'Whatever in it (i.e. the original story) is at all unsuited to the hero or inconsistent with the Sentiment is to be omitted or arranged in some other way.' The same view is maintained in the Nāṭyadarpaṇa and the Sāhityadarpaṇa as well.[22] Thus keeping the hero and the Sentiment in view, the dramatist has to adopt

---

21. DR. III. 24-25

यत् तत्रानुचितं किञ्चिन्नायकस्य रसस्य वा ।
विरुद्धं तत् परित्याज्यमन्यथा वा प्रकल्पयेत् ॥

22. Vide ND. I. 18; SD. VI. 50.

the theme to suit his purpose, and devise a separate beginning and end for it.

Division of the Plot

Although adapted, the dramatic plot naturally has other agents than the hero, and many actions and events. So, a further division of the plot into the Principal and the Incidental is necessary. Bharata defines these in these words: 'The action which succeeds attaining the desired result is the Principal subject (ādhikārika or mukhyā), the rest is Incidental (prāsaṅgika or gauṇa).'[23]

The Principal Subject

The Principal Subject has the hero himself as its agent, as Duṣyanta is in the Śakuntalā, and the other incidents, like the Vidūṣaka incident, the Durvāsas incident, the fisherman incident, etc. are Incidental Subjects. The Nāṭyadarpaṇa observes in this connection: 'No subjects are either Principal or Incidental by themselves. But of all the results, the one to which the poet assigns importance is the desired one. So the subject with the desired end is the Principal.'[24]

The Incidental Subject

Apart from the main subject connected directly with the hero and his activities, the rest is included in the Inci-

---

23. NŚ. XXI. 3

यद् कार्यं तु फलप्राप्त्या सामर्थ्यात् परिकल्प्यते।
तदाधिकारिकं ज्ञेयमन्यत् प्रासङ्गिकं विदुः॥

24. ND. I

इह तावन् न निसर्गतः किञ्चिन् मुख्यमङ्गं वा किन्तु बहुष्वपि फलेषु कवियंस्यात्यन्तमुत्कर्षमभिप्रैति तत् फलमिष्टम्। अनेन च यत् फलवद् वृत्तं तदिह मुख्यम्।

dental. The Incidental is almost inevitable in every plot, but the presentation of it depends on the consideration whether it promotes the Principal. Bharata points out that the Incidental subjects should not be employed for their own sake, nor as having their own ends but only for the improvement of the Principal.[25]

Rāmacandra and Guṇacandra, also observe—'In a drama, only such Incidental matters are to be employed as indirectly promote the main end.'[26] Śāradātanaya exemplifies the Principal and the Incidental subjects in relation to Rāma-legend thus :

> 'From his birth to his coronation, the Principal theme relates to Rāma. The actions of Sugrīva and Bibhīṣaṇa constitute the Incidental Subject.'[27]

In this way the theme is to be divided into two parts —the Principal and the Incidental. But the problem of the dramatist is how to present the theme as a composite whole. He will have to divide the plot into Acts which should be independent so for as a beginning and an end are concerned but they must at the same time, appear as a compact whole when staged or read. How to achieve

---

25. NŚ. XXI. 5.

    परोपकरणार्थम् तु कीर्त्यते ह्यानुषङ्गिकम् ।

26. ND. I

    नाट्ये हि तदेव अवान्तरं वृत्तमायोज्यं यत् पारम्पर्येण प्रधान-फलसाधकम् ।

    Compare this point DR. I. 13 ; SD. VI. 44 ;
    BP. VII. p. 201 lines 7-8.

27. BP. VII. p. 201

    आजन्मनोऽभिषेकान्तं रामस्यैवाधिकारिकम् ।
    प्रासङ्गिकं तु सुग्रीव–बिभीषण–विचेष्टितम् ॥

this ? Bharata answers that there are five Elements of the Plot (arthaprakṛti) which join the whole story. He says :

> 'The five Elements of the Plot are—the Germ (bīja), the Prominent Point (bindu), the Episode (patākā), the Episodical Incident (prakarī) and the Denouement (kārya). These are to be used according to prescription.'[28]

According to Sāgara Nandin the five Elements of the Plot are essential as without them no theme is possible. Of these the Prominent Point is very important as it acts as a connecting link, joining the loose ends. Sāgara Nandin quotes Bharata [29] and says that the Prominent Point works up to the Denouement. He refers to another view also saying—'others hold that the Prominent Point is the reiteration in every Act of the essence of the dramatic theme through a display of depression and energy (i.e. in the case of a heroic theme). This again has to be employed until the end that is the Denouement.'[30] Though anonymous, this view hints at the essential necessity of the Prominent Point and advises its use upto the end. In fact, to connect the links of the main plot, the Prominent

---

28. NŚ. XXI. 22

    बीज–बिन्दु–पताकाश्च प्रकरी कार्यमेव च।
    अर्थप्रकृतयः पञ्च ज्ञात्वा योज्या यथाविधि ॥

29. Ibid. 24

    प्रयोजनानां विच्छेदे यदविच्छेदकारणम् ।
    यावत् समाप्तिर्बन्धस्य स बिन्दुरिति संज्ञितः ॥

30. NLRK. p. 8

    अन्ये तु—यद्धि नाटकार्थस्य प्रकृतिभूतमवमानोत्साहाभ्यां प्रत्यङ्कं परिकीर्त्यते स बिन्दुः············स च कार्यस्य समाप्ति यावत् प्रवर्तयितव्यः ।

Point is indispensable. Of the other four, the Germ is also important. It is the starting poit of the plot and hence of the action. From it issue forth all the actions. The 'Episode' and 'the Episodical Incident' constitute the Incidental Subject and help the development of the main plot by presenting contrasts at times. The Denouement is the end.

Thus after the selection of the theme, the dramatist has to provide these Elements, and with the help of them give it the shape of a dramatic plot. As the plot consists of the Principal and Incidental subjects, it is naturally not necessary to devise all the Elements in every plot. In the absence of Incidental Subject, the two Elements connected with it—the Episode and the Episodial Incident—would be left out. The three Elements connected with the Principal Subject—the Germ, the Prominent Point and the Denouement, however, are indispensable in every plot. Keeping in view the purpose of giving a charming unity to the whole series of events, the dramatist should judiciously use them. As Bharata observes : 'Of these, what serves the purpose or leads to excellence, has to be emphasised, the rest are non-essential.'[31]

The Treatment of the Plot

After fashioning the plot out of the theme, the dramatist has to direct his attention to presenting the events. Needless to say that it is the Principal Subject that demands his full attention. It has already been observed that the dramatist cannot supply all the details relating to the life and action of the hero. He can present only those

---

31. NŚ. XXI. 28

एतेषां यस्य येनार्थो यतश्च गुण इष्यते ।
प्रधानं तत् प्रकर्तव्यं गुणभूतान्यतः परम् ॥

events which, being interesting occupy only a short period of his life. He has also to remember that he has to present only the charming incidents to please his audience. In a plot there are many incidents that have a bearing on the main action but are not charming. Similarly many pieces of information, although essential, belong to the same category. How to acquaint the audience with these matters? —is the next problem facing the dramatist.

Bharata in his characteristic manner speaks of the use of five Explanatory Devices (arthopakṣepaka lit. Communicator of incidents) in drama for giving necessary information of happenings not included in the plot. He enumerates : 'The Explanatory Scene (viṣkambha), the Intimating Speech (cūlikā), the Introductory Scene (praveśaka), the Continuation Scene (aṅkāvatāra) and the Anticipatory Scene (aṅkamukha) are five Explanatory Devices.'[32] These are the five means by which the dramatist is to supply the missing links and effect compactness. Bharata emphasises the necessity of making the drama concise and observes : 'Incidents which are connected with many (persons, places, etc.) are to be compressed by means of the Introductory Scenes or in the Junctures (sandhi).'[33] Sāgara Nandin, explaining the above statement, observes : 'The entire story should not be included in the Acts. The short Acts, having the duration of one or half a day cannot fittingly present all the incidents covering a month or a year, and so short Introductory Scenes should be utilised. Thus by means of the Introductory Scenes the story should

---

32. NŚ. XXI. 108.

33. NŚ. XX. 35

बह्वाश्रयमप्यर्थं प्रवेशकैः संक्षिपेच्च संधिषु च ।

be compressed.'[34] The Explanatory Devices are thus the means of achieving conciseness through the reporting of necessary information.

The later writers have nothing new to add to either the purpose or definition of these. Dhanañjaya and the authors of the Nāṭyadarpaṇa, however, show a novelty in their approach. In order to decide the exact scope of the Explanatory Devices, Dhanañjaya prescribes a further division of the plot into Indicatory (sūcya) and Presentable (dṛśya-śravya), and assigns the reporting of the Indicatory matters to the five Explanatory Devices.[35]

Rāmacandra and Guṇacandra are still more elaborate and carry the argument further to its logical conclusion. They speak of a four-fold division of the plot—'The plot is four-fold--Indicatory (sūcya), Presentable (prayojya), Inferential (abhyūhya) and Negligible (upekṣya),—and define them in the following manner: 'The Indicatory is what is unpleasant and improper; the Presentable is the opposite of it, that is, pleasant and proper; the Inferential consists of such matters as are connected with

34. NLRK. pp. 14-15
आख्यानकं न सर्वमङ्के प्रणेतव्यम् । न संक्षेपाङ्के दिवसकृतं दिवसार्धकृते मासकृतं वर्षकृतं वा सकलमुपदर्शयितुमतः संक्षेपार्थः प्रवेशकः कर्तव्यः । अतः प्रवेशकेन कथासंग्रहणं कार्यम् ।

35. DR. I. 56, 58
द्वेधा विभागः कर्तव्यः सर्वस्यापीह वस्तुनः ।
सूच्यमेव भवेत् किञ्चिद् दृश्यश्रव्यमथापरम् ।
अर्थोपक्षेपकैः सूच्यं पञ्चभिः प्रतिपादयेत् ॥
Also compare BP. VII. p. 214.

these but, can be easily inferred. The Negligible is what is odious.'[36]

Although so elaborately explained, the last two, i.e. the Inferential and the Negligible do not present much of a problem. The dramatist has to avoid both, although he has to remember that his neglect or omission must not involve a vital subject. Even what is Indicatory or Inferential may be presented provided it promotes the Rasa-realisation or is connected with later Action in the drama. The practice of the dramatists warrants the presentation of kissing, embrace or killing or an actual journey on the stage, though avowedly constituting the Indicatory and the Inferential on account of their importance towards the Rasa-realisation.

The first two, i. e. the Indicatory and the Presentable are the same as in the Daśarūpaka. The authors' comment on the above verse clearly defines the scope of both these, which, however, is the same as prescribed by Dhanañjaya. It goes : 'That which is void of relish is unpleasant. Improper is that which although relishable is not befitting to be shown such as, caresses, kissings, etc. These constitute the Indicatory, and are to be indicated by such means as the Explanatory Scene (viṣkambhaka). The opposite of this unpleasant and improper Indicatory is pleasant and proper. It is presented, that is, presented before the eyes of the audience through the histrionic

---

36. ND. I. 10–11

सूच्यं प्रयोज्यमभ्यूह्यमुपेक्ष्यं तच्चतुर्विधम् ॥
नीरसानुचितं सूच्यं प्रयोज्यं तद् विपर्ययः ।
ऊह्यं तदविनाभूतमुपेक्ष्यं तु जुगुप्सितम् ॥

devices of Words and Gestures, etc. So, it is called the Presentable.'[37]

On this point, Viśvanātha follows Dhanañjaya and does not go into the detail of the Inferential and the Negligible. With the inflexibility of a codifier, a characteristic of the later writers, he, however enumarates the exact instances where the Explantory Devices are to be used.[38]

The selection of the theme, shaping the Plot by devising the five Elements, a careful division of the Principal and the Incidental subjects, and then deciding how much is to be presented and what is to be indicated—these are thus the necessary steps of a dramatist.

The Explanatory Devices

Before proceeding to a study of the five Elements of the Plot, it is proper to examine the nature of these Explanatory Devices, and how these assist the playwright in his work.

Dhanañjaya points out that if the plot be charming from the very beginning, no Explanatory Device is required.[39] In such cases, the main events should follow the very exit of the Stage-manager. But if it is otherwise, that is, if a short introduction is required for the presentation

---

37. Ibid. I. 11

नीरसमरञ्जकम्, अनुचितं सरसमप्यनर्हंमालिङ्गनचुम्बनादि, तत् सूच्यं विष्कम्भकादिभिर्ज्ञाप्यम्। तस्य नीरसानुचितस्य सूच्यस्य विपर्ययः सरसमुचितं च प्रयुज्यते—वाचिकादिभिरभिनयैः सामाजिकानां साक्षादिव क्रियते इति प्रयोज्यम्।

38. Vide SD. VI. 51-52.

39 Ibid. III. 28-30.

of the main events, then an Explanatory Scene should be prefixed to the first Act. The same view is maintained by all the later writers.

The Nāṭyadarpaṇa, however, prescribes a gradation of preference of these Devices. After naming these in the order—Explanatory Scene, Introductory Scene, Anticipatory Scene, Intimating Speech and Continuation Scene, the authors observe that the first two i.e. the Explanatory and Introductory Scenes are to be employed for reporting lengthy information, and that the remaining three according to the gradually decreasing volume of information to be conveyed.[40] Although no other treatise speaks of such a gradation, the practice of playwrights does, to a great extent, warrant such an assumption.

The Viṣkambhaka and the Praveśaka

Of the five Explanatory Devices, the Explanatory and the Introductory Scenes are more prominent because of their greater use than the other three. Bharata defines the Explanatory Scene thus:

'The Explanatory Scene should employ male characters of middle rank, such as cultured priests, ministers and *Kañcukin*, etc., and relate to the Opening Juncture (mukha-sandhi) of the Nāṭaka. There are two varieties of this—Pure (Śuddha) and Mixed (Saṃkīrṇa). The former has characters of middle rank only and the

---

40. ND. I. 17

आद्यौ सूच्ये बह्वावन्ये क्रमादल्पे तरे तमे ।

41. NŚ. XXI. 109-10

मध्यमपुरुषनियोज्यो नाटकमुखसंधिवस्तुसंचारः ।

latter, a combination of men of both the middle and lower ranks.' [41]

The Bharatan definition of the Explanatory Scene along with its twofold classification based on the nature of characters employed in it, has been accepted by all the later formulators. The prescription of introducing men only of middle and lower ranks in it points out the inadvisability of employing persons of the highest rank such as gods, kings, etc. for reporting Indicatory matter. Sanskrit being the language of men of middle rank and Prakrit of the lower, a mixture of both these languages is fittingly prescribed. A great number of persons also is to be avoided in such scenes.

The Introductory Scene is also likewise defined by Bharata elaborately. The definition of Dhanañjaya, however, gives all the salient points :

'The Introductory Scene which is quite similar (to the Explanatory Scene) and is performed by inferior characters in language that is not elevated, explains between two Acts, matters that have been omitted.' [42]

The similarities in nature and function of the Introductory Scene with those of the Explanatory Scene are too evident. The only distinctions are in point of language and character. In an Introductory Scene, the use of Sanskrit is ruled out, although there are views which prescribe the use of Sanskrit as well as of characters of

---

विस्कम्भकस्तु संस्कृतपुरोहितामात्यकञ्चुकिभिः ॥
शुद्धः संङ्कीर्णो वा द्विविधो विष्कम्भकस्तु विज्ञेयः ।
मध्यमपात्रैः शुद्धः सङ्कीर्णो नीचमध्यमैः कृतः ॥

42. DR. I. 60-61 (Tr. C. O. Haas).

middle rank there also. The Bhāvaprakāśana refers to the view thus—'Some scholars prefer the employment of Sanskrit-speaking persons like the Viṭas, hermits, old men, sages and Kañcukin, etc. in the Introductory Scene as well.'[43]

The other distinction is the prohibition of its use in the beginning of the first Act. Bharata has nothing definite to say on this point. The view of Kohala quoted in the Nāṭyadarpaṇa shows that he advocated the use of the Explanatory Scene exclusively in the beginning of the first Act.[44] He thus distinguishes the two by their placing —the Explanatory Scene at the beginning of the first Act and the Introductory Scene at the beginning of any other Act.

Dhanañjaya formulated the generally accepted rule for the use of the two. He is of opinion that the Explanatory Scene may be used anywhere in the Nāṭaka and the Prakaraṇa but the Introductory Scene is to be used only after the first Act is over.

The use of all the Explanatory Devices is prescribed in the Nāṭaka, the Prakaraṇa and the Nāṭikā varieties only. The themes in these, being complex and wider in scope, require such information to make the situation clear. The Nāṭyadarpaṇa observes that the other varieties deal with shorter themes, and so the intervention of the Explanatory Devices would impede the course of events.

---

43. BP. VII. 9-10.

44. Vide ND. I. p. 38

कोहलः पुनरेतं प्रथमाङ्कादावेव इच्छति ।

Cūlikā, Aṅkāsya and Aṅkāvatāra

The Intimating Speech, the Anticipatory Scene and the Continuation Scene are comparatively less important Explanatory Devices. In some treatises, Cūlikā and Aṅkāsya are called Cūlā and Aṅkamukha as well.

Bharata gives the definition of the Intimating Speech thus: 'When some points are explained by characters of high, middle or low ranks from behind the curtain, it is called the Intimating Speech.'[45]

This Explanatory Device takes the form of a statement by any character, made from behind the curtain to report some important but brief information. Generally it is used to introduce a new character as in the Uttararāmacarita. There in the beginning of Act II, a voice from behind the curtain welcomes a female hermit, and thus reveals the identity of the entering character. It is also used to announce the outcome of fierce battles and such other pieces of information.

The reporting of events from behind the curtain suffers naturally from want of interest on the part of the audience, and so the view of the Nāṭyadarpaṇa that the Intimating Speech should be used only to report brief information is justified. It has generally been used in order to be able to observe the rule of the theorists that no characters are to be presented on the stage without an introduction.[46]

---

45. NŚ. XXI. 111

अन्तर्जननिकासंस्थैरुत्तमाधममध्यमैः ।
अर्थोपक्षेपणं यत्र क्रियते सा हि चूलिका ॥

46. Quoted in NLRK. p. 15

असूचितस्य पात्रस्य प्रवेशो नैव विद्यते ।

Aṅkāsya

About the nature of the Anticipatory Scene, there is a difference of opinion among the formulators. Bharata defines it thus : 'When the detached beginning of an Act is summarised beforehand by a male or a female character, it is called the Anticipatory Scene.'[47] Thus, in this Explanatory Device only one character is employed, who gives a summary of the Act to follow. It is clear that the summarisation is necessary, as without it the following Act would appear somewhat unlinked.

Sāgara Nandin gives a different definition. He says that 'the Anticipatory Scene is the furnishing in brief of a summary of all the Acts.'[48] He cites the dialogue between Kāmandakī and Avalokitā in the Mālatīmādhava, Act I, which furnishes all the information about the hero and his designs in a nutshell.

Dhanañjaya, on the other hand, defines it thus : 'The Anticipatory Scene (is so called) because of the allusion by characters at the end of an Act to the subject of the following Act.'[49] The example is furnished from the Vīracarita Act II of Bhavabhūti. There Sumantra enters at the end and asks Janaka, Śatānanda and Paraśurāma to go to meet Vaśiṣṭha and Viśvāmitra, which they do. The next Act thus begins with these very characters. So far as this illustration is concerned, it appears that here also the

---

47. NŚ. XXI. 116

विश्लिष्टमुखमङ्कस्य स्त्रिया वा पुरुषेण वा ।
यत्र संक्षिप्यते पूर्वं तदङ्कमुखमिष्यते ॥

48. NLRK. p. 17

'सूत्रणं सकलाङ्कानां ज्ञेयमङ्कमुखं बुधैः'—येनैकत्र सकलानामङ्कानां सूत्रणं क्रियते तदङ्कमुखं यथा कामन्दक्यवलोकितयोः ।

49. DR. I. 62 also ND. I. 26.

matter to be reported is trivial, and it serves chiefly to observe the convention of introducing characters with proper introduction. The Nāṭyadarpaṇa follows Dhanañjaya in both definition and illustration, and does not refer to the other view at all.

Viśvanātha appears to consider the view of Sāgara Nandin as Bharatan, and gives the same definition. He, however, refers to the definition of Dhanañjaya as an alternative with the comment that some critics hold it to be identical with the Continuation Scene.[50] The device has so rarely been used by the dramatists that the practice of playwrights does not shed any light as to which view should be preferred. On the ground that Bharata expressly prescribes the use of the Explanatory Scene for Nāṭakas only and that of Introductory Scene for both Nāṭakas and Prakaraṇas, Dr. Ghosh observes: "The Aṅkamukha (aṅkāsya) seems to relate mostly to plays other than of the Nāṭaka and the Prakaraṇa types.'[51]

Aṅkāvatāra

The fifth Explanatory Device is the Continuation Scene. About this also there is a diversity of views. Bharata defines it thus: 'The Continuation Scene is so called as in practice it falls between two Acts or within an Act, and relates to the purpose of the Germ.'[52] The definition is not very clear. It appears that this device is intended to bring the Germ of the Plot to the forefront, when it is lost

---

50. Vide SD. VI. 59-60.
51. Vide The Nāṭyaśāstra, M. Ghosh, Calcutta 1950, notes to XXI. 113, p. 398.
52. NŚ. XXI. 115

अङ्कान्तरेऽथवाङ्के निपतति यस्मात् प्रयोगमासाद्य बीजार्थयुक्तियुक्तो
विज्ञेयोऽङ्कावतारोऽसौ ।

sight of, either as the part of an Act or as a separate entity.

Sāgara Nandin holds it to be the indication of the following Act by some character towards the end of the current Act. He illustrates the type by the description of an elephant, suffering from excessive heat in the summer made by Jīmūtavāhana in the Nāgānanda at the end of Act I, which according to him indicates the future love-lorn condition of the hero.[53]

Dhanañjaya defines : 'The Continuation Scene is the occurrence of an Act at the end of (the previous) Act, without separation from it.'[54] The illustration is supplied from the Mālavikāgnimitra of Kālidāsa. There at the end of the first Act, when all are about to start for the 'Theatre' to witness the music competition, the Vidūṣaka says that the sound of the musical instruments would indicate the proper time to go there. The first Act ends and the second begins with the sound of the instruments. Thus, the commentator thinks, the statement of the Vidūṣaka ushers in the new Act and so is an instance of the Continuation Scene. The Nāṭyadarpaṇa gives an identical definition and the same illustration. In the comment, however, the authors refer to another view according to which the Germ of the entire Plot is introduced in the Continuation Scene. The illustration is supplied from the Ratnāvalī Act II where Susaṅgatā justifies and commends the love of Sāgarikā for Udayana, the Germ of the Plot. The same, according to them, is termed Interlude (garbhāṅka) by others.[55]

---

53. Vide NLRK. p. 18.
54. DR. I. 62 (Tr. C.O. Hass)
55. Vide ND. I. 27a.

Viśvanātha follows Dhanañjaya in the definition but strangely enough gives a different illustration.[56] He illustrates the type by the fisherman incident appended to the end of the fifth Act of Abhijñāna Śākuntala. He treats the Interlude separately, which according to him is an independent scene, complete in itself, introduced within an Act.[57] The Interlude thus defined takes the form of a play within the play and cannot be treated as an Explanatory Device.

From a study of all these views and illustrations it becomes clear that there is a confusion regarding the exact nature of this Explanatory Device. The illustrations furnished by Sāgara Nardin, Dhanañjaya and Rāmacandra-Guṇacandra can easily be taken as those of the Anticipatory Scene. There is little difference between the illustration of the Anticipatory Scene from the Vīracarita and that of the Continuation Scene from the Mālavikāgnimitra. The suggestion of his own future sufferings by Jīmūtavāhana through the description of an elephant, in fact, is not related at all to the Indicatory matter, as love for Malayavatī constitutes the Presentable in the play. So the illustration given by Rāmacandra-Guṇacandra is also inadequate.

On the other hand, the illustration given by Viśvanātha has certain distinct features for which it may be taken as a typical example of the Continuation Scene. Although none of the formulators consider the fisherman

---

56. SD. VI. 58–59

अङ्कान्ते सूचितः पात्रैस्तदङ्कस्याविभागतः ।
यत्राङ्कोऽवतरत्येषोऽङ्कावतार इति स्मृतः ॥

57 Vide Ibid. VI. 20.

incident in the Abhijñāna Śākuntala as an example of the Continuation Scene and the greater number of commentators treat it as an instance of the Introductory Scene prefixed to the sixth Act, some special features of this Scene differentiate it from other Explanatory Devices and justify the view of Viśvanātha.

Here is a new type of Explanatory Device. It does not report events like the Explanatory or the Introductory Scenes. The regaining of the ring shown here is apparently without any connection with the main course of events. The characters employed are completely unaware of the importance of the ring in the life of the hero, and so are not in a position to explain the situation. The self-contained scene however, brings out indirectly the motif of the play, that is the restoration of Śakuntalā, to the forefront, and the king is presented immediately afterwards as repenting for his rude behaviour to Śakuntalā. If the phrase '*prayogam āsādya*' in Bharata is taken to mean 'as a distinct spectacle' instead of 'as in practice,' the illustration of Viśvanātha may be considered as truly Bharatan. It is undeniable that the fisherman incident has a definite scenic charm.

The five varieties of the Explanatory Device were conceived by Bharata for reporting important but uninteresting incidents, passage of time, battles, etc. which could not be presented on the stage. The later writers on dramaturgy have all stuck to the founder in maintaining the five-fold classification, though with the passage of time much confusion crept in regarding the exact nature and their function.

From a study of all these varieties and the examples supplied by different formulators, the conclusion is, however, inescapable that all the five varieties cannot be maintained as Explanatory Devices. In the absence of illustrations in the Nāṭyaśāstra, it is impossible to determine the criterion of Bharata's classification. But on the ground of the illustrations provided by his followers, it can be said that the Explanatory and Introductory Scenes should be treated as identical. They have nothing distinctive in them in essence, that can justify their separate enumeration. The mere prohibition of using the latter in the beginning of the first Act can hardly be taken to justify its separate character. The Continuation Scene, as defined and illustrated by Viśvanātha may be taken as a distinct variety, but as demonstrated by others, it ceases to be an Explanatory Device. The Anticipatory Scene, likewise, deserves no separate place. The Intimating Speech, however is a distinct variety.

In fine, only three varieties may be treated as valid Explanatory Devices—the Explanatory (or the Introductory) Scene, the Continuation Scene and the Intimating Speech.

———

CHAPTER IV

THE STRUCTURE OF DRAMA (2)

The Plot, Action and the Link

It will be relevant to recall the statement of Bharata made in reference to Rasa and Bhāva[1] in understanding the conception of the five Elements of the Plot. Bharata speaks of the interdependent nature of the Emotions and Sentiments and, using the simile of the seed and the fruit, points out the various stages of development of the Dominant Emotion (sthāyin) resulting in Rasa-realisation. Already the significance of the simile regarding the funccion of Rasa in the drama has been pointed out. It is the simile again that hints at the basis of the structure of drama.

The drama has been, apparently, conceived to be like a tree which undergoes these steges—the germ, the sprout, the development of the tree in the form of branches and leaves, the flowers, and the fruit. The seed attains fulfilment, so to say, in giving birth to the fruits. The dramaturgist evidently visualiszes the theme from its very inception to its final stage in shaping his drama. As in the case of a tree, the process of its fulfilment passes from the germ to the fruit, so in the case of the dramatic plot as well, there is a Germ which gradually unfolds itself and fructifies in the end.

Again, as in the case of the tree, there is a basic unity running from the seed up to the fruit, linking the life-force of the tree with the various manifestations of it

---

1. NŚ. VI. 38 See above p. 18.

in the form of the sprouts, branches, flowers, etc., so in the case of the drama there is a basic unity underlying the entire plot and a linking of it with its outcome in the form of the actions of the hero. Thus the simile supplies us with three factors—the plot, the action and the link.

Taking the clue from this, the dramatic plot has been conceived as having five steps of gradual development. These are termed as 'arthaprakṛtis' or the Elements of the Plot. Bharata says—[2]

> 'The five Elements of the Plot are designated as the Germ (bīja), the Prominent Point (bindu). the Episode (patākā), the Episodical Incident (prakarī) and the Denouement (Kārya), and these are to be used according to prescription.'

It should, however, be borne in mind that all these five Elements can be had only in such themes as have both Principal and Incidental subjects, as the Episode and the Episodical Incident belong exclusively to the Subsidiary or the Incidental Plot. Thus, the Principal Plot must have the three Elements—the Germ, the Prominent Point and the Denouement, and if Incidental Plots are added then the number of the elements would be five.

These five belong to the plot, the body (śarīra) of the drama and not to the Action which also has its own course of development. The situation and the action go side by side ending in a harmony of purposes and situations. Bharata speaks[3] of five Stages of Action (Kāryā-

---

2. NŚ. XXI. 22 Also NLRK. pp. 6–7; DR. I. 18; SD. VI. 64–65; BP. p. 204.
3. Ibid. 9

प्रारम्भश्च प्रयत्नश्च तथा प्राप्तेश्च संभवः ।
नियता च फलप्राप्तिः फलयोगश्च पञ्चमः ॥

vasthā). These are—Beginning (prārambha), Effort (prayatna), Prospect of Success (prāpti-sambhava=prāptyāśā); Conditional Success (niyatāpti) and Attainment of the Result (phalayoga, phalāgama). Needless to say, everyone ambitious of attaining a particular end must pass through these five stages of action, and thus the conception of these is fully rational.

The linking of the Elements of the Plot and the Stages of the Action is done by the so-called Junctures (sandhi) which also are five in number, viz. the Opening (mukha), the Progression (pratimukha), the Development (garbha), the Pause (vimarśa or avamarśa) and the Conclusion (nirvahaṇa). These five serve as the five chapters[4] in a drama, showing the completion of each Stage of the Action, one after the other. The Junctures are the means of linking the Elements of the Plot with the Stages of the Action. There is a view advocated by Dhanañjaya[5] and his followers that there is a parallelism among these three pentads, which, however, is not tenable as it would make the use of Subsidiary plots compulsory. Bharata says[6]— 'Of these (Elements of the Plot) prominence should be given to those which serve the purpose and embellish (the theme), the others are subordinate.'

---

4. Vide Ibid. 1

   पञ्चभिः संधिभिस्तस्य विभागाः परिकीर्तिताः ।

5. Vide DR. I. 22–23

   अर्थप्रकृतयः पञ्च पञ्चावस्थासमन्विताः ।
   यथासंख्येन जायन्ते मुखाद्याः पञ्च सन्धयः ॥

6. NŚ. XXI. 28

   एतेषां यस्य येनार्थो यतश्च गुण इष्यते ।
   प्रधानं तत् प्रकर्तव्यं गुणभूतान्यतः परम् ॥

A full-fledged theme, having both the Principal and Incidental Plots will have all the Elements of the Plot—the Germ, the Prominent Point, the Episode, the Episodical Incident and the Denouement. It is but natural that the Incidental subject should come later and end ealier so that it might further the cause of the Principal subject. The hero however, has to go through all the five Stages of the Action—Beginning, Effort, Prospect of Success, Conditional Success and Attainment of the Result. In such themes the Elements of the Plot and the Stages of the Action run parallel to one another. If there is no Subsidiary Plot, the third and the fourth Elements of the Plot are dropped but the Stages of the Action remain intact.

The five Elements of the Plot : the Germ

The Germ is considered to be the starting point of the plot. It is sown in the very beginning and at that time it appears to be insignificant but as it develops it assumes greater importance. Bharata defines[7] the Germ in these words—

> 'What appears as small but spreads in various ways and leads to the result, is known as the Germ.'

This definition has been accepted by all the later authorities with slight changes in the words but emphasising the same sense. The Bhāvaprakāśana states—[8]

> 'As the sown seed develops variously in the form of the trunk, branches and flowers, etc. and at the end

---

7. NŚ. 23

अल्पमात्रं समुत्सृष्टं बहुधा यत् प्रसर्पति ।
फलावसानं यच्चैव बीजं तदभिधीयते ॥

8. BP. p. 204

बीजमुप्तं यथास्कन्धशाखापुष्पादिरूपतः ।
तथा नायकमित्रादिरूपोऽन्ते फलवान् भवेत् ॥

brings about the fruit, so do the hero and his friends, etc. attain the result in the end.'

This Element of the Plot is the most important as all the later situations until the end of the plot, ensue from it.

The Germ is normally given out in the Introduction (Prastāvanā) by the Sūtradhāra, as in the Ratnāvalī,[9] or at times, in the Explanatory Scene before the first Act, as in the Mālavikāgnimitra where the conversation of the maid-servants of the queen gives out the Germ. The Introduction is naturally the most fitting place for the Germ to be discovered as, without it, the Introduction would tend to be inadequate. But in such cases, the Nāṭyadarpaṇa insists [10] that the Germ has again to be presented in the very first scene by the hero, the opponent of the hero, the chief minister or the like. As the Sūtradhāra is an outsider, a reiteration of the Germ by such a character is necessary. About presenting the Germ, Sāgara Nandin observes [11] that it should be brought out through Double-meaning words (praśleṣa) as in the Veṇīsaṁhāra, or Similarity of sense (chāyā) as in the Jānakī-Rāghava, or Expression of facts (upakṣepa) as in the Kundamālā.

As without the Germ, there can be no Beginning of the Action and consequently no Attainment of the Result, it is indispensable to every plot. The Nāṭyadarpaṇa rightly

---

9. Rat. I. 6.

10. ND. I. p. 43

नायकप्रतिनायकामात्याद्याश्रयेण विचित्ररूपो बीजोपन्यास इति ।

11. Vide NLRK. p. 7

प्रश्लेषो द्व्यर्थवचनम्, छाया कथासाम्यमुपक्षेप अर्थोपस्थान-

मेभिरङ्गैस्तद् बीजमुच्यते ।

points out[12] the pre-eminence of the Germ and the Prominent Point in a drama on the ground that these two pervade the whole plot.

The Prominent Point

The Germ being provided, the Action follows. There is every possibility of its being diverted from the right track. The second Element of the Plot is designed to check such deviation, and is said to be of equal importance with the Germ. *Bindu* (lit. drop) or the Prominent Point is so called for it spreads like a drop of oil on the water, as explained by Dhanika,[13] or like rain drops that pervade the whole space up to the horizon at the time of rain, according to Sāgara Nandin.[14] The dramatist must be very careful to present the plot as a whole and hence should attempt to unite all the actions with a common link of purpose. This purpose is served by the Prominent Point. Bharata says—[15]

> 'That which sustains the continuity till the end of the play even when the chief object is (for the time being) suspended, is called the Prominent Point.'

Thus whenever the main Action of the play is shrouded by extraneous events and the chief end of the play somehow goes out of sight, the dramatist is to use the Prominent

---

12. Vide ND. p. 42
    बीजबिन्द्वोर्मुख्यत्वं सर्वव्यापित्वादिति ।
13. Vide Commentary DR. I. 17.
14. Vide NLRK. p. 7.
15. NŚ. XXI. 24
    प्रयोजनानां विच्छेदे यदविच्छेदकारणम् ।
    यावत् समाप्तिर्बन्धस्य स बिन्दुरिति संज्ञितः ॥

Point which restores the continuity. The definition of Daśarupaka—'Avāntarārthavicchede bindur acchedakāraṇam' (I, 17) may be viewed in this light. The traditional meaning of 'avāntarārthavicchede' goes—'when the secondary matter is interrupted' (Hass)—breaking the compound 'avāntarārthasya vicchede. It can as well be construed thus—'When the Principal matter is interrupted by the Subsidiary ones' —breaking the compound 'avāntareṇa (by extraneous matter) arthasya vicchede (jāte).' If we accept this meaning then the saying of Dhanañjaya exactly tallies with that of Bharata who clearly says—'prayojanānāṃ vicchede.'

Evidently it cannot come in the very first Stage of the Action where only the Germ is presented. The scope of the Germ and the Prominent Point is almost the same, both running up to the end with the only exception that the latter comes in from the second Juncture. Sāgara Nandin,[16] however refers to another view which holds that both the Germ and the Prominent Point are to be shown in the Opening Juncture. He personally favours the graded scheme of their use, i,e. the Prominent Point following the Germ.

The view of Kohala on the nature of the Prominent Point has been quoted by Śāradātanaya,[17] which is very clear. According to him the Prominent Point is that connecting factor which reinstates the chief end of the drama in its

---

16. Vide NLRK. p. 24.

बीजबिन्दू मुखे दर्शयितव्यौ इति पक्षान्तरमेतत् । क्वचित् क्रमश एव निर्देशः ।

17. Vide. BP. VII. p. 204

फले प्रधाने विच्छिन्ने बीजस्यावान्तरैः फलैः ।
तस्याविच्छेदको हेतुर्बिन्दुरित्याह कोहलः ॥

full importance when it is lost sight of due to other events arising out of the Germ.

To the question—How is the Prominent Point to be employed ?—the answer is that the dramatist should ensure that the motif of the play is recalled at definite intervals so that the audience may not lose sight of the chief end of the play. Sāgara Nandin exemplifies the Prominent Point from the Veṇīsaṃhāra. The Denouement of that drama is to be the tying of the hair of Draupadī in a knot after defeating the Kauravas, and the dramatist uses almost in all the acts some such statements as enkindle wrath against the Kauravas and give continuity to the plot. His reference to another view regarding the employment of the Prominent Point has already been noted,[18] which prescribes the reiteration of the essence of the dramatic theme in every act. The basic urge of the horo is either the insults or injuries received from the enemy—valid in dramas that are founded upon the Heroic Sentiment, or energetic endeavours to win the beloved—valid in those founded upon the Erotic Sentiment. Hence this view lays down that in every Act reference to either the insults of the enemy or the energetic endeavours should serve as the Prominent Point. The motif of the drama thus will remain in the forefront.

The Prominent Point, thus, is the next most important element, and has its scope and use up to the end. Its chief function is to maintain continuity of the action leading to the Denouement implied in the Germ.

The Episode and the Episodical Incident

The third Element of the Plot is called the Episode or Patākā literally meaning a flag. It is so called as it

18. Sea above p. 37

denotes the full significance of the dramatic theme as does the flag of a king. This element presents a different story altogether having however, a bearing upon the Principal Subject. The Episode and the fourth Element, the Episodical Incident constitute the Incidental Subject. Although the introduction of the Incidental Subject depends on the dramatist and so cannot be considered indispensable, the introduction of it in the Nāṭaka and the Prakaraṇa varieties is advised by all the theorists clearly on the ground that the inclusion of the Incidental Subject adds charm to the Principal Subject by rendering it complex and interesting.

This sub-plot goes side by side with the Principal plot but it must subserve the end of the Principal plot. Bharata defines–[19]

'The subject which is introduced in the interest of the Principal subject, is called the Episode'

The Episode thus brings in a new element in the play. It takes the form of a Sub--plot having a hero with a definite end to achieve, that runs to more than one Junctures. This however must not be independent but is to be used to promote the cause of the chief hero. The examples are the Episodes of Sugrīva or Vibhīṣaṇa in the Rāma legends. Sugrīva or Vibhīṣaṇa do attain their respective ends but they render the activities of Rāma, the hero more complex and interesting than otherwise (normal). That the Episode must not stand aloof but should be linked with the Principal plot is recognised by Bharata. He

---

19. Vide NŚ. XXI. 25.

यद् वृत्तं हि परार्थं स्यात् प्रधानस्योपकारकम् ।
प्रधानवच्च कल्प्येत सा पताकेति कीर्तिता ॥

observes[20] that the Episode should be joined with the main plot by one or more Junctures.

The Episode is however not to be limited to only one Juncture. Bharata grants its scope up to the third or the fourth Juncture. The idea apparently is that the completion of the Episode in the fourth Juncture will help the dramatist to show its ancillary character through the events of the last Juncture. The Nāṭyadarpaṇa however prescribes its operation up to the fourth Juncture, the Pause on the ground that if both the Principal and Incidental plots culminate simultaneously, there would be no distinction between the two. It is however logical that the Sub-plot should definitely come to an end before the Attainment of the Result by the hero as otherwise it would fail to further the cause of the hero. Such a full-fledged Episode is seen in the Prakaraṇa, the Mṛcchakaṭika where the Śarvilaka-episode is successfully joined with the Principal Plot.

The fourth Element of the Plot, the Episodical Incident (prakarī) is almost the same as the Episode. Its only distinction is that while the Episode continues for a number of Acts as a subsidiary story, it is merely an incident. Constituting the Incidental Subject it also aims at enhancing the charm of the Principal Plot. Bharata defines[21] it thus—

> 'That whose result is presented only for the purpose of the other (the Principal plot), and which is free from any sequel, is called the Episodical Incident.'

---

20. Ibid. XXI. 29

एको नैकोऽपि वा सन्धिः पताकायाश्च योजयेत् ।

21. Ibid. XXI. 26.

फलं प्रकल्प्यते सद्भिः परार्थं यस्य केवलम् ।
अनुबन्धेन हीनस्य प्रकरीं तां विनिर्दिशेत् ॥

An example of it is the Jaṭāyu– Rāvaṇa incident in the Rāma legends.

Though included in the general scheme of the dramatic plot, these concern only the Subsidiary plot and hence the use of both the Episode and the Episodical Incident depends entirely upon the nature of the theme selected by the dramatist. Thus, it cannot be held that all the five Elements of the Plot must find a place in the drama. This has been clearly pointed out in the Nāṭyadarpaṇa. While explaining the characteristic features of the Episodical Incident, the authors[22] say—

> 'By the word 'if' (in the definition) is denoted the non-inevitability of it (the Episodical Incident) like that of the Episode. Its difference with the Episode is due to its irregular use and want of own end.'

The Denouement

The last Element of the Plot is called the Denouement (Kārya). It paves the way for the hero to achieve his desired end and herein all his activities culminate. Bharata says—[23]

> 'Denouement is said to be such activities as are directed to achieve that end for which the Principal Plot is judiciously fashioned by the discerning.'

Dhanañjaya does not define this element but the definition given by Viśvanātha is very clear. He says—

---

22. ND. p. 46.

    चेदित्यनेन पताकावदनवश्यम्भावितामाह । क्वचिद्भावित्वात् स्वार्थं-
    निरपेक्षत्वाच्च पताकातो भेदः ।

23. NŚ. XXI. 57

    यदाधिकारिकं वृत्तं सम्यक् प्राज्ञैः प्रयुज्यते ।
    तदर्थो यः समारम्भस्तत् कार्यं समुदाहृतम् ॥

'That which constitutes the chief object and is the root cause of all activities, and for the achievement of which all the accessories are brought in—is the Denouement (Kārya).[24] The definition given by Viśvanātha is clearly an improvement as it indicates the nature of the Denouement.

The Plot and the Action both, having displayed all the possibilities, converge here and the action of the hero is crowned with success. The Juncture prescribed for showing this situation of fulfilment is fiittingly termed the Conclusion (nirvahaṇa).

So far as the compulsory use of the Elements of the Plot is concerned, only the Germ, the Prominent Point and the Denouement are inevitable in every plot. The use of the Episode and the Episodical Incident is optional depending on the discretion of the dramatist.

The Five Stages of the Action

The plot unfolds itself with the introduction of the Germ which in its turn initiates the dramatic action. The action aims at attaining a particular end suggested by the Germ. Being attracted by the end so suggested, the hero feels a strong desire for it and sets himself to work in order to achieve it. These two phases of the hero's action are termed the Beginning (ārambha) and the Effort (yatna). The effort goes on the more vigorously due to many obstacles put in the way of the hero and at last he finds a way, like a ray of light in the dark. This finding of a way may be termed as the climax and this point is known as the third Stage of Action, the Prospect of Success (prāptyāśā). The Effort of the hero to reach the goal transforms itself into the Prospect

24. Ibid. SD. VI. 69–70

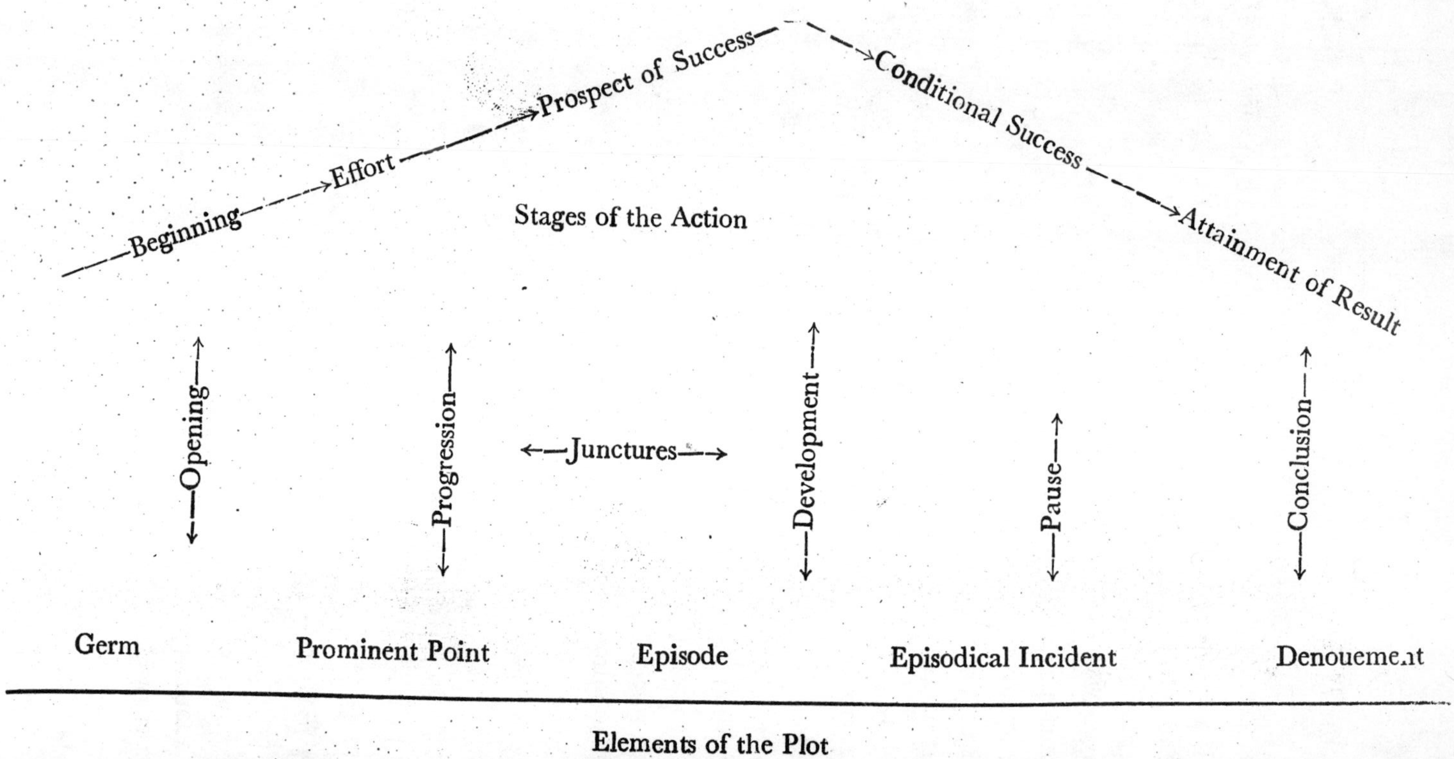
Beginning
Effort
Prospect of Success
Conditional Success
Attainment of Result
Stages of the Action
Opening
Progression
Junctures
Development
Pause
Conclusion
Germ
Prominent Point
Episode
Episodical Incident
Denouement
Elements of the Plot

of Success at which stage the hero feels assured that his longing is going to succeed. As the hero proceeds from this pinnacle of heightened desire and hope, the poignancy of his emotions lessens a bit, and the Prospect of Success strengthens his confidence. He then reaches the stage that is characterised as Conditional Success (niyatāpti) and is definitely a lower state in point of expectancy than the previous one. With further efforts or supernatural assistance, the hero overcomes the remaining obstacle and succeeds in achieving the desired object at the last Stage of the Action, the Attainment of the Result.

From Beginning there is a gradual heightening of emotions up to the stage of Prospect of Success and from thence onwards to the Attainment of the Result a gradual decline, the difficulties being gradually eliminated and success getting nearer achievement. Underlying all these various Stages of the Action there are the five Elements of the Plot and the five Junctures joining the two. The movements of the Plot, the Action and the Junctures may be seen in the diagram.

Beginning

The first Stage of the Action is fittingly called the Beginning (ārambha). Strictly speaking there is no physical action here but only the presentation of a strong desire of the hero. It is the rise of this desire and the consequent eagerness of the hero that constitute the Beginning. Bharata defines it thus—[25]

25. NŚ. XXI. 10.

औत्सुक्यमात्रबन्धस्तु यद् बीजस्य निबध्यते ।
महतः फलयोगस्य स खल्वारम्भ इष्यते ॥

> 'The presentation of eagerness alone for the attainment of the commendable result, ensuing from the Germ is called the Beginning.'

This Stage of the Action is fully dependent on the Germ and so the Beginning follows the Germ closely in every play and they are linked together.

Effort

The desire in the Beginning is immediately followed by the second Stage of Action, the Effort (prayatna) which is characterised by physical striving for the object. Bharata defines[26] Effort thus—

> 'The striving (of the hero) towards the Attainment of the Result when it is not in view, and showing further eagerness (about it); is called the Effort.'

At the Effort stage, though the result is not visualised, expression is given of the determination and zeal of the hero to achieve it through necessary actions. The chief feature of this stage is a great restlessness on the part of the hero. The hero rushes forward with many schemes in his head but somehow fails to reach his goal. This is the proper stage for the cropping up of some other subsidiary episodes, if the plot allows them, which may either retard or encourage him. If it is so, here is introduced the 'Episode' or the 'Episodical Incident'. The Āryaka episode in the Mṛcchakaṭika for example, retards the union of Cārudatta, the hero, with Vasantasenā but helps to save the hero in the end. Thus the action proceeds against heavy odds which at the same time render the desire of the hero more

---

26. Ibid. 11

अपश्यतः फलप्राप्ति व्यापारो यः फलं प्रति ।
परं चौत्सुक्यगमनं स प्रयत्नः प्रकीर्तितः ॥

intense. This intensity keeps on the rise up to the third Stage of Action where the possibilities of success and failure are evenly balanced. So the third Stage can be rightly called the climax of dramatic action.

Prospect of Success

The hero now enters the third Stage of the Action known as the Prospect of Success (prāptyāśā). As the very name implies, the hero at this stage visualises the success as a possibility and resolves to proceed ahead. At this stage the emotions of the hero reach almost a breaking point and there is a corresponding desparation in his thoughts and actions. He however overcomes it and is sustained by the prospect of attaining the cherished end. Bharata's definition of the stage is as follows—[27]

> 'When the attainment of the object is slightly suggested by an idea, it is to be known as the Prospect of Success.'

Courageously facing and fighting with all the obstacles the hero finds himself in a position conducive to attain his end. Though there remain many more impediments to surmount, the hero somehow experiences a temporary respite. He divines a correct line of progress by this time. The definition and explanation offered by the joint authors of the Nāṭyadarpaṇa appeal most. It defines—[28] 'The Prospect of Success is a slender expectation of the Result due to only some expedients.'

---

27. Ibid. 12

ईषत्प्राप्तिश्च या काचिदर्थस्य परिकल्प्यते ।
भावमात्रेण संज्ञेयो विधिज्ञैः प्राप्तिसम्भवः ॥

28. ND. I. 35

'फलसम्भावना किञ्चित् प्राप्त्याशा हेतुमात्रतः'—फलान्तरासंबन्धाद-

And explains—'A slight possibility, not a certainty, of attaining the desired end due to expedients that are not linked with other ends and are free from unpredictable impediments is called the Prospect of Success as it shows an expectation of the Result.'

Being free from undesirable results and from other uncertain impediments in the means, this Stage of Action presents a hope not a certainty of attaining the desired end.

Conditional Success

The tempo of Action, thus heightened step by step, now begins to fall. The plot gets here most entangled in so many problems. To use the fitting simile of the tree in growth, it is the developing condition of it into branches and leaves. After that naturally comes the flower. So the fourth stage is the flowering of success. A definite but conditional success obviously refreshens the tormented hero. This fourth Stage of the Action is called the Conditional Success (níyatāpti). Here success is dependent upon the surmounting of the final obstacle. Thus in this stage of Conditional Success, the actions of the hero lead him to that comfortable position wherefrom he looks at the Result as a certainty, subject only to the removal of the final obstacle. The hero reviews the whole situation and decides upon a course of action that will remove all impediments. The stage is so called because herein the achievement (*āpti*) appears to be conditioned (*niyatā*) by the final obstacle.

Bharata defines this Stage of the Action thus—[29]

निश्चितबाधकाभावाच्च उपायादीषत् प्रधानफलस्य या सम्भावना न तु निश्चयः सा प्राप्तेः प्रधानफललाभस्य आशा प्राप्त्याशा ।

29. NŚ XXI. 13

नियतां च फलप्राप्तिं यत्र भावेन पश्यति ।
नियतां तां फलप्राप्तिं सगुणस्तु विनिर्दिशेत् ॥

> 'When the Attainment of the Result, although conditional, is visualised as a certainty, it is known as the Stage of Conditional Success, by the experts.'

For the Attainment of the Result, however some efforts are still required on the part of the hero but now the possibilities of success by far outweigh those of failure.

Attainment of the Result

The remaining obstacle is overcome in the last Stage of the Action which is fittingly called the 'Attainment of the Result' (phalāgama). Bharata defines—[30]

> 'When the desired and appropriate Result appears in its fullness at the end of all events, it is called the Attainment of the Result.'

In this stage, the striving of the hero is crowned with the attainment of the desired object. The final obstacle is removed by some extra-ordinary or unusual agency. The theorists hold that the Marvellous should play a part in this stage so that the achievement is rendered unique and impressive. Heavenly bodies or sages with super-natural powers make their appearence and grant success to the deserving hero. Here sincere human efforts find success through a sanction of the divine powers—the artistic way of upholding the divine without belittling the human.

This Stage of the Action is naturally related with the last phase of the Plot. The dramatic Plot, having exhausted all possible situations to put to test, so to say, the mettle of the hero, reaches the Denouement which along

---

30. Ibid. 14

अभिप्रेतं समग्रं च प्रतिरूपं क्रियाफलम् ।
यद् दृश्यते निवृत्ते तु फलयोगः स उच्यते ॥

with the final stage of the hero's Action constitute the last Juncture known as the Conclusion. A harmonious blending of situations and activities is brought about and the curtain is rung down.

The Five Junctures

It has been observed that the Junctures have been conceived as the means of linking the Plot and the Action. With the unfolding of the Plot, the hero finds himself in varying situations and embarks upon a course of action, conducive to reaching at the goal, which, starting with the Beginning, has five stages ending in the Attainment of the Result.

Bharata has not given any precise definition of the Junctures but has indicated its function. According to Bharata[31] the Junctures break the Plot into sections which are five in number. Although they divide the Plot, they do not put asunder the sections so divided. The word *Sandhi* literally means joining and in its technical sense also it serves both the purposes—breaking the plot into sections and maintaining a link. The basis of this division and linking is clearly the thoughts and the different Stages of the Action of the hero. We have already noted that the five stages of the dramatic action have been conceived on the basis of the five stages of human effort in achieving a particular end. So, we can hold that the Junctures are so conceived as they mark the completion of these Stages of the Action in a play.

---

31. Vide Ibid 1.

इतिवृत्तं तु काव्यस्य शरीरं परिकीर्तितम्।
पञ्चभिः संधिभिस्तस्य विभागाः परिकीर्तिताः ॥

The relation of the Junctures with the plot is also noteworthy. It can be said that the plot supplies the base on which the hero acts. When the dramatist selects a plot, say from the legends, he has to find out a particular Germ and a Denouement that will mark off his theme. He cannot accept the story in full from the legends where it may have some undramatic beginning and end. Thus selected, the theme requires a new arrangement of events which would properly represent the different stages of the hero's action. This purpose is served by the Junctures.

The Junctures help the dramatist in dividing the Plot into sections with reference to the Actions of the hero. Thus it is with the five Stages of the Action that the Junctures are chiefly related.

The view of Sāgara Nandin is very clear on this point. He observes[32] that the Junctures knit together the various events of the Plot. He refers to the derivative meaning of the term and says, 'By these (Junctures) the events are mutually joined (Saṃdhīyante) and so they are called Junctures.'

Although Viśvanātha follows Dhanañjaya in his definition of the Junctures, he clearly points out[33] the dependence of the Junctures on the Stages of the Action. Dhanañjaya supplies[34] the definition that has been widely

---

32. NLRK
संधिः परस्परं कथार्थानां संघटनम् । संधीयन्तेऽर्थाः परस्परमेभिरिति संधयः ।
33. SD. VI. 74.
34. DR. I. 23
अन्तरैकार्थसम्बन्धः संधिरेकान्वये सति ।
Compare also SD. VI. 75.

accepted. In his view 'Juncture is the connection of one thing with another, when there is a single sequence (of events).' This device, thus aims at joining the many events taking place during the particular time and situation in the life of the hero, and effecting a graded arrangement of the Plot helps the dramatist to present the theme as a composite whole.

The five Junctures are concerned with the Principal Plot and the Actions of the hero. For presenting the development of the Incidental Plot, if any, Bharata prescribes[35] the use of Secondary Junctures (anubandha) but does not go into a detailed description of them. The main purpose of these Secondary Junctures appears to be to link the Episode with the Principal Plot. Dhanañjaya neither defines nor enumerates them but merely says[36] that the Episode should have 'one or more Sub-junctures less.' He calls them Sub-junctures (anusaṃdhi) which is the same as the Bharatan Secondary Juncture (anubandha).

Bharata speaks[37] of a further use of some twenty-one Special Junctures (sandhyantara). These, he says, are almost like the Subdivisions of the Junctures (aṅgakalpa) and aim at enhancing the charm of the Junctures. The Special Junctures are: Conciliation (sāma), Dissension (bheda), Giving Gifts (pradāna), Chastisement (daṇḍa), Killing (vadha), Presence of Mind (pratyutpannamatitva) Blunder in Addressing (gotra-skhalita), Rashness (sāhasa), Terror (bhaya), Intelligence (dhī), Deceit (māyā),

---

35. NS. XXI. 29

एको नैकोऽपि वा संधिः पताकायाश्च योजयेत् ।
प्रधानार्थानुयायित्वादनुबन्धः स उच्यते ॥

36. DR. III. 27.
37. Vide NŚ. XXI. 48–51.

Anger (krodha), Strength (ojas), Concealment (saṃvaraṇa), Error (bhrānti), Ascertainment (avadhāraṇa), Messenger (dūta) Letter (lekha), Dream (svapna), Portrait (citra) and Intoxication (mada).

The list consists of actions, qualities, emotions and expedients which have, however, nothing peculiarly dramatic in them except that they may figure in a play as they do in life. So in a representation of human life, these might naturally come in. Any especial enumeration of these is hardly called for. Dhanañjaya realised the superfluity of the Special Junctures and hence left them out in his treatise. He merely refers[38] to the Special Junctures along with some other matters, considering a separate enumeration of these redundant on the ground that 'they are included in the States of Joy, Energy, and the rest and their embellishments.' The later theorists also follow him in this respect.

The five Junctures and their Sub-divisions are however unanimously accepted as indispensable to a drama. Bharata says—[39]

> 'The five Junctures in the drama are—the Opening (mukha), the Progression (pratimukha), the Development (garbha), the Pause (vimarśa or avamarśa) and the Conclusion (nirvahaṇa).

All the treatises maintain that these five should be employed in the Nāṭaka and Prakaraṇa varieties. These two varieties are therefore known to have all the Junctures

---

38. Vide DR. IV. 83-84.
39. NŚ. XXI. 37

मुखं प्रतिमुखं गर्भः विमर्शस्तथा हि।
तथा निर्वहणं चैव संधयो नाटके स्मृताः ॥

(pūrṇasaṃdhi). In shorter plays however a few of these are dropped. Such varieties of the Drama are described as 'deficient in the Junctures' (hīnasaṃdhi).

The Opening Juncture is concerned with the Beginning, the Progression with the Effort, the Development with the Prospect of Success, the Pause with the Conditional Success and the Conclusion with the Attainment of the Result. Needless to say, the Principal Plot underlies all these Stages of the Action which start with the Germ, is carried on through the Prominent Point and culminate in the Denouement. The Episode and the Episodical Incident are conveniently incorporated in this fabric.

The Opening

The first of the Junctures, the Opening has been defined by Bharata thus—[40]

> 'That part of a play, in which the Germ is brought into being as the source of many objects and Sentiments, is called, in consideration of its body, the Opening.'

The Opening constitutes the first section of a play. The Germ is here and so is the Action arising out of it. The Juncture indicates the prevailing Sentiment as well. The Nāṭyadarpaṇa observes that in all the Junctures the Sentiment should be treated as fundamental. The authors hold[41] that the entire dramatic method being vitalised by

---

40. Ibid 39

यत्र बीजसमुत्पत्तिर्नानार्थरससम्भवा ।
काव्ये शरीरानुगतं तन् मुखं परिकीर्तितम् ॥

Also compare NLRK. p. 24; ND. I. 38; SD. VI. 76; DR. I. 24,

41. Vide ND. I. 68a.

the Sentiment, all the Junctures should be suggestive of it. In short, when the Germ, the Action and the Sentiment are brought to play together to stir the plot into movement, we have the Opening Juncture.

That the Germ should find a place in the Opening is unanimously accepted. The Prominent Point also should be used along with the Germ in the Opening—so runs a view quoted by Sāgara Nandin. The Germ of the Plot being evolutionary, it cannot but give rise to newer situations, and these may necessitate the employment of the Prominent Point, the chief function of which is to unify the main events when these get clouded by other events. So, the use of the Prominent Point in the Opening Juncture can neither be prescribed nor prohibited, as that depends entirely on the nature of the Plot. The dramatist should see whether all the events are advancing smoothly and tending towards the Denouement or not, otherwise he should bring in the Prominent Point to restore the perspective.

However, the Opening is primarily concerned with the Germ, the Beginning and the Sentiment. The Prominent Point may or may not be there. From this also it becomes clear that the Junctures are primarily concerned with the Stages of the Action and not with the Elements of the Plot. A strict parallelism of the three pentads, as advocated by Dhanañjaya, has already been discounted. As the Prominent Point may be placed any where, so the Germ also may find a place almost at every Juncture. only the Denouement cannot evidently come in any other Juncture but the final one. The Episode also generally cannot be introduced in the Opening as an advanced Stage of the Action is required for its appearance. Still it is possible for a Plot to begin with an Episode. For the Episodical incident as well there is no fixed Juncture. Discussing the relative importance of these, Rāmacandra and Guṇacandra observe—[42]

'Due to their all pervading nature, the Germ and the Prominent Point are of the greatest importance. Of the 'Episode', the Episodical Incident and the 'Denouement', the importance of one, of both or of all the three are relative to the fact of their being useful to the desired result......... If the 'Episode' or the 'Episodical Incident' be insignificant or wanting, the Denouement becomes the chief.'

So the introduction of an 'Episodical Incident' in the Opening Juncture should not be considered a violation of the graded scheme of their employment. The scheme only points out the natural order but does not settle or limit the scope of their use.

The Progression

The second Juncture is called the Progression and aims at showing the second Stage of the Action, the Effort of the hero. The Germ, having come to light in the Opening, now assumes a greater importance and allures the hero who embarks upon a vigorous search to get at the result suggested by the Germ. Thus the alluring, though elusive, Germ and the vigorous efforts of the hero to get the desired object suggested by it constitute the Juncture of Progression. Bharata in his definition points to the relation of the Progression and the Germ

42. ND. I. 48

तत्र बीजबिन्दोस्तावन् मुख्यत्वमेव सर्वव्यापित्वात् । पताका-प्रकरी-कार्याणां तु मुख्यफलं प्रति उपयोगापेक्षया एकस्य द्वयोस्त्रयाणां वा

thus—[43]. 'The Progression is the uncovering of the Germ placed at the Opening, in a manner that it is perceptible and not perceptible by turns.'

The hero is forcibly drawn towards the Germ, which however, having once revealed itself gets lost and thus increases the tempo of the Action. Due to a further development of the Plot, the Prominent Point may have a place here to maintain the proper direction of the events. Thus the Germ, the Prominent Point, the Effort and above all, the Sentiment are displayed in the Progression. The view of Dhanañjaya[44] that the Progression shows the sequence of the Prominent Point and the Effort can only be taken in a general way. It is not the Prominent Point but the Effort that is fundamental here, for the former may be there as it may be elsewhere in the Drama.

The Development

The course of events then brings the hero to the Stage of the 'Prospect of Success'. Surmounting very many difficulties he reaches a position wherefrom he finds a way, runs to follow it but again falls into a whirlpool of troubles but still dose not lose heart. In this Stage of Action there is a tumultuous restlessness both in the emotions and the actions of the hero. The Juncture showing this situation and the third Stage of the Action called the Prospect of

---

मुख्यत्वमन्येषां चामुख्यत्वम्············। पताका-प्रकर्योरल्पत्वेऽभावे वा सर्वत्र कार्यस्य मुख्यत्वमिति।

43. NŚ. XXI. 40

बीजस्योद्घाटनं यत् तु दृष्टनष्टमिव क्वचित्।
मुखे न्यस्तस्य सर्वत्र तद्वै प्रतिमुखं स्मृतम्॥

44. Vide DR. I. 30.

Success is known as the Development. Bharata defines[45] the Juncture thus—

> 'The sprouting of the Germ, its attainment or non-attainment and search for it, is called the Development.'

In this Juncture, the Germ appears in its full-fledged form and the Attainment seems near. But the hero cannot have it for certain due to other complexities. The attainment eludes the grasp, and the hero begins a renewed search for it. Although not realised, the Germ grants a heartening prospect of success to the hero who is now quite hopeful of achievement. This Juncture marks the climax of the dramatic action. Sāgara Nandin[46] says that being the central section of the drama, it is called *Garbha* (Development, lit. middle).

Dhanañjaya, with his somewhat unreasonable theory of parallelism between the Junctures and the Elements of the Plot, finds it difficult to associate the Episode with this Juncture. The Episode, as has already been observed, cannot be assigned to a fixed Juncture, and neither Bharata nor any other theorists say that the Junctures should go on uniting the Elements of the Plot quite mechanically. Hence Dhanañjaya has to say[47] that in the Development 'there may or may not be the Episode but the Prospect of

---

45. NŚ. XXI. 41

उद्भेदस्तस्य बीजस्य प्राप्तिरप्राप्तिरेव वा।
पुनश्चान्वेषणं यत्र स गर्भ इति संज्ञितः ॥

46. Vide NLRK. p. 30

नाटकस्य गर्भत्वाद् गर्भः ।

47. DR. I 36

पताका स्यान्न वा स्यात् प्राप्तिसंभवः ।

Success (must be there)'. In this connection, it may be mentioned that Dr. Haas's rendering of this portion of Daśarūpaka as '(In it) there should be an Episode or (else) there should not be Prospect of Success' can hardly be maintained. The text should be rendered as '(In it), there may or may not be an Episode but there must be the Prospect of Success' which finds support in the commentary of Dhanika.

Thus the Juncture, Development by name, shows the hero in the stage of a hopeful eagerness for the result. But the result belongs still to the realm of possibility and not to that of certainty. It is this Prospect of Success that urges the hero onward to the next stage. The Nāṭyadarpaṇa makes this point clear while distinguishing between the Development and the Pause, the next Juncture. It states—[48]

> 'Her e in the Juncture called the Development, the sense of non-attainment prevails, marked as it is by only the possibility of the result, otherwise it would mean surety of the result. Whereas, in the Juncture, Pause the sense of attainment rules, as it is marked by the surety of the result—that is the difference (between the two).'

The Pause

The Prospect of Success leads the hero to a close proximity of the desired end. After this, the tempo of action becomes leisurely. The heap of perplexities dwindles

48. ND· I. p. 56.

इह गर्भसन्धौ अप्राप्त्यंशः प्रधानं फलसंभावनात्मकत्वात् अन्यथा फलनिश्चयात्मक एव स्यात् । अवमर्शसंधौ तु प्राप्त्यंशः प्रधानं फल-निश्चयरूपत्वादिति विशेषः ।

away, and an easy way presents itself to the hero. He now reaches a position where he can stop for a while and consider his own progress, the distance still to be covered and the shortcomings. Considering the pros and cons, he realises a partial success. The fourth Juncture, the Pause shows the fourth Stage of the Action, known as the Conditional Success. Bharata's definition of the Pause is—[49]

> 'One's pause (vimarśa) over the Germ that has sprouted in the Development, on account of some temptation, anger or distress is called the Juncture of that name (i.e. Pause).'

In this section of the drama, the Germ passing through the Development, and putting on an attractive form allures the hero on the one hand and, on the other he is confronted with formidable obstacles. With the assurance of success realised in the previous stage, he now turns to a deliberation of the situation. Due to this nature the Juncture is called Vimarśa which literally means a deliberation. There is thus a review of the situation in this Juncture. The Result appears now to be near at hand and becomes a certainty. Still there is some apprehension. Though most of the complications have come to an end, the hero feels afraid and almost loses heart. This perplexity makes the success conditional. These conditions arise out of calamities, anger, lust, curses, etc. According to Sāgara Nandin[50] they are due to three causes—allurement, anger, and calamity. Dhanañjaya also says the same. The Nāṭya-

---

49. NŚ. XXI. 42

गर्भनिर्भिन्नबीजार्थो विलोभनकृतोऽपि वा ।
किञ्चिदाश्लेषसंयुक्तो विमर्शः स इति स्मृतः ॥

50. Vide NLRK. p. 33

स विमर्शस्त्रिधा भवति—विलोभनसमुद्भवः क्रोधजः, व्यसनजश्च ।

darpaṇa[51] gives no fixed number but states broadly—'Thus the Juncture of Pause comes about due to many causes.' These causes make the hero pause and deliberate.

The desirability of putting such obstacles in the Pause has thus been outlined in the Nāṭyadarpaṇa—[52]

'This Juncture, though it falls within the scope of the Conditional Success Stage of the Action and there can be no misgiving about the possibility of the Attainment of the Result, is full of doubts due to the reason that the forces for and against the attainment of the Result are equally powerful in it. Moreover, the principle that 'great men strive to the utmost even when confronted with so many obstacles' conditions the attainment of the result. Furthermore, to show that although 'prosperity is attended with so many difficulties', one should not flinch, inspite of their onslaughts, when the result is near at hand—the difficulties must be put in this Juncture.'

The Conclusion (nirvahaṇa)

The last Juncture is fittingly named the Conclusion. Up till now all through the Junctures the Germ, the Prominent Point, the actions, the emotions—all these were tending towards the culminating point of fulfilment. Now an end of all his strivings and sufferings awaits the hero. The machinations of the inimical forces have now

---

51. ND. p. 58 एवमनेकहेतुजो विमर्शसंधिः ।

52. ND. I. 39

नियतफलावस्थया व्याप्यत्वेऽप्यस्य संधेः संभावनानन्तरं सन्देहस्याप्राप्तावपि च फलं प्रति जनकविघातकयोस्तुल्यबलत्वात् सन्देहात्मकत्वम् । 'विघ्नैरपि हन्यमानाश्च महात्मानो विशेषतो यतन्त' इति तत्त्वतो नियतफलाप्तिरूपत्वम् । श्रेयांसि बहुविघ्नानि भवन्तीति विघ्नहेतुसंपातेऽपि प्रत्यासन्नवर्तिनि फले न निवर्तनीयमिति च व्युत्पादयितुमवश्यमत्र संधौ विघ्नहेतवो निबन्धनीयाः ।

been completely overcome. Even the supernatural obstacles are removed, and the hero enjoys the possession of his desired object attended with benediction from Heaven. The Conclusion shows this stage and marks the end of the play. Bharata defines[53] the Conclusion as follows:

> 'Bringing together the objects (of the Junctures) such as the Opening, etc. along with the Germ, when they have attained fruition, is called the Conclusion.'

The Plot, both the Principal and the Subsidiary, and the action converge together and bring about the desired result and thus the Germ sown at the Opening attains maturity here and bears fruit.

Although all the later treatises follow Bharata in defining the Conclusion, the definition given in the Nāṭyadarpaṇa points out all its important features very lucidly. According to the authors[54] 'the Conclusion is veritably that Juncture wherein the Germ in its entirety, all the Stages of the Action, the different emotions and feelings, the Junctures such ,as the Opening etc., reach the desired

---

53. NŚ. XXI. 43

समानं च समार्थानां मुख्यार्थानां सबीजिनाम् ।
फलोपसंगतानां च ज्ञेयं निर्वहणं तु तत् ॥

54. Vide ND. I. 40

बीजस्य विकृतं विकार उत्पत्त्युद्घाटफलोन्मुख्यादिका: सह बीजविकृतेरवस्थाभिश्च प्रारम्भादिभिर्वर्तन्ते । नाना विचित्रा भावा: स्थायि-व्यभिचारि-सात्त्विका अथवा भावयन्ति फलं साधयन्ति भावा उपाया बिन्दु-पताका-प्रकरी-कार्याणि यत्र········मुखादयो मुख-प्रतिमुख-गर्भ-विमर्शा: । फलेन मुखसाध्येन नायक-प्रतिनायक-नायिकामात्यादिव्यापारै: सम्यग् औचित्येन युज्यन्ते सम्बध्यन्ते यस्मिन् प्रधानवृत्तांशे स फलागमावस्थया परिच्छिन्नो निर्वहणसंधि: । ध्रुवमिति प्रारम्भस्य निर्वाहाविनाभावित्वात् सर्वरूपकेष्वस्यावश्यम्भावमाह ।

end'. They explain that in this final Juncture the Germ succeeds in reaching its fruit and naturally the dramatic action comes to a successful conclusion granting proper results to different persons such as the hero, the heroine, the opponent of the hero and the like. This Juncture, they maintain, is as indispensable as the Opening, following the natural law that every action must have a beginning and an end.

The Junctures and the forms of Drama

An employment of all these Junctures is prescribed in the Nāṭaka and the Prakaraṇa varieties and in the Nāṭikā as well, included as it is in the broader scope of the Nāṭaka class. Bharata states[55] that 'the dramatists should know that these are the Junctures of the Nāṭaka and the Prakaraṇa.' Sāgara Nandin points out that the use of all the five Junctures is not compulsory. He states,[56] with reference to Bharata's statement, that 'the rule is binding only where all the five Junctures can be had by an elaboration of the Subsidiary Plot that promotes the Principal theme. It should not be taken as compulsory.'

Bharata however makes a provision for omitting one or the other Junctures if necessity so demands[57] in a different context. On this omission, are based the different forms of drama. For example, the varieties known as the Aṅka, the Prahasana, the Bhāṇa and the Vīthī have only two Junctures—the Opening and the Conclusion as opposed

---

55. NŚ. XXI. 44

एते हि संधयो ज्ञेया नाटकस्य प्रयोक्तृभिः ।
तथा प्रकरणस्यापि······················· ॥

56. NLRK. p. 20

प्रासङ्गिकस्याधिकारिकस्यार्थे वर्तमानस्य यदि विस्तारात् संधयो विधातुं पञ्चापि शक्यन्ते तदायं नियमो नावश्यकर्तव्यतयाभ्युपगन्तव्यः ।

57. Vide NŚ. XXI. 18 हीनसंधिस्तु कारणात् ।

to the Nāṭaka and the Prakaraṇa which have all the five. Abou^t^ the omission of the Junctures, an order of preference is prescribed by Bharata. It is stated[58] that 'if one is to be omitted, it should be the fourth, i.e. the Pause if two, then the third and the fourth, i.e the Development and the Pause are to be dropped, and if complete omission is to be effected then the second, the third and the fourth, i.e. the Progression, the Development and the Pause should be left out.' The Opening and the Conclusion being indispensable, must remain in all the varieties. On this the commentary of Abhinavagupta runs as follows: 'It will be said that the Dima and the Samavakāra are of four Junctures—there the Pause is omitted. The Vyāyoga and the Ihāmṛga should always have three Junctures—here the Development and the Pause are to be abandoned. The Prahasana, the Vīthī, the Aṅka and the Bhāṇa are of two Junctures—in these the Progression, the Development and the Pause are to be omitted. In the phrase 'dvitīyatricaturthānām' the word 'tri' (three) means tritiya, i.e. the third. The Opening and the Conclusion are however, indispensable everywhere. [Dimaḥ Samavakāraśca catuḥsaṃdhī iti vakṣyate, tatra avamarśasya lopaḥ. 'Vyāyogehāmṛgau cāpi sadā kāryau trisaṃdhikau'—ityatra garbhavimarśayor lopaḥ. 'Dvisaṃdhi tu Prahasanaṃ Vīthyaṅko Bhāṇa eva ca'—tatra pratimukhagarbhavimarśānāṃ lopaḥ. Triśabdena dvitīyatricaturthānām ityatra tṛtīyo lakṣyate. Tatropakramopsaṃhārau tāvat sarvatrāvaśyambhāvinau—A. Bh. Vol.III. p. 11.]. Thus it appears that the use of all the Junctures depends on the nature of the Plot, and no compulsion is implied here.

58. Vide Ibid. 19

एकलोपे चतुर्थस्य द्विलोपे त्रिचतुर्थयोः।
द्वितीयत्रिचतुर्थानां त्रिलोपे लोप इष्यते ॥

The Sub-divisions of the Junctures

These five Junctures have been allotted twelve or thirteen Sub-divisions (saṃdhyaṅga) each, the total number of which is sixty-four (64). According to Bharata, the Opening has twelve Sub-divisions; the Progression thirteen; the Development thirteen; the Pause thirteen and the Conclusion fourteen. Although thus the total (12+13+13+13+14=65) comes to sixty-five, Bharata maintains the total as sixty-four. Dhanañjaya removes this discrepancy by reducing the number by one in the Development. So maintains the Bhāvaprakāśana. The Sāhityadarpaṇa and the Nāṭyadarpaṇa, on the otherhand follow the Nāṭyaśāstra strictly in the distribution of the Sub-divisions but observe that the last two Sub-divisions of the Conclusion (viz. Kāvyasaṃhāra and Praśasti) should be treated as one, and thus remove the discrepancy regarding the total number given by Bharata.

Bharata and following him, all the later writers on dramaturgy, attach much importance to these sub-divisions which literally mean 'limbs of the Junctures.' Bharata declares—'Just as a man, deficient in limbs, is unable to fight a battle so is a play, deficient in 'limbs', unfit for production.' He further maintains that a play even poor in theme, if provided with adequate 'limbs', will certainly be charming because of the brilliance of its production. On the other hand, plays with lofty theme would fail to charm, if deficient in the limbs.'

The definition of these given by Bharata have been mostly accepted by the later theorists who, on their part, have supplied examples of these in their treatises. To the modern mind, this elaborate classification must appear as hair-splitting and redundant to a great extent. The prescription of the five Junctures is enough for suggesting the broad outline of the structure of the play and the course of progress of the dramatic Action. A further elaboration of these into a number of Sub-divisions amounts to making the scheme too mechanical. Moreover, no playwright can utilise all the so-called 'limbs' and as such all play would be deficient in them. Bharata himself is however conscious that in the drama, display of Sentiments is of prime importance, for which no fixed scheme can be prescribed. So regarding the use of these 'limbs' the dramatist should be given freedom to work within the broad limits suggested by the Junctures as otherwise he would merely follow the rule and fail in his mission of effecting Rasa-realisation.

In spite of this observation, it is necessary to give an account of these sixty-four Sub-divisions of Junctures, as they point out the growth of the technical side of dramaturgy. It will be seen from the scheme that these Sub-divisions were conceived for making the Junctures capable of presenting the different Stages of the Action. Taking the Action in general, the theorists speak of these Sub-divisions which supply, as it were, a pre-fabricated structure of a building. Being unrelated with any particular type of the Action, a careful selection of these is needed for their use. A blind following of these in respect of handling the theme and collocating the incidents would clearly take away the initiative of the playwright and tend to make his art mechanical.

The Sub-divisions of the Opening

Bharata speaks[59] of twelve Sub-divisions of the 'Opening'. These are—

59. References to the Sub-divisions and their definitions are to be made to NŚ XXI.59–105.

1. Suggestion (upakṣepa),
2. Enlargement (parikara),
3. Establishment (parinyāsa),
4. Allurement (vilobhana),
5. Resolve (yukti),
6. Success (prāpti)
7. Settling (samādhāna)
8. Conflict of feelings (vidhāna),
9. Surprise (paribhāvanā),
10. Disclosure (udbheda),
11. Activity (karaṇa),
12. Incitement (bheda).

It will be noticed that the Sub-divisions of the Opening have only one aim that of inspiring the hero to begin his activities. It goes to the credit of the founder of Drama that all the Sub-divisions are very general in nature. From Suggestion to Incitement all the Sub-divisions are concerned with preparing the proper atmosphere for the hero to act. The object may be anything—the love of a beautiful lady or winning back the lost kingdom. The Sub-divisions are so conceived that the hero first resolves in his mind for the success and ultimately starts his activity which however meets with obstacles. The Opening through its twelve Sub-divisions places the object before the hero and urges him to activity. There must be 'Allurement', 'Conflict of Feelings' and last of all 'Incitement' that is the urging on to further activities as the situation warrants. These may be considered the very steps for the action to move forward.

A strict use of all these Sub-divisions is not prescribed by the later treatises. The dramatist is given freedom to use these according to necessity. Dhanika, the commentator of the Daśarūpaka observes—[60] 'Of these, 'Suggestion,' 'Enlargement,' 'Establishment,' 'Resolve,' 'Disclosure' and 'Settling' must be employed.' But about the compulsion, there may be diversity of opinion, so from a liberal and practical view point it may be said that the dramatist is to consult his own mind and employ the Sub-divisions accordingly.

The view of the Nāṭyadarpaṇa regarding this is valuable. The authors observe[61] that these Sub-divisions may be classified into two groups. One will consist of those which are to be used exclusively in the Opening and the other will consist of those which may be used in other Junctures as well. They say that the Sub-divisions, viz. the 'Suggestion,' the 'Enlargement' and the 'Establishment' should be used in the very beginning and in the same order. The 'Settling' should come according to the composition somewhere in the middle of the 'Juncture'. The 'Disclosure' and 'Activity' should be placed at the end. Excepting for 'Activity' the remaining five Sub-divisions along with 'Resolve', according to the authors, belong exclusively to the Opening Juncture. The other six may be used in other Junctures as well. They further observe that Incitement must be used at the end of all Junctures and after the Introductory and the Explanatory Scenes as well. These Sub-divisions should be employed after the Introduction is over, as it is outside the pale of the dramatic Plot.

---

60. Vide Commentary on DR. I. 29.

61. Vide ND. p. 59

तत्रापि उपक्षेप-परिकर-परिन्यासानां यथोद्देशक्रममादावेव, समाधानस्य तु रचनावशान् मध्यैकदेश एव, उद्भेदकरणयोस्तु उपान्ते निबन्धः। उपक्षेपादीनि करणरहितानि युक्तिसहितानि षडत्रावश्यं भवन्ति.................................।

Thus the Opening Juncture, having for its base the 'Germ' and the 'Beginning', pushes on the hero to attain his desired end through these twelve steps.

The Sub-divisions of the Progression

Likewise, the second Juncture of Progression has thirteen sub-divisions. These are—

1. Passion (vilāsa),
2. Pursuit (parisarpa),
3. Rejection (vidhūta),
4. Torment (tāpana),
5. Joke (narma),
6. Amusement (narmadyuti),
7. Controversial Talk (praśamana),
8. Frustration (nirodha),
9. Courtesy (paryupāsana),
10. Thunderbolt (vajra),
11. Gallantry (puṣ pa),
12. Intimation (upanyāsa),
13. Combination of the Castes (varṇasaṃhāra).

With the Incitement at the end of the Opening Juncture, it can be surmised that the theme passes on to the next stage which is marked by a strong desire of the hero —the Sub-division of Passion (Samīhā ratibhogārthā). This passionate longing engages the hero in the 'Pursuit' (dṛṣṭanaṣṭānusaraṇam) of his object which once shown has again disappeared. As a result of that everything soothing in nature appears to the hero as void of all charm and he feels Frustration (vyasanasaṃprāpti). Next follows 'Torment' (apāyadarśanam) and gradually the hero proceeds through the vicissitudes of emotions. All the sub-divisions of the 'Progression' aim at exhibiting the 'Effort' of the hero to attain his end while the 'Germ' and the Prominent Point—these two Elements of the Plot urge him.

The Daśarūpaka reads 'praśamana' (controversial talk) of Bharata as 'pragamana' meaning the same thing. It appears that the reading 'pragamana' is the right one though the variant reading of the word in the Nāṭyaśāstra is 'pragaṇana' and 'pragayaṇa' which do not make good sense. On the other hand, all the other treatises have accepted it as pragamana with the same definition. The Daśarūpaka further, excludes the Sub-divisions of 'Torment' (tāpana) of Bharata and includes instead 'Alleviation' (śāma), a new one. This 'Alleviation' is accepted only by the Bhāvaprakāśana while the others follow Bharata. These two are diametrically opposite to each other. It seems that in the Juncture of 'Progression,' 'Torment' is more befitting than 'Alleviation.'

The Nāṭyadarpaṇa gives a few new names but hardly adds anything to the main idea. The authors follow Bharata strictly and refute the definition of vidhūta as given in the Daśarūpaka (vidhūtaṃ syād aratiḥ—Unrequitedness) and accept that of Bharata (kṛtasyānunayasyādau vidhūtamaparigrahaḥ—Rejection). They use *anusarpaṇa* for *parisarpa*, *dhūnana* for *vidhūta*, *rodha* for *nirodha*, *sāntvana* for *paryupāsana*. About the meaning of *Varṇa* in the last Sub-division, *Varṇasaṁhāra*, there is a difference of views. Dhanika[62] in his commentary on the Daśarūpaka, takes the term to mean caste and explains it as 'Combination of the Castes.' He illustrates its use from the Mahāvīracarita of Bhavabhūti where in the third Act, all the different castes, the Brāhmaṇa, Kṣatriya,

62. Vide Commentary on DR. I. 35.

etc. are presented at one place. Viśvanātha[63] accepts this but refers to the view of Abhinavagupta who takes *varṇa* to mean characters. To him Varṇasaṃhāra is a drawing together of all the different characters at one place. The Nāṭyadarpaṇa follows this view and observes[64] that it is the combination of all the characters like the hero, the opponent of the hero, the heroine, their assistants, etc. at a time for a fixed purpose. In addition to the view of the Daśarūpaka, it refers to another view also according to which Varṇasaṃhāra is the 'Admonition of the Stated Matter' (varṇitārthatiraskāra).

About the use of these Sub-divisions of the second Juncture, Dhanika obesrves[65] that of all these, Pursuit, Alleviation, Thunderbolt, Intimation and Gallantry are the most important, the others are to be used at the discretion of the dramatist. The Nāṭyadarpaṇa replaces Alleviation by Controversial Talk (uttarottaravākya) as it does not recognise the former, and prescribes the compulsory use of Gallantry, Controversial Talk, Thunderbolt, Intimation and Pursuit in the Progression. The authors further observe that the Juncture should start with Passion. They argue that the Dominant Emotion of the Sentiment with which the drama opens must be nourished by a display of Passion in the beginning of the Progression. If the theme is erotic, then this Passion would be for the beloved; if heroic, for the desired object and so forth.

---

63. Vide SD. VI. 93 (a).

64. Vide ND. p. 73

पृथक् स्थितानां पात्राणामोघः कार्यार्थं मीलनं वर्णयन्त इति वर्णानां नायक-प्रतिनायक-नायिका-सहायादिपात्राणां संहृतिरेकत्रकरणम् ।

65. Vide DR. I. 35.

The Sāhityadarpaṇa also prescribes the use of the same Sub-divisions in this Juncture.

Although the use of the Sub-divisions should be left to the discretion of the dramatists, the observations of the theorists regarding their selection are interesting. The authors of the Nāṭyadarpaṇa show their keen understanding when they advise the use of Passion in the beginning of the Juncture. Sentiment being fundamental in dramatic creation, the dramatist must be careful to handle his theme in a manner that would successfully effect Rasa–realisation. Passionate longing for the object thus deserves a place in this Juncture which has to show the Effort of the hero. The scheme of their use advocated in the Nāṭyadarpaṇa is quite reasonable. Passion having supplied the urge for progress, Gallantry adds a new charm to the hero's speech. Then comes a terrible obstacle—the Thunderbolt—thwarting the dramatic action, which again is overcome by a reasonable Intimation. Lastly comes Pursuit which helps the Plot to jump over to the next Stage of the Action.

The Ṣub-divisions of the Development

The Development has thirteen sub-divisions according to Bharata, the Nāṭyadarpaṇa and the Sāhityadarpaṇa. The Daśarūpaka gives the number as twelve excluding the Sub-divisions called Prayer. These are—

1. Mis-statement (abhūtāharaṇa)
2. Indication (mārga),
3. Supposition (rūpa),
4. Exaggeration (udāharaṇa),
5. Progress (krama),
6. Propitiation (saṃgraha),
7. Deduction (anumāna),

8. Prayer (prārthanā),
9. Revelation (ākṣipta),
10. Quarrel (toṭaka),
11. Outwitting (adhibala),
12. Dismay (udbheda or udvega),
13. Consternation (vidrava).

Of these, the Nāṭyadarpaṇa stresses the use of these five—Revelation, Outwitting, Indication, Mis-statement and Quarrel. The commentator of the Daśarūpaka also speaks of the comparative superiority of these five.

According to them, these five may suitably be used in the Development to help bring about the climax. The order of their use may be like this—Revelation of the Germ comes first and gives a new momentum to the Action that would lead the hero to a Prospect of Success in this section. But he has to face Mis-statement, Outwitting and Quarrel. He however carves out a way out of this difficult situation through Indication, a reference to his real purpose. Needless to say, here also, as elsewhere, the choice entirely depends on the dramatist and he can use any number of Sub-divisions. The treatises only hold that these five should definitely be used in this Juncture. Thus the Development, with these Sub-divisions, shows the hero in the Stage of the Prospect of Success.

The Sub-divisions of the Pause

Bharata enumerates thirteen Sub-divisions of the Pause. These are—

1. Censure (apavāda),
2. Altercation (saṃpheṭa),
3. Tumult (vidrava),

4. Challenge (śakti),
5. Assertion (vyavasāya),
6. Reverence (prasaṃga),
7. Rebuke (dyuti),
8. Disappointment (kheda),
9. Despair (niṣedhana),
10. Opposition (virodhana),
11. Summary (ādāna),
12. Humiliation (chādana),
13. Foresight (prarocanā).

The Daśarūpaka inserts three new items—'drava' (Contempt), 'chalana' (Humiliation) and 'vicalana' (Boastfulness) instead of 'kheda' (Disappointment), 'niṣedhana' (Despair) and 'chādana' (Humiliation). Of these three, 'chalana' of Daśarūpaka is equal in purport to the 'chādana' in Bharata. The other two are new.

The Nāṭyadarpaṇa accepts almost all the Sub-divisions of Bharata with some differences in essence, e.g. 'śakti' according to Nāṭyadarpaṇa is 'Appeasement' where as according to Bharata, it means just the opposite, Challenge. 'Saṃrambha' is also a new Sub-division accepted by Nāṭyadarpaṇa instead of 'niṣedhana' of Bharata. 'Saṃrambha' means 'Boastfulness' whereas 'niṣedhana' is 'Despair'.

Dhanika in his commentary advocates the definite use of Censure, Challenge, Assertion, Foresight and Summary in this Juncture. Excepting for Censure, the remaining four constitute the compulsory group of Sub-divisions of this Juncture according to the Nāṭyadarpaṇa. However, it too interprets Śakti as Appeasement and not Challenge.

In this section the dramatist has to present the Conditional Success, the fourth Stage of the Action. The Juncture (Pause) is so called because here the hero takes stock of the situation and realises a partial success which renders him confident of the final one.

The Sub-divisions may be utilised in the following manner. The hero starts with Censure directed against him and passes through Altercation, Tumult and Challenge to Assertion, a decision to carry out the plan of Action (vyavasāyastu vijñeyaḥ pratijñāhetusaṃbhavaḥ). He then faces, among the rest, Disappointment, Despair and Opposition. Undaunted he reaches at Summary, a view of the Germ and the Denouement that grants him Foresight of the Conclusion.

The Sub-divisions of the Conclusion

The last stage now appears, and the dramatist has to face the problem of bringing the drama to an end. He now accordingly brings in the final Juncture of Conclusion in order to unite all the loose ends with the final Stage of the Action, the Attainment of the Result, bringing about Rasa-realisation.

The 'Conclusion' has fourteen Sub-divisions. These are—

1. Junction (saṃdhi),
2. Vigilance (virodha),
3. Hint (grathana),
4. Narration (nirṇaya),
5. Conversation (paribhāṣaṇa),
6. Confirmation (dyuti),
7. Graciousness (prasāda),
8. Bliss (ānanda),

9. Deliverance (samaya),
10. Unforeseen Circumstance (upagūhana),
11. Expression of satisfaction (bhāṣaṇa),
12. Anticipation (pūrvavākya),
13. Termination (kāvyasaṁhāra),
14. Benediction (praśasti).

All the later treatises accept these Sub-divisions. The Daśarūpaka, however reads vibodha for virodha, meaning the same thing—a seeking for the Denouement, Kṛti for Dyuti meaning the same Confirmation of the result attained. The Sāhityadarpaṇa also follows the Daśarūpaka in this. The correct reading of Bharata might be vibodha as virodha hardly conveys the sense intended. Pūrvavākya (anticipation) is Pūrvabhāva in the Daśarūpaka.

The commentator of Daśarūpaka does not enumerate the most important Sub-divisions of the Juncture. The Nāṭyadarpaṇa also maintains that all of these should be used. The Sāhityadarpaṇa however refers to a view that in the Conclusion, the last two—Termination aud Benediction must be used in the order prescribed. This view is clearly based on the actual practice of the playwrights. The former takes the form of a question—'What can I do for you ?' that precedes the final Benediction in every Sanskrit play.

It is clear that these Sub-divisions are designed to bring about the Attainment of the Result. Junction shows the Germ and Vigilance, a seeking for the Denouement. Then follow Bliss in the form of attainment of desires, Confirmation, and unforeseen Circumstance that register an experience of something wonderful. Lastly, Termination grants a boon to the hero and in the fulness of his heart he speaks the Benediction, praying for all-round happiness and prosperity.

The Junctures and their use

Regarding the use of the Junctures and their Sub-divisions, theorists have granted full autonomy to the dramatist, subject only to a single consideration. This concerns the Rasa. It has been severally accepted and announced by all of them that the Rasa is of prime importance in drama. Bharata declares—[66] 'First of all, I shall speak of Sentiment, because without Sentiment nothing issues forth.' Accordingly, like the Elements of the Plot and other techniques in the drama, the Junctures and their Sub-divisions also should be used in order to support the chief Sentiment of the play. Bharata says—[67]

> 'After a consideration of Sentiments and Emotions, expert playwrights should use these Sub-divisions in the appropriate Junctures of the drama.'

This stress on the consideration of Sentiment and Emotion finds elaborate support in the Nāṭyadarpaṇa.[68] The authors observe that all through the drama the self-same Sentiment is to be nourished, which has found an opening in the very beginning. The rdamatist should use his talent not to follow merely the rules laid down in the treatises but to develop the Sentiment of the piece. In support, the authors quote the statement of Dhvanikāra,[69]

---

66. Ibid. VI. p. 71
तत्र रसानेव तावदादावभिधास्यामः । न हि रसादृते कश्चिदप्यर्थः प्रवर्तते ।
67. Ibid. XXI. 106
इत्येतानि यथासंधि कार्याण्यङ्गानि रूपके ।
कविभिः कार्यकुशलैः रसभावानवेक्ष्य तु ॥
68. Vide ND. I. p. 115.
69. Dhv. III. 12
संधिसंध्यङ्गघटनं रसव्यक्तिव्यपेक्षया ।
न तु केवलशास्त्रार्थस्थितिसम्पादनेच्छया ॥

which holds that the Junctures and their Sub-divisions are to be employed for the suggestion of Sentiments and not merely for justifying the tenets of the Code.

Such a mechanical following of the Code leads to a loss of propriety as is the case with Veṇīsaṃhāra. In the second Act of Veṇīsaṃhāra, Passion, the Sub-division of the Progression is used; but it apparently leads to indecency, as dallying with one's beloved is entirely improper when a fight is imminent. The king, Duryodhana, goes to meet his queen, ordering the Kañcukin to make ready his war-chariot. But he engages in dalliance with her. Here, though scripture is followed, the Heroic Sentiment of the drama is clearly impaired.

The Nāṭyadarpaṇa further says that the purpose of using the Junctures is to give a unity to the plot. Until and unless there is a communion among all the incidents and events, no impression can be possible. The Sentiment, for its revelation, requires a well-linked subject-matter. For this purpose, the dramatist is granted freedom to use the Junctures and the Sub-divisions judiciously. There can be no hard and fast rule, the Nāṭyadarpaṇa concludes, regarding the use of the technique prescribed by the treatises. If suitable, the Sub-divisions of the different Junctures may be employed in all the Junctures. As to what constitutes this suitability, the authors[70] leave it to the judgment of the real poet who knows the secret of

---

70. Vide ND. I. p. 115

अमीषां (संध्यङ्गानाम्) च सर्वसंधौ सन्ध्यन्तरे च योग्यतया निबन्धः। योग्यतां च रसनिवेशैकव्यवसायिनः प्रबन्धकवयो विदन्ति, न पुनः शब्दार्थग्रथनमात्रमदिष्णवो मुक्तकवयः। तेनैकमप्यङ्गं रसपोषकत्वादेकस्मिन्नपि संधौ द्विस्त्रिर्वा निबध्यते।

suggesting Sentiments. It is, however, not known to those who feel puffed up by their skill in mere versification. That is why there is no bar in using the same Sub-division twice or thrice in the same Juncture, if that promotes the Rasa-realisation. Sentiment being the chief factor, all attention is to be focussed on it and a choice of the Sub-divisions of the Junctures is to be made carefully from the available profusion of these. For a proper selection due skill in suggesting the Sentiment is required on the part of the poet. Only a skilful collation of meaningful words is vain, as is observed rightly by the authors of the Nāṭyadarpaṇa.

It can also be noted here that theorists have treated the drama not as an artificial structure but as something full of life. As human life, as a sign of its life force, follows a scheme of acceptance and rejection, so the drama also should move, making a choice between the useful and the dross at every step. Simply because sixty-four Sub-divisions are enumerated by Bharata, one should not consider the use of all these as obligatory. On this point, Abhinavagupta observes—[71] 'The sage, Bharata has pointed out that the utility of the Sub-divisions is only to render the Plot interesting so that it may lead to Rasa-realisation, and not accruing of virtue or dispelling of obstacles like those of the Pūrvaraṅga.' As the dramatist aims, to use the phrase of Abhinavagupta,[72] at 'showing the success of one

---

71. Dhv. III. 12. p. 340
भरतमुनिना सन्ध्यङ्गानां रसाङ्गभूतमितिवृत्तप्राशस्त्योत्पादनमेव प्रयोजनमुक्तम् न तु पूर्वरङ्गवददृष्टसम्पादनं विघ्नादिवारणं वा ।

72. Ibid. p. 337
तेनोपायक्रमेण प्रवृत्तस्य सिद्धिः, अनुपायद्वारेण प्रवृत्तस्य नाश इत्येवं नायक-प्रतिनायकगतत्वेनार्थोपायव्युत्पत्तिः कार्या ।

who follows the right path and the failure of the other who adopts the wrong one' through the activities of the hero and the opponent of the hero, it is natural that his method should be a flexible one. That is why the theorists have granted great liberty to the dramatist and left him free to employ his judgment regarding the use of the Junctures and their Sub-divisions.

The Junctures and the Acts

At the very outset a natural relation between the Junctures and the Acts of the drama suggests itself. One is tempted to think that the five Acts of the average drama are based on the five Junctures. In fact, it is not the Junctures that determine the number of Acts because, if so, there would be only five Acts, no more, no less. But the number of Acts in the Nāṭaka and the Prakaraṇa varieties is said to vary between five and ten. It is thus the Stages of the Action with which the Acts correspond. The dramatist has the liberty to elaborate a particular Stage of the Action over more than one Act. If the five Stages of the Action are depicted, one in each Act, the number of Acts is five which is the minimum for the Nāṭaka and the Prakaraṇa varieties, and the maximum would be ten where the Stages of the Action continue for two Acts each.

The Nāṭyadarpaṇa clarifies the point thus—[73] 'When there are Acts, one for each Stage of the Action, there are five Acts. But when one Stage of the Action is divided by a (separate) beginning and end, due to some purpose, there are six................ If all the Stages are thus divided,

73. ND. I. p. 36

यदा एकैकस्यामवस्थायामेकैकोऽङ्कस्तदा पञ्चाङ्काः। यदा तु कार्यवशेन काप्यवस्थोपक्रमोपसंहाराभ्यां छिद्यते तदा षट्......सर्वावस्थाभेदे तु दश इति।

then ten.' Thus, though the number of Acts may go up, that of the Junctures remains the same, covering all those Acts relating to the respective Stages of the Action so extended. As is the case with the Veṇīsaṃhāra where the third Stage of the Action, the Prospect of Success, continues for three Acts—the third, the fourth and the fifth—but all the three comprise the same Juncture, the Development. Needless to say, as in the use of the Sub-divisions of Junctures, it is the judgment of the dramatist that is to decide which Stage of the Action should be extended.

The division of the Drama into Acts

Supplying thus the method as to how the Plot and the Action are to be handled, the theorists prescribe next a division of the drama into Acts. The Acts constitute a characteristic feature of the dramatic form. Bharata clearly observes—[74] 'The Drama is characterised by the Acts and the Introductory Scenes.' Like the five divisions of the Stage of the Action, this division also aims at ensuring the unity of the Plot and the Action. Beginning, for example, is complete in itself as a distinct Stage of the Action but is a part of the whole, as the Attainment of the Result causally follows it. The partial completion of each Stage of the Action effects the total completion of the dramatic Action and the Junctures and their Sub-divisions are devised for fulfilling this purpose. Without these, the Action imitated would lose unity of purpose, and the play tend to be a series of incidents without any internal link.

The Acts, likewise, aim at dividing the whole drama into parts in order to give an organic unity to it.

---

74. NŚ. XX. 11

अङ्कप्रवेशकाढ्यं भवति हि तन्नाटकं नाम ।

Secondly, the Acts satisfy the time factor. The Action may continue for many days but for its presentation in a play, it is necessary, to put a limit to its duration as otherwise it would lead to a feeling of incongruity on the part of the spectators. Acts thus divide the whole dramatic Action into parts with reference to time. A third reason for the division into Acts may be said to be a practical one. Although the theorists do not say so, definite breaks in the course of staging a play are necessary and helpful for both the actors and the audience.

To the question—'What is an Act ?' Bharata answers,[75] 'The Act, (aṅka) is a conventional term (rūdhiśabda). As by means of (a display of) the Emotions and the Sentiments, it helps the theme to develop (ruh=to grow) through certain rules (technical), it is called the Act.' In the long descriptive account, Bharata then clarifies all the points relating to the Act—its nature, function, composition and lastly duration. The Act thus is a characteristic section of the dramatic form of literature, wherein a particular phase of the Action terminates. It must be attended with the Prominent Point so that later Acts may organically follow. This association of the Prominent Point with the Act, it should be noted, is not called for in the final Act where the Attainment of the Result puts an end to the dramatic Action.

Sāgara Nandin observes—[76] 'The Act divides the dramatic theme. It should be formed on the basis of a

---

75. NŚ. XX 14–31.

76. Vide NLRK. p. 11

अङ्कश्चाख्यानभागस्य परिच्छेदयिता। स च सन्ध्यङ्गवशादस्यैव नाटकस्यावस्थां प्रसमीक्ष्य बिन्द्वादीनां विस्ताराद् वा कर्तव्यः।

consideration of the Stage of the Action of the drama either through the Sub-divisions of the Junctures or an extension of the Prominent Point or the like.' The consideration is necessary as, otherwise, there is a great chance of its being dissociated from the context. No Act should stand separate. To make the point clear, the simile of a garland may be employed. The flowers may vary in their colour as well as in their odour. So may the 'Acts' in their content, i.e. the Rasa. But there must be some likeness or an internal unity among all the flowers to make them appear as a garland and that uniting factor running invisible through the flowers is the thread. Similarly in the case of the dramatic Plot, this factor is fulfilled by the Junctures, so far as the Action is concerned, and by the Prominent Point with regard to the Plot. It is evident that the success of the dramatist depends much upon his skill in maintaining this unity in the diversity of Acts. There are many such examples of feeble dramatic attempts which may be termed as a collection of Acts but never a drama.

Bharata describes[77] the contents of an Act thus: 'The Act should present the direct exploits of the prescribed characters in different situations and should not be made too long. It is to contain the various Sentiments arising out of the actions of the hero, the heroine, attendants, priests, ministers and merchants (or leaders of army—Abhinavagupta). Persons who enter the stage in an Act should all go out after performing their functions in accordance with the Germ and the proper Sentiments.'

---

77. NŚ. XX. 17, 18. 26
ये नायका निगदितास्त्तेषां प्रत्यक्षचरितसंयोगः । नानावस्थान्तरितः इत्यादि ।

Sāgara Nandin gives a slightly different explanation of the first verse which has been rendered here following Abhinavagupta. He interprets 'avikṛṣṭastu' as 'linked' instead of 'not long' and explains thus—[78]. 'In a drama there should be four or five chief characters, and a relish of their Actions. The Act should display different situations. The relish of these Actions should be linked (avikṛṣṭa), that is should not drift away from the subject–matter. It should be well linked with the Principal Subject.'

Bharata further speaks[79] of what should not be directly presented in an Act. The non-presentables according to Bharata are: feats of anger, favour, grief, pronouncing a curse, running away, marriage, showing of a miracle taking place, a battle, loss of kingdom, death, seige of a city and the death of a renowned hero. It should be noted that Bharata does not totally rule out death in the drama. Death of the hero is excluded but that of others may take place in the course of a drama. Such deaths however should not be directly displayed on the stage but are to be reported through Explanatory Devices. In fact, Bharata discusses[80] elaborately the mode of the presentation of death.

To this list of Bharata, Dhanañjaya adds[81] a few more, and includes long journey, revolt, eating, bathing, intercourse, anointing the body and putting on clothing.

78. Vide NLRK. p. 11

नाटके नायकाश्चत्वारः पञ्च वा स्युः तेषां चरितसम्भोगः। नानादशायुक्तोऽङ्कः कार्यः। अविकृष्टश्च स चरितसम्भोगः—आख्यानवस्तुना रवतीं कर्तव्यः। य आधिकारिकस्य सन्निधीयत इत्यर्थः।

79. Vide NŚ. XX. 20–22.

80. Vide Ibid. VII. 85.

81. Vide DR. III. 34–36.

In the Sāhityadarpaṇa[82] the definition of an Act includes all the features referred to by Bharata and Dhanañjaya. Although Bharata does not specifically prescribe the number of characters to be introduced in an Act, on the basis of his caution against the introduction of a horde of characters in the Nāṭaka and the Prakaraṇa, Dhanañjaya clearly says[83] (and is supported by Viśvanātha) that 'an Act should be arranged with a single purpose exemplified by the doings of a single day, with the hero thus engaged, and with three or four characters–these making their exit at its end.' He also emphasises the importance of Sentiments of various kinds and the use of the Episode—indications in it, along with the Germ and the Prominent Point.

Time factor in the Act

Duration is one of the primary factors in a drama. Complete success of a play depends upon the time factor, that is, on the period of time required to perform the actions presented in the play. So it is necessary that all the 'Acts' should be allotted a fixed time limit. On this Bharata says—[84] 'Depending on the Germ, the Act should present the actions relating to a single day, and there should be no conflict with the routine duties. At times, a skilled playwright may present many Actions but these should not come in the way of the necessary duties.'

From this, it becomes clear that in one Act the Actions of a single day are to be shown. There may be various Actions but the single-day rule is to be kept in

82. Vide SD. VI. 12–19.
83. DR. III. 36–37.
84. NŚ. XX. 24–25.

mind. If within the span of a single Act some such Actions are presented as require more than a day for their performance, it is natural that men will disapprove of it as implausible. Hence the general rule says that such Actions should constitute an Act as may be performed within a single day. An Act thus presents only one day in the life of the hero. This single-day rule has been accepted by Dhanañjaya and others in relation to the duration of an Act.

But there may be other difficulties. For example, the hero, as in Śākuntala, leaves a certain place and reaches another. This journey definitely requires more than one day. How the dramatist is to present this lapse of time? Bharata prescribes 'Termination of the Act' (aṅkaccheda) and the use of the Introductory Scene for the purpose. According to him, all such Actions as cannot be performed within the span of a single day—a long journey undertaken, for example—are to be reported in the Introductory Scene after terminating the Act. Bharata further determines the duration of such incidents as well. He holds that events thus reported should not have a duration of more than one year. Bharata says—[85] '(Incidents) that may take place in the course of a month or a year are to be presented after 'termination of the Act' but (those covering) more than a year should never be treated in such a manner.'

It is clear that such incidents come under the Indicatory matter (sūcya) for which the use of the five Explanatory Devices is prescribed. As such, reporting of such incidents can be made by the Explanatory Scene as well.

---

85. Vide NŚ. XX. 29

अङ्कच्छेदं कुर्यान् मासकृतं वर्षसंचितं वापि ।
तत्सर्वं कर्तव्यं वर्षादूर्ध्वं न तु कदाचिद् ॥

That is why, although Bharata speaks only of the Introductory Scene in this connection, the later theorists approve of the use of the Explanatory Scene (viṣkambhaka) in addition for this purpose. They have done so apparently on the basis of the practice of eminent playwrights who have freely used both—the Introductory as well as the Explanatory Scenes. Kālidāsa, for example, uses an Explanatory Scene after the termination of Act III in the Abhijñāna Śākuntala to report : (1) Śakuntalā's marriage with Duṣyanta; (2) the return of the hero to his capital ; (3) the anxiety of Anasūyā and Priyaṃvadā and (4) the curse of Durvāsās. All these incidents refer not to a single day but to a couple of days.

Logic and practice of the playwrights, thus urged Dhanañjaya to deviate from Bharata and include[86] this feature of 'explaining parts of the story that have happened or are about to happen, in the definitions of the Explanatory and Introductory Scene. His definition has been accepted by all the later writers on dramaturgy.

Similarly, on the basis of the practice of playwrights, the later theorists discarded the insistence of Bharata on the limit of one year's duration with reference to the events to be reported by means of the Explanatory Devices. Bhavabhūti, for example, relates the passage of twelve long years in the Explanatory Scene in between the first and the second Acts of the Uttararāmacarita.

Accordingly the dramatists have freely taken themes which cover several years but have not ventured foolishly to show marriage and child-birth in the same Act. Their sense regarding the unity of time seems to have been very

---

86. Vide DR. I. 59.

rational. It is evident that the dramatists while following Bharata strictly in presenting events in a single Act, have also taken help of the technique of 'aṅkaccheda' i.e. the putting of either the Introductory or the Explanatory Scenes in order to indicate the passage of time. Several years thus may pass between two Acts but never so in a single Act. Further, single Acts can by no means refer to such happenings as are separated from the main happenings by a long gap of time.

As an example, we can refer to the time analysis of Kālidāsa's Śākuntala. The whole Action continues for a period hardly less than six years. But each Act covers only a part of a day though years have elapsed in between the incidents depicted. Between the second and the third Acts there is a slight interval and between the third and the fourth, a number of months pass. Two or three days pass again before the fifth Act comes and the longest interval of four or five years falls between the fifth and the sixth Acts.[87]

The problem of time thus boils down to this, that, as a rule, the incidents in one Act should be confined to one day. But in such cases as require an indication of a lapse of time, the dramatist is to terminate the Act, and use the Explanatory Devices.

Of all the later theorists the view of Rāmacandra and Guṇacandra regarding the Act deserves special mention. They define an Act by three factors—[88] Character-

87. For more delails see Time-Analysis of Sanskrit Plays, A.V.W. Jackson, JAOS. Vol. XX.

88. ND. I. 19

अवस्थायाः समाप्तिर्वा च्छेदो वा कार्ययोगतः ।
अङ्कः सबिन्दुहृस्यार्थश्चतुर्यामो मुहर्ततः। ॥

istic (lakṣaṇa), Nature (svarūpa), and Duration (kālamāna). According to them, when a particular Stage of the Action ends it is an Act, or when a break is caused in the middle of the Stage of the Action for the purpose of showing a journey or the like, that also is an Act. This the authors treat as the Characteristic of the Act.

An Act secondly must be attended with the Prominent Point, and everything in it must be visible. This is the Nature of the Act.

Thirdly, an Act should last for any period beginning with forty-eight minutes (one muhūrta) to twelve hours (four yāmas). This is the Duration of the Act.

Explaining the question of duration, the authors allot a period of 48 minutes (2 ghaṭikās or 1 muhūrta) for the shortest and a period of 12 hours (4 yāmas) for the longest one. According to them, there will be no fulness of presentation if an Act lasts less than 48 minutes and, on the contrary, if it continues for more than 12 hours, it will cause the attention of the audience and the patience of the actors to flag, creating at the same time disadvantages in the performance of their daily duties. The reasons for both these observations are unimpeachable. But we cannot grasp the import of the authors' view which tolerates the duration of an act for 12 long hours. If a drama consists of five Acts of such duration, it is difficult to imagine how it can be staged. So far as the minimum time limit is concerned, 48 minutes is adequate and a drama having five or seven Acts of such length will last for four hours or five hours and a half. But a duration of 12 hours for a single Act is barely conceivable.

The view of Rāmacandra and Guṇacandra, so far as the two factors of Characteristic and Nature of the Act are concerned, is essentially Bharatan. Showing up a Stage of the Action, making all the exploits visible and providing a link by means of the Prominent Point—these are accepted by all as definite features of an Act. Their view, however, regarding Duration is unconventional. Though the authors have shown great liberality of view, as they have not laid down any rigid time limit but given extremes, the view is neither based on dramatic tradition nor on the practice of playwrights. No extant drama conforms with either the minimum or the maximum time limit so far as the Acts are concerned. It may however be observed that all the dramatists follow the golden mean regarding the duration of the Act, and in this sense the authors deserve appreciation for supplying a comprehensive view regarding the duration of the Act.

Acts and the varieties of the Drama

All the ten varieties of drama have been allotted a fixed number of Acts—from one to ten. The Nāṭaka and the Prakaraṇa varieties are considered to be complete in every respect—the Elements of the Plot, the Stages of the Action, the Junctures and Sentiments. These two, accordingly, must have five Acts as a rule, but this number can go up to ten, if necessary. The number of Acts allotted to other varieties will be discussed later.

CHAPTER V

THE PŪRVARANGA

Bharata has given an elaborate account of staging a play of the Dima variety, Tripuradāha by name, on the valley of Kailāsa mountain to please Śankara with the newly-devised drama. There he says that before the exact play began, he performed the Pūrvaranga (Preliminaries). 'What is this 'Pūrvaranga ?' and 'What is its relation with the dramatist ?'—these two questions naturally come up.

To the first question a direct answer is not available. But Bharata, by his descriptive definition of the Preliminaries has explained the meaning. The creation and the first successful staging of the drama are associated with the disturbing Demons (asuras) against whom all the gods protected Bharata. Bharata, on his part, as a mark of gratitude to the gods, performed a ceremonial worship of all of them, and made it compulsory for all his followers, the 'Bharatas'. This worship of the Gods with the prayer for protection constitutes what is called Pūrvaranga. Bharata makes it obligatory for the actors and actresses and not for the dramatist saying—[1]

> 'He, who will stage a play without worshipping the (gods of the) Stage, will be reborn in the animals, and all his knowledge would be futile.'

This function of worshipping the gods is intended for the party of the actors. The Stage-manager, as the

---

1. NŚ. I. 122

representative of the troup, performs the ceremony, the elaborate form of which has been laid down by the Sage in the third Chapter.

The Preliminaries have as many as eighteen parts. Before the beginning of the drama, the Stage-manager arranges everything in proper order. The placing of the orchestra, dancers, singers, actors—all this is done beforehand. The 'raṅga' means the stage and as all these are performed at the beginning on the stage, these taken together are fittingly named the Preliminaries (Pūrvaraṅga). Since all these refer not to the drama or the dramatist as such but only to the actors, it is not necessary to dilate on them. But of all the Sub-divisions of the Preliminaries, the Nāndī (Benediction) and the Sūtradhāra (Stage-manager) require special attention due to their importance.

Defining the Nāndī Bharata says —[2] 'The Nāndī is so called as it constitutes a benedictory eulogy of the gods, brāhmaṇas or the kings.' Bharata has clearly assigned its use for the actors and before the commencement of the play. As it does not come under the scope of the dramatist, Dhanañjaya has left it untouched in his treatise. The first confusion arises on the point whether it is the duty of the dramatist to supply this Benediction. Apparently it is not. The Benediction being the twelfth part of the Preliminaries, has nothing to do with the dramatist. Viśvanātha[3] quotes a statement of Bharata according to which 'the poet is to begin from the Raṅgadvāra,' the fourteenth part of the Preliminaries. Although the front

2. NŚ V. 24.
3. Quoted by Viśvanātha, SD. VI. p. 264.

curtain is removed with the tenth part, it is not until the fourteenth part that the dramatist takes over. As the reciter of the Benediction, the Stage-manager also has nothing to do with the play itself, and his function is only to prepare the actors and the audience. He goes out after performing the Preliminaries and the drama begins thereafter. It is highly probable that he never faces the footlights at all.

The authors of Nāṭyadarpaṇa also find it unnecessary to define the Preliminaries in detail. They only deal with the Benediction and consider it to be the chiefest of all the parts. They hold that the other parts of the Preliminaries might be neglected but that the Benediction is essential. They remark :[4] 'The formal unchangeability of the Benediction is accounted for by its indispensableness as is proved by the fact of its regular application. The claim of the Benediction to being recited prior to the opening of a play stands fast as long as play-acting is there.'

The chanting of the 'Benediction' being compulsory for the actors, the authors rightly thought it to be the most important part of all the eighteen. In fact, later on the Benediction begins to signify the entire Pūrvaraṅga and as a result, the first line of all the dramas is 'nāndyante sūtradhārah' (Enter the Stage-manager after the Benediction). The authors are clear enough when they say—whenever there is a stage-performance, there must be this benedictory verse. In this connection, the Nāṭyadarpaṇa

4. Vide ND. IV. p. 192

अहरहः प्रयोज्यत्वाद् वा नित्यत्वम्। यावद्धि रूपकस्याभिनयस्तावदेषा नान्दी प्रयोक्तव्यैव। रूपकस्य नाटकादेर्मुखे प्रारम्भे नान्दी—प्रयोगस्थानकथनमेतत्।

advises[5] that in case the poet does not supply the Benediction, the Stage–manager should furnish one.

From this statement arises another question which has found expression in the Sāhityadarpaṇa. There are some dramas which bear the direction 'After the Benediction' after the benedictory verse composed by the dramatist is given. 'Do verses, such as '*Yā sṛṣṭiḥ sraṣṭurādyā*', etc. (Śāk.), constitute the Benediction ?—is the question. Though these have all the qualities of the Benediction, being prayers to gods, kings and the like for protection, these do not adequately fulfil the demand of the Codes as regards the number of metrical lines to be used in it. Bharata maintains[6] that it should not exceed twelve words (*pada*) and may be composed with eight, and the number given in the Nāṭyadarpaṇa[7] is six or eight. In no way do the verses in question satisfy the rules. Hence the conclusion reached by Viśvanātha is quite logical. He does not accept these verses as constituting the Benediction so defined, and says—[8] "That is why in old books the verse 'Vedānteṣu', etc. (the Benediction in the Vikram. of Kālidāsa) is found placed after the phrase—'The Stage-manager after the Benediction.' Where, on the other hand, the phrase 'The Stage-manager after the Benediction' is written after the

---

5. Vide ND. IV. p. 192

यत्र तु कविकृता नान्दी न दृश्यते तत्रापि रङ्गसूत्रणकर्तृकृता द्रष्टव्या ।

6. NŚ. V. 106—107.
7. ND. IV. p. 192.
8. SD. VI. 25. pp. 264-65

अत एव प्राक्तनपुस्तकेषु 'नान्द्यन्ते सूत्रधारः' इत्यनन्तरमेव 'वेदान्तेषु' इत्यादिश्लोकलिखनं दृश्यते । यच्च पश्चात् 'नान्द्यन्ते सूत्रधार' इति लिखनं तस्यायमभिप्रायः—नान्द्यन्ते सूत्रधार इदं प्रयोजितवानितः प्रभृति मया नाटकमुपादीयत इति कवेरभिप्रायः सूचित इति ।

verse, it would mean—'the Stage-manager presented this after the Benediction—from here I present the drama.' Thus is the intention of the dramatist indicated." This clarifies the whole situation. The Benediction is an indispensable part of a play, not for the dramatist but for the party of the actors. The dramatist only hints at the proper placing of it by such directions as 'Enter the Stage-manager after the Benediction' or simply 'After the Benediction.'

That the Benediction is connected with the party of the actors is known even from the role of the Stage-manager.

Sūtradhāra

The Stage-manager is the actor who is to recite the Benediction. Bharata prescribes the reciting of the Benediction by him in an equable voice. The Stage-manager forms thus a chief part of the Benediction portion of the Preliminaries; with the drama proper, however he has nothing to do. Bharata does not allot the function of presenting the drama to him but prescribes his exit after the chanting of the Benediction is over. Though, in later dramas, it is the Stage-manager who introduces the play, yet the Bharatan Stage-manager does not introduce the play but goes out after reciting the Benediction.[9]

The Introducer

The presentation of the drama itself and the statement of the preliminary facts such as the names of the play and the playwright, the occasion of the performance and the announcement of the entrance of the different dramatic characters—are the duties of the Introducer (sthā-

9. Vide NŚ. V. 106-163.

paka), who resembles the Stage-manager in manners and appearance.[10]

A confusion arises over the role of the Introducer. Excepting in the dramas of Bhāsa and a couple of others the Bharatan Introducer has no place. Everywhere his duties are assigned to the Stage-manager. Viśvanātha[11] gives a plausible explanation. He says that with the gradual discontinuance of the fullfledged Preliminaries, the single Stage–manager comes to perform both the functions—those of the chanting of the Benediction and of the announcement of the preliminary facts regarding the drama and the dramatist.

It may be surmised that the employment of two different characters—the Stage-manager and the Introducer began to be felt superfluous, and consequently the elimination of the latter took place, to save time and to avoid complications which might have cropped up in the presentation of the play.

Such a view is expressed in the Nāṭakalakṣaṇaratnakoṣa by Sāgara Nandin. He concludes[12] his long discussion on the Preliminaries, the Benediction and the Stage-manager by saying—'As it would be difficult (to follow) in the assemblies of men, the order of the Preliminaries, as prescribed by Bharata, has not been shown.' This difficulty hinted at here refers plainly to the unnecessary lengthening of the Preliminaries, the simple and chief aim of which is to arrange the party of the actors in the proper order and begin the play.

10. NŚ. V. 164.
11. Vide SD. VI. p. 265.
12. Vide NLRK. p. 49
यस्तु भरतोपदिष्टक्रमः स खलु मानुष्यां सभायां संकटतया नोपन्यस्तः ।

Thus, with the passage of time, the role of the Introducer lost its independent importance, and the limelight was monopolised by the Stage-manager. The Stage-manager-cum-Introducer is the first actor to appear before the audience, and he recites the Benediction as well as performs the functions assigned to the Introducer. Bharata speaks of the qualities and functions of the Introducer in the following way—[13] '(The Introducer) having pleased the audience by reciting verses consisting of charming phrases and different Emotions and Sentiments as prescribed, should announce the name of the poet; then introduce the play by a reference to the Beginning in accordance with the Germ, along with a praise of it, assuming a divine character if the subject relates to divine bodies, or a human character in the case of a mundane subject, or a semi-divine character if the story is a mixed one. The Introducer should go out after thus introducing the play.'

The dramatist accordingly should take into consideration the following facts in relation to the role of the Introducer. The Introducer is to use sweet and charming sentences to draw the attention of the audience; announce the name of the dramatist and finally introducing the Germ of the play in a befitting manner withdraw from the stage. The Introduction should be as short as possible and aim at arousing eagerness in the spectators for the play that is to follow. Regarding the duration of the Preliminaries, Bharata clearly points out that too much time should not be devoted to the songs, instrumental music and dances as these are bound to create monotony, undermining, as a consequence, the exact representation as well as the proper appreciation of the dramatic piece.

13. NŚ. V. 167—71.

The same restriction should be laid on the Introducer. Though Bharata does not say so in respect of the Introducer, it can be inferred on the basis of his repeated stress on the brevity of his performance. It should be borne in mind that the Introducer has no interest of his own, and hence his role should be as brief as possible.

The Agnipurāṇa assigns[14] a five-fold function to the Stage-manager. According to it the function of the Stage-manager is (1) to announce the names of the teachers of the poet; (2) to praise his clan; (3) to eulogise the poet; and finally (4-5) to state the relation and utility of the piece. This observation, it should be noted, seems to be made by one who is not interested in the main function of the drama, viz., to actuate Rasa-realisation. It is almost useless, if not meaningless, to announce the names of the teachers of the dramatist or his forefathers before a throng of people assembled to witness a dramatic performance. Moreover, the greatness of the poet is not a thing to be established by mere praising; it depends upon his skill in presenting his theme. It is the 'satisfaction', as hinted by Kālidāsa,[15] of the 'Sahṛdaya' that establishes the real greatness of the poet. All the great and successful dramatists, however, knew this fact and so in their works the portion devoted to their personal introduction is very brief. Bhāsa does not even mention his own name and Kālidāsa merely gives it without any elaborations. So far as this is concerned, only the name of the dramatist is essential, as observed by

---

14. AP. XXXIII. 8

नान्द्यन्ते सूत्रधारोऽसौ रूपकेषु निबध्यते ।
गुरुपूर्वक्रमं वंशप्रशंसां पौरुषं कवेः ।
सम्बन्धार्थौ च काव्यस्य पञ्चैतानेष निर्दिशेत् ।

15. AS. I. 2.

Bharata. Though the name of the dramatist does not help in the Rasa-realisation, it is essential from another point of view. In ancient times it was difficult for people to know a particular poet, as books, being handwritten, were scarce. There was no other machinery to introduce the poet to the people at large. Hence the necessity of the laudatory introduction of the poet. So long as drama in Sanskrit was on the rise, the dramatists were very careful and conscious about their function as dramatists, but in the decadent period, the dramatist relied more on the observance of the letter of the rules and, as a consequence, many dramas were written which can hardly be called by that name fittingly. But they indulged however in eulogistic references in high flown language to the writer, irrespective of his achievements.

The first use of the Stage-manager as the Introducer

The first innovator to use the Sūtradhāra as the Sthāpaka was, perhaps, the poet Bhāsa. Bāṇa Bhaṭṭa hinted, it seems, at this special feature of Bhāsa-dramas when he acclaimed the works of Bhāsa saying—[16] 'Bhāsa attained fame through his plays, like the temples, that are begun by the Stage-managers (sūtradhāra = craftsmen), and have many roles (bhūmikā = storeys) and many episodes (patākā = flags).' Were it a custom to begin the drama with the Stage-manager, the phrase 'begun by the Stage-manager' apparently would have conveyed no special meaning. From it appears the possibility of his being the first dramatist who replaced the Introducer by the Stage-manager. This innovation, it thus appears, elicited appreciation from the later poets.

---

16. Harṣacarita I. 16
सूत्रधारकृतारम्भैर्नाटकैर्बहुभूमिकैः ।
सपताकैर्यशो लेभे भासो देवकुलैरिव ॥

Thus it is clear that the Introducer comes to be replaced by the Stage-manager quite early in the history of Sanskrit drama, and all the famous playwrights right from Bhāsa assign to the Stage-manager the function originally meant to be performed by the Introducer. The theorists prescribe five different modes for the Introduction (prastāvanā) of a play. The dramatist is at liberty to chose any of these and can introduce the play through the Stage-manager alone or may use one or two additional characters as well for the sake of variety. In every mode, however, brevity and charm should be maintained. The more artistic and charming the Introduction is, the more it is impressive.

Bharata prescribes that the Stage–manager should present himself either as a divine person or a human being or a mixture of both in accordance with the subject-matter. If the subject-matter comprises events both mundane and celestial, the Stage-manager should be a semi-divine being.

Bharata prescribes[17] the use of Sanskrit language by the Stage-manager as his speech is to follow the Verbal Style (bhāratī vṛtti). The Verbal is one of the four dramatic Styles relating to speech in general, and the Stage-manager should use it while introducing the play. Bharata divides the Verbal Style into four varieties—the Laudation (prarocanā), the Introduction (prastāvanā or āmukha), the Vīthī, and the Prahasana. According to Bharata,[18] the Laudation in the Preliminaries ensures victory, pros-

17. Vide NŚ. XXII. 25

या वाक्प्रधाना पुरुषप्रयोज्या स्त्रीवर्जिता संस्कृतवाक्ययुक्ता ।
स्वनामधेयैर्भरतैः प्रयोज्या सा भारती नाम भवेत्तु वृत्तिः ॥

18. NŚ. XXII. 27.

perity, good fortune, etc. and as it belongs typically to the Preliminaries; does not concern the dramatist. The third and fourth varieties form respectively two varieties of drama of the same name and so these are not defined by Bharata in the chapter on the Style (XXII). The Introduction, on the other hand, relates exclusively to the Stage-manager. It has five modes and the Stage-manager is to introduce the play through any of these modes.

Five modes of Introduction

Bharata enumerates the varieties of the Introduction thus[19] 'The five modes of the Introduction are–the Accidental Interpretation (udghātyaka), the Opening of the Story (kathodghāta), the Entrance of a Character (pravṛttika) and the Transference (avalagita).' Of these, the first (udghātyaka) and the fifth (avalagita) form the two sub-divisions of the Vīthī as well. The definitions of these, though undergoing slight changes from time to time, have yet retained their original character.

Udghātyaka

Udghātyaka or the Accidental Interpretation is that mode of Introduction which is executed, according to Bharata[20], through a different interpretation given to a particular statement by a change of the context, which brings about the entry of the main character. In it the Stage-manager says something which is overheard and

---

19. NS.XXII. 30

उद्घात्यक: कथोद्घात: प्रयोगातिशयस्तथा ।
प्रवृत्तिकावलगिते आमुखाङ्गानि पञ्च वै ॥

20. Ibid. XX. 121

पदानि त्वगतार्थानि यैर्नरा: पुनरादरात् ।
योजयन्ति पदैरन्यैस्तदुद्घात्यकमुच्यते ॥

construed differently by one of the main characters who thus enters the Stage. Viśvanatha accepts the definition and exemplifies its use from the Mudrārākṣasa. The Stage-manager in the Mudrārakṣasa reads out a verse[21], the simple meaning of which is related with the eclipse of the moon. But the moment he utters—'the demon Rāhu wishes to overpower Candra (the moon),' Cāṇakya, the chief minister of Candragupta enters, enraged to hear the defeat of his favourite King, Candra. Here the words of the Stage-manager have got nothing to do with Candra, the king but only with the moon. But Cāṇakya takes it in a different light, and thus the dramatist ushers him on the stage. So this mode is known as the Accidental Interpretation because of its having two different sets of meaning.

The Bhāvaprakāsana follows Daśarūpaka regarding the definition of the Accidental Interpretation. Dhanañjaya[22], unlike Bharata, sub divides it into two varieties, and according to him, the first variety is a series of questions and answers, having a hidden sense, and the second variety takes the form of a conversation. The commentator has exemplified both from the Vikramorvaśīya and the Pāṇḍavānanda respectively. Of these, the first example does not form any part of the Introduction while the second might have constituted the Introduction of the lost play. The Nāṭyadarpaṇa[23] defines it as a dialogue having a hidden sense but does not sub-divide it into two. His example is also the Introduction of the Pāṇḍavānanda.

21. MR. I.
22. DR. III. 13.
23. Vide ND. II. 100
परस्परं स्यादुद्घात्यं गूढभाषणम् ।

The Sub-divisions made by Dhanañjaya are without any speciality. Both the varieties take the form of a conversation between two men, having a second meaning, with the help of which the dramatic characters are introduced on the stage. The main point to be noted in this mode, is its hidden sense. The dramatist may use it in any form whether conversational as in the Pāṇḍavānanda or general as in the Mudrārākṣasa.

Kathodghāta

The second means in the hands of the dramatist for the purpose of introducing his characters is the Opening of the Story (kathodghāta), another mode of speech designed for the Stage-manager. This mode has been used by many great dramatists. According to Bharata[24] when the character enters the stage either repeating the very words of the Stage-manager or considering the meaning of what is said by him—that type of the Introduction is known as the Opening of the Story. The Introduction of Yaugandharāyaṇa in the Ratnāvalī is executed in this way. The Stage-manager reads out a verse[25] proclaiming the omnipotence of Fate and immediately Yaugandharāyaṇa, the chief minister of the hero, enters repeating the same verse and appreciating the truth of the statement. As here the character enters with the very words of the Stage-manager, it is of the first variety.

Sometimes the character enters, not repeating the exact words of the Stage-manager, but weighing the mean-

---

24. NŚ. XXII. 32

सूत्रधारस्य वाक्यं वा यत्र वाक्यार्थमेव वा ।
गृहीत्वा प्रविशेत् पात्रं कथोद्घातः स कीर्तितः ।।

25. Rat. I. 6.

ing of it. That is the second variety of this type. Bhaṭṭa nārāyaṇa supplies an example of it in the Veṇīsaṃhāra. The Stage-manager recites there a verse having a double meaning, the last line of which runs—'Let the sons of the king of the Kurus live in peace.'[26] Though the apparent meaning of the verse is in favour of the Kauravas, the implied meaning is just the opposite due to paronomasia. But Bhīmasena, the hero, cannot swallow any praise of his opponents and so immediately he enters cursing the Stage-manager as a liar and challenges boldly how the sons of king Kuru can live in peace so long as he is alive.

One thing more is to be noted regarding this. The hero or any other dramatic character should not meet the Stage-manager. The dramatist should remember the fact that the Stage-manager is an outsider, and his function is only to introduce the characters. So he first enters as an officer of the dramatist to announce the names of the author and the play and, by his well-contrived speech, to help the entrance of the real characters of the play. So the first response to his spoken words or their sense comes from behind the curtain (nepathya) and the Stage-manager being thus interrupted, explains the behind-the-curtain response. Thus he supplies the link, and leaves the stage. Immediately afterwards enters the hero repeating once more what he had said from behind the curtain. So the rules[27] place the elaboration of the dramatic theme after the Introduction is over.

---

26. VS. I. 7

27. Vide DR. III. 22

…………………ततो वस्तु प्रपञ्चयेत् ।

Prayogātiśaya

The third type is called the Particular Presentation. Bharata defines[28] it as one in which the part or performance of the Stage-manager is superseded by another in such a manner that a character is suddenly brought on the stage. The example supplied by Viśvanātha shows its nature. In this type the performance of the Stage-manager gets interrupted by someone else from behind the curtain and he interprets the interruption in such a way that the interpretation itself provides for the presentation of the dramatic character on the stage. Diṅnāga's Kundamālā supplies the example. When the Stage-manager (of that play) is about to call his fellow-actor, he hears the call of someone else and finds it to be the call of Lakṣmaṇa leading Sītā to the forest. Thus, by his interpretation, he helps Lakṣmaṇa to come on to the stage.

The views of Dhanañjaya and Śāradātanaya

The Daśarūpaka and the Bhāvaprakāśana differ in their definitions of this mode. According to Dhanañjaya, in this mode of Introduction, the character is introduced by the Stage–manager by such sentences as 'Here comes the hero' or the like. The example given by the commentator, Dhanika,[29] is from the prologue of Śakuntalā where the Sūtradhāra ends with the words—'Like this king Duṣyanta (distracted) by the running antelope.'[30] The Bhāvaprakāśana[31] simply accepts this definition and illustration and does not mention the Bharatan definition at all.

---

28. NŚ. XXII. 33

    प्रयोगेऽत्र प्रयोगं तु सूत्रधारः प्रयोजयेत् ।
    ततश्च प्रविशेत् पात्रं प्रयोगातिशयो हि सः ॥

29. Vide DR. III. 11.
30. AS. I. 5.
31. Vide BP. VIII. p. 229.

This might have been taken as a new variety of the Particular Presentation, were the same illustration not claimed by Viśvanātha as an example of the Transferrence type.

Pravṛttika

This mode of Introduction has been differently called by Dhanañjaya and Viśvanātha. Dhanañjaya calls it 'pravṛttaka' whereas Viśvanātha's reading is 'pravartaka.' Though the names differ, both the codifiers mean the same thing. Bharata defines[32] the Entrance of a Character (pravṛttika) as that mode of Introduction where the character enters on the basis of a description by the Stage-manager of the action in progress. Dhanañjaya[33] replaces action by season and holds it to be the entrance of a person hinted at by the similarity of the season described. In this as well as in the definition of Viśvanātha[34] the word 'kāla' is found instead of 'kārya' in the Nāṭyaśāstra.

The proper reading of Bharata was, it seems highly probable, 'kālam' as is taken by Dhanañjaya. The Stage-manager being the very first character of the drama and his chief function being to introduce the dramatic characters, cannot be in a position to talk of the action in progress (pravṛttaṃ kāryam). But while describing the season, he may very easily serve his purpose of introducing the characters. So if the variant reading *'Kālaṁ pravṛttam āśritya'* be accepted, there would be no discrepancy.

---

32. NS. XXII. 34

प्रवृत्तं कार्यमाश्रित्य सूत्रभृद् यत्र वर्णयेत् ।
तदाश्रयाच्च पात्रस्य प्रवेशस्तत् प्रवृत्तिकम् ॥

33. Vide DR. III. 10

कालसाम्यसमाक्षिप्तप्रवेशः स्यात् प्रवृत्तिकम् ।

34. Vide SD. VI. 37.

This mode, then, belongs to that type of prologue where the Stage-manager describes a particular season in such phrases as to represent the hero by it and ushers him in. Both the Daśarūpaka and the Sāhityadarpaṇa illustrate this from an anonymous drama where the Stage-manager describes the season of autumn making it one with the hero, Rāmacandra.

Avalagita

Transference or avalagita is the fifth variety of the Introduction. Like the Accidental Interpretation, this also forms a part of the Vīthī. Bharata defines[35] it thus—'When (anything) occuring in (relation to) something, is made to accomplish something else, it is to be known as Transference by the dramaturgists'. Viśvanātha has illustrated Bharata's definition by the prologue of Śakuntalā in his Sāhityadarpaṇa. According to him, in this mode, the Stage-manager arranges something to serve his own purpose, but suddenly applies that to introduce the hero. In the prologue of Śakuntalā, the Sūtradhāra asks the actress to sing a song to please the audience but suddenly leads in the hero cleverly with a reference to that song.

Dhanañjaya, however gives[36] a different interpretation. According to him, 'avalagita' has two varieties and both of these, while aiming at different purposes, help the Stage-manager to introduce the dramatic characters. Illustrations of these two varieties are taken from the Uttararāmacarita and the Chalitarāma (untraced) but, peculiarly, these illustrations do not belong to the Intro-

---

35. NŚ. XX.122

यत्रान्यस्मिन् समावेश्य कार्यमन्यत् प्रसाध्यते ।
तच्चावलगितं नाम विज्ञेयं नाट्ययोक्तृभिः ॥

36. Vide DR. III. 14-15.

duction of either drama. Perhaps the commentator, Dhanika, his brother and contemporary, could not find out any prologue answering to the definition, and hence the discrepancy. As a type of the Vīthī, one of the ten chief forms of drama, this definition and illustration may hold good but as a mode of the Introduction this is clearly inadequate.

Prayogātiśaya & Avalagita

The forms, Particular Presentation and Transference are, moreover almost similar. Both these bring about the entrance of the hero with the help of a matter meant for some other purpose. The definitions of these two are also similar in the Nāṭyaśāstra.[37] This similarity is further proved by the illustration of the Particular Presentation in the Daśarūpaka. Dhanika exemplifies it by the prologue of the Śakuntalā, which is an illustration of the Transference in the Sāhityadarpaṇa. In point of time Viśvanātha came after Dhanañjaya, and he undoubtedly owes much to the latter for many of his definitions regarding dramaturgy. Perhaps Viśvanātha noticed the inadequacy of the illustration of the Transference as given in Daśarūpaka and, as a result, resorted to the Bharatan definition and supplied the example of the Particular Presentation anew and used the same old example as an illustration of Transference.

In fact, of all these modes of the Introduction, the Opening of the Story (kathodghāta) with its two Sub-

---

37. The definitions of these two as given by Viśvanātha are also overlapping in nature. He defines the Prayogātiśaya as :

'यदि प्रयोग एकस्मिन् प्रयोगोऽन्यः प्रयुज्यते'

and the Avalagita as :

'यत्रैकत्र समावेशात् कार्यमन्यत् प्रसाध्यते' ।

The difference is mostly verbal.

divisions, the Entrance of a Character (pravṛttika) and the Transferenec (avalagita) have special features. The other two—the Accidental Interpretation (udghātyaka) and the Particular Presentation (prayogātiśaya) can very easily be included in the Opening of the Story and the Transference respectively.

On the Introduction, the view of Rāmacandra and Guṇacandra deserves special mention. They define[38] the Introduction as 'the dialogue of the Stage-manager with the Vidūṣaka or with an actress or with his associate in plain or ambiguous terms, aiming at suggesting the Subject-matter' and thus emphasise that the Stage-manager is to use either a ḍirect statement or an indirect one to introduce the characters. This Introduction can be executed by means of anyone of the following devices—the Word (vākya), the Meaning (artha), the Season (samaya) and Calling by name (āhvāna). All the five above mentioned varieties of the Introduction are included in these four devices. The authors do not go into a detailed discussion of these nor do they give any special name to any of them.

The dramatist has to select any one of these and use it in the Introduction. He should remember that the real drama begins not in the Introduction but after it is over. So he must be very careful to make this portion as charming as possible and save it from all unnecessary details. The advice of the authors of the Nāṭyadarpaṇa is very

---

38. ND. III. 105

विदूषक-नटी-मार्षैः प्रस्तुताक्षेपि भाषणम् ।
सूत्रधारस्य वक्रोक्त-स्पष्टोक्तैर्यत्तदामुखम् ॥

appropriate. They say—[39] 'Any one of these means of introducing dramatic characters that is spectacular, should be employed. Otherwise an overdoing of the introductory part may lead to the undoing of the Principal theme.'

Unnecessary detail is to be left out at all cost. Brevity, the acclaimed soul of literature in general, is typically so in the case of drama, and the dramatist must keep his eye on this requirement.

The necessity of the Stage-manager

The typical feature of beginning the play with the Stage-manager has decided merits. Rasa-realisation being the basic purpose, the dramatist has to take all necessary steps to ensure it. The device of Introduction through the Stage-manager should be viewed from this point of view. Cursorily looking, the role of the Stage-manager may appear rather prosaic, but looking at it from the viewpoint of the dramatist, we have to accept that this is a very effective device of gradually drawing the attention of the audience to the dramatic theme. A song attended with musical instruments is followed by the Benedictory verse (nāndī) which again is followed by some information regarding the play, the playwright and the occasion of the performance and last of all a reference to either the hero or the theme, with which the Stage-manager retires and the main characters enter the stage. The Introduction, thus, paves the way so to say, for the spectator to go forward to the realm of the dramatic fancy to which the Stage-manager just initiates him.

---

39. Ibid. p. 155

एषां च नाट्यपात्रप्रवेशप्रकाराणामन्यतम् एवैकश्चमत्कारकारी निबन्धनीयः । अन्यथा पात्रप्रवेशग्रन्थबाहुल्येन प्रस्तुतार्थविघातः स्यादिति ।

Keeping the above observation in view, probable objections against the device may be discussed. The objections may be enumerated thus :

(1) There is no necessity for the Stage-manager as an introducer, as the audience know full well that they are to witness a drama ;

(2) The name of the dramatist also may be known from other sources ; and

(3) The Stage-manager being entirely an outsider, reminds the audience that they are witnessing something that is artificial, which mars the identification of the audience with the actors.

As against these objections, a few arguments can be advanced in support of introducing the Stage-manager. The first objection can be very safely controverted by saying that though the audience may happen to know the subject-matter of the drama, they do not know how the dramatist will be dealing with it. What the Stage-manager does is to supply the clue to the main Action which facilitates the understanding of the audience. The objection rests, it seems, on a misunderstanding of the function of the Stage-manager. It should be carefully noted that he does not supply the whole story in miniature but only suggests the nature of the plot.

Secondly, the objection against announcing the name of the dramatist also does not stand to reason. We must not forget the fact that the rules of the Sanskrit drama were laid down long ago when the printing press was beyond even imagination. Now-a-days printing facilities have made this announcement redundant. People, now, no longer stand in need of knowing from the actor the name of the dramatist, a piece of information they can get very easily from so many other sources. But in those days the dramatist, to be known among men, had to rely upon his own pen and the dramatic characters. Hence the convention of the Stage-manager's announcing the necessary information. It may further be maintained that this convention is even now in vogue as in the cinema where the names of the author, the cast, etc. are flashed before the actual drama begins.

The third objection may also be refuted by saying that the Stage-manager does not appear as an outsider inspite of his functioning as the announcer. On the contrary, he plays the part of a bridge between the stage (raṅgamañca) and the audience. He first functions as a representative of the audience and secondly as one who has close connections with the dramatic characters. Thus he keys up the audience to the mental state conducive to the appreciation of the play, transporting them as it were, to the age and clime depicted in the drama.

The question of beginning the play on the Stage is a very important one. Even to-day we can realise the difficulty. Before the drama begins, there reigns a confused noise in the auditorium, and the dramatist must devise a plan to attract the attention of the audience to the play. To achieve this, the Sanskrit Codifiers have suggested the various forms of the Introduction (prastāvanā). The Introduction is composed in such a manner as to facilitate a quick appreciative response to the drama from the audience. All the same, if unheard by the audience, it does not hinder the said response. The danger of in-attention on the part of the audience, thus, passes over by the time the

Stage-manager announces the hero. The audience thus become fully attentive to the play.

To avoid this difficulty, it may be argued, Shakespeare employed the scenes of a crowded street, a ghost-haunted place and a deserted place with three wild-looking witches in his *Julins Caesar*, *Hamlet* and *Macbeth* respectively. The attention of the habitually noisy audience immediately gets riveted to the unfolding of the dramatic plot and by the time they are 'mentally ready' they find themselves in the presence of the hero or the main Action.

The Greek drama also had its Prologue. But apparently that cannot be compared with the Sanskrit Introduction. The flow of eloquence in them was considered to be undramatic even at the time of their composition and the greatest tragedians did not introduce them. Sikes points out[40]—"To judge from the 'Life of Euripides', his prologues were commonly regarded as a bore," and again—"This device was fair game to comedy for more than one reason; it was an innovation not used by Aeschylus or Sophocles, and it was essentially undramatic."

The Introduction of the Sanskrit drama, on the other hand, can never be characterised as undramatic. The economy of speech and the artistic way of introducing the characters, the maximum of suggestion with a minimum of words are the special features of the Sanskrit Introduction which stands unique in the domain of dramatic devices. In fact, the employment of the Stage-manager by the master-artists like Bhāsa, Śūdraka, Kālidāsa, Viśākhadatta, etc. evokes unstinted appreciation.

40. The Greek View of Poetry, E. E. Sikes, p. 56.

CHAPTER VI
THE PROBLEM OF DRAMATIC STYLE

The Codes, after giving all the details concerning the accessories to the drama, lay down the mode in which the theme (vastu) is to be treated. The frame-work of the entire drama, divided into the Elements of the Plot on the basis of the Stages of the Action, the Junctures and the Explanatory Devices etc,. having been made, the question arises as to how the matter will be arranged.

This question of arrangement is typically important in the field of drama as a distinct form. Each form of literature has its distinct scheme of arrangement of the matter. On this point, as well, drama has a speciality of its own. In other forms, especially in Mahākāvya and Kathā, the arrangement is what may be called expository, the events coming one after another quite plainly. On the contrary, the arrangement of the dramatic events is quite different. The element of regular 'shock and surprise' must be maintained throughout. In drama, surprise is expected at every turn even up to the very end. The eagerness and curiosity of the audience have to be regularly intensified, otherwise one would not willingly sit through three or four hours to witness the show.

The arrangement as the tail of a cow

In order to sustain throughout this curiosity of the audience in respect of the dramatic events, the dramatist has to follow a principle established by the Codifiers. Bharata, himself being an actor, has supplied the principle that ensures success in this direction. He formulates[1] that the 'bandha' or the arrangement of the drama should be like the end of the 'tail' of a cow' and that the lofty ideas are to be displayed towards the end.

Similarly Sāgara Nandin observes—[2] 'Having considered the Subject matter, the drama should be enlarged in the first half, and compressed in the latter half. All the lofty ideas should be placed there.'

Both these views lay down that the lofty ideas (udāttā bhāvāḥ) should be placed in the latter portion. The former portion of the drama should be broad and wide while the latter one should be concise, and present all the the lofty ideas.

Regarding this arrangement of theme, Dhanañjaya is strangely silent. The reason is unknown. But Viśvanātha, a later exponent, again quotes Bharata and gives his own explanation.

In giving a very detailed account of the 'Nāṭaka' in general, Viśvanātha observes[3]—'The arrangement of the matter (in the Nāṭaka) is like that of the end of a cow's tail,' and in explaining this he gives two views, the second being

---

1. NŚ. XX. 46

   कार्यं गोपुच्छाग्रं कर्तव्यं काव्यबन्धमासाद्य ।
   ये च उदात्ता भावास्ते सर्वे पृष्ठतः कार्याः ॥

2. Vide NLRK. p. 38

   नाटकमिदं कथाबन्धमालोक्य पूर्वभागे विस्तारणीयम् । पश्चार्धे च संहरणीयम् । तस्मिश्च य उदात्ता भावास्ते अवधारणीयाः ।'

3. SD. VI. 11

   गोपुच्छाग्रसमाग्रं तु बन्धनं तस्य कीर्तितम् ।

his own. The text goes—[4] 'According to some the term 'like the end of the cow's tail' means that the Acts should be gradually shortened. Others say that as in the cow's tail some hairs are short and some long so in the Nāṭaka some events come to an end in the Opening and some in the Progression. Similarly, in other Junctures too other (events end).' From the statement above, the first view, which advocates a gradual shortening of the Acts, appears to be that of Sāgara Nandin and the second is an echo of the author's predecessors—Rāmacandra and Guṇacandra. These two authors also compare the arrangement of the theme (prabandhavastūni) to the hairs in the tail of a cow. According to them,[5] as the hairs in the tail are not all equal in length—some reach up to the end, some upto the middle, while some others fail to reach even the middle—similarly in the drama some events reach upto the end, some to the middle and some other exhaust themselves in the very Opening 'Juncture'.

Thus, it seems that, regarding the arrangement of the theme, Viśvanātha supports the view of the authors of Nāṭyadarpaṇa by the words, 'others say'.

The merits of the above formulation must be discussed here as it is one of the most important factors in the structure of the drama. Judged from every point, this scheme of arrangement is one of the best proofs of the keen insight of the formulators. The demand of 'surprise

---

4. Ibid. p. 259
गोपुच्छाग्रसमाग्रमिति क्रमेणाङ्काः सूक्ष्माः कर्तव्या इति केचित्। अन्ये त्वाहुः यथा गोपुच्छे केचिद् बाला ह्रस्वाः केचिद्दीर्घास्तथेह कानिचित् कार्याणि मुखसन्धौ समाप्तानि कानिचित् प्रतिमुखे। एवमन्येष्वपि कानिचित् कानिचिदिति।
5. Vide ND. I. 17.

and shock' which a drama is required to satisfy accounts for this scheme of arrangement. All the Acts in a drama, whether five, seven or ten, must show such events as may atonce sustain and increase the interest of the audience and give the drama an organic unity and render it impressive. There may be plays in which there is no dearth of events but which, not being arranged properly, or rightly speaking dramatically, become nothing but an assortment of eventful Acts and by no means successful stage-plays. This scheme of arrangement of the subject-matter saves the dramatist from such a danger and hence all the treatises, with only the exception of the Daśarūpaka, have given proper importance to it.

It may be asked—'What does this shortening mean ?' The answer is, it means the shortening not necessarily of the bulk but of the complexities. The more the dramatic action advances towards the climax, the more should it be free from complexities. Thus, removal of the factors impeding the advance of the Plot and the Action towards the Attainment of the Result being the fundamental point of this arrangement, both these methods for achieving that end are equally efficacious. One may follow the process of elimination, so to say, by solving the problems in the successive Acts or he can proceed ahead, after solving the additional problems in the early part, leaving the chief problem of the hero to be solved in the Denouement.

The use of the Patākāsthānakas

Of all the various methods thought of by the theorists to give savour and charm to the play, the use of the Episode-indications (Patākāsthānakas or sthānas) commands a prominent position. These 'Patākāsthānakas' add a peculiar charm to the plot by their suggestive power.

These serve, to a great extent, the same function as the 'dramatic irony' in Shakespearean plays, and hence are highly appreciated by the cultured audience.

What is this Episode-indication ? In answer to this, Bharata says[6] that it is a statement that conveys a definite meaning in its own context but which, on further thought, refers to some future events in the play. He speaks of four different types of it. The general definition and classification of Bharata have been accepted with a nominal change of words in the later treatises,[7] viz. the Nāṭakalakṣaṇaratnakośa, the Nāṭyadarpaṇa and the Sahityadarpaṇa. Dhanañjaya,[8] although following Bharata in his definition, speaks of only two types. All the treatises[9] however hold this to be an embellishment (maṇḍana) of high order in the drama.

Nāṭyadarpaṇa provides a very clear definition of the Episode-indication. It says—[10] 'The matter that, aiming at a particular purpose or measure, leads to the achievement of another purpose or measure promoting thereby the chief end of the play, is called the Episode-indication.' The Episode-indication thus serves two purposes, the

---

6. Vide NŚ. XXI. 81

   यत्रार्थे चिन्त्यमानेऽपि तल्लिङ्गार्थः प्रयुज्यते ।
   आगन्तुकेन भावेन पताकास्थानकं तु तत् ॥

7. Vide NLRK. p. 42 ; ND. I. 30 ; SD. VI. 45.
8. Vide DR. I. 14.
9. Vide NLRK.—शोभाहेतूनि; ND.—मण्डनम्; SD.— अत्यन्तमुपादेयानाम् आदि ।
10. ND. p. 44

    अध्यवसितात् प्रयोजनादुपायाच्चान्यस्य प्रयोजनस्योपायस्य च प्राप्तिर्यत्रेतिवृत्ते उपकारिणी प्रधानफलोपकारिका तदितिवृत्तं पताकास्थानकम् ।

further purpose being the more important. Charmingly it relates one thing with the other, both of which may have no apparent connection. That is why all the treatises hold it to be an ornament of the drama.

Thus the Episode-indication signifies the apt use of some statement in order to give a special charm to the play. The use of one statement, apparently meant to express one sense but really suggesting something more significant, gives rise to an intellectual pleasure in the audience. In fact, the right use of these is considered to be the proof of the dramatists' skill, and the works of the master-artists abound in these.

The most apt and artistic use of this by Kālidāsa in the Śakuntalā, in the very first Act will vouch for the truth of the epithet of 'embellishment' given to it. Riding on his chariot the king Duṣyanta is chasing a deer. Meanwhile the hermits of the Kaṇvāśrama come between the king and the deer and request the king not to pierce with his too strong arrows the tender deer. They say—[11]

> 'Don't, oh Don't hurl your arrow on this tender body of the deer, like fire on the flowers. Oh, where is the too unsteady life of the poor deer and where are the thunderlike and sharp-piercing arrow of yours !'

This saying of the hermits apparently is related to the hunting of the deer but another suggestion crops up from it that[12] strikes at the heart of the 'sahṛdaya', the noble-hearted. They realise instantly the fact that the

11. AS. I. 10.
12. Śakuntalā, Prāchīn Sāhitya, Rabindranath Thakur.

love-arrows of this king, experienced in love-making, will prove as fatal to the innocent girl, Śakuntalā. This suggestion is definitely an ornament to the dialogue and it arouses increased interest among the onlookers, who get eager to know the future course of events.

Such double-meaning statements have rendered equally the dramas of Shakespeare highly enjoyable. It should also be noted that such Episode-indications are meant for the cultured one only and not for the common men assembled at the theatre-house. Needless to say, this limitation does not, therefore, lessen its utility. The common man enjoys the simple meaning which is apparent and is pleased whereas the cultured one catches the suggested meaning and admires the poet and his skill.

The four types of the Episode-indication are also accepted by almost all the later formulators, following the lead of Bharata. In fact, no fixed number of this should be mentioned. The dramatist, according to his skill and fancy, can put it in various forms keeping in view its general function of hinting at the future happening, whether auspicious or inauspicious, by words that are suggestive as well as indicative.

Bharata has given no illustrations of these but only the definitions. We shall take up the illustrations supplied by the later writers and discuss their aptness.

In the Nāgānanda[13] of Śrī Harṣa, the hero, Jīmūtavāhana, out of his benevolence, decides to save Śaṅkhacūḍa the Nāga by offering himself to be devoured by Garuḍa. But the Nāga does not agree to this proposal and consequently does not give him the red garment to be

13. Nāgānanda IV. 20.

worn by the victim. Jīmūtavāhana is distressed in not being able to save the Nāga. At that very moment a messenger comes and offers a red garment to him, sent by his mother-in-law. The red garment is sent to him for a quite different purpose but the hero takes its help to fulfil his determination of self-sacrifice. Though there is no direct foreshadowing of the future, the hero finds a new significance of the red garment and uses it for a different purpose that promotes the chief end of the play.

This is the first type, the definition of which in the Nāṭyaśāstra is[14]—'The sudden development of a meaning due to an indirect suggestion.' This illustration is supplied by Sāgara Nandin. Rāmacandra and Guṇacandra define[15] it as 'a sudden gaining of the desired thing', and illustrate its use from the Ratnāvalī[16] like Viśvanātha in the Sāhityadarpaṇa.[17] There we find the hero, Udayana, suddenly getting Sāgarikā within his embrace, mistaking her to be the queen, Vāsavadattā.

The second type is defined by Bharata[18] as—'The use of words having clearly two meanings.' For example, in the Introduction of the Veṇīsaṃhāra, the Stage-manager says[19]—'.................Let the sons of the King of the Kurus

---

14. NŚ. XXI. 32

सहसेवार्थसम्पत्तिगुंणवत्युपचारतः ।

15. Vide ND. I. 31

सहसेष्टार्थलाभश्च........।

16. Rat. III. 17.
17. Vide SD. VI. 46.
18. Vide NŚ. XXI. 38

वचः सातिशयं श्लिष्टं काव्यबन्धसमाश्रयम् ।

19. VS. I. 7.

who have adorned the earth with devotion and have put an end to fighting be happy, along with all their servants.' Here though apparently it is a prayer for the prosperity of the Kurus, yet the pun on the words *rakta* (devotion and blood), *vigraha* (fight and body) and *svastha* (happy and dead) hints at their impending defeat and their bodies being maimed and blood-stained as a consequence.

The illustration of it in the Nāṭyadarpaṇa[20] is taken from the drama, Rāmābhyudaya. There we find Sugrīva conveying a message to Sītā in these words—'What is the use of too much talk ? O Lady, if you be even on the other side of the sea, Rāma will restore you to your proper place by his side within no time.' In this message the reference to the other side of the sea is too true when we consider the subsequent course of events leading to Sītā's actually being carried across the sea. Hence it serves as an Episode-indication.

The third type is also based on paronomasia. This type may be called the best of all the four as it demands a careful composition of the dialogue on the part of the dramatist. Bharata speaks[21] of it as a dialogue, carrying a double-meaning, that suggests with courtesy the object of the play. Examples of this type are numerous.

The Nāṭyadarpaṇa illustrates it from the Mudrārākṣasa. In this type we get a conversation between two persons. One of them comes all of a sudden and makes a remark which shows that he has no knowledge of what

---

20. Vide ND. p. 45.
21. Vide NŚ. XXI. 34

अर्थोपक्षेपणं यत्तु लीनं सविनयं भवेत् ।
श्लिष्टप्रत्युत्तरोपेतं तृतीयमिदमुच्यते ॥

has just been uttered or thought of by the other person but is conveying some information or expressing some thought which will serve his own purpose. But this very remark comes so pat with a bearing upon the earlier utterance or thought of the other that the two statements taken together begin to convey a meaning which may be desirable or otherwise to the man spoken to. In the Mudrārākṣasa[22] we find Cāṇakya anxiously thinking about how to subjugate Rākṣasa. While he soliloquizes—'Will the wicked Rākṣasa be captured', a messenger enters and says—'O Sir, captured' as if to satisfy his query. This statement uttered to describe entirely a different situation is made to support another and thus adds to the charm of the piece.

As observed by Viśvanātha, the hinted sense is not necessarily auspicious for the person addressed to. He illustrates how such a statement may cause apprehension as well, from the Veṇīsaṃhāra.[23]

Duryodhana, while dallying with his queen, Bhānumatī, refers to his thighs. At that very moment enters a messenger uttering the words—"O Lord! broken." The juxtaposition of these two pieces of dialogue hints at the very grim reality which is to take place.

Similar but much more tasteful is the use of this type of Episode-indication by Bhavabhūti in the Uttararāmacarita.[24] Rāma recites a verse in praise of Sītā, which ends with these words: 'What (of Sītā) is not charming? The only unbearable thing about her is (her) separation.'

22. Vide MR. I.
23. VS. II. 23.
24. UR. I. 38,

No sooner he concludes than enters the door-keeper saying, —'O King! has come' to announce the arrival of an attendant. That the pangs of separation are already come, is accentuated by the word 'has come' (upasthitaḥ), though uttered in a different context.

The fourth veriety is a slightly variant form of the second. It is also a statement having two senses. Here also paronomasia functions to bring about the second meaning. Bharata defines[25] it as 'the use of words with a double-meaning couched in well-knit poetic language.' Explaining the term 'double', the Nāṭyadarpaṇa says[26] that the second meaning should supplement the theme.

The illustration is taken from the Ratnāvalī.[27] In the first Act the 'Vaitālika' sings a song in praise of king Udayana, the last link of which runs—'All the kings are anxiously looking up to the feet of Udayana, pleasing to the eye like the rays of the rising moon.'

This statement serves two purposes. Firstly it announces the time by a reference to the rising moon and secondly, due to the pun on the word 'udayanasya', it serves the other purpose of acquainting Sāgarikā, the heroine with Udayana. The heroine, indeed, responds immediately to it by saying—'Oh! this is the king Udayana to whom my father betrothed me'.

---

25. Vide NŚ. XXI. 35

द्व्यर्थो वचनविन्यासः सुश्लिष्टः काव्ययोजितः ।

26. Vide ND. I. 31

द्व्यर्थः श्लेषादिवशात् प्रस्तुतोपयोग्यर्थान्तरोपक्षेपिणी इत्यादि ।

27, Rat. I. 23

प्रीत्युत्कर्षकृतो दृशामुदयनस्येन्दोरिवोद्वीक्षते' ।

Thus all the Episode-indications have in them the general characteristic of informing the audience of something that is to take place in future, whether auspicious or inauspicious. Since such information are not supplied directly but demand an intellectual awareness of the audience, the Episode-indications give a special pleasure to the connoisseur. This quality of adding charm to the easy flowing plot is the reason for describing it as the 'embellishment' (maṇḍana or śobhāhetu) of the drama.

Saṁdhis and the Patākāsthānakas

How many such Episode-indications should be used in a drama ? On this question, Bharata says[28] that 'the poetical composition meant to be acted should have four Episode-indications, Sāgara Nandin,[29] keeping in view this statement of Bharata, holds that 'the Episode-indications should be employed in all the Junctures excepting the Conclusion.' The reason as to why he disapproves of its use in the final Juncture appears to be that in the Conclusion, being the last Juncture, there can be no more future events to which a reference can be made by the Episode-indications.

This prohibition, however, has not been accepted by any of the later formulators. The Nāṭyadarpaṇa does not at all mention this but observes—[30] 'Even one Episode-

---

28. Vide NŚ. XXI. 36
चतुःपताकापरमं नाटके काव्यमिष्यते ।

29. Vide NLRK. pp. 42, 44
पताकास्थानानि चत्वारि काव्यस्यालङ्कारभूतान्यपि निर्वहणसन्धिवर्जं कार्याणि ।......अस्य प्रयोगो मुखसंधिचतुष्टये क्वापि विधातव्यः ।

30. ND. p. 44
एकमपि पताकास्थानकं नाट्यकाव्यस्यालङ्करणं किं पुनर्द्वे त्रीणि चत्वारि वा । एतद्विहीनं रूपकं न कर्तव्यमित्यर्थः ।

indication is an embellishment of the drama—what to say about two, three or four? No drama should be composed without this.' Viśvanātha,[31] after quoting this view, rejects it by saying that as the Episode-indications are quite enjoyable in themselves, these can be used anywhere in the play to indicate something auspicious or otherwise, and that the discretion of the dramatist is final in this respect.

In fact, the use of this device is seen to be successful even in the last Juncture. For example, in the fifth Act of the Nāgānanda, the father of Jīmūtavāhana is found expressing the fulfilment of his life. Unaware of the predicament of Jīmūtavāhana at that time, he concludes,[32] '.........To-day, successful as I am in every respect, the only object of my concern is death.' Immediately enters Sunanda and says—'of Jīmūtavāhana.' This is clearly an Episode-indication of the third type and though the full sentence is—'Of Jīmūtavāhana am I sent to know the whereabouts,' it foretells the hero's doom.

It can, thus, be safely stated that the observation of the succeessful use of these even in the last Juncture has convinced the later formulators of the feasibility of its use anywhere in the play. The latter view thus definitely proves to be an improvement on the former one.

The discussion on the Episode-indication, though done in detail, cannot possibly be complete without a

---

31. Vide SD. VI. 49, p. 275

एतानि चत्वारि पताकास्थानानि क्वचिन् मङ्गलार्थं क्वचिदमङ्गलार्थं सर्वसन्धिषु भवन्ति ।···एषामत्यन्तमुपादेयानामनियमेन सर्वत्रापि सर्वेषामपि भवितुं युक्तत्वात् ।

32. Nāgānanda V. 3

'······चिन्त्यो मया ननु कृतार्थतयाद्य मृत्युः ।

reference to the Daśarūpaka. The reason is that the view expressed by Dhanañjaya is quite a different one, and belongs to a class by itself.

The definition given by Dhanañjaya, though it appears to be different from that of Bharata, may be said to be the same in import. The definition of the Daśarūpaka is—[33] 'An indication, by the mention of something extraneous, of a matter that is begun or is about to happen (is called) an Episode-indication which is characterised by similar situations or attributes.'

The definition is quite clear and it fully stresses the prime function of the Episode-indication, which is to hint at future events. But it does not divide it into four varieties but speaks of only two. According to it the indication can be effected by the use of either similar events (saṃvidhāna) or attributes (viśeṣaṇa).

This view is definitely a very liberal one. It does not enter into a hair-splitting differentiation of the various types but speaks of only two. And it can be very easily said that all the four varieties may safely be included in these two forms.

From the discussion above, it becomes clear that all the theorists of the drama consider the Episode-indication as a very effective device to add a peculiar charm to the dialogue. Startling revelation of future events through statements apparently not intended for that purpose proves the skill of the playwright and so he is given freedom to employ the device anywhere he deems fit.

The Episode-indication, if used by a master artist, may indicate the future through Suggestion (vyañjanā) and thus

---

33. DR. I, 14 (Tr. C. O. Haas).

transform the drama into the best variety of the 'Kāvya' (the Dhvanikāvya of the Ālaṅkārikas). Kālidāsa's Śakuntalā may be cited as an example. In the first Act we find the hermits greatly upset at the sudden and disturbing arrival of King Duṣyanta and his retinue in pursuit of wild animals. What they say clearly reveals their feeling of distress—[34]

> 'Distracted by the sight of the chariot, here enters the elephant that has hit hard the trees, with one of its tusks piercing its neck and legs enmeshed in the creepers uprooted, into the holy hermitage like the impediments of our penance personified.'

This verse is bound to suggest to the mind of the discerning the fact that king Duṣyanta is just like the distracted elephant, who has entered the hermitage to disturb the enveloping peace of the place. This meaning, it is needless to say, does not come by Denotation (abhidhā) nor by Indication (lakṣaṇā) but by Suggestion (vyañjanā). These are very subtle examples of the Episode-indication, and such examples are rare.

Rasa and the various types of the Drama

It has already been noted that Rasa is the soul of drama, and Rasa originally did mean the 'nāṭyarasa' only. The form of a drama, as a result, depends much upon the Rasa factor of the piece. If the theme is based on the Heroic or the Erotic Sentiment, a change in the form of

---

34. AS. I. 29

तीव्राघातप्रतिहततरुः स्कन्धलग्नैकदन्तः
पादाकृष्टव्रततिवलयासङ्गसंजातपाशः ।
मूर्तो विघ्नस्तपस इव नो भिन्नसारङ्गयूथो
धर्मारण्यं प्रविशति गजः स्यन्दनालोकभीतः ॥

the drama takes place. The drama consequently is divided into ten varieties according to the Sentiment it displays.

In addition to the Sentiments, Dhanañjaya speaks of the theme and the type of the hero as well, as the bases of the different varieties. According to him—[35] 'Dramas are classified according to Subject-matter, Hero, and Sentiment.' Of these, the last factor is the most important. Dhanañjaya endorses the view of Bharata—[36] 'Nothing moves without the Sentiments (in the drama)' by pointing out—[37] 'All the ten varieties are based on the Sentiments,' and thus puts stress on the Sentiment of the piece in determining its variety.

On the basis of the Sentiments, the drama is divided into ten chief varieties including the Nāṭikā which is not separately counted.

According to Bharata[38] we may classify the following varieties from the viewpoint of Sentiment.

No.	*Types*	*Sentiments*
1.	Nāṭaka	All the Sentiments (sarvarasa)
1 (a)	Nāṭikā	The Erotic (ratisaṃbhoga)
2.	Prakaraṇa	All the Sentiments
3.	Samavakāra	Three types of the Erotic (triśṛṅgāra)

35. DR. I. 11
वस्तु नेता रसस्तेषां भेदकः ।
36. NŚ. VI. p. 71
न हि रसादृते कश्चिदप्यर्थः प्रवर्तते ।
37. DR. I. 7
······दशधैव रसाश्रयम् ।
38. Vide NŚ. XX. 10-116.

4.	Īhāmṛga	The Heroic (dīptarasa)
5.	Ḍima	The rest, without the Erotic and the Comic (ṣaḍrasa)
6.	Vyāyoga	The Heroic (dīptarasa)
7.	Aṅka	The Pathetic (Karuṇarasaprāyakṛta
8.	Prahasana	The Comic (hāsopahāsa)
9. & 10.	Bhāṇa & Vīthī	All the Sentiments (sarvarasa)

Of these, the Prakaraṇa and the Nāṭaka may have five to ten Acts ; the Nāṭikā should have four Acts ; the Samavakāra type is allotted three Acts ; the Ḍima has four Acts; the Vyāyoga, Bhāṇa and Vīthī each should have one Act. The number of Acts in the Aṅka, Īhāmṛga and Prahasana are not explicitly mentioned in the Nāṭyaśāstra.

According to Sāgara Nandin the Nāṭaka and Prakaraṇa may have five to ten Acts, as said by Bharata. Nāṭikā is also to be as defined in the Nāṭyaśāstra. The Vyāyoga should have the Heroic or the Furious Sentiments with one Act. The Aṅka has the Pathetic. The Ḍima has four Acts, and the Heroic or the Furious as the chief Sentiment. The Samavakāra has three Acts and the Heroic Sentiment. The Īhāmṛga should have four Acts and the Heroic Sentiment attended with a romantic theme. The Prahasana has two Acts, and the Bhāṇa and the Vīthī each is allotted one Act.

For a clear understanding of the views of the different formulators, it will be helpful if we draw a chronological table of the formulators and give their different views regarding the number of Acts, Junctures, and Sentiments in the various types of the drama. We will arrange the formulators in this order—Bharata, Sāgara Nandin, Dhanañjaya, Rāmacandra and Guṇacandra, and Viśvanātha.

It will be clear from the table that so far as the number of Acts and Junctures are concerned, the later theorists are almost one with Bharata. Where Bharata has not given the number of Acts, it has to be decided on the basis of the number of Junctures. That is how the Aṅka and the Prahasana have been allotted one Act each, and the Īhāmṛga four Acts, though Bharata has not given the exact number. The number of Junctures allotted to each variety has already been discussed.[39] But regarding the type of Sentiment to be displayed, the later theorists appear to be more rigid than Bharata. Where Bharata liberally allows free choice for the dramatist by not specifically mentioning particular Sentiments for the varieties, the later theorists from Dhanañjaya onwards fix them specifically. Whereas Bharata allows all the Sentiments for certain varieties, and six for some or the exciting ones (dīptarasa), i.e. the Heroic, the Terrible or the Odious for others, Dhanañjaya and his followers bring it down to only one. Thus the Nāṭaka and the Prakaraṇa which could display all the Sentiments are confined to either the Heroic or the Erotic only. The freedom of choice has thus been taken away by the later theorists who mention the type of Sentiment specifically for each variety.

It is however remarkable that all the Sentiments, excepting only the Terrible, the Odious and the Marvellous, have been allotted separate media for their display as the chief Sentiment. So much so that even the Pathetic has the Aṅka variety as its medium. The exclusion of the Terrible, the Odious and the Marvellous from being the chief Sentiment does not however mean that these may not have any scope in the drama. All the Sentiments

---

39. See above p. 83.

may find a place but one of them should be the chief in the different varieties.

It should also be remembered in this connection that so far as its realisation is concerned the Sentiment is, at bottom, only one. The bottles may be of different colours but the wine is the same and when tasted the effect also is the same. That is why the Pathetic does not cause sorrow to the man witnessing the display of it, nor does the Erotic arouse the feeling of lust in the onlooker. But all the various types of the Rasa give birth to an ineffable joy. and that is why Rasa is described as 'equivalent to the realisation of the Brahman' by Viśvanātha.[40] In fact, by witnessing the spectacle of extreme suffering, say of Cārudatta (Mṛcchakaṭika) or the lovelorn Duṣyanta, the audience is not grieved by it, even though weeping at their distress, but experiences a sublime delight which is, for this very reason, 'alaukika' or supramundane.

The different Sentiments are to be so treated that they to not contradict but complement one another. It should not be thought that where a particular Sentiment is displayed no other Sentiment can be introduced. The dramatist is only to see to the fulfilment of that Sentiment which he selects as the chief one (aṅgī) for his play. The Codifiers enjoin upon the dramatists the caution that they should not make an agglomeration of different Rasas but maintain the supremacy of the chief Rasa. Here also the sense of proportion (aucityabodha) is the only guide for the dramatist. This sense will point out to the dramatist the fact that the comic should get no ascendency over the Heroic Sentiment, if the latter happens to be the chief

40. Vide SD. III. 2

ब्रह्मास्वादसहोदरः ।

Rasa. In this case, the comic, however can be displayed to effect what is called 'dramatic relief' by Western formulators, through various means, as for example, through the character of the Vidūṣaka.

So the question of the chief (aṅgi) and the subsidiary (aṅga) Sentiments, boils down to this. The dramatist must make one Sentiment prominent in his play, and he is at liberty thereafter to introduce any other which is not incompatible with the chief one.

The chief Rasa of the Nāṭaka and the Prakaraṇa

The Nāṭaka variety being the most appealing one, Bharata and others, with the exception of only Dhanañjaya and Viśvanātha, hold that it can be the vehicle of any of the nine Sentiments. But later on, this view came to be qualified, and Dhanañjaya was the first to opine[41] that either the Heroic or the Erotic is to be the chief Rasa in the Nāṭaka and Prakaraṇa varieties. Though this view seems to be dogmatic, yet the later dramatists finding the Erotic to be the most appealing, displayed it exclusively in the Nāṭaka and Prakaraṇa. But there are a few instances of other Rasas being successfully used as the chief Rasa in the Nāṭaka. There can be hardly two opinions to-day on the rather stereotyped nature of the decree enforced by Dhanañjaya. Even if the Śṛṅgāra Rasa is best suited for the Nāṭaka and Prakaraṇa forms, other Rasas can also be successfully displayed in them. The Nāṭaka, as a fine art, can be the medium of all the human emotions and feelings. Hence we may hold, with all due respect to the views of Dhanañjaya and Viśvanātha, that the Nāṭaka

---

41. Vide DR. III. 33

एक एव भवेदङ्गी शृङ्गारो वीर एव वा ।

should not be limited only to the Heroic and the Erotic Sentiments.

Omission of the Junctures and the varieties

Reference has already been made[42] to the rule of omission of the Junctures in the different varieties of drama. Only the Nāṭaka, the Prakaraṇa and the Nāṭikā are to have all the five Junctures. Of the remaining eight Bharata says—[43]

'The Ḍima and the Samavakāra are to have four Junctures, and the playwright should not introduce Pause in them. The Vyāyoga and the Īhāmṛga are to have three Junctures. There should be no Development and Pause in these two, and the Graceful Style (kaiśikī vṛtti) also has no place in them. The Prahasana, the Vīthī, the Aṅka and the Bhāṇa are to have only two Junctures which should be the Opening and the Conclusion and their style should be the Verbal one (bhāratī).'

Thus there are two four-Juncture varieties—the Ḍima and the Samavakāra. These should have four and three Acts respectively. Three—Juncture varieties are the Īhāmṛga and the Vyāyoga. The remaining four are two-Juncture varieties. About the number of Junctures in these, all the later theorists agree with Bharata excepting Sāgara Nandin who allots to the Vyāyoga two Junctures perhaps to justify its one Act. About the number of Acts in the Īhāmṛga there is some difference of opinion. Bharata does not specifically mention the number but says[44] that in other respects it should follow the Vyāyoga.

42. See above p. 84 and footnote.
43. NŚ. XXI. 45-47.
44. Vide Ibid. XX. 85-86.

Apparently due to this statement of Bharata, Rāmacandra and Guṇacandra, and Viśvanātha fix the number at one or four. The alternative number of four Acts is allotted to the Vyāyoga by Sāgara Nandin and Dhanañjaya perhaps on the basis of these Junctures. The practice of the playwrights does not shed any light on this as it is a very rare variety. The only Īhāmṛga[45] of a very late date has four Acts following the prescription of Dhanañjaya. Of the four two-Juncture varieties, the number of Acts in the Prahasana has been a matter of disagreement. Bharata does not give the number but as all the other two-Juncture varieties are allotted one Act, it is also allotted one by all excepting Sāgara Nandin and Viśvanātha who allow one to two Acts to it.

Regarding the correspondence of Junctures and the Acts, the general rule appears to be like this. Two Junctures will have one, and four Junctures three or four Acts. Three Junctures should logically have one or at the most, three Acts, allowing one Act to each Juncture; the number four appears to be incompatible with the comparatively short theme of such varieties.

The justification for this ommision of the Junctures is not far to seek. It should be remembered that the drama depicts a journey—the journey of a man from a particular point, the Beginning (ārambha) to the Attainment of the Result (phalāgama). This journey begins in the Opening and ends in the Conclusion. These two Junctures are thus indispensable in any form of the drama. But where the Plot is confined to a short period its movement must be quick. In order to effect this, the dramatist may

45. Rukmiṇīharaṇa by Vatsarāja (12th Century).

use only two Junctures—the Opening and the Conclusion. The other Junctures are omitted, and the Stage of the Action corresponding to these are merely hinted at. Generally in such types, the Development, the Pause and the Progression are dropped.

Thus there are two types of Plot-movement—slow and quick. The slow-moving Plot is seen in the Nāṭaka, the Prakaraṇa and the Nāṭikā, which have all the Junctures. The quick-moving Plots, on the other hand, are employed in the Ḍima, the Samavakāra, the Īhāmṛga, the Vyāyoga, the Prahasana, the Vīthī and the Aṅka varieties where one, two or three Junctures are left out. By dropping the Junctures, the tempo of the Action is heightened, and naturally in these varieties the theme is shorter and less complicated than in the Nāṭaka and the Prakaraṇa.

These two Plot-movements can be compared with the movement of the passenger and the mail trains. The Nāṭaka, the Prakaraṇa and the Nāṭikā are like the passenger train that stops at each station and after taking in new elements at every stop reaches the destination. The other varieties, on the other hand follow the mail train which passes on speedily stopping only at important stations. It should be however remembered that the courses of movement in both the cases is the same, and so all the five Stages of the Action must be there in both the types of plays. Only in the quick-moving varieties these are not elaborated as in the all-Juncture varieties.

Though in all the varieties where the chief Sentiment is other than the Erotic, one or the other Junctures are omitted, it should not be thought that the other Sentiments cannot be displayed in full. Any Sentiment in fact can be shown in full with the aid of the Junctures. This restriction should apply only to those plays in which the field and time of action are limited. Naturally one cannot demand the slow stages of the Development and the Pause in the case of the exciting Sentiments, viz. the Heroic, the Furious and the Odious. Any omission of these does not untowardly affect the course of drama other than the Nāṭaka and the Prakaraṇa and hamper the realisation of the Sentiment. The Rasa-realisation being the 'be-all and end-all' of the drama in general, the omission of some of the Junctures in comparatively brief dramas, which facilitates the tempo and artistic consummation of the Plot, is fully justified.

The Theme, the Hero, and the varieties

The three-fold classification of the Subject-matter into legendary, invented, and mixed has already been discussed.[46] Like the Sentiments, this three-fold Subject-matter and the types of the Hero as well distinguish the different varieties of drama. According to Bharata[47] the Nāṭaka, the Samavakāra, the Ḍima and the Vyāyoga are to have legendary themes, and the Prakaraṇa, the Nāṭikā, the Prahasana, the Bhāṇa and the Vīthī, the invented ones, For the Aṅka, he assigns both the types, though his preference is for the legendary. The type of theme in the Īhāmṛga is not mentioned by Bharata. Dhanañjaya, who is followed by Viśvanātha and others faithfully, assigns a mixed theme to the Īhāmṛga, and denies an invented theme to the Aṅka. According to him the theme in the Aṅka should be legendary but be developed by imagination. Although excepting the Īhāmṛga, no other variety is assigned a mixed theme, it is however

46. See above pp. 26-28.
47. Vide NŚ. XX. 10; 49, 60, 66, 82, 88, 94, 98.

evident that the themes of invented class may easily have a mixture of the legendary.

Similarly the different varieties have been assigned different types of Heroes.

Bharata divides[48] human beings into three basic groups of the first-rate (uttama), the second-rate (madhyama), and the third-rate (adhama). Of these, the Hero should always belong to the first two groups. No third-rate person should be chosen as the Hero. The Hero must be self-controlled (dhīra), who again is classified into four types—the Vehement (uddhata), the Light-hearted (lalita), the Exalted (udātta), and the Calm (śānta). The Hero must belong to any of these four types. He further says that the gods are of the Vehement type, the kings belong to the Light-hearted group, the commanders and the ministers are of the Exalted category, and the Calm type consists of the Brāhmaṇas and the merchants.

Bharata expressly allots[49] the Exalted type, the royal sages (like Vaśiṣṭha, Viśvāmitra, etc.) and the kings as the Hero of the Nāṭaka. He seems not to approve of gods as Heroes but they may have a supporting role (divyāśrayopeta) in it. The Exalted heroes, according to Bharata, mean the commanders and the ministers; the royal sages would comprise the Calm type and the kings would be included in the Light-hearted type. Thus it appears that barring the gods, that is the Vehement type, all the other types of the Hero may be chosen for the Nāṭaka. Although this interpretation of the term Exalted widens the scope of the Nāṭaka, relating it with all sorts of human charac-

48. Vide NŚ. XXXIV. 16-19.
49. Vide Ibid. XX. 10-12.

ters, later theorists do not accept it. Dhanañjaya who represents the later theorists, define the four types differently;[50] and allots only the Self-controlled and Exalted (dhīrodātta) Hero to the Nāṭaka. According to him—"The self-controlled and exalted (Hero) (dhīrodātta) is of great excellence, exceedingly serious, forbearing, not boastful, resolute, with self-assertion suppressed, and firm of purpose."

· This restriction is clearly un-Bharatan and the practice of the playwrights does not justify it.[51] On the basis of the Nāṭakas the Bharatan view of choosing the Hero from the first-rate and second-rate human beings seems to be not only liberal but a progressive one. Moreover the terms Vehement, Exalted, Light-hearted and Calm should not be associated with the genus. These are in fact qualifying epithets. Thus the same man may be exalted, vehement, etc. according to his moods. The dramatists is only to choose a person belonging to the class of first-rate or second-rate human beings as the Hero of the Nāṭaka. Moreover, only by selecting such a Hero, can the Nāṭaka be made a fitting vehicle for all the Sentiments and Emotions. Dhanañjaya cannot accommodate Sentiments other than the Heroic and the Erotic as the chief ones in the Nāṭaka because of the fact that other Sentiments would be incompatible with the Exalted type of Hero.

Of the other varieties, the Prakaraṇa is allotted the Calm type, and so it may have a Brāhmaṇa, a merchant, a minister or a priest as the Hero. The Nāṭikā is to follow

---

50. Vide DR. II. 3-6 (Tr. C. O. Haas).

51. See below Part II.

the Nāṭaka in respect of the Hero and so has a king of the Light-hearted type as its hero. The Samavakāra, the Ḍima and the Vyāyoga are allotted Heroes of the Exalted type. The first two are to have respectively twelve and sixteen such Heroes and the Vyāyoga may have either a royal sage or many heroes like those of the Samavakāra. The Vehement type, i.e. the gods have only one exclusive variety, the Īhāmṛga. The Vīthī, on the other hand may have any of the four types as its hero but the number of heroes should be restricted to one or two. The Aṅka should have no divine character as the Hero, that is, it may have any of the four types excepting the Vehement. The Prahasana and the Bhāṇa are given to third-rate characters.

The later theorists, following the lead of Dhanañjaya, are on the whole in agreement with Bharata. However some changes are introduced by Dhanañjaya with regard to Īhāmṛga, the Ḍima, the Vyāyoga and the Aṅka. He replaces the Exalted type by the Vehement in the Ḍima and the Vyāyoga. In the Īhāmṛga he allows a human opponent to the Hero (pratināyaka); and allots third-rate characters (Prākṛta) to the Aṅka.

To conclude, so far as the other varieties are concerned, the changes, introduced by Dhanañjaya and followed by others, can neither be justified nor rejected as these had become rare even at the time of Dhanañjaya. Bharata, it appears, had himself composed and staged a Samavakāra and a Ḍima.[52] So his views are based on a living tradition, which is not true in regard to those of Dhanañjaya. It is the Nāṭikā and, to some extent, the

52. Vide NŚ. IV. 2, 10. अग्रमृतमथन, a समवकार and त्रिपुरदाह, a डिम

Prakaraṇa which drew the attention of the later playwrights more, and the restriction imposed on them by Dhanañjaya regarding the Sentiments and the Hero may be held to be the reason for these forms being stereotyped.

The Nāṭyālaṅkāras

Bharata elaborately deals[53] with thirty-six Characteristic Marks (lakṣaṇa), ten Guṇas, four Figures of Speech (alaṅkāras) and ten Faults (doṣas). The first three are necessary attributes of literary compositions in general and these aim at ornamenting the theme (śobhā-hetu). The Faults, on the other hand, detract the charm and so are to be avoided. As these do not belong exclusively to the dramatic form of literature, a detailed account of them may be excluded from the present discussion as is done by Dhanañjaya and other later theorists excepting only Sāgara Nandin and Viśvanātha.

It is, however, interesting to note as to how the number of the Figures of Speech fixed at only four by Bharata, increased with the passage of time, so much so that by the end of the 17th century we find as many as hundred Figures of Speech. Though the question regarding the use of these may seem superfluous in the Nāṭyaśāstra yet there is a point in its favour. Bharata in prescribing the use of only the Simile, the Metaphor, the Dīpaka and the Yamaka Figures of Speech in the drama, has very justly brought out the fact that these are the most simple and commonly understood Figures of Speech and, for this reason, may be introduced in the drama-form in order to make it more appealing to the audience. The more complex types of figures of speech may fruitfully be

53. Vide NŚ. XVII. 1-42.

employed in the Kāvya, Kathā and such other literary forms but not in the Nāṭya-form. The Kāvya, Kathā and similar other forms of literature are meant for reading and in them the employment of complex figures of speech and other rhetorical devices is fully justified. But in the drama-form which is meant for presentation on the stage and enjoyment of all and sundry, only the simple rhetorical devices may be fittingly and justifiably used. Also there is no time for slow understanding—things are caught quickly or not at all, in a drama.

In fine, regarding the Nāṭyālaṅkāras, this can be said that as drama forms a part of literature in general, all the excellences considered to be useful, may be wisely and tactfully used to add grandeur to it. It should be borne in mind that the figures of speech in a drama must answer to the exigencies of the drama in question. Drama should never be taken merely as a means to make a display of one's mastery of rhetoric.

The Bharata–vākya

As Sanskrit drama begins with an invocation to the gods, so must it conclude with a similar prayer. The hero, attaining the fulfilment of his desires, prays for peace and prosperity to all. This prayer is in verse and is called the Bharata-vākya. The inclusion of the name of Bharata is designed to enshrine the hallowed memory of the illustrious originator of the drama.

Bharata-vākya has not been mentioned by name in any of the dramatic treatises. The name is given, as seen in the plays, to the last verse of every play, always a prayer of the hero for the prosperity of the people in general. This prayer comes, as a rule, in response to a deity or sage who, being pleased with the hero, asks him to pray for some boon. So comes the prayer known as Bharata-vākya.

It has already been noted that all the treatises hold that the two sub-divisions—Termination and Benediction, of Conclusion, the last Juncture must be used in every play. It is this Benediction which has been named Bharata-vākya. It is, however, possible that like the Benediction in the Beginning (nāndī), this also once was related to the actors only and the playwright was not called upon to supply it. That is why it came to be called the Bharata-vākya or the prayer of the actors. In that case, over and above the Benediction forming the final sub-division of the Conclusion, another Benediction used to be recited by the actors. The self-same Bharata-vākya in the Bhāsa-plays perhaps exemplify this Benediction of the actors.

This convention of the Sanskrit drama may be appreciated for more than one reason. The Bharata-vākya celebrates the final success of the hero and, by invoking the blessings of God, pleases the audience in general. The deity or the sage, as the case may be, by showering boons and benedictions on the hero, gets the due respectful appreciation from the audience. In addition, it imbues the drama with a universal appeal by emphasising the fact that in this world the good and righteous are duly rewarded.

A point of similarity with the Greek drama is to be seen regarding the introduction of a divine agent at the end of the Sanskrit drama. In the Greek drama also, we find a deity appearing in the Exodos, the last section of a play, and performing almost the same function as the deity or sage in the Sanskrit drama. This 'deus ex machina', as it is called, is employed to solve the complexity of the plot that otherwisc seemed impossible of solution. The reasons for employing this device are well accounted for by P. W. Harsh.[54] As Sanskrit drama also exhibits the Marvellous Sentiment in the last stage and brings a super-natural character to the forefront, the account may be quoted.

"A deity furthermore, can explain or interpret the action with an authority far beyond that of the Chorus. Deities can also place the seal of finality and divine approval upon the solution of a play. Lastly, the appearance of a deity makes a highly spectacular closing tableau."

The introduction of a deity or a super-human being and his conferring the final benediction, it can be seen, have been utilised to serve the self-same purpose in the Sanskrit drama.

The Question of Language

'Bhāṣāvidhāna' or the question of language to be spoken by the different characters in a play does not come, strictly speaking, within the fold of technique. It depends entirely upon the dramatist to decide what the form of the language to be spoken by the king or the cobbler should be. Needless to say, any rule aiming at fixing the nature of the king's speech would seem impossible. And to a dramatist of the modern times such a question never arises. But in ancient times, Sanskrit being the language of the cultured class, the use of Sanskrit was prescribed for them. Hence Bharata has prescribed rules regarding this question of speech in the Nāṭyaśāstra.

54. A Handbook of Classical Drama, p. 17.

The eighteenth chapter is of special interest to the linguist and historian. It deals elaborately with the four kinds of Bhāṣā and their sub-divisions; the Sanskrit and Prakrit; and the various Prakrit dialects in use from one corner of India to the other. According to Bharata, the king, the queen, the minister, the Purohita and such others, in short, those who belong to the upper class, should converse in Sanskrit though at times they may express their feelings in Prakrit. Particularly, when these persons allow their good sense to be eclipsed by the lust for wealth or when they wallow in the rut of poverty, they are to speak in Prakrit.[55] Does it throw any light on the controversy whether Sanskrit was ever a spoken tongue? It appears from such a rule that Sanskrit was always the language of the court where it was used as the medium of expressing 'polished' (saṃskṛta) or sophisticated thoughts and outside the court none used it to express his 'natural' (prākṛta) or spontaneous feelings. Sanskrit was, so to say, a customary means of expression used chiefly on formal occasions, and hence the use of Prakrit was resorted to when one was in ordinary moods.

However, the rules regarding the speech-form point out a few facts which must be carefully noted by the aspiring dramatist.

The first point is that the dramatist needs always to be careful to ensure that the characters depicted should appear life-like. Not only in their dress but even in their speech, the characters should follow the way which is natural to them. All the men belonging to the upper or

55. Vide NŚ. XVIII. 31

ऐश्वर्येण प्रमत्तस्य दारिद्र्येण प्लुतस्य च ।
उत्तमस्यापि पठतः प्राकृतं संप्रयोजयेत् ॥

the cultured class used to converse in Sanskrit in the time of Bharata ; hence the rule that these men should speak in Sanskrit. In order to maintain naturalness, the Nāṭya-śāstra has emphasised this question of language. It is in the fitness of things that the man on the street should speak in Prakrit. Different types of characters belonging to different social strata are not to speak in the same tongue. The dramatist must give them such language as befits them and their stations in life.

The Nāṭyaśāstra enumerates many dialects and says that the dramatist is to employ one or the other according to the nature of the characters. The final statement of Bharata regarding this is very liberal. After giving the names of the various dialects to be used by different types of characters, he says—[56] 'Whatever has been omitted by me should be gathered by the wise from the people.'

The dramatist should observe minutely the forms of speech used in different places and by different types of people and in introducing a character in his drama, he must conform to the use of that particular form of speech that is natural.

Conventional use of speech

While truth to life or a certain kind of approximation to realistic representation is emphasized in respect of the use of language, dramatic conventions allowed such devices as are typical to drama and very useful. These are enumerated by Bharata[57] as Speaking to the Sky (ākāśavacana), Soliloquy (ātmagata), Confidence

---

56. Vide Ibid. 49

अथ नोक्तं मया यत्तु लोकाद् ग्राह्यं बुधैस्तु तत् ।

57. Vide Ibid. XXVI. 79-87.

(apavāritaka) and Personal Address (janāntika). The nature and utility of these forms of conventional speech deserve special attention as these are almost invariably used by all the playwrights.

Speaking to the Sky

Speaking to the Sky is a talk with an imaginary person beyond the stage, in which questions and answers are both given by a single person. The man on the stage is supposed to see and talk to one who is far away. He anticipates the answer and by giving it out helps the unravelling of the plot. Thus, by means of an 'Ākāśa-vacana', a single character can supply the audience with much information. It is to be noted here that though this device helps to elicit information, yet it is not an Intermediate Scene. Unlike the latter, it reports only happenings of the immediate present. Thus it helps the play-wright in the reporting of simultaneous occurrences without bringing in a great number of persons on the stage.

The Soliloquy

The Soliloquy, likewise, helps the play-wright in disclosing a character's personal feelings (*hṛdayasthaṁ vacaḥ*). It is thus an expression of one's own desires or ideas to one's own self. This device is very useful in all forms of drama and is resorted to by all play-wrights.

Confidence and Personal Address

These two types of speech are designed to give out some secret information or a matter of deliberation and feeling by one to the other in the presence of many. As in the Soliloquy, in Confidence and Personal Address too, persons other than the one addressed are supposed not to hear what has been said. Bharata prescribes for both these modes of speech a particular gesture of hand—the Tripatākā i.e. three outstretched fingers, which is indicative of the exclusion of those who are not supposed to hear the confidence.

The distinctive features of these two are, however, not very clear. Abhinavagupta refers[58] to a view which appears to distinguish the two. According to it, although both these modes of speech belong in general to the Personal Address category, both being spoken in the presence of others (janānta) to a particular person exclusively, the intention of the speaker in the case of a Confidence is to allow others to hear it if they so desire. The Nāṭyadarpaṇa observes[59] that a Personal Address is meant for the hearing of many to the exclusion of one particular person whereas a Confidence is just the opposite, that is, it is not to be heard by many and is intended for one particular person. Sāgara Nandin puts[60] it differently. According to him, in the Personal Address two speak together with the intent of deceiving another with the help of the gesture of the hand. Dhanañjaya accepts[61] both these modes, and prescribes a new gesture for the Confidence. The speaker is to bend over to the side of the person addressed in giving out the secret information in Confidence.

---

58. Vide. Abhinava Bhārat. p. 424

अन्ये त्वाहुः—उभयमप्येतज्जनान्तिकमेव यावतो हि जनस्य तद्वक्तव्यं तावतोऽन्तिके सामीप्ये तदुच्यते, यत्तु तस्मात् परमुद्दिश्य नोच्यते अथ च परः श्रृणोत्वयमेवाशयो वचने तदपवारितकेन निगूढेन भावेनाशयेन संयुक्तम् ।

59. Vide ND. p. 31

इह यद्वृत्तमेकस्यैव गोप्यं बहुनामगोप्यं तज्जनान्तिकम्, तद्विपरीतमपवारितम् ।

60. Vide NLRK. p. 95.

61. Vide DR. I. 65-66.

In short, a Personal Address relates to some serious deliberation or strong feeling of the speaker, and a Confidence to some secret information. In the former, the speaker should make the gesture of three outstretched fingers and in the latter, he is to bend over to the side of the person addressed. Although strict adherence to this prescription is not observed in the plays, both the modes of speech have been widely used.

The two Practices

The use of these modes of speech comes under Conventional Practice as these are typical to the drama. Bharata discusses[62] the two practices—the Realistic (lokadharmī) and the Conventional (Nāṭya-dharmī) in detail. According to him, 'If a play depends on natural behaviour (in its characters) and is simple and not artificial, and has in its (plot) professions and activities of the people and has (simple acting and) no playful flourish of limbs, and depends on men or women of different types, it is called Realistic.' The Conventional practice, on the other hand has some of those very elements, in general, that are prohibited in the Realistic. For example, the appearence of inanimate things used by people or of objects like a hill, aerial car, weapon, etc. as endowed with human qualities, the changing of the role of the same person, the playful movement of characters, the artificial representation of strong feelings, the hearing of what has not been uttered at all and non-hearing of words uttered in proximity and such other extra-normal things constitute Conventional Practice. The use of both the practices is prescribed by Bharata, and the dramatist is required to use his judgement in determining how much of conventional means

62. Vide NŚ. XIV. 69-81.

should be employed. It is to be noted that an excess of the Realistic may equally mar the play as an excess of the Conventional. The former would render the play too matter-of-fact while the latter, too artificial. Hence a judicious employment of these by the playwright is counselled.

The Conventional Practice owes its origin to the limitations of the stage. The showing of a hill or say, the disc of Lord Viṣṇu as obeying the order of the Lord on the stage would be impossible without allowing them human form or conduct. The Conventional Practice as defined by Bharata permits the use of such means as are unavoidable. The later formulators, however, do not discuss this point and so it is not possible to assess the development of stage-craft in the post-Bharatan period.

The Conventions of the Stage

Of the two practices—the Realistic and Conventional, the latter makes allowance for the use of certain conventional means in a play. The means sanctioned are apparently connected with the limitations of the stage. On the same grounds, a large number of things are prohibited from being presented on the stage. These non-presentables taken together may be called dramatic conventions, a clear understanding of which is necessary for every dramatic artist.

The conventions, though it may sound paradoxical, were not in the least conventional in the beginning. Conventions, whether social or literary, are the creations of human ingenuity necessitated by the desire to overcome practical difficulties which crop up from time to time. Whenever mankind is faced with such problems, practical or ideal, which appear to be without a solution, the conventions come to their rescue. In each of the conventions, consequently, we find a sagacious approach to practical problems. True it is that these persist conventionally even when the original problems have been solved by newer inventions or devices.

So, all the conventions, especially those pertaining to the drama, can be traced to two problems—the practical and the ideal or moral, for their origin.

Drama being connected with the Stage and Acting, there are many difficulties regarding the presentation. Particularly in the ancient times the stage was much simpler than that of to-day. No revolving stage was there nor the elaborate scenic arangements of the modern stage. Hence the dramatist had to depend much upon his dialogue, which he had to conceive in such a manner as to give an idea of the back-ground or the scene. Too many men could not enter the stage and it was not possible to show a battle, a siege, an elephant or a chariot on the stage. To solve this difficulty, the convention of not presenting these before the audience came into being. The number of non-presentables has changed from time to time but Bharata can be well appreciated even to-day for his general verdict of not presenting the following which are practically unmanageable on the stage. Bharata rules out the presentation of a battle, loss of a kingdom, death, the siege of a city and forbids the introduction of a chariot, an elephant, a horse and a palace on the stage. Reference has already been made to these[63] and it has been observed that in order to avoid overcrowding of the

63. Vide Ibid. XX. 21-43.

stage the convention of introducing a limited number (three to four) of persons at a time also came into being. In this connection it is remarkable that there is a striking similarity between the stage-conventions in the Sanskrit and the Greek dramas. The Greek theorists forbade the display of violent deeds on the stage, and in the dramas of the great Attic masters, we find a total absence of such scenes.[64]

The Sāhityadarpaṇa provides us with a long list of non-presentable subjects. This list can be held to be the last one as, after Viśvanātha, no treatise on dramaturgy worth any notice was composed. The Sāhityadarpaṇa holds[65] the following as non-presentable on the stage—

Calling from afar, murder, fighting, revolt of a kingdom or province or the like, marriage, eating, cursing, excretion, death, intercourse and such other reproachable acts as biting, nailing, sleeping, kissing, etc., the siege of a city, bathing, and anointing the body.

Though these are not allowed for a show on the stage, these may however be reported, if necessary, by the Introductory or Explanatory Scenes.

While most of these conventions owed their origin to the necessity of overcoming practical difficulties in presentation, some of these originated due to the consideration of the moral sense prevalent at the time. To this consideration are due the conventions of not presenting death, coition, etc. The staging of a drama generally formed part of some gay ceremony in which the display

---

64. For a detailed discussion see 'Sanskrit Drama in a Comparative Light', Dr. K. C. Pandeya, JGJRI. Vol. V. part IV.

65. Vide SD. VI. 16-18.

of pathetic and cruel scenes seemed naturally repulsive. The hero, it is stated, due to the same consideration, should not meet his death on the stage. It should not even be reported. So we find no tragedy in Sanskrit in spite of Bhavabhūti's waxing eloquent on the merits of the Pathetic Sentiment.

The observation of these conventions became customary and, as a result, they ruled throughout. Though there were innovators now and then, the greater number proved the truth of the saying—'All men are conventional'.

The Unities

Like the Greek drama, Sanskrit drama also observes the unities of time, action and place. In the Sanskrit drama, an Act being the unit, we find these unities maintained in each Act. An Act generally deals with events at a single place and in a single day. Whenever more than a day is to be covered, the Code advises division of the Act and introduction of either a separate Act or any one of the five Explanatory Devices. Though an interval of several years is seen between two Acts, the passage of time does not militate against the sense of reality of the audience as the link is supplied by some Introductory Scenes.[66]

The Nāṭyavāras

Bharata speaks[67] of the Nāṭyavāras or the appropriate time for staging plays. This mainly concerns the producer rather than the play-wright. The later theorists have, for this very reason, left it out of their treatises. The

66. For details see 'Time-analysis of Sanskrit Plays', A.V.W. Jackson, JAOS. Vol. XX & XXI.

67. Vide NŚ. XXVII. 85-95.

view however points out the practice of staging plays even in daytime in ancient India, and may have some relation with the allotment of different Rāgas to different periods of day by the musicologists.

Bharata divides the night into three periods—the early part beginning with dusk, the midnight and then the last part ending with day-break. Similarly the day is divided into two periods—forenoon and afternoon. Of these five periods, Bharata rejects midnight and prescribes the remaining four as the proper periods of time for staging a play. This time-scheme has an intimate relation with the display of the different Sentiments. Accordingly, plays with a religious theme are to be staged in the forenoon, those with heroic theme in the afternoon, and those having romantic and pathetic themes are to be staged during the first and the last parts of the night respectively[68].

It is, however, not very clear why midnight has been excluded. In fact, people today would prefer a midnight performance extending from 10 p. m. to 2 a. m. to a late night one from 2 a. m. to day break.

The Style of Procedure

The Vṛtti or the Style of Procedure is a well-known term in the field of drama, and though it has been described elaborately in the Nāṭyaśāstra,[69] there prevails some confusion regarding it. Even by reading the various texts on dramaturgy, one finds it rather difficult to form a comprehensive idea of it. From the viewpoint of technique,

---

68. For a detailed account of the Nāṭyavāras see, 'The Time of Staging a Sanskrit Drama—A Note, K. R. Pisharoti, IHQ. 1950.

69. Vide NŚ. XXII.

however, two questions are important—'What is the Style of Procedure?' and 'How far is it related to the art of dramatisation?'

The Styles of procedure are four—the Verbal (bhāratī), the Grand (sāttvatī), the Graceful (kaiśikī) and the Energetic (ārabhaṭī). Bharata treats[70] all these Styles of Procedure as the 'mother' of all literary creation and holds that the ten forms of drama originated from the representation of these Styles. They are thus the sources of origin as far as the forms of drama are concerned.

As to the origin and characteristics of the Styles of Procedure, Bharata has given a long story. The story, may however be legendary but its bearings are worth-noticing. He says that at the time of killing the twin demons, Madhu and Kaiṭabha, the Lord Viṣṇu invented the four-fold Styles of Procedure. The exchange of words that preceded the fighting constituted the Verbal Style the anger and such other violent emotions at that time gave rise to the Grand Style, the girding up of his loins to face the enemy constituted the Graceful Style, and the actual fighting brought about the Energetic Style. Citing this incident, Bharata has fixed the definitions of the four Styles on the basis of words (bhāratī), the temperament (sāttvatī), the preparation (kaiśikī) and the gestures (ārabhaṭī) of Lord Viṣṇu.

He then observes that the four Styles—the Verbal, the Grand, the Graceful and the Energetic, are derived from the Ṛg, the Yajus, the Sāma, and the Atharva Vedas

---

70. NŚ. XX. 4

सर्वेषामेव काव्यानां मातृका वृत्तयः स्मृताः ।
आभ्यो विनिःसृता ह्येतद् दशरूपं प्रयोगतः ॥

respectively. In the same manner, the four histrionic devices—Words (vācika), Representation of the Temperament (sāttvika), Costumes and Make-up (āhārya) and Gestures (āṅgika) are founded upon the representation of these four Styles of Procedure.

Excepting Sāgara Nandin none of the formulators has discussed the Styles in detail. According to Sāgara Nandin[71] 'speciality in relation to dress, song, instruments, Sentiments, emotions, acting, dance, etc. constitutes the Style of Procedure.' Another view recorded by him holds that the Style is 'the order of presenting the graceful (actions and moods).' Following Bharata, he further observes—'These Styles are based on the four Vedas. They have in them respectively the predominance of words, temperaments, grace and physical action—Words in the Verbal; Temperaments in the Grand, Costumes and make-up in the Graceful, and Gestures in the Energetic.'

Dhanañjaya accepts the four styles as defined by Bharata and merely says[72] that the Styles of Procedure are based on the conduct of thc Hero. Following the same, Viśvanātha holds[73] these to be 'the special mode of conduct of the Hero and others in the drama.'

Thus, the Verbal Style is the speech itself, the other three respectively present the grand, the graceful, and the

---

71. Vide NLRK. p. 44
नेपथ्ये गीतवादित्ररसभावाभिनयनृत्यजातीनां क्वापि विशेषे वर्तनमिति वृत्तिः कथिता। अथवा विलासविन्यासक्रमो वृत्तिरिति। एता वृत्तयश्चतुर्वेदीसमाश्रयाः। यथाक्रमं च वाक्सत्त्वलीलाव्यायामप्रधानाः। वाचिकं भारत्याम्। सात्त्विकं सात्वत्याम्। आहार्यं कैशिक्याम्। आङ्गिकमारभट्याम्।
72. Vide DR. II. 47.
73. Vide SD. VI. 123.

energetic dispositions of the chief characters in the drama. Leaving aside the Verbal Style, the other three Styles are related more with the actor than the playwright. The dramatist is to supply the speech and, as such, must be careful about the Verbal Style. It does not however mean that he can ignore the other Styles. On the contrary, it is the dramatist who is to supply the situations and appropriate speech which will call forth the display of the Grand, the Graceful and the Energetic Styles.

Bharata has allotted[74] the different Styles to the different Sentiments. He assigns the Graceful Style to the Erotic and the Comic, the Grand Style to the Heroic. the Furious and the Marvellous, the Energetic Style to the Terrible, the Odious and the Furious, and the Verbal Style to the Pathetic and the Marvellous Sentiments. This allotment of Styles does not mean any exclusion of one from the other. It is apparently based on the predominance of the Styles in the different Sentiments. Thus this prescription does not eliminate the Energetic Style in the Erotic or the Comic Sentiments but suggests that the Graceful is the chief Style in these two. This is clear from the allotment of both the Grand and the Energetic to the Furious and that of the Grand and the Verbal to the Marvellous Sentiment. Likewise neither can the Verbal Style be limited only to the Pathetic and the Marvellous Sentiments. The same is true in the case of the Grand and the Energetic Styles as well. In fact, wherever there is a representation of the temperaments, the Style is Grand, wherever the action is graceful, the Style is Graceful, and wherever physical gestures are called forth,

74. Vide NŚ. XXII. 65-66.

the Style is Energetic. The Verbal Style, on the other hand, signifying speech in general, is basic everywhere. By assigning, for example, the Verbal to the Pathetic and the Marvellous, Bharata merely points out that these Sentiments do not call forth any major display of the Grand, the Graceful or the Energetic Styles. Thus the Verbal Style is all-important while the other Styles are exclusively concerned with the attitudes, moods, and actions of the characters. In this way these Styles serve the important purpose of making the Verbal Style, that is, the speech variegated and dramatic.

This is why the Nāṭaka and the Prakaraṇa are said to be 'endowed with all the Styles of Procedure' by Bharata.[75] As these two forms of drama can have all the Sentiments, Emotions and Actions, all the Styles are naturally present in them. In Veṇīsaṃhāra, for example, which is pre-eminently a drama of the Heroic Sentiment, there are all the Styles. The view of Dr. V. Raghavan on this is worth quoting. He concludes[76]—

'Thus speech or Bhāratī also may be graceful or terrible and there can be a Kaiśikī-Bhāratī in the exchange of sweet words between the lover and the beloved. So Kaiśikī-Ārabhaṭī and Kaiśikī-Sāttvatī.'

The Audience and the Actors

Mention has already been made of the two other factors, the Actors and the Audience which, besides the dramatist, play a very important role in a drama. Though the dramatist is not directly concerned with them in

---

75. Ibid. XX. 7 सर्ववृत्तिविनिष्पन्नम् ।

76. Vide The Vṛttis, Dr. V. Raghavan, JOR Vol. VII. p. 33, Madras.

composing his play yet he has to depend much on them for the success of his drama.

That the Sanskrit dramatist was very conscious of his audience is demonstrated by his Very first statement through the Sūtradhāra. The Sūtradhāra begins by saying that—'This is a learned assembly' and adds that his aim is to satisfy it. From this the desire of the artist, to see his work presented before cultured people of taste, becomes clear.

Bharata echoes this very desire of the dramatist in giving a description of the qualities that should mark an audienee. In as many as thirteen verses[77] he speaks of the requisite attributes of an ideal audience. The spectators should be conversant with all the factors, such as 'the Costumes and Make-up, the rules of the dialects, the four kinds of histrionic representation' that constitute the drama. They should have a keen appreciation of the Sentiments and the States presented, and be able to identify themselves with the dramatic characters. Void of prejudice, they should be imbued with a deep sympathy without which real appreciation of art is not possible. He concludes by saying that 'one who is capable of assuming a particular role by imitating the States of the latter, can be said to be a qualified spectator (prekṣaka).'

Apparently an audience of such spectators is an impossibility. Rightly says Bharata that in an audience composed of superior, mediocre and inferior types of men, the appreciation cannot be uniform or universal. The inferior men cannot be expected to appreciate the performance of the superior ones. Moreover the disposition

77. Vide NŚ. XXVII. 50-62.

of men and women, young and old would naturally vary. So, an ideal audience is practically an impossibility. Still all of these spectators may and should derive pleasure from the drama. The young people are pleased to see the representation of love, the old men derive pleasure from the Puranic legends and tales of virtue whereas the women, children and the common men are always delighted with the Comic Sentiment and the Costumes and Make-up.

A dramatist thus should be conscious of the audience and his obligation of pleasing all the sections of it.

In addition to a generous and appreciative audience, the success of a play depends on a set of accomplished actors. The histrionic art is one of the most difficult and subtle arts. So, for the success of his play, the playwright stands in great need of a set of good and qualified actors. Bharata has given[78] a list of all the qualities essential for the roles of the Stage-manager, the Hero, the Heroine, the Viṭa, the Vidūṣaka, the Śakāra, etc. The list furnishes all the essential requirements of head and heart of the different actors.

Though these two, the audience and the actors, are not directly connected with the playwrights' composition, it is they on whom the success of a dramatist finally rests. Drama being an object to be presented before a congregation of people, the dramatist cannot be indifferent to the importance of these two factors.

---

78. Vide Ibid. XXXV. 45-76.

PART II

CHAPTER VII

THE TECHNIQUE AND ITS APPLICATION

Section—1 : Nāṭaka : The First Period

Having surveyed the conception and structure of drama of all variety, we may now proceed to see the playwrights at their writing table. The topics discussed in the previous pages are important in their bearing on the composition of successful dramatic pieces. Whether the composition falls in the ten major forms or the eighteen minor forms, the dramatist has to be particularly careful in handling his theme along the lines suggested by the Doctrinaires.

In following any particular line faithfully, there is every risk of the intellectual output getting totally stereotyped and, we are afraid that with the passage of time, the rules laid down by Bharata became more and more binding upon the playwrights and consequently we find that few artists ventured to adopt an original method. This may be the reason as to why Sanskrit drama, in spite of such rich legendary sources which it could draw upon, could not attain to that sublimity and charm that we find in the Tragedies of West. The dramatists became so very conventional that they never tried their art in illustrating the Karuṇa Rasa in the Nāṭaka though the later has been acclaimed as having all the Sentiments (nānārasa). Not only the Karuṇa but all other Rasas were more or less neglected. The predominant Sentiment in the dramas became the Erotic.

The predominance of thc Erotic Sentiment may be traced back to the period of its successful use by Kālidāsa. The Erotic which suited Kālidāsa so excellently, could not be treated in a like manner by other dramatists. And as a result, so many plays are there, the themes of which are romantic no doubt but are void of savour and charm.

The ideal of Trivarga and the abundance of the Nāṭaka

. In the history of the development of Sanskrit drama one other fact is significant. Dr. S. N. Das Gupta has rightly pointed it out in his history, which may be quoted. Discussing the influence of the ideal of Trivarga (dharma, artha and kāma) Dr. Das Gupta says—'It is for this reason that the Sanskrit poets of India instead of portraying mere characters or giving expression to ardent love or other sentiments as such, or devising their plots at random from their everyday sphere of experiences, had to adopt a particular scheme, a framework of types, within which limitations they had to give vent to their poetic effusions. The scheme or the frame should be such that the fundamental principle that Dharma, Artha and Kāma should not transgress one another leading to disastrous results, may be observed.'[1] It is this preoccupation of the poet's mind with the religious ideal that is responsible for the predominance of the Nāṭaka variety which has been taken to be the best form to execute the plan of exhibiting Kāma attuned with Dharma. And again it is this consideration which restrained the greatest playwrights to compose pieces having secular plots such as the Prahasana or the Bhāṇa.

---

1. H.S.L. p. Ixxxi.

The problem of Chronology

Besides these limitations, another difficulty is to be taken notice of in our attempt to trace the development of drama on the lines prescribed by the treatises on technique. It is the question of chronology. If the history of Sanskrit literature lacks anything, it is exact date. Hardly there is any unanimous view about the dates of so many celebrated dramatists. Śūdraka, a very distinguished dramatist, is still lost in uncertainty as to the proper time of his dramatic creations.

Without going into the details of the problems of chronology, we shall follow, in general, the chronology supplied by Dr. S. K. De in the History of Sanskrit Literature. According to it, Aśvaghoṣa is the earliest dramatist, the fragments of whose dramas have been unearthed by H. Luders. Stray references to some other dramas of approximately the same or earlier period, are to be found in different treatises. Since these dramas exist only in name, there cannot be any discussion on their merits.

The age to be covered in the following pages can be divided as follows — (1) the first period—predecessors of Kālidāsa—Aśvaghoṣa, Bhāsa ; (2) the second period —Kālidāsa; (3) the third period--successors to Kālidāsa —Śūdraka and others and (4) the last period—the later dramatists. However, to facilitate the discussion of the gradual development of the different types of drama, we propose to deal with them according to their varieties.

The first period—Aśvaghoṣa

Aśvaghoṣa is the writer of the earliest extant drama. Many other dramas are mentioned here and there and also in the Nāṭyaśāstra itself but none of them is traceable and so these may be ignored.

The drama of Aśvaghoṣa is a 'prakaraṇa' and is named—Śāradvatīputra-or Śāriputraprakaraṇa.

The Prastāvanā

Unfortunately the first portion of the drama is not available so what type of a Sūtradhāra was utilised by Aśvaghoṣa, is difficult to ascertain. But the Pāripārśvaka being present, it can be said that the dramatist was fully conversant with the dramatic practice and that he had definitely more than one models before him. Regarding this the amazement expressed by Dr. Keith is quite understandable. He observes[2]—'On the contrary, it is amazing how much literature must have preceded to permit of the setting up of the main types of drama, some of which were evidently represented by many specimens, though others doubtless rested on a small basis of practice.'

The type of the Drama

The type has been clearly denoted by the playwright himself to be a Prakaraṇa. The hero accordingly conforms to the rules laid by Bharata by being a Brāhmaṇa of the Calm type (dhīraśānta). Besides the nature of the hero, the number of the Acts also corresponds to the number prescribed for such a type. Śāradvatīputraprakaraṇa has got nine Acts.

The Rasa of the piece

The Rasa of a Prakaraṇa may be any one of the nine types according to Bharata. Though the later formulators like Dhanañjaya and Viśvanātha restrict the use of all Rasas excepting the Śṛṅgāra and Vīra in the Nāṭaka and Prakaraṇa varieties, it was not so before.

2. Sanskri Drama p. 31.

It seems that while formulating such a rule these two theorists had not taken into account the Sāriputraprakaraṇa which possesses neither of these two Sentiments. The Prakaraṇa of Aśvaghoṣa has got the Quietistic Sentiment, as the plot aims at the conversion of two Brāhmaṇas—Śāriputra and Maudgalyāyana to the Buddhistic faith. The use of the Quietistic Sentiment in this Prakaraṇa is remarkable and proves that Bharata's dictum regarding the free use of any Rasa was in consonance with the practice of the age.

The Vastu and Netā

The Vastu or the subject-matter of the piece also conforms to the Śāstra. The plot is invented, though it has its origin in the Mahāvagga. The 'netā' or the hero, likewise, is one of the 'vipra-vaṇik-saciva'. We do not know whether the heroine was a courtesan or a lady but the other characters like the Vidūṣaka and others prove that the playwright never went astray from the formulations of the treatise.

The Saṁdhis and other techniques

In the absence of the full text, it is difficult to form a concrete idea of the different Junctures and the Stages of Action. Still the gradual development of the plot presupposes the frame-work of it. The benedictory verse, that is, the Bharata-vākya, proves unquestionably the fact that it was considered essential in the time of Aśvaghoṣa. It is noteworthy here that Bharata also considers this to be the most essential sub-division of the Conclusion.

Conclusion

From the above account, we can form the following ideas regarding the position of the dramaturgic art at the time of Aśvaghoṣa. If we accept the view of Prof. M. M. Ghose regarding the date of the Nāṭyaśāstra which he thinks to be the 1st Century B. C.[3], we can safely say that Aśvaghoṣa, a poet in the court of Kaniṣka (circa 58 B. C. to 120 A. D.) was converasnt with the rules laid down by Bharata. Though it is not in the least necessary to have a Śāstra to be consulted while composing a drama yet it must be accepted that no serious deviation is noticed in the works of the poet. Aśvaghoṣa's work may not conform to all the rules laid down by the later theorists but this fact does not prove his ignorance of the Śāstra. On the other hand, his work, it seems, was not appreciated by the later critics, perhaps due to his conversion into Buddhism, and gradually it might have lost its hold on the Indian mind. The neglect suffered by all his works including the Buddhacarita accounts for the want of reference to his works in the treatises on Dramaturgy and Poetics alike.

Leaving aside the thorny question of chronology, we must appraise the intrinsic merits of Aśvaghosa's drama. Aśvaghoṣa stands alone in his use of Śānta Rasa in a 'Prakaraṇa and the charm of his style induces one to believe that his drama was highly appreciated in his time. The drama, now being available in a fragmentary form, makes it well-nigh impossible to attempt at an integrated appreciation of its worth. Even then the very fragments speak highly of the artistic and literary attainments of this almost pioneer dramatist. The cogent appreciation of A. B. Keith is worth-quoting in this connection. Keith says "...........in the main the Sanskrit is excellent and

---

3. The Date of Bharata Nāṭyaśāstra, Journal of Calcutta University.

the fragments show traces of the able versification and style of Aśvaghoṣa.'[4]

The anonymous fragments

Along with the manuscript of the Sāriputraprakaraṇa, the fragments of two other plays were also discovered by H. Luders. These two are so fragmentary that no consistent idea can be formed regarding them. The names of these are nowhere mentioned, not even the name of the author. In all probability these plays might have been written by Aśvaghoṣa but there is no conclusive proof of their being so.

Of these two, one is allegorical and as such resembles the Prabodhacandrodaya, a work of Kṛṣṇa Miśra belonging to the second half of the 11th century. In it we find the personifications of abstract notions such as—Fame *krīti* Firmness *dhṛti* Wisdom *buddhi* and the like. Along with these, the Buddha also appears in person and all of them speak in Sanskrit. The plot ts apparently religious aiming at the glorification of the Buddha. The number of Acts or any such details is not available.

The second one might have been a Prakaraṇa of the Mṛcchakaṭika type. In it we find, in addition to the hero, a Vidūṣaka, Kaumudagandha by name, a courtesan, Magadhavatī, a prince, a rogue and Śāriputra and Maudgalyāyana. By the very nature of the characters, we may hold safely that it was also a religious piece perhaps aiming at the conversion of the down-fallen to the Buddhistic faith. In the absence of material, we cannot reach any definite conclusion regarding this piece.

---

4. Sanskrit Drama, p. 86.

In respect of these two pieces, the important factors may be enumerated thus. The allegorical piece is definitely the first of its type and if the playwright was Aśvaghosa himself, appreciation is due to him for the invention of such a device. The only thing worth-notice in the second piece is its stage-direction. The dramatist was definitely an innovator in giving the directions in the respective dialects of the characters. That is, when the character speaks in Sanskrit, the direction is also given in Sanskrit and in case of Prakrit-speaking characters the directions likewise are in Prakrit.

Were Aśvaghosa the actual composer of these fragmentary dramas, his mastery in the field of drama must go unchallenged. In any case, these plays are the first of their type in the domain of Sanskrit drama.

Bhāsa

From the point of view of the development of technique all the thirteen plays ascribed to Bhāsa are important. The reference of Bhāsa in the works of Kālidāsa[5] speaks of his wide popularity not only among the people in general but also among the aspiring dramatists. All the later dramatists, important critics and other litterateurs have expressed appreciation of Bhāsa's works. Beginning from Kauṭilya, the politician down to Rājaśekhara, the literary critic, so many men have referred to Bhāsa in their respective works. The great popularity and honour thus enjoyed by Bhāsa entirely depended on his dramas. The qualities which arrested the attention of all are given below by way of a critical appreciation of Bhāsa's method.

---

5. Mālavikāgnimitra, prastāvanā.

Three factors of judgment

Dhanañjaya, we have already seen, lays down three factors as the determining criteria of the types of drama and these are—the Plot, the Sentiment and the Hero. These successfully distinguish the ten forms of drama from one another and as such an examination of these will lead us safely to form an idea of Bhāsa's attainments as a dramatist and the conditions in which he found and left the art of dramaturgy.

Vastu

So far as the Plot is concerned, Bhāsa has used all the three types of it viz. the Legendary, the Invented and the Mixed in his plays. Though all the dramas have their origin in the Rāmāyaṇa, the Mahābhārata, the Bhāgavata or the Bṛhatkathā yet the poet has not followed the sources blindly. His inventive and creative brain has worked upon them and as a result, we find in his works all the three types of the plot. Strictly Legendary are the Pratimā, Abhiseka, Dūtavākya, Ūrubhaṅga and Bālacarita. The Invented are Svapnavāsavadattā, Pratijñāyaugandharāyaṇa, Avimāraka and Cārudatta. The Mixed are Pañcarātra, Madhyamavyāyoga, Dūtaghaṭotkaca and Karṇabhāra.

Thus it is clear that the chief sources of Bhāsa are the Rāmāyaṇa, the Mahābhārata and the Bṛhatkathā. Though the last one exists merely in eulogistic references to its illustrious author, Guṇāḍhya in other works, it must have been well-known in the times of Bhāsa. Guṇāḍhya has all along been honoured for this work and we do not know whether the book in its famous Paiśācī form was known or not to Daṇḍin, Bāṇa or Dhanañjaya. All of them, however, speak highly of him. Bṛhatkathā has been mentioned clearly as a source of dramatic themes in th Daśarūpaka.[6]

In the face of such wide popularity of Bṛhatkath it may seem wrong to class the Svapnavāsavadattā, Prat jñāyaugandharāyaṇa, Avimāraka and Cārudatta as havin Invented themes. Though it is a fact that the illustriou hero, Udayana found a great favour with the drama turgists and there are, as a result, three to four dramas o his various amorous activities, the stories of Avimārak and Cārudatta, especially of the former, were less notice by the dramatists. To a modern student of the dram these fall under the category of the invented plot. Bu Bhāsa did not invent them. He simply collected ther from legendary sources.

Thus we find that all the thirteen dramas ascribe to Bhāsa fall under two general classes—the Legendar and the Mixed. Though the dramatist has taken th plots freely from the legends, he has never hesitated t alter the theme according to his convenience.

The plays which have been classified under the head ing Mixed theme, are so called because of the fact that i spite of their characters being legendary the plots of ther are entirely invented. Thus although Pañcarātra based on the Virāṭa Parvan of the Mahābhārata, th peculiar situation depicted in the play is original. Th conclusion of the drama as shown by Bhāsa is not onl his own creation but is contrary to the Mahābhārat We find in it the king Duryodhana handing over half c his kingdom to the Pāṇḍavas to fulfil his promise mad earlier to Droṇācārya. Now, such a thing would hav

6. DR. I. 68.

topped the great war of the Kurukṣetra which is not the :ase with the Mahābhārata. Thus, though the characters n the play are well-known in the Mahābhārata, the ituation is entirely differently presented.

Likewise, the Madhyamavyāyoga is also an inven-ion of the poet. The meeting of Bhīma, the second 'āṇḍava (madhyama) with Ghaṭotkaca, his son through Iiḍimbā, in the way in which the play depicts is entirely magined by the poet.

The Dūtaghaṭotkaca also is a creation of the poet. 'here is no mention of such a sending of messenger in the Aahābhārata.

The Karṇabhāra, which is in all probability, a ragmentary portion of a much bigger drama, also proves he fact that Bhāsa was the first and last dramatist to ealise the tragic greatness of the character of Karṇa. 'he plot is entirely created by the poet by his fancy, hough some of the events have been taken from the reat epic.

Hence in the background of the above discussion, om the point of view of the Vastu, the thirteen plays nay be classified as forming the following types—

Vo.	*Name of the play*	*Acts*	*Rasa*	*Types*
1.	Svapnavāsavadatta	6	Śṛṅgāra	Nāṭaka
2.	Pratijñāyaugandha-rāyaṇa	4	Dīptarasa	Nāṭikā
3.	Avimāraka	6	Śṛṅgāra	Nāṭaka
4.	Cārudatta	4	Śṛṅgāra	Prakaraṇa
5.	Pratimā	7	Sarvarasa	Nāṭaka
6.	Abhiṣeka	6	Vīra	Nāṭaka

7.	Bālacarita	5	Vīra	Nāṭaka
8.	Pañcarātra	3	Vīra	Samavakāra
9.	Madhyamavyāyoga	1	Vīra	Vyāyoga
10.	Dūtavākya	1	Vīra	Vīthī
11.	Dūtaghaṭotkaca	1	Vīra	Vyāyoga
12.	Karṇabhāra	1	Dīptarasa-Karuṇapradhāna	Vīthī
13.	Ūrubhaṅga	1	Karuṇa	Aṅka

The allotment of the types, it should be noted, to these plays does not conform strictly to the rules of the Śāstra. Bhāsa's dramas betray some points of deviation from the prescribed formula. As for example, the Pratijñāyaugandharāyaṇa, which appears to be a Nāṭikā in four Acts, has been styled as a Prakaraṇa by Bhāsa himself. This drama appears to be a Prakaraṇa from the point of view of the main character. Yet it has in it certain other features which unmistakably are those of a Nāṭikā.

Deviation from Bharata

While strict adherence to Bharatan rules was not obligatory, though literary practice, more or less, demanded it, Bhāsa at times struck out a new way and thereby deviated from the master. These peculiarities we shall show as these occur in the plays, one by one, so that the achievements of Bhāsa as a dramatist may be clear. The question whether Bhāsa was anterior to Bharata or not is not relevant to our discussion. A dramatist may very well take a new path even if the Śāstra directs otherwise. Moreover, it is an undeniable fact that the definition and rules of Bharata are too elastic in comparison with those of the later Law-givers. In following Bharata one may very easily strike a new path without in the least violating totally the rules of Bharata. But none can do so with the rules of Dhanañjaya or Viśvanātha. As a result, we shall see that a few dramas of Bhāsa do not come under the categories allotted to them if viewed from the Daśarūpaka-point of view. As for example, the type known as Vīthī is said to have only the Śṛṅgāra Rasa in the Daśarūpaka and its followers, whereas Bharata does not limit it to only one Rasa. His definition says that Vīthī may have any Rasa.[7] This clearly points out that the strictness of rules is a later outcome and belongs to that age when instead of being the expositors of dramatic practice, the Law-makers began to claim a controlling hand over all creative work. Naturally the rules laid down by men who had no direct concern with the stage, could not answer the need of the playwrights. On the contrary, Bharata was himself a law-giver as well as a playwright.

The deviations are to be considered not as transgresion of the laws of Bharata but should be acclaimed as the landmarks in the gradual development of the drama. The chief deviations are—the presentation of death on the very stage in the Abhiṣeka (Act I) and the Ūrubhaṅga, the speech of Sūtradhāra in Prakrit in the Cārudatta and the new function of Sūtradhāra in Bhāsa's dramas.

As regards the killing of Vāli in the Abhiṣeka, we may say that the dramatist could have avoided it by resorting to the use of a Viṣkambhaka or Praveśaka but so far as the death of Duryodhana is concerned, it was indispensable. And as the latter is an Aṅka in form,

---

7. NŚ. XX. 117, 135

सर्वरसलक्षणाढ्या; रसैर्भावैश्च निखिलैर्युक्ता वीथी प्रकीर्तिता ।

having Karuṇa as its Rasa, we may say that death-scene in such forms of drama could hardly be avoided. The rule that no death is to be presented came, it seems, as a result of a consideration of the technical difficulties in presenting it. The killing of one by an arrow on the stage seems even to-day incredulous and ludicrous instead of being awe-inspiring and effective. A consideration of this fact is most probably responsible for the elimination of death-scenes. But the death of Duryodhana in Ūrubhaṅga is of another type. There he is not directly killed on the stage. He dies due to the mortal blow of Bhīma, which is not shown. As a result, his death becomes much more pathetic and effective. So, as a technique, the presentation of death by Bhāsa, it may be said, is successful in the case of Ūrubhaṅga and is flat in the Abhiṣeka.

The use of Prakrit by Sūtradhāra

The Sūtradhāra in Cārudatta uses Prakrit instead of Sanskrit. This is the only drama of Bhāsa which has got a Prakrit-speaking Sūtradhāra. It is definitely a remarkable deviation from the Śāstra and it may be due to the influence of another current of thought which attempted at giving the dramatic directions in the Prakrit. Whether this was actually the case, cannot be determined but this much can be said safely that the two fragmentary Buddhistic plays referred to earlier,[8] have the dramatic directions in both Sanskrit and Prakrit according as the persons, speech, and it is just possible that Bhāsa was also half in a mind to adopt Prakrit for the Sūtradhāra who talk with generally Prakrit-speaking men or women. It should be clearly stated that this is completely a hypothesis

8. See page 186 above.

and the case may be just the opposite. It may, as well, be due to the editing of Bhāsa's plays, later on, by others. Though significant, it is not important as it could not influence the later practitioners in the field.

Prastāvanā

The most remarkable feature of Bhāsa-plays is their Introduction. The speciality of it has been marked by many, especially by Bāṇa who speaks of the plays of Bhāsa as having the special feature of beginning with the Sūtradhāra. Though the beginning of all the dramas in Sanskrit is done by the Sūtradhāra, the statement of Bāṇa, as already observed, has got a special meaning. The role of the Sūtradhāra of Bhāsa is of a singular type and as such forms a class by itself. All the thirteen plays ascribed to him show the speciality of this technique of Introduction.

The Introduction has got two aspects according to Bharata. The first is the Pūrvaraṅga ending with the Nāndī-śloka and the second is Prastāvanā or the proper introduction of the play. The former is allotted to the Sūtradhāra and the latter to the Sthāpaka. It has already been pointed out[9] that the Pūrvaraṅga does not come under the proper jurisdiction of the dramatist and his work begins with the Sthāpanā. Accordingly, Bhāsa eliminates the Pūrvaraṅga or rather allots it to the body of actors and begins his play with the Sthāpaka whom he gives the name of Sūtradhāra. His practice was so much appreciated, it seems, that in the later Śāstras we find no mention of Sthāpaka whose functions are entirely assigned to the Sūtradhāra.

---

9. See Part I, page 111

Apart from this, the Introduction in Bhāsa, which is styled as Sthāpanā (which also points out the fact that Bhāsa was conscious to make the change) is remarkable for its brevity. Bhāsa has shown a great skill in finishing off the Introduction portion of his plays with the greatest economy of words. The number of lines used by the Sūtradhāra in all the plays is given below—

1.	Svapnavāsavadatta	7 lines
2.	Pratijñāyaugandharāyaṇa	9 lines
3.	Avimāraka	18 lines
4.	Cārudatta	80 lines
5.	Pratimā	13 lines
6.	Abhiseka	19 lines
7.	Pañcarātra	10 lines
8.	Madhyamavyāyoga	18 lines
9.	Dūtavākya	8 lines
10.	Dūtaghaṭotkaca	14 lines
11.	Karṇabhāra	10 lines
12.	Ūrubhaṅga	20 lines
13.	Bālacarita	10 lines

From this it will appear that whether the plays belong to the bigger types, viz: Nāṭaka, Prakaraṇa, Samavakāra, or to the smaller, viz : Vyāyoga, Vīthī, etc., Bhāsa introduces them with equal ease and brevity. The only exception is the Cārudatta which has 80 lines in the Sthāpanā. All the Introductions display a similarity not only on the point of brevity but also in the method of execution.

The success of Bhāsa in this respect is remarkable. The technique of Introduction by a Sūtradhāra is typical to the Sanskrit plays and serves many purposes. The chief of all is that the Sūtradhāra supplies the link, to the audience, of the subject-matter of the play. It is a very difficult task to lead one, completely ignorant of the theme, to the understanding of the very first scene unaided. This is effected by the Sūtradhāra, and the successful dramatists have shown remarkable skill in this respect. The best type of Introduction is that which introduces the main events without much ado. The test of the successful dramatist, so, lies in his power to begin a play with as brief a preamble as possible. Bhāsa is undoubtedly one of the best dramatists from that point of view.

Another fact is also to be taken notice of regarding the Introduction. The Sāstra says that if the motif interfused with the proper Sentiment can be shown from the very beginning, no Explanatory Devices (viz. the Explanatory or the Introductory Scene) should be used. The main characters are then to be introduced on the stage just after the Introduction. It is a rare skill to introduce the royal personages on the stage through the Sūtradhāra who belongs to the commonality. But the Sūtradhāra is to introduce characters like Rāma, Kṛṣṇa and Duṣyanta and the like. There is no denying the fact that in between the Sūtradhāra and the royal personages there is a wide positional gap which makes it almost impossible for the former properly to introduce the latter. In order to obviate this difficulty and lessen the hiatus, a second character is introduced who is nearer to the royal personages than the Sūtradhāra. This second character presented through the Explanatory Devices (generally Viṣkambhaka) paves the way for the appearence of the Hero. However, the introduction of this second character betrays a weakness in the art of the dramatist who should set the ball rolling, as far as the main theme is concerned, with as little delay as possible.

The Introductions in Bhāsa show how this difficult aim can be easily attained. The Sūtradhāras in Bhāsa are not mere announcers, they are practically a set of characters who lead the audience directly to the presence of the hero or to the centre of action. In all the thirteen plays, Bhāsa uses only three Viṣkambhakas to introduce the hero on the stage. In the Abhiṣeka, a Nāṭaka, the Ūrubhaṅga, an Aṅka, and the Bālacarita, a Nāṭaka—Explanatory Scenes are used before the proper action begins. The best of the Bhāsa-plays is Svapnavāsavadatta which has an Introduction of only seven lines and the dramatist ushers in all the main characters before the audience in a very successful manner.

Bhāsa very often uses the two dramatic devices—'Speaking from behind the Curtain' and 'Speaking to the Sky' for the sake of brevity. All his Introductions have a speech or sound from behind the curtain. By way of explaining that, the Sūtradhāra ushers in the main character or hints at the main event. The later treatises on dramaturgy, however, have overlooked this technique and have not enumerated it as one of the means of introducing the hero on the stage.

Another technique of Bhāsa should also be noticed. This is 'Speaking to the Sky.' This technique is very helpful to the dramatists in giving so much information by a single character.

Of the five Explanatory Devices, Bhāsa uses only two—the Explanatory and the Introductory Scenes. (Viṣkambhaka and Praveśaka). Herein also Bhāsa shows his skill in the economy of words. His Explanatory Devices are usually short.

With reference to the usual practice of ending a drama with a Benediction (generally known as Bharata-vākya), some are of the opinion that Bhāsa dispensed with it and left this task to the Stage-manager, which can be surmised from the fact that the same verse appears at the end of most of Bhāsa's dramas. It would have been otherwise, had the poet himself furnished the same, as he could have written any number of them, did he so choose.

The one-act plays and the Samavakāra

The one-act plays of Bhāsa are his masterpieces. The Madhyamavyāyoga, the most famous of them, has got the theme of Bhīma's meeting with his son, Ghaṭotkaca. The dramatist is highly successful in introducing the old brāhmaṇa, Keśavadāsa and his family pursued by the Rākṣasa, Ghaṭotkaca. The Sentiments — Karuṇa, Bhayānaka and Vīra—are beautifully developed. The Hāsya also illumines the course of the events. The brief drama is so skilfully conceived and executed that it can be said to be the best one-act play in Sanskrit.

Bhāsa is also a master of the Erotic Sentiment as is seen in the Svapnavāsavadatta. But his mastery of the Pathetic Sentiment is unparalleled. The Ūrubhaṅga speaks highly of his power of treating a tragic plot. The presentation of Duryodhana as a tragic figure is not only unique and singular but very important. No other dramatist ventured to depict the career of the great Kuru king as a hero. Bhāsa is the dramatist who selected Duryodhana as his hero and gave the grand Aṅka, Ūrubhaṅga. The delicate pathos therein has always evoked the most sincere appreciation from the audience.

The Dūtavākya, Dūtaghaṭotkaca and Karṇabhāra—all the three speak highly of Bhāsa's power of dramatisation.

All these are one-act plays. In their execution Bhāsa shows remarkable skill of characterisation and the presentation of the theme. Though his characters are legendary yet he infuses new life and interest in them and consequently the characters, in the hands of Bhāsa, undergo a sea-change into something rich and strange.

The one-act plays, further, are remarkable for their unities of action and time. All the events presented in them happen in a single day and the action gets completed with the very exit of all the characters in the end. It is a very rare power of integration of all the aspects of the drama, which marks all these plays. Though brief, they are never fragmentary.

The Pañcarātra is a Samavakāra. The dramatist has followed Bharata in having ten to twelve chief characters in it. The plot begins with an intrigue and ends in its peaceful solution. The characters are of the Mahābhārata but the theme is Invented. The main action begins after a Viṣkambhaka and there are only three Acts according to the rules of the Śāstra.

Conclusion

To sum up, Bhāsa's contributions in the domain of Sanskrit drama are great. It is not possible for us to form any idea regarding the condition of Sanskrit drama before Bhāsa. Excepting the fragmentary pieces of Aśvaghoṣa nothing older than Bhāsa's works being extant, his plays serve as the first specimens of Sanskrit drama. Though pioneering efforts, his plays betray no smack of primitiveness in them, which speaks eloquently of the great achievement of Bhāsa. His mastery of the composition of all the ten varieties, conception of interesting plots, the art of characterisation, display of the subtle feelings of human beings and his keen sense of proportion are unsurpassed. The originality shown in the handling of legendary themes speaks of his high dramatic acumen. To crown all, his artless but superb diction and intelligent use of technique are rarely equalled in the long history of Sanskrit drama.

Though it is not possible for us to surmise what was the precise condition of the dramatic art before his advent, his plays prove beyond doubt the greatness achieved by the dramatic art in his hands. He left Sanskrit drama, a successful vehicle of all the Rasas and Bhāvas and opened up newer avenues before the next generation of dramatists.

—

B. The Second period—Kālidāsa

About the predecessors of Kālidāsa we know only the names of Bhāsa Saumilla and Kaviputra mentioned by himself as famous dramatists.[10] Of them, only the works of Bhāsa are extant. The other two are still now lost in obscurity. In the absence of material, no idea can be had of the process of development during the period beginning from Bhāsa and culminating in Kālidāsa. Consequently, Kālidāsa is the next playwright to arrest our attention after Bhāsa.

Though we are focussing our attention on Kālidāsa directly, it cannot be overlooked that there must have been many playwrights paving the way for the advent of one of the greatest Indian dramaturgists. The perfection of the plays of Kālidāsa presupposes regular attempts at dramatic creation during the interval. True it is that they are all shrouded in mystery still the difference between the plays of Bhāsa and Kālidāsa compels one to believe that there were a number of artists who followed Bhāsa and heralded the advent of Kālidāsa. The reason as to why none could shine in this interregnum is given by Dr. S. K. De. He observes—"It is, however, the effect also of the tyrannical dominance of a great genius that it not only obscures but often wipes out by its vast and strong effulgence the lesser lights which surround it or herald its approach."[11]

---

10. Vide, Introduction, Mālavikāgnimitra.
11. History of Classical San krit Literature, p. 118

The features of Kālidāsa as a dramatist

Kālidāsa is pre-eminently a poet. In his hands the classical Kāvya reaches its consummation and perfection. He, it has been accepted unanimously by both eastern and western critics, is one of the greatest poets not only of India but of the world. The fact of his being regarded as one of the greatest of poets of all times proves his universality.

Though a poet of the first rank, Kālidāsa's dramatic genius can hardly be minimised. His greatness as an artist does, in fact, rest much upon his rare creative genius which proved excellently capable of producing both poetry and drama which are, to a great extent, respectively subjective and objective in nature. As a dramatist Kālidāsa shows a gradual development in his art. Among his plays, the first two, Mālavikāgnimitra and Vikramorvaśī, are definitely inferior to the last and the best, Abhijñāna Śākuntala in charm and appeal. His fine diction and beautiful versification, the various dramatic devices used in his plays, and above all the stamp of originality on them, especially on the Abhijñāna Śākuntala, are such factors as are never surpassed and rarely equalled. His genius reaches its zenith in Abhijñāna Śākuntala, the appeal of which is universal even now. His other plays, however, have a popular appeal and show to a great degree his skill as a successful dramatist. Kālidāsa is a worthy successor of Bhāsa whose greatness he himself admits but is ever careful not to copy his illustrious predecessor and to give something original and new.

Another feature to be noticed is his modesty. Unshakably believing that his permanent fame as a dramatist would depend only upon the intrinsic merits of his dramas, he followed the footsteps of his forerunner, Bhāsa in steering clear off all self-praise in the Introduction. The effacement of individuality, the chiefest of all the requisites of a successful dramatist, is to be seen in all his works. He not only refrains from personal eulogies but infuses an individuality into all his characters making them appear life-like and not as mere shadows of the poet himself.

The plays of Kālidāsa have got a typical poetic charm. The fact that he is the greatest of the Sanskrit poets helped him as a dramatist as well. The fine poetic element of his plays succeeds wonderfully in charming his audience and leading them to the delectable realisation of the ineffable joy which literature produces. So we can say that the real appeal of his dramas lies in the effective fusion of poetry and drama.

The language of kālidāsa

It has already been noticed that all the Formulators have denounced the attempts at a display of learning in the dramas. Bharata clearly says that the diction of a playwright must be very simple so that any layman can appreciate it. Bharata denounces the use of difficult and quaint words saying—[12]

'As the associatian of a prostitute with a Brāhmana carrying a Kamaṇḍalu is anomalous and revolting so is the use of such difficult terms as *cekrīḍita*, etc. by the dramatists.' The restraint of speech, as a result, has been held as one of the foremost qualities of a playwright.[13] Kālidāsa is a perfect artist in this respect. His works are

12. Vide, NŚ. XXI. 132.
13. See page 17 above.

remarkable for the measured use of words. He makes his characters speak nothing more, nothing less and thus makes characterisation effective. Kālidāsa knows the art of concealing art so well that his style is marked by the stamp of that sublime simplicity which never fails to arrest attention of all. If all art consists in the removal of surplusage, it is there in the dramas of Kālidāsa.

The three Dramas

Kālidāsa composed three dramas—Mālavikāgnimitra, Vikramorvaśī and Adhijñāna Śākuntala. This is the chronological order in which the dramas were written according to the consensus of critical opinion.

Mālavikāgnimitra

Mālavikāgnimitra is a drama of five Acts and is based upon the wooing, ending in marriage, of Mālavikā by Agnimitra, a king of that name of the Śuṅga dynasty. The plot entirely depends upon the love-intrigue of the King for Mālavikā which gets interrupted by Irāvatī, the second queen of Agnimitra.

The Vastu or theme is taken from contemporary history and herein lies a departure from the established practice. Kālidāsa was thus the first to introduce in his play the story of a comparatively modern king, Agnimitra and Kālidāsa's success induced the later Formulators to include contemporaneous characters in the list of heroes. The life of contemporary kings had been previously discarded as unfit for dramatic presentation, since it could not properly impress the audience. Whereas kings of antiquity commanded a very great influence upon the imagination of the audience. It was due to this reason that kings of antiquity had been given preference to the contemporary kings. But the success of Kālidāsa with

Agnimitra as the hero suggested that even royal personages of contemporary times could be properly presented as dramatic heroes. There is thus ground for the presumption that Abhinavagupta and later on Rāmacandra and Guṇacandra modified the statement and accepted contemporary characters as fit for dramatic representation.

The Structure of the Plot

The five Acts of this play bring about the five Stages of Action and plot successively. There is the Marvellous Sentiment in the end as well. No remarkable deviation from Bharata is noticeable. Kālidāsa does not depict the details of events nor does he deal with the psychology of the hero. The otherwise plain story is laden with the complexity as to how the king can get the hands of Mālavikā, a handmaid, in marriage in the teeth of opposition from other queens. The king is assisted by his friend, the Vidūṣaka and Vakulāvalikā, a friend to Mālavikā who plays as a go-between. The opposition comes from the second queen, Irāvatī who wields a great power. The play begins with the desire of the king to get Mālavikā whom he loves at the very first sight and ends with the marriage of the king and Mālavikā who is presented to the king by the chief queen, Dhāriṇī after the revelation of the fact that she is a princess.

Prastāvanā

The Introduction of this play is very brief and has got only seventeen lines including two verses. The names of the already famous playwrights referred to in it are three—Bhāsa, Saumilla or Saumillaka and Kaviputra. Judged from the view-point of technique, it can be very easily said that Kālidāsa owed much to his predecessors. It is not out of mere courtesy that he refers to Bhāsa and others but he follows, in fact, their way. How far he was influenced by Saumilla and Kaviputra is difficult to ascertain but his Introduction speaks clearly of the influence of Bhāsa over him. The Introduction of Kālidāsa is as simple and brief as that of Bhāsa. This brevity and simplicity, it should be noted, are the signs of perfection attained by the great artists.

That Kālidāsa's dramas were prior to the Agnipurāṇa is proved by the fact that these do not conform to rules prescribed therein. There is however, no reference to Kālidāsa in Agnipurāṇa, the rules of which, it is maintained, might have been formulated on extant dramas of a decadent period when authors indulged in self-laudation in a manner disproportionate to their achievements.

The Explanatory Devices

The play begins with an Explanatory Scene of the mixed type. It is a bit long but the playwright manages beautifully to introduce the name, nature and attainments of the heroine by it. The attempt of keeping away Mālavikā from the sight of the king is also spoken of here and so when the king enters after the Explanatory Scene, his eager search for some plan to meet the heroine is not inconsistent and unnatural. Hence when the very plan is explained by the Vidūṣaka to the king, the Germ of the drama is sown.

There are altogether three Explanatory Devices—an Explanatory Scene in the first Act and two Intermediate Scenes in the third and fifth Acts respectively. This minimisation of reportable facts *(sūcya)* speaks eloquently of the great attainments of Kālidāsa as a dramatist. He thus introduces directly the main characters in other Acts without any assistance of the minor characters. Though these scenes are not charming in nature, laden with facts as these are, the dramatist exhibits a great skill in making these very brief.

Act I, an Aṅkāvatāra?

Dhanañjaya speaks of the first Act of Mālavikāgnimitra to be an Aṅkāvatāra. His view is that the second Act is commenced by the very characters of the first one. The words of the Vidūṣaka in the end of the first Act—'athavā mṛdaṅgaśabda eva na utthāpayiṣyati' and the sound of the musical instruments in the beginning of the second, link up the two Acts. As the characters in the end of Act I usher in the next, Dhanañjaya considers it to be an Aṅkāvatāra.

But such a view is not tenable. Aṅkāvatāra being an Explanatory Device cannot have all the chief characters in it. Like the Explanatory or the Introductory Scenes, etc. it should also be formed by minor characters and assume the form of a brief scene. The exact Aṅkāvatāra is found in Śākuntala in between the fifth and sixth Acts. So the device used by Kālidāsa in ushering in the second Act is to be considered as one of the serious and highly original histrionic devices employed by him.

The Characters

The characters of Kālidāsa are in general well-drawn. The king, the queen and all other royal personages in the drama are presented in a very befitting manner. It may be said that the love-lorn king, the jealous queen, the Vidūṣaka and all such characters are so drawn that all of them become more or less models to the later playwrights.

The time analysisof the play

Mālavikāgnimitra is the only play of Kālidāsa in which the dramatic action occupies a period of about a week. The analysis as given by A.V.W. Jackson is as follows—[14]

Act	I & II	part of one day (Interval, hardly more than a day
Act	III	part of one day (Interval, slight, if any)
Act	IV	part of one day
Act	V	the next day.

The whole time occupied by the action is thus abou a week. This compactness is remarkable and it prove amply the great skill of the playwright.

The End

According to Bharata each play should have the Marvellous Sentiment in the end. Kālidāsa has obeyed this principle. The end brings about the surprising revelation of the real identity of Mālavikā and thus fulfils the course of the Action in the proposed marriage of the King and Mālavikā. The Bharata-vākya is spoken by the hero and it prays for heavenly benediction for all the people ruled by king Agnimitra.

Vikramorvaśī

Vikramorvaśī is the second drama of Kālidāsa. Herein he depicted the love of king Purūravas for Urvaśī, the famous danseuse of Heaven. In the treatment of a love affair between a denizen of Heaven and

---

14. Vide Time-analysis of Sanskrit Plays, JOAOS, Vol. XX.

a mortal man, the poet is in a great difficulty to bring about a happy union between the two. The story, as it runs, should have ended in tragic separation but somehow the poet manages the incidents and makes the two lovers unite. There is thus 'a decided weakness in general treatment.'

The Source

Dr. S. K. De observes—'The romantic story of the love of the mortal king, Purūravas and the divine nymph, Urvaśī is old, the earliest version occuring in the Ṛgveda—X, 95; but the passion and pathos, as well as the logically tragic ending, of the ancient legend is changed, in five Acts, into an unconvincing story of semi-courtly life with a weak denouement of domestic union and felicity, brought about by the intervention of a magic stone and the grace of Indra.'[15] Though references to the love of Purūravas and Urvaśī are found in the Vedas, Purāṇas and the Śatapatha Brāhmaṇa, the exact source of this play of Kālidāsa is difficult to ascertain. He has taken the kernel of the plot from any or all of these books, but has given altogether a new form to his play. He has changed, so to say, the 'la belle dame sans merci' of the Vedas and Purāṇas into a loving and loveable heroine. Even though the story may be weak, the characterisation of the poet is remarkably magnificent. Purūravas, Urvaśī and the jealous queen, Auśinarī are not mere shadows of Agnimitra, Mālavikā and Irāvatī or Dhāriṇī of the preceding play. Even the Vidūṣaka of this play differs from that of the Mālavikāgnimitra. Herein the Vidūṣaka speaks always of his appetite and thereby causes laughter. This character-

15. Vide HSL. p. 138.

istic of the Vidūṣaka, it is to be noted, owes its origin to Kālidāsa. It is Kālidāsa who represented, first of all, the Vidūṣaka as a hungry fellow. And a man, speaking of appetite in season and in out of season, is bound to be classed as a fool. As a result, the formulators define, later on, a Vidūṣaka as—

"Kusumavasantādyabhidhaḥ karmavapurveśabhāsādyaiḥ
Hāsyakaraḥ kalaharatir vidūṣakaḥ syāt svakarmajñaḥ"[16]

and explain Svakarma ase ating, etc. (*bhojanādi)* That the Vidūṣaka is meant for supplying the Hāsyarasa, is admitted but it is not intelligible why for making others laugh one should always go on speaking of his appetite. The Daśarūpaka speaks only of the Hāsyakāritā of the Vidūṣaka. The explanation of the term Svakarma in the Sāhityadarpaṇa as eating seems erroneous and such a meaning owes its origin to one or two such characters of ancient dramatists. The real meaning should be appropriate actions. That is, the Vidūṣaka is to perform all such acts as may cause laughter among the audience.

The Name of the Vidūṣaka

The Śloka in question from Sāhityadarpaṇa (III,42), further fixes up the names of the Vidūṣaka. It says that the Vidūṣaka should have such names as Vasanta (the Spring) or Kusuma (flower). Such a formulation is undoubtedly dogmatic and here also the influence of great playwrights is obvious. The naming of the Vidūṣaka in the beginning must have been done by the playwrights according as their choice. Consequently, the Vidūṣakas of Bhāsa have got these names—Vasantaka in Vāsavadattā

---

16. SD. III. 42.

and Pratijñāyaugandharāyaṇa; Santuṣṭa in Avimāraka; and Maitreya in Cārudatta. Even if the term Kusumavasantādyabhidhaḥ is explained, as it is done, as to mean names purporting to Kusuma or Vasanta, this rule cannot be applied to Bhāsa. Vasantaka is all right but Santuṣṭa and Maitreya have got nothing to do with Kusuma or Vasanta.

The names of the Vidūṣaka in the plays of Kālidāsa also do not conform to this definition. The names—Gautama and Mānavaka, the Vidūṣakas of Mālavikāgnimitra and Vikramorvaśī respectively, have got nothing to do with flower or spring. Only that of Abhijñāna Śākuntala tallies with the above formulation. Mādhavya has got the sense of spring in it, Mādhava meaning the spring season. On the ground of so many names of Vidūṣaka given by the master-playwrights, the view of Viśvanātha does not stand. It seems, on the other hand, that the formulator was too much influenced by the successful character of the Vidūṣaka of the Abhijñāna Śākuntala and considering the name of this Vidūṣaka, directed that such names should always be given to these characters.

Vikramorvaśī—a new form ?

Sāhityadarpaṇa speaks of a new kind of drama, Troṭaka by name. According to it the Troṭaka is a drama which rests upon the story of divine and mortal beings, has got the character of Vidūṣaka in every Act and has, further, seven, eight, nine or five Acts in it.[17] The Rasa of a Troṭaka is said to be the Śṛṅgāra. The formulator finds it difficult to illustrate the form and names

17. SD. VI. 273

only two plays by way of example. The example of a seven-Act Troṭaka is given as Stambhitarambha and that of a five-Act one is the Vikramorvaśī.

It is obvious that on the ground of such a data no new form can be established. Nothing is known about the first one, i.e. the Stambhitarambha but so for as Vikramorvaśī is concerned the definition is not applicable in its fullness. The story, no doubt, comprises of characters divine and mortal both, but the Vidūṣaka is not seen in each Act. The first Act is void of Vidūṣaka. Whether only one element that of bringing together the divine and mortal characters should be considered weighty enough to class it as a Troṭaka is doubtful. Save this element, Vikramorvaśī is a full-fledged Nāṭaka with five Acts just like the Mālavikāgnimitra.

Simply for such a negligible variation from the Nāṭaka type, it is not sound enough to define an altogether new form. This is the reason why the form has not received universal acceptance. The variation may be noted but no new form should be based upon this.

Apart from this treatment of heavenly and mortal beings together, another element of this play demands attention. It is the song element in it. The fourth Act presents the king in mad pursuit of his beloved Urvaśī who is lost. There are many songs which run as a commentary while the king runs in utter bewilderment asking everything, animate or inanimate, about his beloved. The scene is highly romantic and full of pathos. Though the scene has got almost no action, still the lyric element raises it high above the common-place. 'The fourth Act on the madness of Purūravas is unique in this sense. The scene is hardly dramatic and has no action, but it reaches an almost lyric height in depicting the tumultous ardour of undisciplined passion.'[18] Kālidāsa has shown in this Act a rare power of making a soliloquy highly charming and effective.

The Prastāvanā

The Prastāvanā of Vikramorvaśī is of the Bhāsa type. There is a pathetic cry for immediate help, which is explained by the Sūtradhāra and thus the main story is ushered in. The poet introduces the hero and heroine in the very first Act without any of the Explanatory Devices.

In this play there are three Praveśakas and one Viṣkambhaka. All the four are very short and indispensable and as such bear glowing testimony to the finished art of Kālidāsa. The Praveśakas take place firstly in the beginning of the second Act to indicate the repercussion on the life and attitude of the king of his meeting with the nymph; secondly before the fourth Act where two nymphs disclose how Urvaśī is metamorphosed into a creeper while dallying with the king in the Kailāsa mountain and the pathetic pursuit of the king after his invisible beloved; and thirdly in the beginning of the fifth Act wherein the Vidūṣaka announces the return of the king from the Kailāsa regions and the startling news of the loss of the magic stone which brought about the union of lovers. The Viṣkambhaka is placed in the beginning of the third Act wherein two disciples of Bharata, the preceptor of drama, acquaint us with the fact that while playing in the drama, Lakṣmī-svayamvara, in the court of Heaven,

18. Vide HSL. p. 139.

Urvaśī forgot her own part and spoke out the name of Purūravas as her choice husband instead of the name of Viṣṇu which she ought to speak as Lakṣmī. Further, they announce that Indra sent Urvaśī, out of his appreciation of Purūravas, a friend of his, to the world in order to satisfy both the longing lovers.

The unity of time is fully maintained in this drama. The playwright has introduced one or the other Intermediate Scenes to indicate the passage of time and consequently the play has got an integrated dramatic form. The time analysis is given below[19]—

Act	I	part of one day (Interval—one or two weeks)
Act	II	mid-day of one day
Act	III	the same afternoon and evening (Interval—twelve years)
Act	VI	indefinite but condensed into a single day of the rainy season
Act	V	part of one day, probably the next.

Thus the action covers a period of about 12½ years.

The Song Element

The fourth Act of the play is full with so many songs in the Gāthā form. 'The Apabhraṃśa of the type found in them is suspicious in a drama of such an early date' and these are not found in the south Indian recension of the text. Whether the songs in the Apabhraṃśa are of Kālidāsa or belong to a younger editor of the play is

---

19. Vide Time-analysis of Sanskrit Plays, JOAOS, Vol, XX.

doubtful but it must be accepted that these songs, intended to be sung from behind the curtain, add much to the pathos of the scene. The verses in Sanskrit as well are superb in the Sanskrit literature as the best examples of Vipralambha–śṛṅgāra-rasa.

Abhijñāna Śākuntala

Abhijñāna Śākuntala is the last and best play of Kālidāsa and in it the art of Kālidāsa, through a gradual process of development reaches its meridian. Much has been said by the critics of East and West alike on its charming plot, subtle and grand characterisation, sublime theme, etc. which it is useless to reiterate. We shall discuss the play from the view point of dramatic technique and structure.

The Prastāvanā

The Prastāvanā of Abhijñāna Śākuntala is the best of all the Prastāvanās of Kālidāsa. The type is known as the Prayogātiśaya. The Sūtradhāra with the assistance of a Naṭī introduces the hero himself, using not more than twentyfive lines and in a manner which is highly artistic and charming. Herein also Kālidāsa shows his sense of artistic modesty in not mentioning anything else but the names of his patron, Vikramāditya, the play and the playwright. To repeat what has been already said, Kālidāsa always relied upon the perfection of his art and never bragged of his attainments by means of well chosen phrases of self-approbation. The most important requisite of the dramatist, namely, the effacement of his own personality impresses all from the very beginning of the play.

The Vastu

The source of the play is Mahābhārata. Though there is a Śakuntalopākhyāna in the Padmapurāṇa as well, critics hold that Kālidāsa was no borrower from the latter.[20] The plot of the play is thus of the legendary type. Kālidāsa however, did not follow the Mahābhārata story in toto but showed great art in bringing novel situations which heightened the sense of drama. The artistic worth of these new devices can hardly be overlooked or under–estimated by anyone. Like Shakespeare, Kālidāsa, also took the liberty of changing the original material as the exigencies of art demanded and hence the curse of Durvāsas, the two companions, Anusūyā and Priyaṃvadā, and so many other deviations from the source.

The justification of such deviations by great artists is supplied by the English critic, Stopford A. Brooke in his book entitled—'Ten Plays of Shakespeare', which may here be quoted for its convincing judgment. He writes—'Then, again, a creative genius, having collected his materials, feels his mastery over them and uses them as he pleases. He is going to make a greater matter than that which actually happened; something that will endure when the historical events have become dreams........' This observation, though made in connection with Shakespeare's handling of Plutarch, may very aptly and justifiably be applied to Kālidāsa's handling of the Mahābhārata. As a result, the shrewd, straightforward and taunting girl of the Epic is transformed into the shy, dignified and pathetic heroine, while the selfish conduct of her practical lover in the Epic, who refuses to recognise her out of policy, is replaced by an irreprehensible forgetfulness which obscures love. A dramatic motive is thereby

20. Vide Notes. S. K. De, HSL., p. 140; also Winternitz, HIL. III, p. 215, who finds no reason to hold that Kālidāsa was the borrower.

supplied, and the prosaic incidents and characters of the original legend are plastically remodelled into frames and shapes of beauty.'[21]

This remodelling, it has been well said, has supplied the play with a motive. What is the motive underlying this play? A very magnificent exposition of that is given by the poet, Rabindranath Tagore in his article on Kumārasambhava and Śakuntalā[22] which should be quoted in order to make full justice to Kālidāsa's deviations. He says—'Kālidāsa has recognised the power of that love which defies all restraint, and overwhelming the man and woman, hoists its banner of victory over the ruins of the castle of restraint but the poet has not surrendered himself to it. He has shown that the riotous dalliance, which makes men and women irresponsible, is blasted by the curse of the lord, frustrated by the curse of the sage and ruined by the wrath of the gods' (Translation mine).

The Structure of the Play

After the Prastāvanā is over, Duṣyanta, the hero enters riding on a chariot, chasing a deer. The first Act begins here and the Germ of the plot is sown in it. The intervention of the disciples of Kaṇva, the entry of the king into the hermitage and his meeting with Śakuntalā and her two comrades—Anasūyā and Priyaṃvadā—all these happen one after another very briskly. Kālidāsa brings before the audience without delay the main theme—the attraction of the king and Śakuntalā to each other and supplies the necessary information as to the heredity

---

21. Vide HSL. p. 140-41.
22. Vide Prācīna Sāhitya, pp. 18-19.

of the heroine and the like from the very happy discourse that follows. The scene is so conceived that there remains not the slightest doubt in anybody's mind as to the growth of the sentiment of love in the two—Duṣyanta and Śakuntalā. The introduction of Anasūyā aud Priyaṃvadā, though a deviation, makes the scene more lively and interesting.

The Act, thus, having sown the Germ ends with a warning from the sages who cry at the top of their voice cautioning the inmates of the hermitage for the protection of the frightened animals at the sudden advent of king Duṣyanta with his retinue. This warning in the end as well as that in the beginning (e.g. Na khalu na khalu vānaḥ.........etc.) of the Act, has got a great bearing upon the course of events in the play. The suggestion in both the places is that Duṣyanta is somewhat a foreigner to the hermitage from whom everyone should be kept under careful protection. The absence of this protection, it may be pointed out, proves fatal in the case of Śakuntalā.

The gradual development of the plot goes undisturbed upto the third Act. The hero is invited by the sages of the hermitage to save them from the disturbances made by the demons, which the king willingly accepts. But his longing for Śakuntalā makes him eagerly enquire of her and so, fittingly does Kālidāsa place an Explanatory Scene in the beginning of the third Act to let us know the success of Duṣyanta in curbing the demons, and also the illness of Śakuntalā. After this, the pursuit of Duṣyanta of the heroine follows easily and the Act abounds in charmingly romantic expressions.

Kālidāsa does not present the marriage scene. Though a marriage is not necessarily something (vrīḍākara) shameful and is accepted as presentable yet it is omitted to impress upon the audience the effect of unbridled passion which considers nothing else but itself. Kālidāsa informs us of the marriage of the two and the return of the king by means of another Explanatory Scene. The passage of a few weeks is also denoted herein.

The introduction of the curse of Durvāsās proves once more the great skill of Kālidāsa as a dramatist. Without this, nothing could ennoble the character of the hero, who, it is said in the Epic, did not, later on, recognise Śakuntalā out of the selfish consideration of his own good name. The dramatic effect of the curse, thus not only adds a noble dignity to the king's career, but, in addition, suggests the truth that such a union as is motivated by passion and lust is bound to be cursed by the sages. To Śakuntalā, it comes as a punishment for her neglect of duties. This influence of the supernatural is not in the least discordant with the Indian view and, as such, criticism of Kālidāsa on this score is unjustified.

The fourth Act is remarkable for its sublime pathos. The sage Kaṇva comes for the first and last time on the stage in this Act and bids farewell to his foster-daughter. The pathos comes out so movingly that the verses have been acclaimed to be the best of the type and universal in their appeal. The blessings showered upon the departing daughter by the sage are so very appealing that these have become a part of common usage. The emotional outbursts of the companions of Śakuntalā, Gautamī and Kaṇva are made more impressive by the dramatist by his sense of restraint and proportion. In the depiction of sentiments Kālidāsa is never sentimental.

Nature and Kālidāsa

The utilisation of nature by Kālidāsa deserves attention. As a poet Kālidāsa is fond of nature and has given so many beautiful pictures of the various seasons. It is to his great credit that he has manipulated successfully the entire hermitage to add a new colour to his play. From the very beginning he suggests that Śakuntalā is a child of nature. The entire background of her life consists of very many trees, creepers and wild-eyed stags. The great self-restraint shown by the poet-dramatist is particularly noteworthy here. Though fond of natural beauty, he never mars the advancement and development of the plot by poetic effusions. The short but impressive reference to and description of nature here and there has added a charm peculiar to it. His mastery in depicting nature as a living character of the play is so perfect that everyone takes to be true the saying of Priyaṃvadā that the entire hermitage is weeping at the departure of Śakuntalā. (Act. IV, 14)

The soothing atmosphere of the hermitage has its contrast in the fifth Act, the court scene of the famous king Duṣyanta. The effect of quiet nature of the previous scene is used masterfully to hint that anyone from such a plain and simply beautiful sphere is bound to be duped at the royal court where urban sophistication rules. The idea of probable denunciation of Śakuntalā thus occupies the mind of the audience who are aware as well of the curse of the sage. The failure of Śakuntalā in producing any proof of the king's connection with her is rendered very keen and appealing by means of the grand dialogue of the characters.

Kālidāsa resorts to supernatural to reassure the audience that though jilted she suffers no harm and is borne to the heavens by an angel, mothered as she was by a nymph.

The Aṅkāvatāra

Kālidāsa uses the Explanatory Device known as *Aṅkāvatāra* to bring back the lost ring of Śakuntalā. It is Kālidāsa, who, it can be said on the basis of extant dramas, used this for the first time. The use of it is highly successful. Unlike the Explanatory and the Introductory Scenes, it has no such characters who can relate the past events and hint at the future. On the contrary, it is a scene complete in itself. The fisherman here has no knowledge of the love affairs of the king, neither the policemen know the matter. The entire scene is, so to say, unconnected with the main event. It is the dramatic worth that attracted the playwright to put an *Aṅkāvatāra* and his attempt proved successful. Though it is the first *Aṅkāvatāra* in the history of Sanskrit Drama, it is the foremost of all in charm and impression.

The sixth Act reveals to the audience the king's reaction to the recovery of the ring. The king is shown in a penitent mood, ruefully thinking of his cruel denunciation of Śakuntalā. So many years have passed by and the king is engaged in drawing a portrait of his beloved, which never reaches the mark of perfection. There is no sign of valour left in the king, weeping always as he is. The king is skilfully aroused from his lethargy by the poet. He brings in the charioteer of Indra who frightens the Vidūṣaka of the king in order to rouse the king to regain his old valour. The suffering of Vidūṣaka at the hand of the unseen foe, Mātali, serves two purposes. Firstly, it lifts the king from the state of torpor and inspires him to action. Secondly, it supplies a great dramatic relief. Previous to this there was no merry-making in the king's palace and a heavy sadness hung upon the place. The cry of the Vidūṣaka is the first symptom of a welcome change in the atmosphere. The element of ludicrous which is patently manifested in the cry, is a successful effort of the dramatist to give an occasion to laugh to the audience. The king, then, goes to Heaven to help Indra and the Act ends.

The last Act (VII) shows the king and the charioteer, Mātali, coming down to the earth. The king has successfully performed his duty of vanquishing the enemy of Indra and they are presented as talking to each other While passing by the aerial region where lives the sage Kaśyapa, the king decides to pay his respects to the grea sage and they get down from the chariot. Kālidāsa set this scene high above the earth apparently to show tha the penance of the king for his sin of not recognising Sakuntalā has purified him and made him fit for the blissful re-union with his so long discarded consort. Kālidāsa brings about the re-union of the two hapless lovers in a very highly artistic manner. The king is shown left alone as Mātali goes to inform the sage about the arrival of Duṣyanta. Then comes a boy whose very sight gives rise to filial affection in the heart of the king. The boy is too much self-willed and inspite of the protests of the Tāpasīs is bent upon counting the teeth of a lion-cub. A surprising similarity between the appearence of the king and the boy is marked by all. Considering the embarrassment of the king in asking directly the name of the boy's mother, Kālidāsa reveals the identity of the boy very dramatically. One of the Tāpasīs asks the boy to look at the beauty of a toy-bird in order to save the lion-cub from the determined boy. The dramatist uses the word '*Śakunta-lāvaṇyaṁ paśya*,' and immediately the boy cries out, hearing the two words spoken together, 'Where is my mother?' The king hears this and the hope of getting his much wronged wife back wells up in his eager heart. The incident of the magic stone also is interesting. Not only the king is anxious to know the real identity of the boy but the Tāpasīs also become eager to know who is this man resembling so closely the boy. When the king touches the magic stone, inspite of the protestations of the Tāpasīs, nothing unusual happens. This stone has the potency of being changed into a serpent if touched by anyone excepting the father and the mother of the boy. This fact as well speeds up the anxiety and expectation of the king, and the dramatist presents Śakuntalā before him almost immediately. The recognition of each other then takes place and the re-union is made permanent by the blessings of the great sage, Kaśyapa. The ephimeral attraction of a man and a woman is thus shown to have risen above the banality of unenduring passion and in the process, both the lovers have undergone the chastening ordeal which has sufficiently proved their sincerity.

The greatest achievement of Kālidāsa as a dramatist is the element of universality with which he imbues his plot, characterisation and motive of the play. The subject matter of Abhijñāna Śākuntala is love which was, is, and will remain a thing of beauty and joy for ever. Not only the love of the lovers but the affection of a father for his daughter, the comradeship of friends, the attraction for one's own son—all these are matters which command universal appeal. The tragic disavowal of true love and the reception of the most sincere emotional appeal with ridicule and contumely are also matters which deserve universal condemnation.

Characterisation

Characterisation of Kālidāsa also deserves high appreciation. No where his characters appear as the spokesmen of the dramatist. On the contrary, all his characters exhibit individuality of their own. The greatest proof of this success is the fact that the drama of Kālidāsa has superseded its original in the Mahābhārata in sheer beauty and charm. Duṣyanta, as presented by Kālidāsa, has become the real Duṣyanta after being shorn off the hard-heartedness which stains the character of his original in the Epic.

Moreover, in the presentation of characters, Kālidāsa never emphasises upon those specialities of his characters, which are typically Indian, specialities which may not be appreciated by the foreigners. He presents Kaṇva not while performing a Yajña ceremony, nor even engaged in teaching or penance but as a loving father with a noble character, thus making him also universally appealing. The Kaṇva of Kālidāsa may, as a result, be highly appreciated even by one who has not the least knowledge of the Indian sages and their mode of living. The greatest success attained by the dramatist is that if rendered in any language of the world, the play will remain equally charming and appealing throughout the ages. The subtle psychological sense exhibited by Kālidāsa in the presentation of characters gives him a position in the galaxy of world's best dramatists. The illustrations of this power of the dramatist are spread all over the entire drama and one must pause at their charming subtlety while perusiug the play.

Conclusion

To sum up, Kālidāsa shows Sanskrit drama in its richest stage. Though all his plays are based on romantic themes and he excels in the display of Śṛṅgāra yet his plays are so charmingly unlaboured and void of all artificialities that these speak eloquently of the greatest achievements possible to be attained by Sanskrit drama. The charm and simplicity of style and diction of his plays unmistakably point out the capacity of Sanskrit drama to depict all the phases of human life in it. As a grand successor of Bhāsa, Kālidāsa raises the drama to a highly refined level and though his plays appear to be more polished in nature than those of Bhāsa, the fine alchemy of Kālidāsa's art invests them with a universal appeal which never fades. It is useless to search for the naivete of the type of Bhāsa in Kālidāsa's plays which by their nature are products of a more cultured and sophisticated age. This, however, takes away not a whit from the intrinsic charm of the plays.

C. The third period—Śrī Harṣa

In the field of Nāṭaka, Harṣa comes after Kālidāsa. A long gap is to be jumped over in our attempt to reach Harṣa, the last Hindu king of Thaneswar of the seventh century A.D.

The fame of Harṣa as a dramatist depends upon three dramatic pieces—a Nāṭaka and two Nāṭikās. In the field of Nāṭikā, he is to be regarded as the first dramatist as no other older Nāṭikās have come to light. Regarding this species we shall discuss in its proper place. Here we shall judge the merits and achievements of Harṣa as a writer of Nāṭaka and attempt at forming an idea of his dramatic technique, success and his contribution towards dramatic literature.

The Nāṭaka and its subject matter

Nāgānanda is the Nāṭaka composed by Harṣa. The source of the play is Bṛhatkathā wherein the self-sacrifice of Jīmūtavāhana is narrated. Harṣa, it is held by the historians, was a Buddhist but at the same time he was liberal in his attitude to other faiths. In the quinquennial assemblies held by him at Prayāga, he used to worship—Śiva, Viṣṇu and Buddha, all in turn. In his drama also we find the influence of his religious liberality. He selects a theme which is Buddhistic in essence, that of universal benevolence, and invokes the Buddha in the benedictory stanzas in the Prologue but introduces the goddess Gaurī not only as a presiding deity but as the Deus ex machina in the end to bring the drama to a successful close.

The subject-matter is peculiar and there are two clear cut directives that guide the actions of the hero. Jīmūtavāhana, a Vidyādhara prince, accompanies his old father to the forest for the purpose of serving him as a dutiful son. He denounces all the worldly pleasures and is so benevolent and compassionate that he wishes to sacrifice even his own life for the benefit of others. With such a resigned and dedicated attitude, while moving about on the Malaya mountains, the hero and the Vidūṣaka, Ātreya by name, suddenly meet Malayavatī, the beautiful daughter of the Siddha king, Viśvāvasu in the temple of Gaurī. This meeting gives rise to amorous feelings and both become the prey of the God of love. Within short, the brother of Malayavatī comes to meet the hero and offers the hand of his sister to him. The hero declines for his love for the unknown Malayavatī. However, the refusal is withdrawn with the discovery that the object of love of the hero and Malayavatī are the same person and a happy marriage follows. The one of the two directives spoken above ends here.

The next directive begins from the third Act and continues upto the end. In this portion, Jīmūtavāhana is again presented as a resigned prince who is regardless of all pomp and pleasure of the royal life. His ideal of plain living and high thinking and the resigned attitude make his former romantic life appear as deviation from the correct path. He is callous even at the news of his kingdom being overthrown by an enemy and dissuades Mitrāvasu, his brother-in-law, from taking any steps by preaching non-violence and renunciation. While moving about on the sea shore where the above discussion takes place, he sees the skeletons of the Nāgas or serpents lying in heaps and from a distance appearing like small mountain heads. Coming to know that these are the remains of the wretched Nāgas that have been devoured up by Garuḍa as a regular custom, he feels pity for the Nāgas and on meeting Śaṅkhacūḍa, the snake ordained to be the food of Garuḍa that day, he asks the Nāga to retire and decides to offer himself instead. Garuḍa then comes and sets upon his prey unaware of the fact that his prey is not a Nāga. In the end, the father, mother and wife of the hero come to the place directed by the Nāga and Garuḍa is ashamed to realise his mistake. Garuḍa is further overwhelmed by the nobility of the hero and agrees to abide by his request of not to kill Nāgas any more. Jīmūtavāhana dies and Garuḍa goes to heaven to secure nectar to bring him and all the dead snakes back to life. At this juncture when the grief-distracted relatives are ready with the funeral pyre, Gaurī, the goddess, appears and brings Jīmūtavāhana back to life and restores his kingdom to him.

The weakness of the story is apparent. The love episode of the first three Acts has got nothing to do with the later and more important episode. The dramatist fails to bring in a dramatic unity between the two episodes and consequently, as far as dramatic art is concerned, the first episode appears superfluous. Moreover, the characterisation of the hero suffers greatly by a serious self-contradiction in him. The intensity of the hero's love for Malayavatī conveyed through phrases common to the romantic hero of the Sanskrit plays does not, in the least, match with the extreme disregard of her, at the time of his noble self-sacrifice. One is at a loss to account for the romantic hero's sudden disregard for his beloved. In fact, the chief weakness of the play is this anomaly between Jīmūtavāhana, the lover and Jīmūtavāhana, the apostle of self-sacrifice. The dramatist fails to effect a harmonious blending of the two phases. Consequently, there follows a Rasa-doṣa. The two divisions of the play have got Śṛṅgāra and Śānta as their chief sentiments and these are contradictory to each other. The denouement also suffers from this. The Germ of the plot has nothing to do with the love-affair as it is Vairāgya, and as a result the denouement, wherein Gaurī fulfills all the possible and probable desires of the hero, seems anomalous in view of the fact that the hero has actually no desire in his heart.

Though the play thus suffers from a serious artistic breach between the two parts, it has found favour with all the critics and codifiers. The Rasa-doṣa referred to above has been neglected by all. They hold, on the contrary, that the presentation of such contradictory Rasas is to be condemned only when they are introduced simultaneously. But in Nāgānanda, both the Rasas have their special fields. One does not over-lap the other. Moreover, sufficient recompense for this weakness, they say, is supplied by the interception of Adbhuta-rasa in the statement—'*Aho gītam ! Aho vādyam*' of the hero (Act I). The Adbhuta–rasa acts as a line of demarcation, so to say, between the two sentiments. And Sāhitya-darpaṇa holds Jīmūtavāhana to be a Dayā-vīra, one of the four Vīra-nāyakas. (SD. III, p. 181). This apparently makes it a play of Vīra-rasa.

This classification is based, it is clear, on the famous statement '*Aṣṭau nāṭya rasāḥ smṛtāḥ*' of the Nāṭyaśāstra (Ch. VI.) and in order to avoid the difficulty of admitting the Śānta-rasa as the dominant rasa of a play, the codifiers have tried toa rgue that the Rasa of this play is a variant of Vīra. This classification and the arguments adduced in its support are rather dogmatic. That the play has got in it the Śānta-rasa, particularly in the latter portion, is clearly evident. The self-sacrifice of the hero to save the Nāga is prompted not only by a temporary fit of emotion but by the deep-rooted sense of renunciation which is presented as the keynote of the character.

Nāgānanda, then, should be considered rightly as a play of Śānta-rasa. In spite of the codifiers trying to prove the contrary, it is definitely a non-conventional play with the Śānta-rasa as the dominant Sentiment. The romantic as well as the quieter phase of the hero's life has been ably executed and presented side by side, in their fulness. In fact, the romantic situation presented in Nāgānanda is not so laudable, since a better handling of such situations can be found in Harṣa's Nāṭikās. But the most appealing feature in it is the calm universal benevolence of the hero for the sufferers and the wretched. The denunciation of insolent youth (Act I, 6) with which he begins and the annoucement that he wishes to help others even sacrificing his own body can lead him, in all probability, only to sacrifice his own life in order to save the Nāga and not to dally with a princess. The aim of the dramatist, as it is evident, is to emphasise upon the aspect of renunciation and not on dalliance and self-indulgence. The attempts made to fulfill this aim are praiseworthy with this limitation that the dramatist does not succeed in making the two aspects blend in a harmonious fusion.

The Prastāvanā

Harṣa successfully introduces the hero in the very beginning and in it he takes help from the Prologue of

Śākuntala. In fact, the introduction of the hero with the phrase–'*Vanaṁ yāmyahamadyaiva yathā jīmūtavāhanaḥ*'– reminds one unmistakably of the line–'*Eṣa rājeva duṣyantaḥ sāraṅgenātiraṁhasā*' of Abhijñāna Śākuntala. The type of the Prologue, accordingly, is Avalagita

The Nāndī also deserves attention. It is an invocation to the Lord Buddha who maintained calmness of mind even when frightened by Māra and his associates. The verse suggests, it may be said, the fact that the hero of the play also is a man of similar fixity of purpose, whom the attraction of Malayavatī could not dissuade from his determination of self-sacrifice for the protection of the helpless.

The Structure of the Play

The play is divided into five Acts. The Stages of Action exhibited in these may here be denoted. The first Act begins with the hero, Jīmūtavāhana, Ātreya, the Vidūṣaka, Malayavatī, the heroine, her handmaid and a hermit. The Germ of the plot is sown here. The mental bent of the hero is evidently detached, still his attraction for the beautiful lady marks the opening of the plot and as well the first Stage of Action (*ārambha*). The second Act shows the next Stage of Action (*yatna*). In it both the lovers are anxious to have each other intimately and both of them go to a particular place. The love-sick condition of the heroine is first reported by a Praveśaka which exposes her sickness and the fact that she wishes to go to the calm bower known as 'candramaṇiśilātala'. The dramatist brings about their first meeting very skilfully while the hero unfolds his love-sick heart to his friend, the eaves-dropping Malayavatī gets disappointed and jealous of the unknown lady-love referred to by the hero. She does not know that the lady referred to and drawn on the marble slab by the hero is none else but she herself; and to crown all, when she sees how the hero rejects the marriage proposal of her brother Mitrāvasu who has come there for the purpose, utter frustration takes her into its grip and she attempts to hang herself from a tree. The hero also, in his turn, is unaware of the fact that the sister of Mitrāvasu is none else than his unknown beloved and so he rejects the latter's proposal. This comedy of errors, however, ends when the hero proceeds to rescue the heroine and recognises her as his own beloved and then removes her apprehension by showing the picture he has drawn. With the announcement of another maid-servant that Malayavatī has been welcomed as the bride of his son by the father of Jīmūtavāhana, the second Act ends.

The third Act is again preceded by a Praveśaka. This Praveśaka, with the Viṭa, Ceṭa, Ceṭī and Vidūṣaka in it, supplies us with the information that the marriage ceremony of Jīmūtavāhana and Malayavatī has ended. Much amusement has been derived by befooling the Vidūṣaka in this Praveśaka and thus it gives rise to a robust laughter. The Act proper brings in the happy couple engaged in loving chat. Herein the fourth Stage of Action, the Niyatāpti, is reached. Though the hero attains his end of having Malayavatī as his wife, the discordant note is struck by the news which is conveyed to the hero by Mitrāvasu. Mitrāvasu comes in with the news that an enemy has invaded the kingdom of Jīmūtavāhana and asks his permission to quell the invader.

The next two Acts concern with Jīmūtavāhana, the detached, and compassionate. He pacifies the angry Mitrāvasu saying that he cares little for the kingdom and it is better to live without one. Then, one after another, events take place, which lead him towards the noble self-sacrifice for the sake of the suffering Nāgas.

The playwright has averted the tragic ending of the play by introducing what is known as the divine assistance in the end. He contrives to grant the hero all his desires by bringing in goddess Gaurī who restores him to life, his parents, wife and kingdom. All the dead Nāgas also are revived by the repentant Garuḍa who showers nectar over them.

A few specialities may be noted here. Śrī Harṣa is the pioneer in introducing the Viṭa in a Nāṭaka and the use of the Patākāsthānakas. The successful use of these are found in the fourth and fifth Acts. It is perhaps from this play that Bhavabhūti derives the idea of using these devices. The third thing which is remarkable in this play is the unconventional Sentiment (Rasa) used in it. Acknowledging even the classification of Jīmūtavāhana as a Dayāvīra (a variety of vīra) hero, one must recognise in it the Śānta-rasa which is best exemplified in the calm and noble self-sacrifice of the hero.

Viśākhadatta

Viśākhadatta, the writer of Mudrārākṣasa, occupies an important place in the field of Nāṭaka. Though his exact date is controversial, most of the historians affix his date approximately between 750 and 850 A. D.

The Vastu

The chief merit of Viśākhadatta lies in the fact that he struck a new note. He is the first dramatist to handle successfully a historical theme in his play. The subject matter of the Mudrārākṣasa is the winning over of Rākṣasa, the wise minister of the dead Nandas to the side of Candragupta, the new king by his crafty well-wisher and guide, Cāṇakya. The play naturally abounds in innumerable political and diplomatic conspiracies contrived by both the ministers. Rākṣasa is sincerely loyal to his vanquished master and is ever active to undermine the new government of Candragupta as a retaliation for the defeat of his lord. Cāṇakya, also in his turn, is ever vigilant to safeguard the interests and security of Candragupta. Thus the play takes the form of a political intrigue with these two characters in the centre.

In addition to being political, the theme is historical as well. The fight between the Nandas and Candragupta the Maurya, is historical. Accordingly, the drama depicts the course of events that begins with the declaration of Cāṇakya to win Rākṣasa over to the side of Candragupta as his minister and ends with the fulfilment of his promise.

The Prastāvanā

The Prastāvanā is also of a new type. Unlike Kālidāsa, Viśākhadatta uses a new technique known as Udghātyaka. The Sūtradhāra says to the Naṭī that there can be no eclipse of the moon and this is heard by Cāṇakya from behind the curtain. The negation coming in the end of the sentence is not heard by Cāṇakya, and so he gets infuriated with the idea, taking Candra to mean Candragupta, the king (Act I, 6). He shouts from behind the stage that none can subdue (*grahaṇa*) Candra(Gupta) whose interests are protected by him. Thus the playwright introduces the main character and brings to light his strong determination to uproot all the enemies of Candragupta.

The drama is divided into seven Acts. The Germ (*bija*) of the plot is sown in the first Act which also depicts the first Stage of the Action (*ārambha*). There are no Episodes (*patāka*) or Episodical incidents (*prakarī*) appended to the theme. The second Stage of the Action that is efforts to attain the end have been depicted through all the five Acts. The last stage of Attainment of the Result is reached in the seventh Act. The third and fourth stages viz: Prāptyāśā and Niyatāpti are almost suppressed excepting a few references by the two chief characters, Cāṇakya and Rākṣasa, while they weigh their success.

The technical device, Patākā-sthānakas, is frequently used by the playwright and in all such places (especially in the first and fourth Acts), the victory of Cāṇakya is hinted at. In a play where political intrigue and espionage are two important factors such oblique statements are particularly effective.

Though the theme is too complex, the dramatist is admirably successful in giving all the events a grand dramatic unity of both time and action. The period of time covering all the seven Acts consists of ten to fifteen days. Only two Praveśakas are used in the play—one in the beginning of the fifth Act and the other in the beginning of the sixth. These expose in short how the subtle policies of Cāṇakya are nearing fulfilment.

The Nāṭaka is greatly remarkable for its peculiar plot and execution. The subtle art of the playwright succeeds in giving it a rare charm not to be found in any other Sanskrit play. A political tug-of-war between Cāṇakya and Rākṣasa has been so effectively dramatised that all the Acts of the play speak of the great accomplishments of the playwright. The working of the spies of both the parties has been so adroitly depicted that it has become highly interesting. The playwright has very successfully proved in this play that romantic theme is not the only theme for Nāṭaka. Another feature of the drama is the lack of important female characters. Only three women are there and of them two are female gate-keepers and the other is the wife of Candanadāsa, an ally of Rākṣasa, who, however, plays no important role.

The hero and the Rasa

Though the play has got the king Candragupta as one of the dramatic characters, he can never be considered to be the hero. The chief character who starts and attains the result of the action is decidedly Cāṇakya. As a Brāhmaṇa, Cāṇakya cannot be the hero of a Nāṭaka and so all the commentators try to prove Candragupta to be the hero of the play. We feel, however, that the play-wright is non-conventional in choosing his hero. He keeps Candragupta throughout as a minor character and presents Cāṇakya as the pivot of all the actions in the play.

There is a controversy regarding the type of Rasa of this play. The commentators who follow the dicta of the Daśarūpaka and the Sāhityadarpaṇa, assign Vīra-rasa to Mudrārākṣasa to prove the truth of the saying—'*Śṛṅgāro vīra eva vā.*' But the study of the play proves it to be otherwise. There is Vīra-rasa no doubt but there are other rasas as well. In fact, the play tallies with the statement of Bharata—*Sarvarasabhāvāḍhyam*—so far as the question of Rasa is concerned. No particular Rasa is made here principal. Vīra, Karuṇa, Raudra and Adbhuta all these four Rasas are to be seen in the play intermingled with one another. So this play presents most unconventionally, a number of Sentiments that come together without clashing with one another.

The place of Mudrārākṣasa in the history of Sanskrit drama is unique. Not only in the subject matter, the dramatist has shown his dramaturgic skill in devising so many rich dramatic situations. One can never overlook the third Act in which a feigned quarrel between Candragupta and Cāṇakya takes place by the very orders of the latter. This ruse is an attempt to put Rākṣasa on a wrong and misleading track and thus catch him napping.

In characterisation also the powers of Viśākadatta are amply exhibited. Cāṇakya, the greatest of Indian diplomats, has been depicted in such a masterly way that his greatness as an astute politician is nowhere hidden. His constant concern to see his disciple well placed in the newly founded kingdom of the Mauryas has been brought to light by all his activities. This Brāhmaṇa, though honoured by the king as his lord, leads a life of extreme simplicity, the characteristic feature of the Brāhmaṇas. He lives in a hut and runs not after wealth and material prosperity. He is depicted as a Sannyāsin who has taken up the vow of capturing Rākṣasa and to make him accept the chief ministership of the new king, Candragupta. So, the very moment, Rākṣasa is captured, he pays his homage to Rākṣasa and requests him to take over the office which he so long held unduly.

The opponent is presented in no less grandeur. All the qualities of Rākṣasa have been displayed and his loyalty to the house of the Nandas has been shown through his talks and activities. Though Rākṣasa is an enemy of Candragupta, the great loyalty shown by the former to his vanquished and deceased lord arouses the attention and appreciation of Cāṇakya and he leaves no stone unturned to have and place such a loyal man as the minister of Candragupta. The evaluation of Rākṣasa by Cāṇakya as the most devoted, loyal and reliable statesman has been proved true by the playwright's skill of characterisation.

Conclusion

Mudrārākṣasa is, thus, one of the finest Nāṭakas in Sanskrit literature. No other playwright took up a similar historical theme full with such varied activities. The transfer of a crown and the chaos and conspiracies that went with it form a very interesting dramatic theme but unfortunately all the later historical plays lack in such themes. The example of Kālidāsa and Bhavabhūti led all the dramatists towards the romantic themes which, however, became hackneyed and insipid in the hands of mediocre dramatists.

The diction of Viśākhadatta also demands our attention. His Prastāvanā is brief and charming; his prose is generally free from long compounds and, so, easy to follow; his verses, though at times many in number, are simple and unlaboured and his Explanatory Scenes are remarkable for their brevity and interesting nature. Nowhere the dramatist suffers from what is sarcastically called *kāvya-kaṇḍūḥ*—the vanity of parading one's poetic skill. Last but not the least, he possesses the best of the qualities of a dramaturgist—the quality of complete self-effacement.

Bhaṭṭanārāyaṇa

Bhaṭṭanārāyaṇa follows Viśākhadatta as a writer of Nāṭaka. Exact date of his literary career is difficult to

16

ascertain. But the historians hold, almost unanimously, on the ground of references made to his Nāṭaka in other works, that he should be placed somewhere earlier than 800 A.D.

The idea of dramatising the main events of the Mahābhārata occured first perhaps to Bhāsa who composed, in all, six Mahābhāratan plays. All of these are one-Act plays excepting only the Pañcarātra which has got three Acts. The next playwright who chose Mahābhārata as his source is Bhaṭṭanārāyaṇa and he is successful in presenting the fight of the Kauravas and Pāndavas in the most interesting manner.

The Vastu

The subject matter of the Veṇīsaṃhāra is, as it is evident from the name, the drawing together of the hair into a braid. The drama depicts how Bhīma fulfilled his pledge of drinking the blood from the chest of Duḥśāsana and breaking the thighs of Duryodhana, both of whom were responsible for the molestation of Draupadī in the royal court of the Kurus. The pledge of Bhīma was that Draupadī should not tie her hair until Bhīma killed Duḥśāsana who had pulled her by hair, and broke the thighs of Duryodhana who had insulted her with the order to shampoo his legs.

The playwright begins with the Pāṇḍavas' resolution of war with the Kurus and ends with the death of Duryodhana. The course of events is too long and full of fights that are not presented. As a result, the playwright resorts to long Praveśakas in order to report the fight as it goes on. Though such scenes are a bit tedious, the playwright is very successful in dramatically presenting a few Mahābhāratan characters and in making the dramatic dialogue very savoury and full of heroic sentiment.

The Prastāvanā

The Prastāvanā of the play is, it appears, influenced by that of the Mudrārākṣasa. Herein also we find the Stage-manager reciting a verse having two meanings. The last line of the verse in question runs—'*svasthāḥ hhavantu kururāfasūtāḥ sabhṛtyāḥ*' Act I, 7). The meaning intended to be conveyed by the Sūtradhāra is—'Let the sons of the Kuru king go to heaven' but the pun on the word Svasthāḥ gives the other sense—'Let them rest in peace', which is strongly condemned by Bhīma who thunders at the Sūtradhāra from behind the scene, just like Cāṇakya in the Mudrārākṣasa, saying how can the Kauravas rest in peace while Bhīma lives. Recognising the voice to be of Bhīma, the Sūtradhāra retires alarmed, and the Act proper begins with Bhīma and Sahadeva, his brother. The prefatory verses are four in number which could have been easily and profitably reduced to only two. However, the verses suggest the tenor of the play.

In the formation of Acts also, Bhaṭṭanārāyaṇa's skill is admirable. All the Acts have only a limited number of persons agreeing with Bharata's prescription—'*ye tatra kāryāḥ puruṣāḥ catvāraḥ pañca vā te syuḥ*' (NŚ. XX, 40). [The men in action in an Act should be four or five in number]. The first Act likewise has got only five characters. The first Act presents before the audience the enraged Bhīma who is intolerant of Yudhiṣṭhira's compromising attitude. He reiterates his pledge of killing all the Kauravas and condemns in bitter terms Kṛṣṇa's policy of appeasement. There then appears Draupadī who further enkindles the violent Bhīma and in the end the Kañcukin enters and announces the failure of the proposal of compromise. As it bids fair to certain battle, Bhīma feels exulted and exits to join the war and fulfil his pledges. Herein the Germ of the plot is also brought to light by the pledge of Bhima that he will tie up the hair of Draupadī into a braid with his hands, red with the blood of Duryodhana. Through this announcement and his joining the battle the first Stage of the Action is also exhibited.

Viṣkambhaka

The second Act brings us face to face with the great Kuru king, Duryodhana. A considerable number of days have passed between the first and the second Act. The passage of time has been denoted by prefacing the Act by a Viṣkambhaka. A Kañcukin is introduced who reports that Abhimanyu has been killed by a band of great warriors and that Duryodhana desires to meet his queen, Bhānumatī first and then to go to the battle field to congratulate the warriors who have jointly killed Abhimanyu. From this it becomes clear that Bhīṣma, the first Commander-in-Chief of the Kuru army is defeated and Droṇa has stepped into his shoes. The amorous intention of Duryodhana to meet his queen appears silly in the context of the blood-red battle field and the criticism of the audience has been put in the mouth of the Kañcukin who condemns the habit of amorous dalliance of the king in the harem even at that critical stage of the battle.

After reporting the passage of time and the position of the two armies by the Viṣkambhaka, the playwright presents the queen, Bhānumatī and her attendants. She is greatly troubled by a vision which she dreamed on the previous night. The dream is ominous and at the request of the attendants the queen narrates it to them. She saw a mongoose which killed 100 snakes. The dream is apparently indicative of the defeat of the one hundred sons of the Kuru king at the hands of the Pāṇḍavas. While she narrates the dream, Duryodhana with his Kañcukin reaches there and overhears the story. The Sanskrit term for mongoose is *nakula* which is also the name of the fourth Pāṇḍava. The playwright uses the pun and Duryodhana suspects the chastity of his wife and decides to kill her instantly. But his misunderstanding is removed as he listens her story upto the end. The queen decides to worship the Sun-god for the welfare of her husband and when she is about to offer the *arghya* to the Sun, Duryodhana enters and the offering is interrupted. Then follows a very romantic exchange of loving words between the king and the queen which is out of tune with the context, and the critics rightly condemn it as irrelevant as has already been observed. The only thing which can be said in favour of the playwright is that his object is to show the great weakness of Duryodhana's character. This scene proves the fact that one is bound to be defeated, who dallies with his sweet heart at a time when the enemy is knocking at the door. This may be considered to be the tragic flaw in the character of Duryodhana.

A very apt Patākā-sthānaka is used in this Act. When Duryodhana is referring to his own thighs as the fittest seat for his queen, the Kañcukin enters suddenly and says,—'O Lord, broken'—thus the very ominous suggestion is given that the thighs of Duryodhana are going to be broken. Duryodhana startles at the news and asks—'By whom ?'. The confused Kañcukin answers—'By Bhīma'. The suspense is too intolerable to Duryodhana and he demands a clear utterance. Then the Kañcukin gives a full verse which conveys the news that by a terrible (bhima) stroke of the tempest, the flagstaff of the king's chariot is broken. (Act II, 23). The feeling of suspense caused by this elaborate Patākā-sthānaka is highly dramatic and interesting. This sudden interference totally ruins the amorous atmosphere, and immediately afterwards the playwright introduces the mother and wife of Jayadratha. Duryodhana consoles the mother and wife of Jayadratha, who are terrified at the pledge of Arjuna. They say that at the death of Abhimanyu, Arjuna has pledged either to kill the killer of his son or to commit suicide if he is unsuccessful. Duryodhana assures the distressed ladies and says that he will arrange an alert guard for Jayadratha and that it is Arjuna who will have to commit suicide as his pledge must go unfulfilled. He then rushes out to the battlefield for the preparation, and the Act ends here.

Praveśaka

A few more days pass before the third Act begins. So a Praveśaka has been preceded to this Act. The Praveśaka has got only a pair of Rākṣasa who reports the present position of the two armies. It is reported by them that the Pāṇḍavas have lost Ghaṭotkaca in addition to Abhimanyu. Further, by way of explaining the cause of a great confused noise, they report that the noise is caused by the sudden decapitation of Droṇa, the Kuru commander, by Dhṛṣṭadyumna. After this, they announce the arrival of Aśvatthāman, and retire.

The Act proper deals with a quarrel between Aśvatthāman and Karṇa. Duryodhana rejects the proposal of making Aśvatthāman the next general of the Kuru forces in favour of Karṇa. This along with the killing of Droṇa infuriates Aśvatthāman and he brags loudly of his own valour. Karṇa unable to put up with this, hints at the fact that Droṇa did throw down his weapon just like a coward. This comment is too much for Aśvatthāman to swallow and he gets ready to kill Karṇa who also turns angry at the abusive reference to his birth. The quarrel has been presented by the playwright too masterfully. Duryodhana, quite upset at this, however, succeeds in disentangling the two warriors at last but Aśvatthāman leaves his arms saying that not until Karṇa dies he will take up his arms again. This quarrel is an invention of the playwright and he is highly successful in suggesting by this that such internal dissension leads but to defeat. Suddenly the voice of Bhīma reaches them, who challenges all the Kauravas and asks them to protect Duḥśāsana from his clutches. Karṇa and Duryodhana immediately rush to save Duḥśāsana. Aśvatthāman resolves to break his vow, and take up his arms again to save Duḥśāsana from the clutches of Bhīma but a voice from the heavens orders him, not to break his vow. The sincere feeling of Aśvatthāman for Duryodhana is nicely shown by the playwright in the last sentence he speaks to Kṛpa. He realises that out of his wrath against Karṇa he has committed a blunder but as what is done cannot be undone, he asks Kṛpa to go to the help of Duryodhana. With their exit the third Act ends.

The actual fight being excluded as non-presentable on the stage, the playwright sets the fourth Act just on the border of the actual battle-field. The senseless Duryodhana is carried away by his charioteer. The terrible fight is going on and the triumphant voice of Bhīma announcing the death of Duḥśāsana comes from afar. Recovering his senses, Duryodhana reproaches the charioteer for having carried him out of the battle-field but hearing the news of Duḥśāsana's death, he again faints. A soldier is then introduced who is in search of Duryodhana. In his quest, he presents a picture of the pall of gloom hanging over the battle-field. After reaching Duryodhana, he narrates to the king how Duḥśāsana was killed and then how the young son of Karṇa heroically fought and at last died in the hands of Arjuna. He reports further that Karṇa is also in a critical position and that he is sent by him with a written message to the king. The message is touching and reveals the nobility of Karṇa. It conveys Karṇa's despair at his failure to redeem his pledge. It also contains a pathetic appeal for an all-out action to save the day. Duryodhana is highly shocked and orders to bring a new chariot to carry him to the battle-field. But in the meantime, the chariot carrying Dhṛtarāṣṭra, Gāndhārī and Sañjaya is seen. Duryodhana wishes to avoid them first but then decides to meet them. The Act ends here.

The fifth Act follows as a continuation of the previous one. The Act shows the attempt of Dhṛtarāṣṭra and the party to persuade Duryodhana to sue for peace. This proposal is angrily rejected by Duryodhana on the ground that at this stage when all his brothers and so many kings are dead for his cause, it will be sheer cowardice to seek a treaty with the stronger party for the safety of his own life. While they talk thus the news of Karṇa's death is conveyed to him and Duryodhana loses, as it were, all his energy for the moment. It is at this stage that Aśvatthāman enters and says to the king that all the braggings of Karṇa have been rightly proved to be futile and that he is now ready to fight the Pāṇḍavas. But Duryodhana declines his assistance for his having spoken ill of Karṇa, Duryodhana's dearest friend. The conceited Brāhmaṇa is greatly shocked at this denial and leaves the place. Dhṛtarāṣṭra, however, orders Sañjaya to meet Aśvatthāman and call him back after apologising for the rude conduct of Duryodhana. The playwright has also brought in Bhīma and Arjuna as well on the stage and shown the meeting of the two parties. The meeting takes place just before the arrival of Aśvatthāman and Bhīma challenges Duryodhana to a single combat the next morning.

The sixth is the last Act. In it the efforts of Bhīma, the hero, reach the stage of fulfilment. The playwright has employed a novel device, to bring about the Denouement in this Act. He first presents Yudhiṣṭhira and Draupadī who are anxious to know the whereabouts of Duryodhana who is said to be in hiding. Yudhiṣṭhira is the more troubled since Bhīma has pledged to kill Duryodhana that very day failing which he will commit suicide. That very moment a messenger comes from Kṛṣṇa, who reports to Yudhiṣṭhira that Duryodhana has been found out and that his single combat with Bhīma has commenced already.

The playwright then introduces a man in the guise of a hermit who soliloquises that he would ask for water to quench his thirst to get an entry into the Pāṇḍava-camp with a view to deceive Yudhiṣṭhira with a false report. This hermit is actually a friend of Duryodhana. He meets Yudhiṣṭhira and relates to him that Bhīma and Arjuna both have been killed by Duryodhana. This false news upsets Yudhiṣṭhira and Draupadī both and broken-hearted they decide to jump into the fire. When they are about to do so, the frightened Kañcukin brings the scaring news that Duryodhana is approaching with the terrible club in his hand. Bhīma, in fact, is then presented, whose body is besmeared with blood and who looks ghastly. The false story of Bhīma's death has so much perplexed them that neither Yudhiṣṭhira nor Draupadī can recognise the new-comer to be Bhīma. The perplexity reaches its climax when Yudhiṣṭhira advances to strike at Bhīma. Bhīma is also entirely puzzled at this and is out of his wits. The Kañcukin fortunately recognises Bhīma and reconciliation takes place. Bhīma then fulfils his pledge of tying the hair of Draupadī with his hands stained with the blood of Duryodhana. The breathless suspense created by the introduction of the disguised friend of Duryodhana is highly dramatic.

The happy ending is brought about by the offer of blessings by Kṛṣṇa who enters in the end along with Arjuna. He announces that the man in disguise who came with the false report was a Rākṣasa and that he is now a prisoner at Nakula's hands. The forthcoming coronation of Yudhiṣṭhira is also announced by him. With the Bharata-vākya spoken by Yudhiṣṭhira the drama ends.

Characterisation & Diction

In point of characterisation, Bhaṭṭanārāyaṇa can very easily claim his place among the greatest of Sanskrit dramatists. He has exhibited rare skill in delineating the characters of Bhīma, Duryodhana, Karṇa and Aśvatthāman. These characters have not lost any grandeur granted to them by the great Epic. On the contrary, the dramatist has very successfully brought out the very spirit of these characters. Bhīma has been very aptly depicted as a great hero who believes only in strength. His great spite and ire for the Kauravas have been expressed through all his talks. His strong resentment at the very proposal of compromise, his determination of avenging the wrongs done to them and finally his pledge to tie up the hair of Draupadī with his hands stained with the blood of his enemies are expressed in grand heroic declamations.

The playwright is very careful to show the nature of Bhīma, the great lover of strength, in his conversation with Draupadī by means of such words as speak of his strength and revenge. The contrast between Bhīma and Arjuna is also shown in the fifth Act where they meet Dhṛtarāṣṭra and Gāndhārī. The very mode in which Bhīma presents himself to Dhṛtarāṣṭra expresses his character while the manner of Arjuna is quite different and more sober in comparison. The employment of Ārabhaṭī Vṛtti to the speeches of Bhīma is very apt and effective. Bhaṭṭanārāyaṇa employs admirably the appropriate mode of speech to appropriate persons. Like a true historical dramatist he lends a spirit of universality to his characters by fashioning them as the age-old tradition makes them out.

The quarrel scene between Karṇa and Aśvatthāman is also rendered charming by the proper use of words. He has contrasted the characters even by the mode of their speech which speaks of his great skill. Duryodhana, the opponent of the hero (*pratināyaka*), is also given a characteristic speciality of his own. In his speeches, movements and actions the great Kuru leader presents himself as an arrogant enemy who does not have the least concern for the Pāṇḍavas. His softer qualities, however, have not been overlooked—his sincere love for Karṇa is remarkably shown in the play. Draupadī comes on the stage only twice but the playwright presents her in life-like reality which is granted to her by the great Epic. The character of Yudhiṣṭhira also is presented in a like manner. His excellence as a poet has been accepted by the rhetoricians who quote freely verses from the Nāṭaka to exemplify Vīra and Raudra Rasas.

The hero of the Nāṭaka is Bhīma. He is the man who starts the dramatic action and it is he who brings about the Veṇīsaṃhāra by fulfilling his vow to Draupadī. But the traditional view announces Yudhiṣṭhira to be the hero on the ground that he, as the chief of the Pāṇḍavas, reaps the fruit of the dramatic action. This argument is weak and untenable. If this view is accepted then all the heroic activities of Bhīma will have to be disregarded. Hence it will be absurd to make Yudhiṣṭhira, the hero of the action displayed in the play.

From the view-point of Rasa, Veṇīsaṃhāra is a Nāṭaka of the Vīra-rasa, the heroic feats of Bhīma forming the bulk of the play.

Conclusion

The place of this play in the Sanskrit literature is elevated. This is the first Nāṭaka in which the theme of Kuru-Pāṇḍava war has been successfully dramatised. The success of Bhaṭṭanārāyaṇa in this respect led many later dramatists to make bold dramatic assays with this theme. In fact, the play is remarkable for its bright characterisation, significant conversation and highly dramatic situations. The use of a limited number of characters and accessories prove his knowledge of and contact with the stage as well.

Bhavabhūti—the Pathetic

In addition to the Prakaraṇa, Mālatīmādhava, Bhavabhūti presents two Nāṭakas on the life of Rāma, the great hero of the first Indian Epic, the Mahāvīra-carita and the other Uttararāmacarita. In these two Nāṭakas, he represents almost the whole life of Rāma. The theme of Mahāvīracarita covers the most important portion of Rāma's life till his coronation at Ayodhyā. The second Nāṭaka deals, as the very name suggests, with Rāma's life after that period. Bhavabhūti covers the first six Kāṇḍas of the Epic by his former Nāṭaka and the last or the Uttara Kāṇḍa by the latter. He is second only to Bhāsa in choosing the life of Rāma for dramatisation. Bhāsa also composed two full-fledged Nāṭakas on Rāma legend—the Abhiṣeka and the Pratimā.

The life of Rāma, as is narrated in the Epic, suits the purpose of the playwright which is to show Rāma as a great hero (Mahāvīra). Vālmīki's manner of presentation has hardly any dramatic potentiality in it. There should be in a dramatic theme a motive behind the actions, and Bhavabhūti faced this very problem in dramatising the theme. If the theme began with the taking away of Sītā by Rāvaṇa then that could have served the purpose for Rāma's attack on Rāvaṇa. But Bhavabhūti wanted to present the life of Rāma from before his marriage. So he reshaped entirely the original story as found in the Rāmāyaṇa. His innovations, though too bold, are commendable as these render the theme much more dramatic.

His innovations are—the presentation of Rāvaṇa as a suitor of Sītā, vying with Rāma ; the plot of Rāvaṇa's minister Mālyavat to pitch Paraśurāma against Rāma and also to send Śūrpaṇakhā in the guise of Mantharā to work out the exile of Rāma and the presentation of Vālin as an ally of Rāvaṇa.

Needless it is to say that the presentation of Rāvaṇa as a rival of Rāma from the very beginning of the play supplies the necessary dramatic motive behind the enmity of the two, which is almost fortuitous and pre-ordained in the Epic. In fact, all the innovations of Bhavabhūti increase the dramatic interest of the play. Thus the plotting of Mālyavat brings to light the unfriendly forces that are working against Rāma. The sudden arrival of Paraśurāma and his implacable wrath get a reasonable basis in the conspiracy of Mālyavat and the playwright also gets the chance to show the strength of Rāma. The introduction of Sūrpaṇakhā as Mantharā saves the queen Kaikeyī from a very mean allegation and the alliance between Vālin and Rāvaṇa acquits Rāma of a very disgraceful accusation that he killed Vālin like a thief. Thus Bhavabhūti is successful in supplying a grand motive to the theme of the Epic. He was perhaps attracted by the grand character of Rākṣasa (Mudrā-rākṣasa) which may be considered as the model of his Mālyavat.

The Prastāvanā

The Prastāvanā of the Nāṭaka too shows a novelty. The Sūtradhāra enters with a paper and reads out the matter contained in it. There is in it a request of the people to stage such a Nāṭaka as has the heroic sentiment and is full of all the embellishments of a Nāṭaka. The Sūtradhāra obeys the request as an order and announces that such a Nāṭaka is the Mahāvīracarita. Bhavabhūti is always too much eloquent about his own identity and learning, and here also the Sūtradhāra repeats almost the same long phrases as are found in his Mālatīmādhava by way of introducing the playwright to the audience. He then says that the play presents the great and illustrious life of the immortal hero of the Rāmāyaṇa. Vālmīki, the Ādikavi, is also referred to by him. Wherefrom the play begins is also reported skilfully. An actor enters and says that all have been satisfied with the selection but as it is a new Nāṭaka, the exact point of beginning should be announced. The Sūtradhāra then says that the beginning of the Nāṭaka is laid in the hermitage of Viśvāmitra who has brought with him Rāma and Lakṣmaṇa and whose desire it is to marry Rāma to Sītā. At the invitation of Viśvāmitra, Janaka, the king of the Videhas, has sent his brother, Kuśadhvaja with Sītā and Ūrmilā to Viśvāmitra's hermitage. With this the prologue ends.

The Prastāvanā is such a one that cannot be classed under the five accepted types. Nevertheless the manner of introducing dramatic theme is rather attractive. The Prastāvanā is shorter than that of his former play, Mālatimādhava, the Prakaraṇa.

The Structure of the Play

The Prastāvanā introduces six characters—the king Kuśadhvaja, Sītā, Ūrmilā, Viśvāmitra, Rāma, Lakṣmaṇa. The first Act reports the following events—Viśvāmitra's proposal to effect the marriages of Sītā and her three sisters with Rāma and his three brothers, acting on behalf of Daśaratha, and Kuśadhvaja's agreement; the indifference to Rāvaṇa's proposal of marrying Sītā; the killing of Tāṭakā and other Rākṣasas by Rāma; the presentation of the '*divyāstras*' (divine weapons) by Viśvāmitra to Rāma; the breaking of the bow of Mahādeva and their departure for the capital of the Videhas. The messenger of Rāvaṇa, who is astounded to see Rāma's valour and disheartened at the refusal of Rāvaṇa's proposal, goes to Mālyavat, the minister of Rāvaṇa, to report everything.

Viśvāmitra also sends a hermit to Daśaratha to report and ask him to come to the capital of Janaka with the sage, Vaśiṣṭha, his priest, to officiate at the wedding.

Bhavabhūti, thus, unfolds in this Act the Germ of the entire Nāṭaka. The neglect shown to Rāvaṇa by the cold inattention to his proposal paves the way for the future conflict between Rāma and Rāvaṇa. Thus the first Act successfully shows the complexity of the plot.

Viṣkambhaka

The reaction to the neglect of Rāvaṇa's proposal is shown in the Viṣkambhaka placed before the second Act. Mālyavat, the shrewd statesman, is presented, who is deeply perturbed at the news of Rāma's superhuman valour. He explains his future policy of checking Rāma's powers to Sūrpaṇakhā and starts along with her to the hermitage of the irascible sage, Paraśurāma, the avowed enemy of the Kṣatriya clan. Bhavabhūti presents Mālyavat as a wise statesman who weighs cleverly the position of Rāvaṇa with Rama as his enemy. He shows considerable farsight in judging the future, and political expediency shows him the only way of enkindling Paraśurāma by the news that Rāma has broken the bow of Mahādeva, to whom Paraśurāma is ardently devoted. He succeeds in provoking the sage against Rāma and the sage starts for the capital of the Videhas.

The second Act announces the advent of the angry sage and the meeting of Rāma and Paraśurāma. The marriage is just over when Paraśurāma appears and announces himslf. The dialogue of the two is well executed. Rāma appears as a man of peace and speaks too calmly but Paraśurāma is already angry and at this serenity of Rāma his anger increases the more. The conversation between these two men is very interesting and it reveals the character of these two very clearly. The Act ends with the entrance of Janaka and Śatānanda who send Rāma to the inner apartments to complete the marriage functions. Janaka then asks Paraśurāma to meet Vaśiṣṭha and Viśvāmitra.

The entire third Act comprises a bitter quarrel of Paraśurāma on one hand and Vaśiṣṭha, Viśvāmitra, Śatānanda, Janaka and Daśaratha on the other. All the sages try their best to pacify the angry Paraśurāma who nevertheless sticks to his determination of severing the head of Rāma. The playwright, though makes the quarrel too much real yet fails to make it impressive for his want of balance. Such a long fight of words may suit a narrative but not a Nāṭaka. However, the wordy duel ends with the coming of Rāma whose approach is announced by himself from behind the curtain, and responding to his call, Paraśurāma hastens to meet him.

The second Viṣkambhaka

Scenes of fight being disallowed on the stage, the playwright puts another Viṣkambhaka in the beginning of the fourth Act. This serves also the purpose of showing the future plans of the opponent party. The Viṣkambhaka begins with an announcement from behind the curtain, asking the gods to hold festivities in celebration of Rāma's victory over Paraśurāma. Immediately afterwards enter Mālyavat and Śūrpaṇakhā, and the former wonders to see the gods, rejoicing at the victory of Rāma. His first plan having failed, he conceives another and asks Śūrpaṇakhā to go to the capital of the Videhas in the guise of Mantharā to ask, on behalf of

Kaikeyī, the two boons that king Daśaratha promised to her. At the question of Śūrpaṇakhā, Mālyavat explains his policy in detail.

After the Viṣkambhaka, Janaka, Vaśiṣṭha, Viśvāmitra and Daśaratha are presented, who converse gladly at the victory of Rāma over Paraśurāma. Then Rāma and Paraśurāma are presented and the latter is now entirely changed. He expresses his regards to all and agrees to rest for a while at the request of Janaka. Vaśiṣṭha and Viśvāmitra leave together. Paraśurāma also presents his bow to Rāma and asks him to punish the demons of the Daṇḍaka forest, who disturb the sages, and departs. Thus the humiliation of Paraśurāma covers almost three Acts II–IV. This unnecessary protraction suffers from want of balance on the part of the playwright. Bhavabhūti forgets here his mission and indulges in his fondness for rhetorical effusions.

In this very Act, then, appears ūrpaṇakhā in the guise of Mantharā ushered in by Lakṣmaṇa and begs for the two boons on behalf of Kaikeyī. Amidst universal weeping, Rāma along with Sītā and Lakṣmaṇa starts for the forest to please Kaikeyī.

The third Viṣkambhaka

By a third Viṣkambhaka in the beginning of the fifth Act, the playwright reports through Sampāti and Jaṭāyu (1) the death of Daśaratha and (2) the carrying away of Sītā by Rāvaṇa.

Then he presents Rāma and Lakṣmaṇa, sorrowful and depressed at the loss of Sītā. While they are mourning the loss and condemning themselves, they hear a voice of a woman who cries for protection from a Rākṣasa.

Lakṣmaṇa goes and returns with Śramaṇā after killing the demon. Śramaṇā is a Caṇḍāla woman who meets Rāma and presents him a letter of Bibhīṣaṇa. She further reports that Bibhīṣaṇa has already reached Mount Ṛṣyamūka to live with his friend, Sugrīva. The letter expresses his willingness to serve Rāmā, which Rāmá approves. She leads Rāma and Lakṣmaṇa to Ṛṣyamūka.

On the way, a stranger appears who introduces himself as the Rākṣasa just killed and thereby restored to his lost divinity. He reports that Vālin is approaching to kill Rāma due to his alliance with Rāvaṇa. Rāma welcomes the news and bids adieu to the stranger. Vālin is then introduced. In a monologue Vālin explains that he has no personal grudge against Rāma but he is encountering him only to fulfil his friendly obligations to Rāvaṇa. Rāma and Vālin, then, stand face to face with each other. Each eulogises the other and goes out of the stage to fight. Lakṣmaṇa and Śramaṇā report the stages of the fight which is not presented on the stage. Meanwhile, Sugrīva, Bibhīṣaṇa and others also appear and again Rāma and the wounded Vālin are brought on the stage. Vālin's conferring the kingship on Sugrīva, his request to Rāma to acknowledge Sugrīva as a friend, the formal function of *maitrī-bandhana* (tie of friendship) before fire, Vālin's forecast of Rāvaṇa's defeat indicated by his own condition, and his removal to the precipice (*prapātasthala*) at his order—all these are shown in the Act one after another. The playwright presents Vālin as a liberal and kind-hearted brave being who is well aware of the divinity of Rāma whom he wishes to worship. But he has to fight him to honour his friendly obligations to Rāvaṇa.

The fourth Viṣkambhaka

The playwright puts another Viṣkambhaka in the beginning of the sixth Act with Mālyavat and Trijaṭā, a Rākṣasī. Mālyavat is first presented alone, deeply perturbed by the report of the spies that after killing Vālin, Rāma has sent the monkeys in all directions in search of Sītā. His anxiety increases greatly to learn the death of Vālin at the hands of Rāma and he is very apprehensive of Rāvaṇa's safety. Suddenly enters Trijaṭā, too much afraid, and crying for help. Asked as to the cause of her fear, she reports that a monkey has burnt the golden city of Laṅkā and killed a prince, Akṣa by name. This news startles Mālyavat and he enquires about the date of Kumbhakarṇa's awakening. Unfortunately he learns that the time for his awakening is far away. He then consoles somehow the alarmed Rākṣasī and enters with her into the palace to meet Rāvaṇa who, it is reported, is engrossed in looking at the Aśoka-vana where Sītā has been kept.

The Act proper begins with Rāvaṇa who is presented in a romantic mood. He is so much fascinated by the uncommon beauty of Sītā that he has no knowledge of the affairs of Laṅkā. This is expressed by his queen, Mandodarī who requests him to be prepared for the encounter with the enemy. As a conceited king, he first of all laughs away the apprehension of Mandodarī. He does not rely upon the report of Mandodarī that the enemy has bridged the Sea. But the truth is reported to him firstly by an announcement of the monkeys off the stage that Rāma has reached Laṅkā with his brother, Lakṣmaṇa and friend, Sugrīva; secondly by the commander of his armies, Prahasta who conveys to the King the news that the city is besieged by the foes on all sides, Then the playwright brings in Aṅgada, a messenger of Rāma. He conveys Rama's message to Rāvaṇa that he has to choose between the two, either submission to Rāma or death at his hands. This infuriates the King and he orders punishment for the impertinent monkey who however jumps out of everybody's reach. Rāvaṇa, by now having realised the serious condition, rushes on angrily to kill Rāma and his party.

Very peculiarly Bhavabhūti introduces here Indra, his charioteer and Citraratha. This portion serves the purpose of a Viṣkambhaka as the fight between Rāma and Rāvaṇa and the death of the latter are reported by it. These three men describe the various situations of the battle and at last announce the death of both Rāvaṇa and his son. The Act ends here.

The fifth Viṣkambhaka

The seventh Act presents the coronation of Rāma at Ayodhyā. But before Rāma starts for Ayodhyā, the playwright puts another Viṣkambhaka with Laṅkā and Alakā. These two sister cities converse with each other and the latter consoles the former at the loss of her lord. Through them the playwright reports also the fire-ordeal of Sītā and the joy of all—the gods, the sages, etc. to see Rāma successful. The news of Bibhīṣaṇa's coronation is also announced by them.

In the Act proper Bhavabhūti brings Rāma to Ayodhyā through an aerial journey. The stages of the journey are reported through Rāma's answers about the places passed over, in reply to Sītā's and Lakṣmaṇa's enquiries. All the sages, the two brothers of Rāma, the queens of Daśaratha and a large number of men appear in the end to felicitate Rāma on his return. Thus with the reunion of Rāma and Bharata, the play ends.

The Style

Bhavabhūti suffers badly from over-elaboration. The excess of redundant verses is his main drawback. He does not miss a single chance to display his power of versification. This want of restraint is visible throughout the play, especially in the quarrel scenes between Rāma and Paraśurāma. Nothing but his love of words has made the quarrel linger through almost three full Acts though the victory over Paraśurāma is not at all the main issue of the play, neither is it so much related with the killing of Rāvaṇa. The prolongation of this bandying appears the more inordinate in the background of the actual fight of Rāma with Rāvaṇa, which has been executed in a single Act. Strangely enough, the arch-enemy of Rāma is not granted even as much chance to show his valour as is granted to Vālin. Such a treatment makes Rāvaṇa appear very weak and thereby renders the victory of Rāma over him almost trifling. Though the purpose of the playwright is to present Rāma as a *Mahāvīra*, he fails apparently in doing so.

The innovations of Bhavabhūti are highly successful in the motivation of the plot. But he has failed to manage his theme well. Inspite of his attempts, he does not succeed in giving an impressiveness to Mālyavat as an astute political schemer, like Rākṣasa or Cāṇakya in the Mudrārākṣasa.

The style of Bhavabhūti is also responsible for his unsuccess in portraying the characters in a charming manner. Bhavabhūti's prose, as has been discussed later, is void of charm and is too much laboured. His prose bristles with difficult words and long compounds, whereas his verses are comparatively easy and bright. The dialogue of the characters fails to bring out the characteristic traits of them. All the characters, from a maid-servant to Rāma, speak more or less in the same manner. Such a stiff and rigid language is a great impediment on the way of appreciating the play.

Bhavabhūti the poet, intrudes in the play at all odd places. His egotism can never make him forget the fact that he is a great master of so many branches of learning and so each character speaks more or less as Bhavabhūti likes them to speak, and not as they should in their own right. This has rendered the dialogue artificial and unimpressive.

Conclusion

Despite these limitations, however, the playwright succeeds in presenting a Nāṭaka of *Vīra-rasa*. The play cannot be considered to belong to the highest class but nevertheless it cannot be shunted to the background. There are many charming situations, witty dialogues and above all, a great number of fine verses in this Nāṭaka. The fame of Bhavabhūti rests, so far as this Nāṭaka is concerned, on his poetic excellence and he is rightly honoured more as a poet than an accomplished dramaturgist. His fine and charming poems are still memorised for their soothing quality even bereft of their context.

The Uttararāmacarita

Uttararāmacarita is also a seven-Act Nāṭaka on the life of Rāma, which is a continuation of the Mahāvīracarita as regards the plot. It depicts the life of Rāma after his coronation at Ayodhyā and the word *uttara* in the name means 'later' as well as it indicates the Uttarakāṇḍa of the Rāmāyaṇa, the source of the theme. Thus the desertion of Sītā is the main event of the play.

Dr. S. K. De observes—"In this drama Bhavabhūti idealises conjugal love through the chastening influence of sorrow, and he does this in a way which is unparalleled in Sanskrit, or perhaps in any literature."[23] In fact, the presentation of conjugal love in this play is ideal. The attachment of Rāma and Sītā is not like that of Duṣyanta and Śakuntalā or Agnimitra and Mālavikā. The love depicted in this play has been rendered sublime and pure by means of the sacrifice done by both the parties. In the selection of conjugal love for dramatic representation Bhavabhūti strikes an absolutely new path. None before him attempted to depict a married and, so, common place love affair effectively in a drama. Though in the Nāṭakas of Kālidāsa, Śūdraka, etc. we see the married wives of the heroes yet it is not conjugal love which becomes the object of dramatisation and glorification. But Bhavabhūti is singularly successful in depicting the conjugal love of Rāma and Sītā as an object of ardent appreciation and charm. His poetic genius and exuberant imagination impart an exquisite rainbow-hue and a rare depth of sentiment to the love of this couple. The romantic sentiment finds a full play in the drama in the background of deep pathos.

The Prastāvanā

Bhavabhūti begins his play with the usual Prastāvanā. It is remarkably brief in this Nāṭaka and he does not use

23. HSL. p. 290.

so many high sounding epithets in praise of himself. Like the announcement of the play and playwright by means of a letter in the Mahāvīracarita, he employs here also a new method of introducing the theme of his play. The Sūtradhāra, after announcing the names of the Nāṭaka and the playwright, requests the audience to regard him as a citizen of Ayodhyā during the reign of Rāma. In this new role he loudly enquires about the silence that shrouds the palace at a time when the coronation of Rāma is to take place. Another actor comes in and says that the coronation ceremony is over and all the kings and sages have been bidden farewell by Rāma. He further reports that the mothers of Rāma have also left for the *āśrama* of their son-in-law to participate in his *yajña* sacrifice under the guidance of Vaśiṣṭha and Arundhatī. The identity of this son-in-law is also given and it is also reported that he has begun a sacrifice that will continue for twelve years. For this sacrifice the mothers of Rāma have gone there leaving the pregnant Sītā under the care of Rāma. Bhavabhūti then puts a verse in the mouth of the actor which, as an acceptance of the view of the Sūtradhāra that regarding the truthfulness of women and words men are generally suspicious, announces that many are suspicious even of the purity of Sītā because of her captivity in the house of the Rākṣasa. This report adds that the king is entering into his palace after leaving the court, in order to please Sītā.

The Prastāvanā is remarkable for many qualities. It is firstly very brief and secondly the playwright does not use a single word that is redundant. All the necessary preliminary information is given in it and even the impending separation is hinted at. The economy of words and their significant use speak of Bhavabhūti's culminating dramatic skill.

The first Act is also an example of Bhavabhūti's great artistic skill. He innovates the scene perhaps from a slight reference found in the Raghuvaṃśa (XIV, 25) and uses it wonderfully to show both—the noble love of Rāma for Sītā and the impending separation. The Act is named *Citradarśaṇa.* The scene opens with the entry of Aṣṭāvakra, with a message from Vaśiṣṭha to Rāma. The message of Vaśiṣṭha is significant. He reminds Rāma of his young age, of his new royal quties, and enjoins upon him to take proper care of his subjects. Rāma's statement also is pregnant with dramatic irony. He welcomes the advice, saying that he can forego affection, pity, friendship and even Sītā for the satisfaction of his subjects. Aṣṭāvakra retires introducing Lakṣmaṇa who brings a series of pictures. Lakṣmaṇa tells his brother that the pictures depict the incidents upto the fire ordeal of Sītā. Rāma's angry disapproval of the idea of purification of Sītā and his disbelief in the rumour are significant. The series of pictures arouse various feelings of pleasure and pain in their hearts and Sītā expresses her desire to live in a hermitage along with Rāma. Rāma approves of it and asks Lakṣmaṇa to arrange for the chariot. Lakṣmaṇa exits. Sītā finds herself fatigued and lies down on the arm of Rāma. Bhavabhūti puts a few exquisite verses in the mouth of Rāma, that are unparalleled in Sanskrit love-literature.

Here Bhavabhūti makes a very dexterous use of a Patākāsthānaka. A spy, Durmukha, comes in, and conveys to Rāma the sentiments of the people regarding the chastity of Sītā. The allegation, though unbearable, is respected by Rāma and in order to set at rest the people's suspicion, he directs Lakṣmaṇa to banish Sītā to the forests. After this, Rāma gives voice to all the feelings of his heart. His sorrow wells out of his heart and he dwells long upon the great bliss that Sītā has brought to him. He even prostrates himself at her feet and bids his last farewell not only to her but to married bliss as well. After awakening, Sītā finds her alone and then comes Durmukha to lead her to the chariot, ready to go to the hermitage. The Act ends with the exit of Sītā and Durmukha.

The first Viṣkambhaka

The playwright skips over twelve years before presenting the second Act. The passage of time is indicated by a Viṣkambhaka. The Viṣkambhaka has two characters—Ātreyī, a female hermit and Vāsantī, the goddess of the forest. Ātreyī comes from the hermitage of Vālmīki with the purpose of going to the hermitage of Agastya. In the course of their conversation many events are reported. The arrival of Lava and Kuśa in the *āśrama* and their precocious talent; their reaching the age of twelve years; Vālmīki's composition of Rāmāyaṇa; the desertion of Sītā; the preparation of Rāma for the Horse-sacrifice and the installation of the golden statue of Sītā for the purpose of sacrifice; the starting of the sorrowful mothers of Rāma along with Vaśiṣṭha and Arundhatī to the *āśrama* of Vālmīki after the twelve-year sacrifice of Ṛṣyaśṛṅga and the starting of Rāma to find out the Śūdra ascetic for whom the son of a Brāhmaṇa has died—all these are reported by Ātreyī to Vāsantī who also is reported to be a friend of Sītā. Vāsantī says that the Śūdra ascetic, Śambūka performs his penance at that very place, the Janasthāna, and so she hopes to meet Rāma once more. This prepares the way for the appearance of Rāma just after the Viṣkambhaka. Both of them retire and the proper Act begins.

Bhavabhūti makes his Rāma enter with a dagger in his hand after killing the Śūdra ascetic and he begins by referring to his cruelty done to the pregnant Sītā. The ascetic is then introduced in a divine form who worships Rāma for whom he got back his divine form. He then informs Rāma that the place is Janasthāna and the jungle is the Daṇḍaka where Rāma lived for a time. He then takes leave af Rāma and goes to the hermitage of Agastya to worship him. Rāma being reminded once more of his past life with Sītā gets overwhelmed with grief and the playwright makes full use of his poetic talents to depict it. Śambūka returns again to fetch Rāma to meet Agastya at his invitation.

The second Viṣkambhaka

The third Act is also laid in the Pañcavaṭī. Herein also the playwright puts a Viṣkambhaka to report the condition of Sītā. Two rivers, Tamasā and Muralā, are introduced in human form. Muralā is sent by the wife of Agastya to request the river Godāvarī to be careful about Rāma who will definitely be overwhelmed to look at the places of his former residence along with his dear wife. At this, Tamasā discloses that she is also entrusted with the charge of Sītā by Gaṅgā. She adds that Gaṅgā being apprehensive of Rāma's condition has sent Sītā under her (Tamasā's) care saying that on the occasion of the twelfth birthday of her sons, Sītā should worship the Sun-god for their welfare. Gaṅgā has further given such a charmed attire to Sītā that none will be able to see her.

So saying Tamsā tells that Sītā will serve as the best healer of Rāma in the Pañcavaṭī.

After their retirement, Sītā and Tamasā enter again and Sītā goes on collecting flowers for the purpose of worshipping the Sun-god. Then Rāma is introduced, who has already been charmed by the place where everything reminds him of his beloved, Sītā. He is entirely under a sentimental fit and goes on speaking about those past days when he was united with Sītā. Then the playwright introduces the sylvan goddess, Vāsantī who was a comrade of Sītā. She is already aware of the fact of Sītā's desertion and so charges Rāma bitterly for his cruelty to Sītā. The accusation of Vāsantī makes Rāma and Sītā both highly pensive and Rāma swoons. Vāsantī then realises her mistake and tries to bring Rāma back to his senses. The invisible Sītā then proceeds to nurse the senseless Rāma who is the more charmed at the sudden touch. He weeps helplessly at which Sītā also weeps. Bhavabhūti makes the best use of the situation and gives such a pathetic colour to the event that tears become uncheckable. The search of Rāma for the invisible Sītā is so pathetic that Vāsantī also becomes afraid and tries to change the topic. This Act is so well executed and is so impressive that Bhavabhūti has quite rightly become famous for this Act. Much has been said in praise of the fine expressions put in the mouth of Rāma, which need not be repeated here. Suffices it to say that this Act proves the truth of Bhavabhūti's statement that Karuṇa or the Pathetic Sentiment is the best of all Sentiments. The great attachment of Rāma and his sincere and deep rooted love for Sītā have been well depicted in the Act. The Act is perhaps a bit longer than is necessary but this has been amply compensated by the fine poetry with which it abounds. We must say that the lack of action in this portion of the drama is not allowed to become a rock of offence to critics, by the thrilling expressions of the tenderest pathos of the human heart, which cannot but appeal to the delicate chords of emotion. It is in this context that we must appreciate the split personality of Rāma in which the two aspects—the king and the lover—are at war with each other.

The third Viṣkambhaka

The fourth and fifth Acts are laid in the hermitage of Vālmīki. The fourth Act is utilised to show the repercussions of Rāma's desertion of Sītā on Janaka, and Kauśalyā. By a third Viṣkambhaka, the playwright reports their arrival at the hermitage.

Janaka, the great sage and king, is then presented in a melancholy mood, who broods over the tragic fate of his daughter. He is the more sorrowful because he cannot weep aloud since the mean allegation relates to his daughter. Then comes there Kauśalyā, led by Arundhatī, the wife of Vaśiṣtha, and the Kañcukin. Janaka welcomes Arundhatī with feeling words of honour but does not do so in respect of Kauśalyā though she was a close friend to him. This cold neglect is too much for the wretched lady who has already expressed her inability to look at the distressed father of her daughter-in-law, and she faints. Janaka is taken aback at this and becomes sympathetic to his friend's wife. The psychology of a loving father has been very well studied and represented by the playwright. Janaka recants and helps bring back Kauśalyā to her senses. To a group which is under an emotional fit, the playwright introduces Lava whose appearance attracts the immediate attention of all.

Kauśalyā places the boy on her lap and asks him who he is. The boy can only say that he and his brother are twins and disciples of the sage, Vālmīki. In the meanwhile, the orders of Kumāra Candraketu is announced off the stage, who has come as a guard to the sacrificial horse of Rāma. Lava asks the identity of Candraketu and is informed that he is the son of Lakṣmaṇa. The boy immediately remembers the Rāmāyaṇa and says that Vālmīki has prepared a Nāṭaka on the life of Rāma and sent it to Bharata, the composer of Nāṭyasūtra with the request to stage it. Janaka once more flares up and condemns the evil nature of the people and the hasty action of Rāma but immediately checks his wrath considering the fact that Rāma is verily a son to him. Then a host of āśramite boys comes to fetch away Lava to show him a new animal named horse. The young Lava, unable to swallow the challenging attitude of the royal party, orders the horse to be secured and kept in the *āśrama*. The stage is set for an encounter between Lava and Candraketu.

The fifth Act is a continuation of the fourth and has got almost no action. It is full with wordy warfare between the two champions, Lava and Candraketu. Both of them appreciate each other and wishes to make friends but after a very long conversation they exit to go to a proper place to fight.

The fourth Viṣkambhaka

The fight is reported as usual by a Viṣkambhaka. A Vidyādhara couple is introduced, who go on describing the warfare and the mode of fight of the two. The Viṣkambhaka ends with the announcement of the arrival of Rāma.

The rest of the Act depicts Rāmā's affection for the young Lava and Kuśa who are introduced a bit later. The fight ends with the very arrival of Rāma and he is charmed to see the boy whose appearance resembles Sītā too much. The poet depicts very skilfully the affectionate heart of Rāma who fondles the twin-brothers almost like his own sons. His own cruelty to the pregnant Sītā and the charm of the company of the two boys extort from him expressions of great emotional value. He condemns himself pathetically and finds the world too much for him. Suddenly he listens to the announcement that Janaka, Vaśiṣṭha, Vālmīki, Arundhatī and Kauśalyā all are coming there, alarmed at the news of fight between the boys. Rāma is entirely unnerved at this. He finds no strength left in him to meet the group. The meeting is averted by the playwright by an announcement off the stage that the ladies have lost their senses to see Rāma in that pathetic condition. Rāma rises and advances to meet the elders, led by Lava and Kuśa.

Bhavabhūti uses a new device to bring about the re-union of Rāma and Sītā in the seventh Act. It is a play inside the play. Hamlet of Shakespeare thought that 'Drama is the thing wherein I shall catch the conscience of the king.'[24] In the like manner, Bhavabhūti makes his Vālmīki plan a staging of the episode of desertion of Sītā before Rāma and the assembled people of Ayodhyā. His apparent aim of doing so is to reveal forcefully to the disbelieving world the chastity of Sītā and to prepare the way for them to accept her as the rightful queen.

---

24. Hamlet, Act II, Sc. II.

A similar Denouement is found in the Priyadarśikā of Harṣavardhana. So far as the extant Nāṭakas are concerned, Bhavabhūti is second in time to use the technique but by no means second to Harṣa in other respects. Bhavabhūti's masterly use of the play inside the play is far superior to that of Harṣa.

The miniature play, as performed before Rāma, other important personalities and the populace, has only three characters and two new born babies. Sītā is introduced by the Sūtradhāra. She proceeds to the Ganges with her children to drown herself. Gaṅgā and Pṛthvī appear and restrain her from committing suicide. They advise her to hand over the babies to Vālmīki for bringing them up. This much is the subject matter of this play but the conversation is highly impressive, making Rāma forget that he is witnessing a drama and not participating in real life. Lakṣmaṇa keeps a vigilant eye over him. Again, Pṛthvī gets angry with Rāma for his inhuman cruelty and is pacified by Gaṅgā. Pṛthvī also accepts the truth that the desertion of Sītā is not done out of Rāma's dislike for Sītā but for the satisfaction of the people. This saying does not only please Rāma but helps change the hearts of the people of Ayodhyā. Sītā then disappears with Gaṅgā and Pṛthvī; Rama swoons, and Lakṣmaṇa implores Vālmīki to stop the performance.

Then an announcement from behind the curtain asks the players to disperse and to see the magic performed by Vālmīki. Lakṣmaṇa explains this magic and reports that Sītā is coming out of the water along with Gaṅgā and Pṛthvī. Rāma still lies senseless. Then by another similar announcement, Arundhatī is introduced with Sītā whom Arundhatī asks to nurse Rāma and bring him back to his senses. At her very touch, Rāma recovers and listens to the blessings of Pṛthvī and Gaṅgā, spoken off the stage. Arundhatī then advances to address the people and asks for their approval of Sītā's acceptance by Rāma. Lakṣmaṇa reports their approval. Then at the request of Arundhatī, Vālmiki brings in Sītā's two sons and acquaints them with their parents. The drama ends with the usual Bharata-vākya, spoken by Rāma.

The Style

The Style of Bhavabhūti has already been discussed. His love of exaggeration is to be found even here but in comparison with his former plays, his treatment of the theme is brighter in this play. His verses are fine examples of his great poetic genius. The observation of the critics that—*Uttare Rāmacarite Bhavabhūtir viśiṣyate* is fully justified, though this speciality depends more on his poetic skill than on dramatic dexterity. It is the fine poetry that is more remarkable than the situations or actions of the Nāṭaka.

Karuṇa is the chief sentiment that permeates the whole Nāṭaka. The Nāṭaka, in fact, verges on tragedy and it is in the exposition of the Pathetic Sentiment that the chief merit of the Nāṭaka lies. Even by the happy ending of the play, the note of pathos is not shadowed in the least. Rāma shines as a great pathetic character, and hereby the bold announcement of the playwright—*Eko rasaḥ karuṇa eva* stands amply justified. Even if the chief sentiment be accepted to be the Śṛṅgāra, as is done by the conventional commentators, then also it will be of the Vipralambha type. Whatever it may be, it must be accepted that it is Karuṇa that is charming in the play.

In characterisation also, Bhavabhūti, in this Nātaka, shows a greater maturity of art than in his previous plays. The characterisation of Rāma, Sītā, Vāsantī, Janaka and Kauśalyā demands special appreciation. Rāma has been shown as an ideal lover who has to desert his own beloved wife without the least ill-feeling to her but only to satisfy his subjects. The great personal loss that he sustains is of such a type that he has to endure it without the least demur in consideration of his royal office. His deep and sincere feelings are all brought to light by the playwright in a very fitting manner. Likewise Sītā's character is drawn with rare sincerity, which displays his deep knowledge of human psychology. Minor characters such as Candraketu, Lava, Kuśa and the disciples are also ably drawn. Bhavabhūti's only attempt at humour is also successful, though it is not of that high type as is found in the Mṛcchakaṭika.

His innovations such as the Picture–gallery scene, the Shadow–Sītā, the fight of Lava and Candraketu and the miniature play—all speak eloquently of his imagination and dramatic talent. And even with his inordinate love of verbosity, sometimes even at the cost of action, he shines as the last in the line of great dramatists. Bhavabhūti's success as a dramatist can also be gauged from another factor. It is he who may be held responsible for the Nāṭaka becoming stereotyped. His dramatic skill and appealing poetry captivated the hearts of the later dramaturgists in such a manner that none was bold enough to tread a new path. After him Rāma legend also became too favourite a theme for dramatisation but without any remarkable success. So with him closes the brightest chapter of the history of Sanskrit drama.

Dramatists of the post-Bhavabhūti period

Before entering into a discussion of the technique of the later playwrights who followed Bhavabhūti, a few Nāṭakas should here be taken notice of. About the probable dates of these plays, there is a great controversy and a wide divergence of opinion. Whatever be the dates, we propose to steer clear of the controversy and study the more important question of the technique of these plays. The three Nāṭakas which we will take up, are the Kaumudī-mahotsava of Vijjakā, the Tāpasa-Vatsarāja of Anaṅgaharṣa Mātrarāja and the Āścarya-cūḍāmaṇi of Śaktibhadra. All these plays are remarkable for their originality of theme and treatment, and some of these, especially the Kaumudī mahotsava, give clear stylistic indications of having been written in an old period. The themes of all these dramas are original except that of Tāpasa-Vatsarāja which might have been influenced by the much-in-vogue story of king Udayana.

Vijjakā—Kaumudī-mahotsava

This is a Nāṭaka of five Acts and it has been ascribed to the poetess, Vijjakā by M. Ramakrishna Kavi who first published the play in the Dakṣiṇa Bhāratī Sanskrit Series in 1929. The Nāṭaka is remarkable for its great dramatic quality. The playwright definitely possessed a keen dramatic sense and in this respect she was clearly superior to Bhavabhūti. Her skill is evident in her choice of the theme, the treatment of it and the simple but appealing diction. Her language is free from useless verbiage which vitiates the Nāṭakas that followed Bhavabhūti.

Kaumudī-mahotsava is a historio-romantic Nāṭaka which has for its theme the recapture of the kingdom of

Magadha by the rightful owner, Kalyāṇavarman. The story in brief runs thus.

Sundaravarman, the king of Magadha, had no son and so adopted one, Caṇḍasena by name. Later on a son to the king was born and Caṇḍasena grew jealous of him as his ambition to ascend the throne was nipped ni the bud with the very birth of the prince. The disappointed Caṇḍasena conspired with the Licchavis and had Sundaravarman murdered and announced himself the king. The queens entered into the sacrificial pyre, and the minister and a few faithful servants of the late king contrived to run away with the young prince at night. The servants having subsequently taken to their heels, the helpless prince, separated even from his devoted nurse, found a way into the hermitage of Jāvāli, where he grew up into a youth. The nurse, out of grief, turned a nun and found a respectful place in the royal palace of the king of Mathurā. The minister, however, became successful in creating popular opinion against Caṇḍasena and finally uprooted him engineering a rebellion in the frontier regions. Kalyāṇavarman, the prince, was then called upon by the minister to capture the palace in the absence of Caṇḍasena who had gone out to quell the rebellion and had been defeated and killed there. Meanwhile, the prince had met Kīrtimatī, the princess of Mathurā, near the temple of Durgā in the Vindhya regions. Both of them had fallen in love with each other. Kīrtimatī drew the picture of Kalyāṇavarman which fell in the hands of the nun, Vinayandharā who immediately recognised the prince and recommended their wedding to the father of Kīrtimatī. Kīrtiṣena, the king, approved of the match as Kalyāṇavarman's father had been a close friend of him and as the son was also by that time reinstated in his own kingdom. Thus the wedding took place.

Vijjakā, the alleged playwright of the Nāṭaka shows enough dramatic skill in presenting this interesting theme. She might or might not have been influenced by the dramatic success of Śūdraka's Mṛcchakaṭika, this much is clearly evident that she had an excellent dramatic sense. A few phrases definitely resemble those of Kālidāsa and Bhavabhūti but this alone does not help us in coming to any judgment regarding her model. Her lucidity of style suggests one simply to place her after Kālidāsa and not too much later than Bhavabhūti, if not a bit earlier. We feel that her diction has in it an innate simplicity which leads us to place her before Bhavabhūti whose style suffers from too much ornateness which became the vogue, most probably after Bāṇabhaṭṭa.

The Prastāvanā

The Prastāvanā is short and matter-of-fact. The Sūtradhāra begins with an announcement of the occasion of the staging of the play which is the autumnal full-moon festival and declares that he is going to stage a play that depicts the very early life of the present king. He mentions the name of the poetess as well. The playwright's manner of announcing herself is so unassuming that it reminds us of the plays of Bhāsa, Kālidāsa and Śūdraka. The Prastāvanā, which is named *sthāpanā* according to the Southern dramatic convention, gives place to a Viṣkambhaka.

The first Viṣkambhaka

The Viṣkambhaka placed before the first Act also is very short and has only one character. A disciple of the sage Jāvāli enters and reports by means of *ākāśabhāṣita* that near the temple of Durgā the prince is awaiting the opportune moment to attack the enemy.

The proper Act begins with the prince who is thinking deeply about his past and future. His thoughts are interrupted by the approach of the princess Kīrtimatī with her attendant and Kañcukin. The princess has come to worship the goddess Durgā and on her way she wishes to rest for a while under the tree. The two, thus, are brought face to face and both of them fall preys to the god of love. Kalyāṇavarman comes to know from the Kañcukin everything regarding the lady—her name, her parentage and residence. To the utter disappointment of Kalyāṇavarman, the lady leaves the place. The departure of Kīrtimatī is presented on the model of Śakuntalā's. The Vidūṣaka, almost a worthless fellow, is then introduced who attempts at pleasing the prince but fails apparently as he is engrossed in the thoughts of the beautiful lady. The hero tells everything to the Jester who does not welcome the news but mocks in his own way. Suddenly he finds the pearl-necklace left by Kīrtimatī and presents it to Kalyāṇavarman. Then they exit to have their daily exercise.

Praveśaka

The second Act comes, preceded by a Praveśaka. The Praveśaka, having only two female characters, the attendants of Kīrtimatī, reports the love-sick condition of the princess and that the princess has been seen at night drawing a picture of Kalyāṇavarman and talking with it.

The Act proper introduces the Vidūṣaka who expresses his disgust (in the very manner of the Vidūṣaka of Duṣyanta) at the peculiar love-malady of Kalyāṇavarman. He takes rest under the shade of a tree near a bower. Then enters Nipuṇikā who approaches the bower, in which the nun, Yogasiddhi resides, to take her help in removing the suffering of Kīrtimatī. The nun appears and is seen in a ruminative mood. Then all of a sudden, a picture falls near her feet. She takes it up and immediately recalls Kalyāṇavarman and falls into a swoon. Nipuṇikā approaches near and nurses her. The nun then goes on narrating the story of how the young Kalyāṇavarman was lost, and also comes to know from Nipuṇikā that Kīrtimatī is in deep love with him. The Vidūṣaka, in the meantime, overhears the talk and out of curiosity peeps through the bower. He also recognises Yogasiddhi and appears before her. She gets a pleasant surprise at this. The Vidūṣaka reports the pathetic love-sick condition of the prince. The nun approves of the deep love of Kalyāṇavarman and instructs the Vidūṣaka to give Kalyāṇavarman the picture and also a verse, composed by her. The Vidūṣaka also returns the princess's necklace to Nipuṇikā, and all of them disperse.

The third Act is comparatively short and it contains the presentation of the picture and the verse to the prince. The prince becomes too much pleased to know the fact that the Vidūṣaka has met Yogasiddhi and Nipuṇikā. The Vidūṣaka asks the prince, out of mere fun, to draw a picture of Kīrtimatī by the side of his own picture drawn by her. Kalyāṇavarman, in a gay mood, carries it out. The third Act ends here.

The second Viṣkambhaka

The fourth Act, along with the Viṣkambhaka preceding it, depicts the activities of the royalist party, headed by Mantragupta, the minister of late Sundaravarman. In the Viṣkambhaka, a messenger of Mantragupta is introduced, who meets Āryarakṣita, a disguised agent of Mantragupta, and asks him to meet Mantragupta. Āryarakṣita comes to know from the messenger that Kalyāṇavarman has been summoned by Mantragupta. He rejoices at it and narrates the cruel deeds of Caṇḍasena.

After the Viṣkambhaka, the anxious minister is presented. He is waiting for the arrival of Kalyāṇavarman to whom his messenger has already been sent. Then enters Vīrasena, a soldier whom Mantragupta welcomes and asks about the whereabouts of Kalyāṇavarman. Vīrasena reports that the King is on the way and the enemy is completely crushed. The minister then enquires of the love affair of the King and is told that Yogasiddhi has taken on her the responsibility of uniting the two. The minister says that he has also sent Āryarakṣita to the king of Mathurā for negotiation. Then from behind the stage comes the announcement of the victory of the royalist party and the return of Kalyāṇavarman, the rightful owner of the crown. The minister then sends a messenger to warn everybody about future dangers.

The third Viṣkambhaka

The Viṣkambhaka in the beginning of the fifth Act reports the fulfilment of the plan of Yogasiddhi regarding the marriage of Kīrtimatī and Kalyāṇavarman. The messenger who returns from Mathurā reports to his friend that Yogasiddhi has shown to the king a picture of the two lovers and said that goddess Ekāṅgā has asked her in dream to have these two united in marriage. The king has believed in the oracle, since the moment has coincided with the arrival of Āryarakṣita at Mathurā with the marriage proposal. It is further reported off the stage that the Kaumudī festival will be held at Kusumapura.

Then Yogasiddhi is once more introduced rather uselessly. What she reports is already announced in the Viṣkambhaka. She only says that she has found success by means of a trick and the King of Mathurā has agreed to marry Kīrtimatī to Kalyāṇavarman. She also announces that the royal priest of Mathurā will first meet the King of Magadha and then Kīrtimatī. She then goes to meet Mantragupta.

Then Kalyāṇavarman, now the crowned king of Magadha, and the Vidūṣaka are presented. The king expresses his sorrow in not being able to have his beloved lady. The Vidūṣaka asks him not to lose heart as the priest of Mathurā has come with many presentations to meet the king. The priest is then introduced, who conveys the well-wishes of Kīrtiṣeṇa on the restoration of the ancestral throne to Kalyāṇavarman and then presents an invaluable necklace to the king as token of Kīrtiṣeṇa's affection and admiration. The priest is then asked to take rest and the king goes along with the Vidūṣaka to the pleasure-garden. While the king goes on speaking about his beloved, the playwright introduces there Kīrtimatī and Nipuṇikā who stealthily listen to the talk of the king. The dramatist takes help of the picture, referred to above, to bring, in a very fortuitous manner, the lover and the beloved face to face A somewhat weak explanation is given about the background of these incidents and then we find the king entering the palace with his beloved. The drama ends. The end is unconventional. There is no Bharata-vākya, nor is their any agent to execute the happy union of the two lovers who are united without any assistance whatsoever from others.

The Style

The Nāṭaka is remarkable for more than one reason. The subject-matter of the play should be termed as Invented as it is taken from current history. And the dramatist is admirably successful in presenting such a story in the dramatic form. Most remarkable is her simplicity of language. She never parades her learning and power of versification. Her restraint is also noteworthy. Even in expressing passion she does not lose her sense of proportion. All her verses are simple and bright.

Her knowledge and use of the dramatic technique are notable throughout the play. The Viṣkambhakas are short and nowhere superfluous. Her devices of working out the union of the two lovers, as for example, the picture-incident, are also well executed. The dialogue of the play is admirably simple and charming. The way in which the playwright presents the political conspiracy is also remarkable. Her humour is a bit stale. It is to be noted that the character of the Vidūṣaka was gradually assuming by her time the conventional form that we find in later plays.

In characterisation, she shows enough skill. The character of the loyal Mantragupta, who appears only once, creates such an impression that none can forget him. He is, in fact, like Cāṇakya so far as his part in the restoration of the king and the political intrigue is concerned. But he is by no means a replica of Cāṇakya. He is free from Cāṇakya's egotism and the keynote of his character is the sincere feeling of reverance and loyalty to the dead king, Sundaravarman. His subtle genius is evident everywhere and the playwright has given to this character a grand dignity of its own. Likewise, the members of the royalist party are all brightly drawn. The hero and the heroine are also well delineated. Kalyāṇavarman, the lover has been given greater scope than Kalyāṇavarman, the warrior and leader. It is not for his valour but for his love that Kalyāṇavarman impresses. Kīrtimatī, though there is in her no special point of charm, is drawn well. Nipuṇikā is the typical attendant of the royal house. The character of Yogasiddhi becomes almost superfluous after the second Act. Her entrance in the fifth Act is almost unnecessary. Last but not the least is the peculiarly unconventional ending of the Nāṭaka, for which also praise is due to her.

The unity of time and action is properly maintained in the play. The time analysis shows—

Act	I	One day.
		(An interval of 2 or 3 days)
Act	II	Part of a day.
Act	III	The next day or the day after.
		(An interval, perhaps of 2 days)
Act	IV	The next day.
Act	V	The next day.

The entire dramatic action, thus, covers a period of 10 to 12 days. The actions follow each other in such a quick succession that it lends a special charm to the play. The love affair and the political rising against Caṇḍasena go side by side till the end when both are very happily resolved.

Conclusion

The historical interest along with these qualities has rendered this Nāṭaka very important. It is the only extant successful historical Nāṭaka that can be placed along with Mṛcchakaṭika and Mudrārākṣasa for its containing ample information about the social condition of the time.

Anaṅgaharṣa Mātrarāja

Like the Kaumudī-mahotsava, Tāpasa-Vatsarāja is also an interesting Nāṭaka of six Acts. The writer of this play is Anaṅgaharṣa alias Mātrarāja. In point of theme and technique the playwright should be placed in the creative period of Sanskrit drama. The play is based upon the illustrious life of Vatsarāja, immortalised by Bhāsa and Harṣa. The Vatsarāja-legend was so popular that it supplied materialto a great number of playwrights. There is another extant but incomplete Nāṭaka—Vīṇā-vāsavadatta on the same theme.

Our author dramatises the incidents which are found in the Svapnavāsavadatta with a slight variation. He presents Vatsarāja, turned an ascetic out of his grief for the reported tragic death of his dear wife, Vāsavadattā. Vatsarāja proceeds to Prayāga with his friend, Vasantaka and there meets Padmāvatī who is performing penance to obtain Vatsarāja as her husband. Their marriage, however, takes place, though Vatsarāja is unwilling. Meanwhile, in the absence of Vatsarāja, a battle takes place in the capital and a messenger brings the news of victory of his forces. The time for returning to the capital comes and Vatsarāja poignantly feels the absence of Vāsavadattā, and resolves to destroy his life in fire on the bank of the river. Behind everything that happens is the clever plan of the astute minister who has removed Vāsavadattā and given the king to understand that she is dead, in order to make the king alive to the duties and responsibilities of a king and stop him from dalliance with the queen in total disregard of his royal functions. It is the minister, again, who has engineered the king's marriage to Padmāvatī and it is again he who brings out the hidden Vāsavadattā in front of the king and saves the latter from imminent suicide.

So far as the technique is concerned, the playwright shows his mastery over it. His Prastāvanā is remarkably brief and his control over his pen is also remarkable. He never goes on composing verse after verse for the mere pleasure of versfication. All his verses are, however, well written and charming. There is a situation, similar to that in the third Act of Uttararāmacarita, where Vāsavadattā sees her husband but cannot speak to him. The situation is well managed. The sentimental expressions are not dragged to unnecessary length. The language of the play is also easy and lucid.

Though action is very meagre, the playwright maintains a rapidity in the play. Due to this, the play has attained a stageable character. The Explanatory Devices used are short and never go beyond their scope.

Conclusion

To conclude, this play is a commendable output of the playwright. The naturality and simplicity of the play show that at the time of its composition degeneration did not yet set in the Sanskrit dramatic art. The playwright shows a good knowledge of histrionics and so it is free from all artificial and far-fetched devices.

Śāktibhadra

The third play Āścarya-cūḍāmaṇi, claimed by its discoverer to be one of the oldest extant plays, is also remarkable for its easy diction. The theme of this seven-

Act Nāṭaka is the life of Rāma and the playwright presents in it Rāma's activities beginning from his going to the forest and ending with the reunion with Sitā. The name of the Nāṭaka originates from the *Cūḍāmaṇi* (tiara) of Sītā, which helps to bring about the union of Rāma and Sītā. The device is a pretty one and is dramatically effective.

The Prastāvanā

The technique of the playwright, though following the general trend is yet not totally conventional. The Prastāvanā introduces, in short, the main event and the poet is admirably modest about his own identity.

The first Act presents Lakṣmaṇa engaged in building a cottage when Śūrpaṇakhā, in the guise of a bewitching beauty, comes to him. She expresses her deep love to Lakṣmaṇa who, however, checks himself and rejects her advances coldly. But Śūrpaṇakhā says that Rāma has ordered her to give company to Lakṣmaṇa. He asks her to wait and goes to Sītā and Rāma. The first Act ends with their meeting.

The second Act presents the disappointed Śūrpaṇakhā who comes to Rāma to satisfy her passion after being rejected by Lakṣmaṇa. However, her real nature is exposed and she lifts Lakṣmaṇa up to kill him. Lakṣmaṇa returns followed by the weeping Rākṣasī in her terrifying form which is rendered uglier by Lakṣmaṇa's having severed her nose and ears. Rāma approves of the action of Lakṣmaṇa and the Rākṣasī runs away to report and show her pathetic condition to her brothers, threatening the human beings with dire revenge.

The first Viṣkambhaka

The playwright uses a Viṣkambhaka in the beginning of the third Act to report the killing of the demons—

Khara, Duṣaṇa, etc., and the coming of Rāvaṇa and his persuasion of the unwilling Mārīca to come to his help.

The third Act is a bit long and it begins with the presentation of the magic crest-jewel and magic ring to Sītā and Rāma respectively by Lakṣmaṇa as a gift from the sages. The strange power of these two ornaments is that by the touch of these the delusion caused by the Rākṣasas will disappear and they will be exposed in their real nature and form. Rāma takes the gift and places the jewel in the crest of Sītā and the ring in his finger. Before them, then, appears the illusory deer (māyāmṛga). To fulfil Sītā's desire, Rāma pursues it with his bow, placing Lakṣmaṇa in the cottage to look after Sītā's safety.

After this, Rāvaṇa and Śūrpaṇakhā are introduced on a chariot. At the counsel of Śūrpaṇakhā, Rāvaṇa decides to steal away Sītā. The story is then taken up with the arrival of Rāvaṇa and Śūrpaṇakhā with the intention of stealing away Sītā. It continues upto the departure of Rāvaṇa with Sītā as his captive. In between these two, the chain of incidents follows in the main the narrative as it is found in the epic. The only deviations, all of them creditable for the original and rational approach shown in them, are the presentation of Rāvaṇa in the disguise of Rāma; Śūrpaṇakhā in that of Sītā and the charioteer in that of Lakṣmaṇa. Over and above these, there are a few more deviations of a minor type. The manner in which the playwright presents the carrying away of Sītā shows a rare mastery of the dramatic technique and histrionic skill.

The fourth Act is a very short one and in it Rāvaṇa is exposed to Sītā in his own form as a result of his touching the hair of Sītā. The killing of Jaṭāyu off the stage also occurs in this Act. The chariot then runs to Laṅkā.

A Praveśaka

The fifth Act depicts the situation of Laṅkā. By a Praveśaka, the playwright reports the anxiety of Mandodarī, the wife of Rāvaṇa, who is disturbed by a very inauspicious dream and relates it to her handmaid. Then she proposes to go to the *aśoka-vana* to see how Rāvaṇa is advancing his love to the indifferent Sītā.

Rāvaṇa is, then, presented, who reaches the *aśoka-vana* to induce Sītā to love him. On his way his minister unsuccessfully tries to dissuade him from this immoral act. Rāvaṇa asks him to appoint spies to bring reports of Rāma's designs. He then enters the Aśoka-bower and expresses his love to Sītā. On being rudely rejected, he becomes angry with Sītā and takes up his sword to kill her. At this point Mandodarī, the queen, intervenes and checks Rāvaṇa from committing the sin of killing a woman. Rāvaṇa, a bit ashamed at seeing his queen, retires. Sītā also decides to commit suicide by drowning herself in the nearby lake.

The sixth Act shows the meeting of Hanūmat with Sītā. Hanūmat succeeds in removing Sītā's suspicion about him. Sītā gives up her idea of committing suicide. She gives her crest-jewel to Hanūmat to give it to Rāma as a memento from her and keeps the ring herself. She then bids farewell to Hanūmat.

The second Viṣkambhaka

By the brief Viṣkambhaka before the last Act, the playwright describes the killing of Rāvaṇa and his entire party. The exact fight is so skipped over that it seems that the main object of the playwright is to show the magical influence of the crest-jewel and the ring. A Vidyādhara pair reports the death of Rāvaṇa at the hands of Rāma and goes to convey the same to Indra.

After the Viṣkambhaka, Rāma and his full party are presented. Rāma asks Sugrīva to lead Bibhīṣaṇa into the palace. They start but Sugrīva returns immediately and says to Rāma that Bibhīṣaṇa does not wish to enter the palace until Sītā is freed from the *aśoka-vana.* Rāma then asks him to bring Sītā. On her arrival, Rāma asks Lakṣmaṇa to call Hanūmat and then says to Sugrīva that this lady was never seen by him. None understands the import of Rāma's words. Rāma then points out the beautiful attire of Sītā and comments satirically that such a gorgeous and rich dress really befits one who has been long separated from her consort. Sītā says to herself that the boon of Anasūyā has been turned into a curse on her. Then enters Hanūmat who also does not recognise the brilliantly clad lady to be Sītā whom he saw in the *aśoka-vana.* All of them condemn Sītā as a depraved lady and ask Rāma for her proper punishment. Sītā herself says that she wishes to enter into fire with the permission of her husband. With the approval of Rāma, Lakṣmaṇa leads her. Within short, Lakṣmaṇa reappears and narrates the strange scene of her entering into and coming out of fire unharmed. In the meanwhile, Nārada, the divine sage, is introduced, who shows to Rāma the assembled gods, divine sages and the dead forefathers to whom Rāma and Lakṣmaṇa pay their respects. Nārada then unravels the mystery of Sītā's brilliant appearance. Rāma believes in the saying of the sage and Lakṣmaṇa says that Sītā should immediately be called back honourably because her purity has been vindicated by the gods, sages and fathers. Sītā is brought back and welcomed heartily by Rāma. Bibhīṣaṇa then enters and says that the people of Laṅkā are condemning Rāma's action of suspecting Sītā, saying that darkness cannot impair the pure flame. This pleases Rāma and all of them ascend the *puṣpaka-vimāna* of Kubera at the instance of Nārada and start for Ayodhyā. Nārada blesses Rāma and the Nāṭaka ends.

Conclusion

The technique used in this Nāṭaka shows unmistakably the fact that Śaktibhadra, the playwright, possessed a thorough knowledge of the dramatic art along with its practical side of presentation on the stage. His language, particularly the beautiful prose dialogue, speaks of his mastery over his art. He is not a poet but is endowed with the capability of expressing emotional feelings in a poetic way and this has added a charm to his Nāṭaka. It is true that his Nāṭaka suffers from a dearth of action, but the swift movement of the plot is remarkable. Nowhere a series of emotional verses impede the way. He goes from Act to Act almost without any Explanatory Scenes. This is a rare quality which is found in the best specimens of Sanskrit drama. He uses only three Viṣkambhakas in this long play, and all these are remarkably short. The use of many and lengthy Viṣkambhakas is an evidence of the playwright's incompetence. A skilful dramatist presents his theme with the least possible number of these prosaic informatory scenes, that impede, more or less, the flow of the main events.

The period of Decadence

With the account of this Nāṭaka, we reach the end of the greatest and most creative epoch of Sanskrit Nāṭaka. All the Nāṭakas that follow are highly conventional, and this period may be labelled as imitative as opposed to the creative. It is evident from these, that the playwrights of this later period had no connection with the stage and they wrote the Nāṭakas in the court and for the court. As a result, simplicity and swiftness of movement are replaced by far-fetched imagination and complex poetic figures of speech. These poets took up Nāṭaka only as a vehicle of their poetic skill and so Nāṭakas became undramatic poems interspersed with laboured prose. Being cut off from the main stream of life, the dramatists became slavish imitators of the old legendary themes. Naturally what we get in the later plays are so many verses, illustrative merely of various figures of speech. The language, as a consequence, stiffened. That the playwrights were conversant with the treatises on dramaturgy, is evident in their conforming to the rules supplied by the Daśarūpaka and not the Nāṭyaśāstra of Bharata, which had lost its sway. The Bharatan liberality, thus, became conspicuous by its absence in these plays.

Characteristic features of the Decadent period

A few characteristics of this later dramatic period from circa 950–1200 A.D. are: (1) long Prastāvanās with many verses on the powers and skill of the playwright; (2) stiff and ornamental prose; (3) a great number of verses aiming not at supplying dramatic charm but the display of the poet's skill in using various poetic figures of speech; (4) the presentation of only the Śṛṅgāra Rasa and (5) gradual substitution of action by mere narration. All these point out the fact that the dramatic practice lost its life and those who composed the plays had the motive of becoming famous not as dramatists but as poets. The rhetorical style of these playwrights reminds one of the view of Bharata regarding the language of drama. He clearly says that the language should be as easily understood as possible and regarding the use of *alaṁkāras* also his views are very rational. He speaks only of four *alaṁkāras* Upamā (with its five kinds), Rūpaka, Dīpaka and Yamaka (with its ten kinds). These *alaṁkāras*, it may be said, are advantageous for dramatic composition as these are easy to follow and charming in appeal. But in the period under discussion, all kinds of *alaṁkāras*, some of which are very far-fetched and cannot be appreciated as soon as they are heard, are to be found in the Nāṭakas.

The condition of this period is finely described by Dr. S. K. De, which can here be quoted. He observes—[25] "It is clear that the whole cast of thought and style, the atmosphere, the stereotyped conventions and limited themes and the highly poetical and affected diction become unfavourable and almost fatal, to the writing of such plays as would be at once poetical and practical. The dramatists themselves do not seem quite to know whether they are composing a play or a poem ; nor are they producing the right kind of either. For the prevailing heroic and erotic drama, poetry is, to some extent, necessary, but the poetry here is of the artificial kind ; the heroic degenerates into the pseudo-heroic and the erotic into the namby-pamby."

During this period of decadence we get a group of playwrights who composed Nāṭakas which are, more or less, marked with the above-mentioned blemishes. The dramatists of this period are—Murāri, Rājaśekhara, Kṣemī-

25. HSL. p. 445.

śvara, Vīranāga, Jayadeva and Kṛṣṇa Miśra. Of them, Murāri wrote a Nāṭaka on Rāma-story, entitled Anarghyarāghava ; Rājaśekhara wrote two-Bālarāmāyaṇa and Bālabhārata of which the latter is incomplete. Kṣemīśvara also wrote two—Caṇḍakauśika and Naiṣadhānanda. Vīranāga's play is Kundamālā and Jayadeva's Nāṭaka is Prasannarāghava. The last playwright of the group, Kṛṣṇa Miśra deserves special treatment as he followed a new path and gave us the first allegorical Nāṭaka (excepting of course the fragments ascribed to Aśvaghoṣa). Of all the Nāṭakas mentioned above, we shall take up only two—Murāri's Anarghyarāghava and Jayadeva's Prasannarāghava. These two Nāṭakas, it can be said, exactly represent the highly artificial form and nature of the entire period and as such will help us in making a survey of the entire period.

So far as the themes are concerned, all the playwrights, excepting only Kṣemīśvara, miserably lack in novelty. All of them take up the old themes of early playwrights and try to use them as a peg to hang their coats on. All the four playwrights choose the Rāma legend and though Kṣemīśvara attempts at dramatising new themes—the story of king Hariścandra and Nala respectively, his treatment is as lifeless as that of his contemporaries. So he can also be included among the same group. We shall however discuss in detail the technique of Kṛṣṇa Miśra's Prabodha Candrodaya.

Murāri

Murāri's solitary Nāṭaka is named Anarghyarāghava. The Nāṭaka is divided into seven Acts and it presents the life of Rāma from his breaking the bow of Śiva at Mithilā to his coronation at Ayodhyā after fourteen years.

The playwright does not show any originality in the play. His theme is borrowed from Bhavabhūti's Nāṭaka and he imitates him so faithfully that all the innovations of Bhavabhūti are to be found in his play with the variations that he makes Jāmbavān, the minister of Vālin, and not Mālyavat, responsible for the Mantharā incident. The change is definitely for worse, since it makes Jāmbavān, a well wisher of Rāma do a thing which causes great suffering to Rāma. The other novelty is that Murāri skips over the fire-ordeal incident of Sītā. In other points he is a steady follower of his predecessor. Everything in the play—the rejection of Rāvaṇa's marriage-proposal in the third Act, the subjugation of Paraśurāma in the fourth, the killing of Vālin in the fifth, the killing of Rāvaṇa in the sixth—all are almost exact reproduction of Bhavabhūti's Mahāvīracarita. His seventh Act is also an imitation but he dwells more on the aerial journey of Rāma to Ayodhyā.

The play is so undramatic and artificial that none will agree to accept it as a true Nāṭaka except perhaps the playwright himself. It is evident that Murāri had no dramatic sense nor he cared for the stage-success of his play. The play is inordinately long. The verses are over-burdened with florid rhetorical flourishes. They are repeated monotonously and the dramatist never cares to substitute dramatic action in the place of stiff and useless verses. Even the prose bristles with difficulties and detracts from the charm of the play. The entire play is rendered stale and insipid by the inordinate love of the playwright for pedantry.

His Prastāvanā is typical of the decadent period. It is too long and contains 13 verses which are entirely useless, as these only speak of the various qualities of the playwright. His mode of Introduction is just like that of Mahāvīracarita.

As there is nothing to present on the stage, it is very difficult to find out any distinction between his Viṣkambhakas and Acts save only that the hero is not presented in the former. Particularly the sixth Act can be said to be fully a Viṣkambhaka divided into two parts. In the first part, which the playwright calls a Viṣkambhaka, Mālyavat, Sāraṇa and Śuka, these three characters announce, by the help of a few announcements behind the stage, the killing of all—Kumbhakarṇa, Indrajit and the Rākṣasa forces and also the starting of Rāvaṇa towards the battlefield. In the second part also, that is in the Act proper, the playwright introduces two Vidyādhara characters to report the death of Rāvaṇa. Thus the entire sixth Act takes the form of a narrative, void of the slightest action.

Likewise, the seventh Act should also be named as a Canto not an Act. In it the poet gives in a series of verses, numbering 133, a description, which is at places ludicrous, of the entire sub-continent of India and also of the aerial regions. This description is put in the mouths of Rāma and his associates, when they are returning to Ayodhyā from Laṅkā. Such an undramatic scene is hard to be found in Sanskrit literature. However, the end comes as they come down from the *vimāna* and meet Vaśiṣṭha, Bharata and Śatrughna, etc. at Ayodhyā. The sage performs the coronation ceremony and the play ends with the Bharata-vākya spoken by Rāma.

Conclusion

The degradation of drama into a mere display of inane poetic skill, as is evident in the Nāṭaka discussed above, makes it almost useless for us to go into a detailed evaluation of the Nāṭakas that followed Murāri's. But in order to see the point to which this degradation reached by 1200 A.D., we propose to examine the technique of Jayadeva's Prasanna-rāghava and close our survey of the Nāṭaka variety with a discussion of Kṛṣṇa Miśra's allegorical Nāṭaka, Prabodha Candrodaya.

Jayadeva

Jayadeva's time has been fixed by the historians in the thirteenth century. Thus he is the last dramatist during the period in question. Like his predecessors, he also takes up the Nāṭaka to show his skill in the use of figures of speech and his mastery over so many things, especially over the metric art.

His theme is, the story of entire Rāmāyaṇa beginning from the breaking of Śiva's bow upto the return to Ayodhyā. The theme that he takes is modelled slavishly upon Murāri's Nāṭaka and he shows little originality in it. The seven-Act Nāṭaka is full with all the characteristic features of the decadent drama. A discussion of his technique will clearly bring to light the stage of extreme artificiality, the drama reached.

The Prastāvanā

That Jayadeva possessed little dramatic sense becomes clear from the very Prastāvanā. His Prastāvanā is tediously lengthy and consists of 23 verses. Even with the help of such a long Prastāvanā the playwright is not able to introduce the main theme but has to use a Viṣkambhaka to pave the way for the hero's entrance. The Prastāvanā does not deal with the subject matter of the play as such but with the poet and his great accomplishments. The Sūtradhāra, after reciting three long benedictory verses begins to talk with his associate, on the request of the audience. The poet unnecessarily makes him dwell upon the skill of his brother. However, he then listens to the request of the people to stage a play, which is given in the form of a verse. This verse is so composed that the name of the Nāṭaka lies hidden in it. The Sūtradhāra discovers it and, after a lavish eulogy of the poet in many verses, retires. The skill of placing the component words of the name, Prasannarāghava in the verse may be expressive of his power but it is entirely useless in a Nāṭaka. The prose of the dramatist is also so ornate that there is hardly any difference between this prose and that of Bāṇabhaṭṭa. In the case of Bāṇabhaṭṭa, the prose is an ornament of great charm since he is a writer of fiction. But in the case of Jayadeva, who is a dramatist, the same type of prose is a blemish.

The first Viṣkambhaka

In the Viṣkambhaka which follows the Prastāvanā, he makes Dālbhyāyana, a disciple of Yājñavalkya, listen to the conversation of two bees in clear Sanskrit. With the help of this, he reports that Bāṇa, the demon, has come to see the bow of Śiva and that Rāvaṇa also is coming to the capital of Janaka.

In the first Act we are shown the tussle between Bāṇa and Rāvaṇa for the hands of Sītā. The dramatist describes the discomfiture of these two Rākṣasas when they fail to lift Śiva's bow. This happens before the advent of Rāma.

The second Viṣkambhaka

The next Act heralds the approach of Rāma and Lakṣmaṇa. The preceding Viṣkambhaka, having two characters, reports that Rāma has killed the Rākṣasī, Tāḍakā and has reached Mithilā with Viśvāmitra. The playwright then presents the most unusual spectacle of Rāma and Lakṣmaṇa on one side and Sītā and her attendants on the other. These characters come to know one another. Then follows a scene which is clearly a rehash of thc courtship scene in Abhijñāna Śākuntala. This scene is devoid of rhyme and reason and it does, in no way, help the movement of the plot. The playwright overlooks the very question of the bow of Śiva and makes Rāma and Sītā profess love to each other with no real gain. Thus his innovation proves a dramatic failure. The Act ends with the dispersal of the group. The women folk retire to the palace and Rāma and Lakṣmaṇa go to meet Viśvāmitra.

The third Viṣkambhaka

The playwright then places a Viṣkambhaka which is next to useless. He can very easily introduce Viśvāmitra without any difficulty but puts a Viṣkambhaka with two characters who report the advent of Viśvāmitra with Rāma and Lakṣmaṇa and the desire of the sage to see the bow of Śiva. The scene is entirely superfluous, barring its slight humour.

However, the Act proper brings in Viśvāmitra, Rāma and Lakṣmaṇa on one hand and Janaka and Śatānanda on the other. The conversation consists of many verses most of which are spoken by Viśvāmitra who describes Rāma's valour and qualities. Many poetic tricks are employed by the poet to suggest Viśvāmitra's desire of marrying Rāma to Sītā. Janaka reminds the sage of his decision regarding the marriage of Sītā and speaks of the bow of Śiva. Viśvāmitra accordingly asks Rāma to use the bow and thus fulfil the oath of Janaka. In the meantime a messenger comes from Paraśurāma to convey to Janaka that he may marry his daughter to anybody but should not be so impertinent as to use the bow of Śiva as a stake for that. The king, however, angrily rejects his warning, and Rāma, to the great astonishment of all, succeeds in bending the bow which ultimately breaks in his hand. The happy Viśvāmitra then settles the marriage not only of Rāma but of all his brothers.

The fourth Act depicts the subjugation of Paraśurāma by Rāma. The quarrel and subjugation are executed after the exact fashion of Bhavabhūti. However, the playwright employs no less than 40 verses to present the quarrel and then after the fight, which takes place beyond the stage, the persons disperse.

The playwright shows a novelty in introducing four rivers—Gaṅgā, Yamunā, Sarayū and Godāvarī along with Sāgara to report the incidents that take place after the marriage of Rāma. He goes to the absurd length of introducing, a swan also as one of the reporters ! The Act, consequently, is void of all action. The rivers report one after another the following incidents–the sending of Rāma and Lakṣmaṇa with Sītā to the forest by Kaikeyī ; Bharata's settling at Nandigrāma ; the arrival and settling of Rāma at the banks of Godāvarī ; the stealing away of Sītā by Rāvaṇa ; the killing of Vālin and enthronement of Sugrīva by Rāma and the sending of the monkeys to different directions in search of Sītā. The entire Act thus takes the form of a long Viṣkambhaka and is fully narrative in nature.

The playwright presents the love-sick Rāma with his devoted brother in the sixth Act. He is here presented almost in the same fashion as the love-sick Purūravas of Kālīdāsa. Rāma wails for Sītā to the Sun, the Moon, the birds. The playwright then uses a very strange and impractical device to show the condition of Sītā at Laṅkā. From the point of view of stageability and logic, the device is hopelessly absurd. While Rāma and Lakṣmaṇa are conversing together, two characters are introduced off the stage. One of them demonstrates his magical power to the other by showing the condition of Sītā at Laṅkā. The scene is shown on the stage and in it we find Sītā, Trijaṭā and Rāvaṇa. Rāvaṇa attempts to win Sītā's confidence and love but she rudely rejects all his proposals and allurements. The angry Rāvaṇa is about to kill Sītā and asks for a *kapāla* (the head of a skeleton used as a pot), when the head of his son falls upon his hand from above. Rāvaṇa startles to see the head of his beloved son, Akṣa and realises that it is the work of Hanūmat. He then leaves the place to punish the monkey. Then Hanūmat is introduced, who conveys the message of Rāma to Sītā and then returns. The magic show ends and Rāma also starts to meet the monkeys, hearing another announcement that Hanūmat has returned with the news of Sītā. The scene is definitely interesting but is not practicable and as such it fails to satisfy the demands of art.

The fourth Viṣkambhaka

The playwright puts a Viṣkambhaka before the last Act, which reports Bibhīṣaṇa's defection. The Act proper presents Rāvaṇa looking at a picture given to him by Prahasta. The news of war is reported to him by means of talks off the stage. In this way he comes to know the death of Kumbhakarṇa and Meghanāda. He then himself starts for the battlefield. Then the playwright introduces a pair of Vidyādharas who report the death of Rāvaṇa by means of so many verses. The narrative is inordinately long. In this very scene the playwright then presents Rāma, Sītā, Lakṣmaṇa, Sugrīva and Bibhīṣaṇa. All of them undertake an aerial journey to Ayodhyā during which the landscape below is described. After a plethora of verses, the drama ends with the words of Rāma—'Let us get down and meet the superiors.'

Conclusion

The entire drama suffers from an exuberant display of rhetorical skill. The prose of Jayadeva is typical of the decadent period and both verse and prose indicate that the playwright was a skilled master of rhetorics. Dramatic art, however, did not receive any impetus from him. Jayadeva's Nāṭaka is a typical product of the period of stagnation of the dramatic art.

So far we have discussed the course of development of the Nāṭaka variety from the point of view of technique upto 1200 A. D. and have observed the following—

1. The Nāṭaka had maintained a very living tradition upto the times of Bhavabhūti after which it began to show signs of degeneration which reached its lowest level by the time of Jayadeva ;
2. The degeneration expressed itself through an all round want of dramatic sense which manifested itself in laboured and highly ornamental prose, excess of verses aiming at displaying the dexterity of the playwright in using the rhetorical figures of speech, replacement of action by mere narration ;
3. There was a growing love for useless formalities at the expense of the soul of mimic art, as is evident

from the contrast between the Prastāvanās[26] in the Nāṭakas of the two periods, and there was a fondness for presenting mere rehashes of the older dramas.

Kṛṣṇa Miśra

The account of the position of the Nāṭaka variety during this period will be complete with a discussion of the Prabodha Candrodaya which marks a new approach. It is the oldest extant allegorical Nāṭaka in six Acts. Kṛṣṇa Miśra seems to have been biassed against the romantic theme and so turned towards the Śānta Rasa, taking up the allegorical theme of the victory of Discrimination (Viveka) over his rival Confusion (Mahāmoha) to illustrate it. We find Kṛṣṇa Miśra showing considerable skill in giving human colour to his abstract theme. Though originally the theme is didactic in nature, he contrives well to present it in a charming and realistic manner and thus making it more dramatic than the ordinary Nāṭakas of the age. The diction of the play, though suffering from artificiality is yet not so tedious as that of the Nāṭakas discussed above. The verses are not excessive in number and are easier than the prose.

The dramatis personae comprises Discrimination (Viveka) as the king, having Reason (Mati), Duty (Dharma), Pity (Karuṇā), Good-will (Maitrī), Peace (Śānti), and her mother Faith (Śraddhā), Forgiveness (Kṣamā), Contentment (Santoṣa), Judgment (Vastuvicāra), Religious Devotion (Bhakti) and others as his followers on one hand and Confusion (Moha) as the rival of Discrimination, having Love (Kāma) and his wife Pleasure (Rati), Anger (Krodha)

26. The contrast between the Prastāvanās of two periods has been shown in appendix.

and his wife Injury (Hiṃsā), Greed (Lobha) and his wife Desire (Tṛṣṇā), their son, Deceit (Dambha) and Egoism (Ahaṃkāra), the father of Greed, Heresy (Mithyādṛṣṭi) described as a courtesan and Materialism represented by Cārvāka as his adherents on the other. Both the two groups are said to have been born of Mind (Manas) and his two wives Repose (Nivṛtti) and Activity (Pravṛtti) respectively. The feud between the two parties starts from their attempt at overthrowing each other. King Confusion is assisted by Jainism, Buddhism, and Brāhmaṇism (Soma cult) and the playwright shows a great satirical skill in presenting these. They all are votaries of sensual pleasure and as such are grouped with the followers of king Confusion. A detailed analysis of the theme will point out the merits and drawbacks of the playwright.

The Prastāvanā

Tne Nāṭaka begins with the usual Prastāvanā which is fashioned after the Veṇīsaṃhāra. The Sūtradhāra states that the king Gopāla has asked him to stage a Nāṭaka of Śānta Rasa to please his friend, Kīrtivarman who is fed up with the Vīra after a surfeit of warfare. He then names the play and playwright and calls upon the Naṭī to arrange for the performance. In his attempt at removing the wonder of Naṭī as to the desire of a king to enjoy Śānta Rasa, he speaks out a verse which announces that the king has vanquished Confusion with the aid of Discrimination, and True Knowledge (Prabodha) has revealed itself to him. This statement of the Śūtradhāra is condemned vehemently by one from behind the stage, whom the Sūtradhāra recognises to be Love (Kāma) and reports that Love with his wife Pleasure (Rati) is approaching in an angry mood. With his depariure the play begins.

The Prastāvanā is very ably executed and the playwright deserves universal praise but for his terse prose. His description of king Gopāla reminds us of the description of Śūdraka by Bāṇa in his Kādambarī, and this apparent imitation is too wooden and undramatic to add any beauty to the drama. The phrases—"*Sakala-sāmanta-cakra-cūḍāmaṇi-marīci-mañjarī–nīrājita-caraṇa-kamalena, balavadarinivahavakṣastaṭakapāṭa-pāṭan a-prakaṭitanṛsiṁharūpeṇa, prabalataranarapatikula-pralayamahārṇavani-magnamedinī-samuddharaṇa-mahāvarāharūpeṇa*—" etc. are all very recondite and can ill suit the language of drama. Otherwise, his Prastāvanā is impressive for its brevity and apt introduction of the main theme.

The first Viṣkambhaka

The playwright, puts a Viṣkambhaka in the beginning of the first Act. Love and Pleasure ushered in by the Sūtradhāra are the two characters in it, who inform us with the fact that Discrimination and his followers and Confusion and his adherents both are the progeny of the same father, Mind by his two wives; that the supporters of Discrimination are active to give birth to Spiritual Wisdom (Vidyā) and True Knowledge (Prabodha), daughter and son respectively to be born to king Discrimination by Sacred Lore (Upaniṣad), who will annihilate the entire force af king Confusion and that the followers of king Confusion are labouring hard to check the advent of Wisdom and True knowledge. Supplying these information, Love and Pleasure, servants to king Confusion, retire indicating at the same time the approach af king Discrimination and his wife, Reason (Mati).

King Discrimination and Reason enter, who are deeply concerned at the increasing sway of Confusion.

The king decides to take definite steps so that True Knowledge can be born and in order to persuade Sacred Lore to marry him, he appoints Śama, Dama, etc. The Act thus presents the Beginning of the Action (ārambha).

The second Viṣkambhaka

By another Viṣkambhaka, the playwright describes the repercussions of the policy of king Discrimination on the group of his enemy. In it Deceit and his grandfather, Egoism are presented. Deceit reports that king Confusion has decided to annex Vārāṇasī, the capture of which will defeat king Discrinination and his forces. The selection of Vārāṇasī, the centre of spiritual culture, as the key-spot for the contention between Discrimination and Confusion is very apt. Deceit announces that he has well served the orders of his king and Vārāṇasī has come within his grip. Then appears Egoism who after a bandy of words recognises Deceit as his grandson and discloses that he has also come to Vārāṇasī to make an on-the-spot study of the situation under the orders of king Confusion. Both of them, then, retire to meet the king.

King Confusion is then presented, who laughs at the folly of the religious men. He pronounces his doctrine of 'eat, drink and be merry.' Then appears Materialism (Cārvāka) with a disciple. He teaches his doctrines to his disciples and the king, listening to them, recognises him to be his friend, Cārvaka, and welcomes. Cārvaka reports that Kurukṣetra has been won over by him to the side of Confusion. He further reports that Devotion is very strong and invincible, whose followers, Cārvaka has failed to overcome. King Confusion gets disturbed at the news and orders the messenger to send Love, Anger, Greed, etc. to kill Devotion. A messenger from Kaliṅga is then introduced, who conveys the message to the king that Peace along with her mother, Faith (Śraddhā) has gone to Sacred Lore as heralds of king Discrimination to persuade her to marry Discrimination. Duty (Dharma) along with Asceticism (Vairāgya) also is gaining ground. This news infuriates the king and he orders the messenger to ask Love to capture Duty and put him in prison. He then sends Anger and Greed to overcome Peace, the daughter of Faith. He then finds out another way to defeat Peace. He decides to alienate Faith from Sacred Lore, as a result of which Peace will die of sorrow. Heresy (Mithyādṛṣṭi), the courtesan is commissioned to achieve this end.

The next Act introduces Peace and her friend Pity. Peace is desperately sorrowful at the absence of her mother and decides to commit suicide. She is checked from doing so by her friend. They both go out in search of Faith. On their way they come across Jainism, Buddhism and Brahmanism one after another, all of whom claim to own Faith. But these Faiths are recognised by Peace and Pity to be *tāmasa* and *rājasa* in nature, the *sāttvika* Faith is found to be missing. The playwright presents these characters very cleverly. The satire heaped upon them is very keen and lively. Kāpālika, representing Soma Cult, wins over ultimately Jainism and Buddhism, not by means of proving the superiority of his Cult but by allurement which comes from the charming embrace of his Faith in the form of Kāpālinī. All of them drink wine and accept the Soma Cult. Then one of them decides to find out and capture Faith, the daughter of Sattva in the interest of king Confusion. They come to know by means of their astrological knowledge that Faith is to be found nowhere but in the hearts of good men, along with Devotion. The same is the case with Duty. The group of the followers of Confusion disperses to try to capture Faith. Peace and Pity also depart to convey this to Devotion. The third Act ends.

The third Viṣkambhaka

The fourth Act is also preceded by a Viṣkambhaka. In it we find Good Will (Maitrī) and Faith conversing together. Faith reports her recovery from the clutches of Mahābhairavī, an assistant of the Kāpālika referred to in the previous Act, in which she was helped by Devotion. Then Faith says that she is going to convey Devotion's message to king Discrimination, the message being an exhortation to the king to crush the forces of Confusion and a promise of help in the action. It adds that she has sent a few goddesses to persuade Sacred Lore to give birth to True Knowledge. Good Will says that she is also interested in the success of king Discrimination along with her other sisters, as ordered by Devotion. Faith then reports that king Discrimination is undergoing penance on the banks of Ganges at Cakratīrtha in the country of Rāḍha (Bengal) for the fulfilment of his union with Sacred Lore.

The playwright then presents king Discrimination considering the ways of defeating the attendants of Confusion, as advised by Devotion. He then calls upon Judgment and orders him to fight with and win over Love. Judgment starts forthwith. The king then decides to defeat Anger by Forgiveness (Kṣamā) and sending for the latter orders her to do so. He then asks Contentment (Santoṣa) to overthrow Greed, and sees him starting immediately for Vārāṇasī to vanquish him. He then sends all the army to fight his enemy and starts himself for Vārāṇasī on a chariot. They reach the temple of Ādikeśava and make it their camp.

Herein also, the phrases used to eulogise the god Viṣṇu are very long and complicated, and as a result, very stiff.

The fourth Viṣkambhaka

The fifth Act announces the total defeat of Confusion and his forces, and also the reaction of it on Mind. The Viṣkambhaka reports the battle and its results. In it Devotion, Peace and Faith are presented. It is reported by them that in a fierce battle all the adherents of Confusion have been routed by the followers of Discrimination. The reaction of it on Mind the father, is painful, and he is contemplating to die. But Devotion says that she has sent Sarasvatī to Mind in order to make the latter seek refuge in Vairāgya.

The Act proper then presents Mind and Will (Saṅkalpa). Mind is very restless and sorrowful at the death of his favourite sons and finding himself abandoned by all, even by his wife Activity (Pravṛtti), he asks Will to prepare a pyre for him. Sarasvatī then appears before him and slowly dispels his sorrow. Wisdom dawns upon him, which changes his outlook and to him, then, appears Vairāgya. Vairāgya consoles his father, Mind, and makes him friendly towards Discrimination. Sarasvatī asks him to accept Repose (Nivṛtti) as his consort henceforward, and advises him to be favourable towards his son, Discrimination and his followers. Mind thus is won over to the side of king Discrimination. The Act shows the fourth Stage of the Action, Niyatāpti, as success, though considerably attained, is yet not entirely attained, without the birth of True Knowledge.

The fifth Viṣkambhaka

The sixth Act shows the Attainment of Result (Phalāgama). The Viṣkambhaka with Peace and Faith relates that Mind is leading a peaceful and happy life and king Discrimination is waiting for Sacred Lore to Whom Peace has been sent as a messenger. Faith relates that Confusion has been defeated by Logic and has thus failed to win over Puruṣa who is now desirous of meeting Discrimination on her advice.

After it Puruṣa is presented, to whom come, one after another, Sacred Lore and Peace, king Discrimination and Faith. Sacred Lore relates to Puruṣa how she suffered at the hands of the Heretics and how she was saved by Viṣṇu. Puruṣa then comes to realise that he is the Soul, the Supreme Being, and a happy union of Puruṣa, Sacred Lore and Discrimination thus occurs. Then a messenger from Devotion arrives who conveys to Sacred Lore the message that she should go to Devotion along with Discrimination and that Wisdom and True Knowledge will soon come into being. Wisdom is to be given to Mind and True Knowledge to Puruṣa. King Discrimination and Sacred Lore follow the order. The playwright announces the divine birth of Wisdon and True Knowledge by a proclamation off the stage. Immediately after, enters True Knowledge and pays homage to Puruṣa, who embraces him. Before them, then appears Devotion who greets and blesses the two. Puruṣa speaks the last benedictory verse, the Bharata-vākya and the Nāṭaka ends.

Conclusion

The Nāṭaka, thus, show a skilful handling so far as the technique is concerned. But however successful Kṛṣṇa

Miśra may be in presenting his theme, the want of human interest in the play is fatal. Such abstract ideas as constitute one's moral being cannot attain a life-like reality and consequently, inspite of admirable presentation, the Nāṭaka fails to appeal.

Inspite of the above drawback, the Nāṭaka has greatly influenced the later formulators. All the Explanatory Devices in the play (five in number), which we have styled as Viṣkambhakas, are, however, according to the playwright, Praveśakas excepting only the first and the fourth. Though these are named Praveśakas, the playwright makes no distinction of these with the Viṣkambhakas. The language and the characters used in them are the same. The general rule that Praveśaka should be in Prakrit language and contain lower characters cannot be applied to these. Peculiarly enough, the dramatist introduces the same characters in a few of the Explanatory Devices, naming one Viṣkambhaka and the other Praveśaka without adducing proper reasons. This is the reason, it seems, why Rāmacandra and Guṇacandra observe that Praveśaka may also be in Sanskrit and can have characters belonging to the upper strata. This later formulation speaks eloquently of the great influence and popularity of Kṛṣṇa Miśra as a dramatist. His play moreover cleared the way for future allegorical plays which, though meagre in number and imitative of this very Nāṭaka, are yet interesting for their novelty of theme.

Thus the chapter on the promising origin, grand development and inglorious decay of the Nāṭaka variety comes to an end. In our survey, we have attempted to cover a long period of time from the inception of Nāṭaka to circa 1200 A.D. In the subsequent chapters we propose to discuss the other forms of drama with special reference to the development of technique.

—

SECTION—2 : PRAKARAṆA

Śūdraka

The history of full-fledged and complete Prakaraṇa may very rightly be said to have begun with Śūdraka, the writer of the Prakaraṇa, Mṛcchakaṭika. In point of time whether Śūdraka was prior to or contemporary with Kālidāsa, is a debatable question. Generally he is taken to be posterior to Kālidāsa. We did not include him in the list of the writers of Nāṭaka simply because he wrote no Nāṭaka. His play is a Prakaraṇa and it is the oldest specimen of the type. The transition from Kālidāsa to Śūdraka rests, to a great extent, upon the difference of their approach to life. So long the playwrights occupied themselves with the portrayal of courtly love but with the advent of Śūdraka, a new avenue opens before us, where instead of any royal personages, Cārudatta, a merchant; Maitreya, a devoted friend; the scheming Śakāra, the favourite of the king; Śarvilaka, the leader of a revolutionery party; Vasantasenā, a courtesan; common, but not common place, characters of gamblers; military officers; a city Magistrate; judges; executioners and a great variety of men are presented on a canvas as wide as to cover ten long Acts. This is for the first time in the history of Sanskrit literature, that there come so many persons of different stations of life, and the playwright is highly successful in presenting them in a charmingly realistic manner.

Śūdraka must have been ingenious enough to realise the fact that after Kālidāsa it was not an easy task to attempt at composing a Nāṭaka and attain fame thereby.

The success of Kālidāsa was so obviously felt that we may easily imagine Śūdraka changing the subject matter of his play. Instead of following the already beaten track of Bhāsa and Kālidāsa, he experimented, so to say, with the new form. In the absence of Aśvaghoṣa's Prakaraṇa, his is to be regarded as the first of the type. Whether he was aware of or modelled his Prakaraṇa upon Aśvaghoṣa's work is a thing of mere conjecture. It must be accepted that his first work is greatly successful and it has placed him among the first-ranking dramaturgists of Sanskrit literature. The observation of Dr. S. K. De, regarding the unique character of the play is worth-quoting. He observes—"It is thus, not the usual type of the dramatic poem, but possesses distinctly dramatic qualities, which make a greater appeal to modern taste and idea. Apart from the graphic picture it presents of some phases of contemporary life, the work is truly worthy of a great dramatist in its skilful handling of a swift-moving plot of sustained interest, in its variety of incidents and characters, in its freedom from the usual fault of over-elaboration, in its sharpness of characterisation, in its use of direct and homely imageries conveyed in a clear, forcible and unaffected diction, in its skilful employment of a variety of Sanskrit and Prakrit metres, in its witty dialogue, in its general liveliness and dramatic effect, in its mastery of deep pathos and in its rare quality of quiet humour."[27]

The author, Śūdraka, the history tells us, was a many-sided genius. He had mastery over many branches of learning. A verse in the Prastāvanā acquaints us with the information that he knew Ṛgveda, Sāmaveda, Mathematics and in addition, so many arts of Vaiśika, Hastiśikṣā

27. HSL. p. 243–44.

and the like, and that he was a worshipper of Śiva, by whose grace he regained his eye-sight and lived for one hundred years and ten days. He has been quoted in many books as a great and valorous king of repute. The authenticity of the verse may be doubted and it must have been a later insertion into the play, still the dramatic dexterity shown in the play, proves beyond doubt the great artistic attainments of the playwright. So far as his handling of the theme is concerned, he must be honoured as a great artist who gives little scope, if any, throughout the long play for any incoherence or want of interest.

The Vastu

The source of the play is uncertain. A very great similarity of the first portion of the play with the Cārudatta of Bhāsa suggests that there must have been a borrowing of plot. But no conclusive proof is there to show who was the borrower. The play is in the form of Prakaraṇa which, according to the definition of Bharata should have an Invented plot with a Brāhmaṇa or a merchant or a priest or a minister or the like as its hero. So far as this statement is concerned, Śūdraka has followed faithfully the Śāstra. Cārudatta is a Brāhmaṇa by caste and a merchant by profession. The plot is also an invented one. The number of Acts in a Prakaraṇa is given as five to ten in the Śāstra, Mṛcchakaṭika accordingly has got ten Acts.

The chief deviation from Bharata is notable in the introduction of the courtesan side by side with the wife of the hero. The Śāstra promulgates that if a courtesan is introduced, there should not be any lady of rank. Śūdraka simply overlooks this law and introduces both—Dhūtā, the wife of Cārudatta and Vasantasenā, the courtesan, and puts almost equal importance upon the courtesan and the lady. The calm, dignified and highly devoted wife of Cārudatta is no less important than the charming courtesan, Vasantasenā in the Denouement of the play.

The Prastāvanā

Śūdraka, it seems, set out with the avowed determination of impressing his audience from the very beginning of the play. The Prastāvanā of the play proves this fact. It is of a peculiar type which attracts attention. The Prastāvanā has got apparently two divisions. The first half seems to be an interpolation. At least the verse in which even the death of the playwright is told, which is in Sanskrit, is surely so. Announcing the name of the play and the playwright in the second half, the Sūtradhāra changes his language of conversation from Sanskrit to Prakrit and calls upon his female associate. Though the Prologue is a bit long yet the mode of Presentation, interspersed with genial humour as it is, is highly interesting. The Sūtradhāra, by the help of the *ākāśabhāṣita*, introduces Maitreya, the friend and Vidūṣaka of the hero, Cārudatta.

The dramatist must have been aware of the fact that his drama being based upon an already famous drama of Bhāsa should have some such new elements as might impress the audience. For this purpose, he adds an Episode to the main theme. According to the saying of the Śāstra, the Episode subserves the fulfilment of the main action along with the success of the episodical hero. The episode of Śarvilaka, a revolutionary and the lover of Madanikā has added much charm to the main plot. This impetuous and resourceless Brāhmaṇa youth is compelled to take to the profession of a thief due to poverty and his desire to buy his beloved, a slave to Vasantasenā, with ransom. His theft of the very ornaments of Vasantasenā from the house of Cārudatta at night is an effective dramatic event and one of the many interesting scenes of the play.

The Variety of Characters

Śūdraka introduces an interesting motley of characters from different walks of life. The list of the *dramatis personae* includes in it, in addition to the hero, heroine, the courtesan and the Vidūṣaka, a Śakāra; a Viṭa; Śarvilaka; Āryaka, a usurper; four Ceṭas (servants) all of whom have got distinct characteristics of their own; a Shampooer (Saṃvāhaka) who becomes firstly a gambler and then turns to a Buddhist Śramaṇaka; a keeper of the gambling house; two more gamblers one of whom is a partisan of the revolutioneries; a judge; two court-officials; two executioners; a military officer; Rohasena, the son of Cārudatta; Madanikā, a slave to Vasantasenā; the mother of Vasantasenā and a few more. Though the list is long yet none is unimportant. The playwright has so conceived and executed the plot that from the very child of Cārudatta each and every person in the play including even the toy clay-cart is important. The big drama of ten long Acts is so very well-knit that there is not a single moment when the reader may feel disinterested. The dramatic situations in each Act are to very well-executed that each eloquently festifies to the great art of the playwright.

Śūdraka—a great realist

The dramatist shows a very fine sense of realism in this play. It is not for the mere conformity with the dictum of the Śāstra, that he brings in such a great number of characters. His keen dramatic sense has imparted to each of them an individuality of his own. Even the two executioners are not identical to each other. The superb characterisation in Mṛcchakaṭika elevates Śūdraka to a higher level than that reached by Kālidāsa. In fact, the characters of Kālidāsa are well-known in legends and as such, much is known about them but the characters of Śūdraka have got no spokesmen for them in the legends. They are, on the contrary, their own spokesmen. And the rare mastery shown in this respect has given Śūdraka an everlasting fame as a master-playwright.

A very faithful picture of the then Ujjayinī is one of the finest instances of the playwright's sense of realism. Though the Prakaraṇa is not an historical one, it has got an historical importance peculiar to its own. The life of the rich and poor, the depiction of the faithful love of a lady and of a courtesan, the preparations of a conspiracy to overthrow the unrighteous ruler, and after all the brilliant presentation of the sophisticated mode of life of the men about town—these are the salient features of the play. The court scene can never be overlooked wherein we find the wicked Śakāra plotting for the death of Cārudatta who appears as the noblest man on earth for whom everyone, even the executioners, cherish a great respect. The high dramatic skill of the dramatist is evident in his success in maintaining an eager suspense throughout the play. The unravelling of the knot is executed by him, one by one. When the execution is imminent, he brings in the news of success in the overthrow of the wicked king and Cārudatta is set free. The revolution does end not only in the attainment of kingdom by Āryaka but it revolutionises the life of the hero as well.

The dramatist has shown his great dramatic acumen in respect of the construction of the plot as well. Apart from the great coherence and succession of revelatory events in the play, there are almost no Explanatory Devices. In such a long play where so many characters with their diversified interests meet, it is a matter of no little skill on the part of the dramatist to use only two Praveśakas. These two are placed in the beginning of the third and the ninth Acts. These are very brief and the characters therein serve merely the purpose of acquainting the audience with the background of the respective Acts. The action moves so smoothly that there is hardly any scope for an Introductory Scene and as a result, these two are not marked as Praveśakas in the text. But the nature of these short pieces of information is such that they should be accepted as Praveśakas.

Bharata assigns the use of all the Rasas in the Nāṭaka and Prakaraṇa varieties. The Sentiment displayed in the Mṛcchakaṭika is Erotic, the Denouement of which lies in the happy union of the two lovers—Cārudatta and Vasantasenā.

The Code and the Dramatist

The history of literature records the neglect shown to this great work of Śūdraka by the theorists.[28] But after a careful study of the play none can support the attitude of these theorists. Though his play conforms almost on all points to the Nāṭyaśāstra of Bharata, the later theorists, it seems, must have been put to exasperation by the vastness of the subject matter of the play. The liberality expressed in the Code of Bharata is, to a great extent, lost in the later works on dramaturgy and we will have to seek the reason of neglect for Śūdraka in this fact. Even

28. Vide HSL. p. 243.

if the later codifiers were put to difficulty by this greatly original and bold attempt of the playwright, they could not possibly overlook the importance of this great drama. In fact, Mṛcchakaṭika influenced to a great extent the later rules concerning the composition of a Prakaraṇa.

The influence is evident in the division of the Prakaraṇa in three classes by the later theorists. The Daśarūpaka gives the classification thus—

> "*Nāyikā tu dvidhā netuḥ kulajā gaṇikā tathā*
> *Kvacidekaiva kulajā veśyā kvāpi dvayaṁ kvacit.*
> ....
> *Ābhiḥ prakaraṇaṁ tredhā saṁkīrṇaṁ dhūrtasaṁkulam*"[29]

According to this statement, the first type is to have a (married) lady as the heroine; the second variety may have a courtesan as the heroine while in the third there is room for both of them. This mixed type may have in addition, a number of rogues and rakes in it to heighten local colour. It is apparent that the third variety, named as *saṁkīrṇa* or mixed, is based upon purely the Mṛcchakaṭika of Śūdraka. The list of Prakaraṇas supplied by the commentator, Dhanika, includes, in addition to Mṛcchakaṭika, two other Prakaraṇas, respectively illustrating the first two varieties. These are—Puṣpadūṣitaka (lady heroine) and Taraṅgadatta (courtesan heroine). Unfortunately none of these are extant to this day and so it is not possible to compare the technique of these with that of the Mṛcchakaṭika.

The treatment of Prakaraṇa in the Nāṭyadarpaṇa is highly interesting. The authors have dealt with the type much elaborately and though no illustrations are

29. DR. III. 41-42.

supplied, the variety has been divided by them into 21 types in all. On the basis of hero, the purpose of the hero and Vastu, the variety is said to be divided into 7 types, according as the imagination of the dramatist works in the conception of these. That is, if the hero is imaginary and the subject-matter and the purpose of the hero are not, there is a type and so on. These seven primary types are again divided into 21 by the intermixture of three types of the heroine—lady, courtesan and both.[30]

The classification according to Nāṭyadarpaṇa, it is obvious, must have been based, among others, on Mṛcchakaṭika as well. It may therefore be surmised that Śūdraka's recasting of Bhāsa's drama may have suggested to the codifiers the possibility of having newer types of Prakaraṇas. In addition, Nāṭyadarpaṇa states that there should be no *Deus ex machina* employed in this type of drama (*divyānāśritam*), as this variety abounds in troublesome situations. A divine character may be successfully introduced where there is a peaceful atmosphere but his introduction in such situations where rogues abound and troubles thrive would lower down his divinity itself. This prohibition of divine character is also, apparently, based upon the Prakaraṇa of Śūdraka, where there is little scope for the appearance of the supernatural.

How much the authors of the Nāṭyadarpaṇa were influenced by other Prakaraṇas which served as models, is difficult to ascertain. Though a good many number of Prakaraṇas, a few of which are said to be composed by the authors themselves, are referred to in the treatise

30. Vide ND. II, 67–68.

(nine in all), almost all of them, barring a few are lost. The three Prakaraṇas which have survived to this day are—Mṛcchakaṭika of Śūdraka, Mālatīmādhava of Bhavabhūti and Kaumudī-mitrānanda of Rāmacandra, one of the authors of the Nāṭyadarpaṇa. In the absence of others, it is not at all possible to determine the influence of these Prakaraṇas on the authors. That he had knowledge of the Puṣpadūṣitaka and the Taraṅgadatta, both of which are quoted by all the formulators down to Viśvanātha, there can be no doubt. But unfortunately none of these s extant and so the only thing which can be said with certainty is the influence of Mṛcchakaṭika on the joint authors.

Another observation regarding the Rasa of the type also seems to have been based upon the Mṛcchakaṭika. It is said that in this variety the hero should be a hard-suffering person. The Kaiśikī style, therefore, cannot have a full scope as it is the conveyor of the Śṛṅgāra Rasa (*Śeṣaṁ nāṭakavat sarvaṁ kaiśikīpūrṇatām vinā*).[31] By the elimination of a full use of the Kaiśikī style, the Nāṭyadarpaṇa points out that Śṛṅgāra and Hāsya should not predominate (*Kleśaprācuryeṇa śṛṅgārahāsyayoralpatvāt*).[32] On this point it criticises the employment of Kaiśikī by Bhavabhūti in his Mālatīmādhava. These facts prove the influence of Śūdraka's play over the later formulators clearly.

The naming of the Play

Śūdraka shows a great originality and novelty in the naming of his play. Previously the practice used to be to christen a drama according to the names of the important

31. ND. II, 69.
32. ND. II, p. 120.

characters or nature of the main incidents, e.g. Abhijñana Śākuntala, Abhiṣeka, etc. But Śūdraka shows originality by not following the beaten track. The name, 'The little clay-cart' is highly significant. The subtle artistic sense exhibited here is unique. The clay-cart, though it comes in the sixth Act as an insignificant toy, turns to be the pivot around which everything moves. The very conviction of Cārudatta is based on the harmless clay-cart. Again, the clay-cart episode expresses the deep yearning in the heart of Vasantasenā for motherhood. Thus the Denouement depends to a great extent upon the clay-cart of the child of Cārudatta and the placing of the golden ornaments of Vasantasenā in it. Śūdraka rightly recognised the importance of the claycart and named the play accordingly. In this respect, he belongs to a class by himself. Unfortunately none followed his method and even the theorists overlooked him, according to whom a Prakaraṇa should be named jointly after the hero and the heroine as the Mālatīmādhava.[33]

Bhavabhūti

Among the extant Prakaraṇas, Bhavabhūti's Mālatīmādhava is one of the most well-known. It found more favour with the theorists than the Mṛcchakaṭika, though it is decidedly much inferior to the latter in point of originality and execution. The approbation it received from the circle of theorists made it a model for later imitations and so later Prakaraṇas, only a few in number, lost all novelty and grandeur. As a writer of Prakaraṇa, Bhavabhūti is decidedly inferior to Śūdraka but it is not in the field of Prakaraṇa that Bhavabhūti excels. His

33. Vide SD. VI, 143.

field is Nāṭaka and we have already discussed his contributions to it.

Bhavabhūti has rightly been regarded as the master of pathos and it is in the depiction of the Pathetic that his poetic powers get free scope. In the Prakaraṇa also he brings in the Karuṇa very successfully but he never loses sight of Śṛṅgāra. Peculiarly there is no other Rasa to be seen in the Mālatīmādhava but the Vipralambhaśṛṅgāra and Bībhatsa. In his handling of the plot, Bhavabhūti proves himself to possess more poetic genius than dramatic. As a result, his versification is grand and highly charming but his prose is flat. Throughout this long Prakaraṇa, we do not come across such an elegant prose as is found in the Mṛcchakaṭika. His prose is stiff, dull and boring at times.

The source and the Story

The plot is entirely of the Invented type. The main plot concerns Mādhava, the hero and Mālatī, the heroine, deeply in love with each other. The chief obstacle in the way of their happy union is the request of the king to marry Mālatī to his friend, Nandana. Bhūrivasu, the father of Mālatī, does not want to go against the desire of the king though he personally wishes to marry his daughter to Mādhava who is the son of his close friend, Devarāta. In order to escape the king's wrath, the father asks Kāmandakī to devise plans for the secret marriage of the two. Kāmandakī plans accordingly as she also wishes to see the pledge of Bhūrivasu and Devarāta fulfilled. These two were fellow-students and had promised in front of Kāmandakī and Saudāminī to solemnise the wedding of their son and daughter. There is a Subsidiary plot as well with Makaranda, a faithful friend of Mādhava as the hero and Madayantikā, the sister of Nandana, as the heroine. Through a very many vicissitudes, the lovers succeed in the end. There is an Episodical Incident too, having Aghoraghaṇṭa, a Kāpālika and Kapālakuṇḍalā, his female associate, in it.

The Prastāvanā

The Prastāvanā of the play is one that has become hackneyed by constant imitation. Bhavabhūti is always verbose in speaking about himself. The Sūtradhāra, accordingly, gives a long description of the poet's parentage, his learning and his great attainments. In this self-advertisement, it must be observed, there is nothing dramatic and the poet resorts to it only in submission to the Śāstra. Bhavabhūti takes the statement—*kavernāmānukīrtayet* of Bharata regarding the function of Sthāpaka to mean a description of the lineage of the poet. As a result, his long self-advertisement gives us so many points of historical interest but decidedly the Prastāvanā loses the dramatic charm which we find in the same of Bhāsa, Kālidāsa, Śūdraka, etc.

However, the self-glorification of the poet in the Prastāvanā is not all bragging. His very bold assertion—'*Utapatsyatesti mama ko'pi samānadharmā*' (I, 6) has definitely proved to be true. Bhavabhūti had his *samānadharmā* not only in his own times but even now he has them to appreciate his dramatic skill. Possessed of a great and sound knowledge of so many branches of learning, his boastful statements remind us of the satirical statements of George Bernard Shaw. However, Bhavabhūti inspired the later dramatists to indulge in self-glorification which in their hands became inane and insipid. Dramatic skill, as a consequence, languished.

The Prastāvanā, though rather tediously long, is markedly novel. The sudden change of the Sūtradhāra and his male associate into two important characters of Kāmandakī and her disciple is interesting and something new.

The Structure of the Plot

The Prakaraṇa is divided ino ten Acts and Bhavabhūti shows enough skill in filling all his Acts with so many marvellous or at least striking incidents. In order to bring in the hero, the playwright finds a difficulty and unlike his predecessor, Śūdraka, he introduces a long Viṣkambhaka to report the situation to the audience. Throughout the play there are eight Explanatory Devices of which four are Viṣkambhakas and the remaining Praveśakas. So many of these, however, hint at the looseness of the dramatic structure.

The five Stages of the Action, however, follow one another smoothly. The *ārambha* or Beginning of the Action is dealt in the first Act wherein the love of Mādhava and Mālatī is expressed. In this very Act, the impediment in the way of their happy union gets also its expression from the talks of Kāmandakī who is introduced as a venerable lady to both Mādhava and Mālatī and who is the brain behind the secret arrangements of the meeting of the lovers. The second and third stages, namely, *yatna* and *prāptyāśā* are seen in the second, third, fourth and fifth Acts. These Acts show the love pangs of the lovers; the various plots of Kāmandakī to effect secret meetings of them; the development of love between Makaranda and Madayantikā, the hero and heroine of the Episode; the presentation of Mālatī to Nandana, the king's friend. To present these facts the dramatist utilises so many devices. He introduces a tiger which attacks Madayantikā who is saved by her lover, Makaranda who kills the beast. This incident binds one close to the other. Similarly the Episodical Incident of the Kāpālika and Kāpālikī is introduced to represent the chivalry of the hero, Mādhava who saves Mālatī from impending death at the hands of the Kāpālika. All these incidents lead the hero towards the Prospect of Success (*prāptyāśā*).

The Niyatāpti and Phalāgama stages are reached in the last five Acts. Temporary union of Mālatī and Mādhava is eflected in the sixth and that of Makaranda and Madayantikā in the seventh Act. The eighth Act shows the fructification of Kāpālikī's plot against Mādhava. The Kāpālikī gets angry with Mādhava as he has killed her preceptor for the sake of Mālatī and steals her. Thus the temporary union of the lovers gets interrupted. The other pair of lovers also faces a great opposition from the enraged and deceived Nandana, the king's friend. The difficulty in which they are landed seems unsurmountable by human beings and so the playwright introduces in the ninth Act, the semi-divine character of Saudāminī, an ascetic lady having magic powers. Through her intervention, all the formidable obstacles are removed and the final Attainment of the Result (*phalāgama*) takes place. Thus the tenth Act brings about the happy union of all the lovers and through the gracious intervention of Saudāmini, the father of Mālatī, the king and his friend, Nandana also approve of the union of these adventurous pairs.

The technique

Bhavabhūti shows considerable skill in presenting his play as much dramatically as he can. Save his weakness shown in his use of so many Explanatory Devices, his effort to give all the incidents a dramatic unity and charm, must be appreciated. From this point of view, the introduction of the tiger, the Kāpālika–incident and the deception of Nandana by disguising Makaranda as Mālatī are highly interesting. These incidents are brought forward for the specific purpose of showing the gradual development of intensity of the ardour of the lovers, and the playwright is amply successful in this respect. But so far as the tiger incident is concerned, one must characterise it as a dramatic weakness, valuing though, at the same time, its importance in showing the sincere love of Makaranda for Madayantikā. Its chief weakness is the fact that such a scene cannot be presented on the stage and consequently the mere report of the incident fails to be effective. Similarly the way in which Bhavabhūti introduces Saudāminī is not dramatically effective. The audience is kept all through in the dark regarding her appearance. Suddenly she comes down from the skies in order to resolve the complexities. This resorting to the supernatural, though common in so many dramas, for the purpose of effecting the happy denouement which concerns the mortals of the world, must be accepted as a weak device. This is the reason why the authors of Nāṭyadarpaṇa explicitly deprecate the introduction of the divine beings in a Prakaraṇa. (*Nāṭake hyaṅgatvena divyo bhavati, prakaraṇe tu tathābhāvo'pi neṣṭaḥ*).[34]

The Kāpālika-incident is highly dramatic and it is one of the most interesting and living incidents of the play. The sudden appearance of the disheartened lover, Mādhava as a rescuer of his beloved Mālatī, estranged by the Kāpālika for the purpose of fulfilling the cruel rite of

34. ND. II, p. 117.

human sacrifice before the goddess, Cāmuṇḍā attracts perforce the attention of all, and everyone rejoices at the success of Mādhava in freeing Mālatī from the clutches of the inhuman Kāpālika and his accomplice.

The crafty device of disguising Makaranda as Mālatī and thereby arranging the elopement of her by Mādhava is also remarkable for its dramatic quality. Bhavabhūti has shown unmistakably his great imaginative faculty in conceiving these scenes. The revelation of Madayantikā's love for Makaranda by herself, elicited through the conversation of Lavaṅgikā and Buddharakṣitā is also well contrived. The long speech of Madayantikā, however, appears to be a little unseemly. It is not found in any other play that a young girl tells her love in so unabashed a manner even to her own friends. Still this frank confession of her love for Makaranda helps the playwright to prepare her for the elopement.

The Vṛtti and Diction

The Vṛtti of the play is chiefly Kaiśikī in conformation to the theme which is thoroughly romantic. The excellence of Bhavabhūti is felt in the presentation of the love-lorn hero. The easy flow of the highly romantic verses depicting the sincere love of Mādhava for Mālatī is so very perfect that Bhavabhūti can claim the epithet of Mahākavi simply for these charming pieces. His versification is elegant and free from all artificialities. The germ of the future announcement of the poet—*eko rasaḥ karuṇa eva*—may clearly be detected in the fact of his mastery in composing verses having the Vipralambha-śṛṅgāra Sentiment. These verses are memorable and everlasting and on these depends the poetic greatness of the playwright.

Though Kaiśikī is the chief Vṛtti in the play, there are other Vṛttis as well employed by the poet in the respective treatment of other Sentiments. The Vīra and Bībhatsa Sentiments, for example, are expressed through a different Vṛtti, viz: the *ārabhaṭī*.

So far as the versification is concerned, Bhavabhūti is to be credited with unreserved praise. Elegance, simplicity and effective charm–all these abound in his poems. But regarding his prose one must be cautious. The prose of Bhavabhūti is stiff and greatly laboured. Moreover, the pieces in prose are at times unusually lengthy and are tedious on this account. He announces himself to be a great scholar and to be one versed in almost all the branches of learning. It is perhaps due to this that he is never able to forget his great mastery over the science of language. The egotistical attitude, which is in direct contravention with the effacement of individuality, the most essential requirement of a dramatist, impairs his prose style. The long compounds, love for quaint and commonly out-of-use phrases, and the prosaic nature of the prose dialogue strike a discordant note in the play. His prose is so flat that it hardly shows any sign of dramatic sense. Whenever he resorts to prose, he loses that charm and impression which mark his verses. Particularly the description of the condition of love-lorn Mālatī and Madayantikā (Act III & VII) is tediously lengthy and void of any charm. Another example of his long and tedious prose is the speech of Saudāminī in the Viṣkambhaka in the beginning of Act IX. In his short conversational prose he is quite all right but whenever he resorts to a lengthy speech, and he often does so, he is a failure. These portions burden the play and affect adversely the easy flow of the drama. His use of commonly out-of-use words (as *saṁstyāya* for *gṛha* and the like) and long compounds reminds of the statement of Bharata—

> *'Cekrīḍitādyaiḥ śabdaistu kāvyabandhā bhavanti ye*
> *Veśyā iva na śobhante kamaṇḍaludharair dvijaiḥ'.*

The employment of the Kaiśikī as the chief Vṛtti in the play is also, it seems on the ground of later treatises, a new thing. Though Bharata says nothing regarding the use of Vṛtti in a Prakaraṇa, the later formulators, particularly Rāmacandra and Guṇacandra, cleary state that Kaiśikī should not be the chief Vṛtti of this type. This observation appears to be unjustified since by the employment of Kaiśikī, the drama does not suffer at all.

Whether Bhavabhūti was influenced by his forerunner, Śūdraka, is difficult to ascertain. Even if it were there, Bhavabhūti did not improve by it. But that he was deeply influenced by Kālidāsa and his plays is plain enough. The entire ninth Act containing the pathetic grief of Mādhava at the loss of Mālatī is modelled upon the fourth Act of Vikramorvaśī. The versification of the play also evinces the influence of Kālidāsaover the playwright.

The originality, which can be marked clearly in the Prakaraṇa, and which is more manifest in his later dramas, chiefly in the Uttararāmacarita, is his fondness for the pathetic sentiment. Whenever the playwright gets a scope and the Prakaraṇa supplies him with many, he gives many charmingly pathetic pieces of great poetic worth. It may be held that the favour shown by the poet to the Pathetic Sentiment is responsible for the conspicuous absence of the character of Vidūṣaka and of the Hāsya-rasa in general. The employment of the Bībhatsa-rasa is also a speciality of this play, and the mastery of the poet in its portrayal is almost unsurpassed. In the Veṇīsaṃhāra of Bhaṭṭanārāyaṇa, there are poems having the Bībhatsa but the gruesome description of the cremation ground by Bhavabhūti is far superior to them in all respects.

Conclusion

As a writer of Prakaraṇa, Bhavabhūti must be credited with a very high position inspite of his failings. Taking for granted his particular poetical bias, he is undoubtedly one of the best dramatists. He is second in position among the Prakaraṇa writers and rightly he may be said to be second only to Śūdraka and to none else. He might not have superseded Śūdraka as a playwright but he has given no chance to others as well to supersede him. His rich imagination and dramatic devices are noteworthy and his versification is almost Kālidāsian in effect and charm. The invention of plot also bears the stamp of his high dramatic sense and it is due to this fact that he should be considered as one of the ablest playwrights in the field of Prakaraṇa type of drama. If Śūdraka gives us the pageant of a new walk of life, where the noble and ignoble meet and the noble comes out victorious proving thus the worth of sincerity of a courtesan as a lover, Bhavabhūti also depicts a newer aspect of life which, although being less rich in variegation, is no less impressive for its vital and emotional appeal.

In conclusion, it must be said that the Mālatīmādhava does not mark any regression in point of charm and interest from the Mṛcchakaṭika.

SECTION—3 : NĀṬIKĀ

It is difficult to ascertain now what Nāṭikās served as models to Bharata at the time of his codification. There must have been a good number of Nāṭikās that preceded the Nāṭyaśāstra but none has survived the ravages of time.

The oldest extant Nāṭikā is Bhāsa's Pratijñā-Yaugandharāyaṇa which has been named as the Pratijñā-Nāṭikā. Though there are many points of dissimilarity between this and the later Nāṭikās, yet the play ascribed to Bhāsa presents the oldest form of the genre and the conception of it in the mind of a playwright.

According to the rules of Bharata, the Nāṭikā has a mixed nature. The plot of it is to be like that of the Prakaraṇa that is, of the Invented type (*utpannaṁ vastu*) and the hero is to be like that of the Nāṭaka, that is, he must be a king. In addition, the plot should have a heroine and the main Sentiment to be displayed should be the Śṛṅgāra. So far as the structure of this type is concerned Bharata allots only four Acts to it, with women as the most important characters. Śṛṅgāra being the chief sentiment, Kaiśikī should be the chief Vṛtti of this type.

Bhāsa

While composing the Pratijñā-Yaugandharāyaṇa, the playwright, it seems, must have been well acquainted with these principles. As a creative artist should, Bhāsa also did not follow the rules in their entirety but introduced new things in it. Simply for these innovations, it will not be justified to call this play by some other name. The nature of the plot and the structure of the play clearly show that the play is composed on the Bharatan lines and falls under the Nāṭikā variety.

The Vastu

So far as the plot is concerned, the plot of the Pratijñā-Yaugandharāyaṇa is romantic in nature and is related to a lady. The story of Udayana's love for Vāsavadattā and her ultimate elopement constitute the theme of the play. The name is derived from the minister of Udayana, Yaugandharāyaṇa by name, who is under a vow to execute both—the freedom of the king from bondage and the marriage of the king with the princess of his love. The play follows the Nāṭyaśāstra also in its number of Acts. There are four Acts according to the prescription of the Śāstra.

The main deviation from Bharata, in this play, is that women have almost no part in the action. Another deviation is this that the playwright is more concerned with depicting the loyal minister's policy than the love affair of the king. But this does not, in the least, lessen the importance of the romance which shines throughout the play and is treated as the motive of the action. As a natural corollary of the second deviation, it is Yaugandharāyaṇa, who is the hero of the play.

The Nāṭikā bears everywhere the stamp of genius of the playwright. His handling of the theme is masterful and evinces a keen dramatic sense. Though he takes up the love affair of Udayana as his theme, he never brings in Udayana or Vāsavadattā on the stage. The love affair and even the elopement of Vāsavadattā take place behind the screen, only the repercussions of these on Yaugandharāyaṇa are presented on the stage. The play is full with action and dramatic charm. It becomes the more charming due to the simple but meaningful use of prose and verse. Bhāsa's style nowhere suffers from exaggeration and so the play is not burdened with a great number of verses, though in the power of versification Bhāsa is one among the best poets.

The Prastāvanā

The Prastāvanā is typical of Bhāsa. It is remarkably brief and it introduces the main action in only eleven lines. The Sūtradhāra announces the play to be a Prakaraṇa, which seems strange. Though the hero of the play is of the nature of the Prakaraṇa variety still the play cannot properly be called a Prakaraṇa due to its structure which conforms to the Nāṭikā. This is perhaps the reason why a new category is accepted by Rāmacandra and Guṇacandra in the Nāṭyadarpaṇa as Prakaraṇī. Quite probably this play by Bhāsa led them to accept this new category. Whatever it may be, the play fits in with the Nāṭikā variety in structure and theme. The theme is Associated with a lady (devīsambandhā). Though neither king Udayana nor Vāsavadattā appears before the audience, they are the central figures around whom the play moves.

The first Act presents Yaugandharāyaṇa, the minister, anxiously directing a messenger to carry a message to king Udayana. The King is out on hunting. The minister comes to know that king Pradyota has laid a trap there to capture Udayana. Knowing that Udayana is famous for his power of taming wild elephants by means of his lyre (vīṇā), Pradyota has prepared a wooden elephant and placed it in a dense jungle. The minister tells all this to the messenger and asks him to be so quick as to reach the king before the next day and check the king from going to capture the elephant. While he writes the message, a messenger from the king arrives and reports that king Udayana has been captured by the enemies and carried a captive to their city. This news upsets Yaugandharāyaṇa but he resolves to free the king from his captivity. Suddenly there arrives a Brāhmaṇa who gives to him a disguise which is magical. The minister accepts it and promises to rescue the king by going there himself in disguise.

The first Viṣkambhaka

The second Act presents the court of Pradyota. The king is in a fix in selecting a proper match for his daughter, Vāsavadattā, for whose hands so many kings have sent their proposals. To none of them the king says anything. This is reported in the short Viṣkambhaka by the Kañcukin.

The Kañcukin then introduces the king who comes thinking about Udayana. The Kañcukin asks him about his decision on a bridegroom for the princess. The messenger of Kāśirāja is waiting for the king's dicision. The king calls upon the queen to discuss the question. He then soliloquises that he is anxiously waiting for the news of Udayana for whose capture Śālaṅkāyana has been sent. Then the queen enters with whom the king goes on discussing the question of his daughter's marriage. The king comes to know that Vāsavadattā is learning to play on the lyre. The queen leaves the choice of a suitable match to the king and asks him to choose one among the kings who have sent their proposals. The playwright here puts a very beautiful *patākāsthānaka*. Suddenly the Kañcukin enters and says—'*Vatsarājaḥ*', which connected with the preceding statement of the king gives the sense that Vatsarāja is the chosen bridegroom. At the question of the king, the Kañcukin says that Śālankāyana has successfully captured Udayana and has brought him to the capital. The king cannot very easily believe the news. However, he then enquires of Yaugandharāyaṇa and orders the Kañcukin to treat Udayana as an honourable guest. Immediately the king and queen decide to marry Vāsavadattā to Udayana. The Kañcukin then brings in Udayana's lyre, Ghoṣavatī by name, and presents it to Pradyota who sends it again to the princess Vāsavadattā. The Act ends.

The third Act shows the arrival of Yaugandharāyaṇa and his party to Ujjayinī, the capital of Pradyota. They all are in disguise. Yaugandharāyaṇa, Rumaṇvat and the Vidūṣaka—all enter and kick up a false row and at last they retire to a house where Yaugandharāyaṇa enquires of Udayana and the Vidūṣaka reports that he has met the king. Yaugandharāyaṇa then asks the Vidūṣaka to go to meet the king once again and to say that the plan of his escape is to fructify the next day. The elephant is ready and everything is well arranged. The Vidūṣaka then relates that the king is not in a mind to submit to the plan. Pointing out the reason of his unwillingness, the Vidūṣaka very humorously states that to the king captivity has become very pleasant since it has given him the opportunity of seeing the princess Vāsavadattā. The loyal minister gets confounded. He then takes the second vow that he will execute both—the freedom of Udayana and the elopement of the princess.

A Praveśaka

A Praveśaka in the beginning of the fourth Act reports the escape of king Udayana and Vāsavadattā. The scene is a very lively one. A royal servant is searching after and calling aloud Gātrasevaka, the mahout of the princess. He finds him after much enquiry, in a tipsy condition and asks him to lead the elephant to the princess. The mahout, however, goes on talking irrelevantly. The royal servant then reports through an *ākāśabhāṣita* that Udayana is going out with Vāsavadattā. Hearing this news, the mahout throws off his disguise and tells that he is not a servant of the royal house but a secret spy of Yaugandharāyaṇa. He then goes in search of Yaugandharāyaṇa and reports that Yaugandharāyaṇa is fighting bravely with the forces of Pradyota, who, however, capture him.

After this the proper Act begins with a group of common people who are making noise and praising the valiant role of Yaugandharāyaṇa in the safe escape of his lord. Then the playwright presents the captivated Yaugandharāyaṇa. Though he is wounded and chained, he is happy for the success of his plans. To him then comes the minister of Pradyota who makes disparaging comments regarding his plot. At this the valiant minister, like a shrewd politician, retorts that the capture of Udayana was also done by means of deception. The minister of Pradyota deprecates the conduct of Yaugandharāyaṇa towards his lord (Pradyota), who honourably treated Udayana. Yaugandharāyaṇa, however, goes on supporting all his activities. In the meantime, the Kañcukin conveys the wish of the king that Yaugandharāyaṇa should accept his friendship, which, however, the latter rejects. Then the news from the palace comes that king Pradyota along with his queen is solemnising the wedding of Udayana and Vāsavadattā represented as bridegroom and bride by their pictures. This news gladdens the minister and he accepts the proposal of friendship and, in answer to the query of Pradyota's minister, utters the Bharatavākya. The play ends.

The Style

The play is very deftly executed. The diction of the dramatist is simple and charming. Short sentences, easy but apt verses and above all, a very successful use of humour—these are the remarkable characteristic features of the play. In characterisation as well, Bhāsa is superb. The character of Yaugandharāyaṇa has been depicted in such a manner that none can but praise it. The loyal feelings, strong determination and keen talent of the minister—all are presented in a charming manner. The play is full of action and Bhāsa uses only two Explanatory Devices which are cleverly executed.

Conclusion

We have already seen how Bhāsa's talents raised the Nāṭaka variety to a high standard of excellence. In his Nāṭikā as well, the same elevated standard is maintained. It is regrettable that the later playwrights, perhaps due to their ignorance of Bhāsa, could not take a leaf out of his book. They were masters of the Śāstras, but they singularly lacked in the dramatic talents of Bhāsa.

Harṣa

The next playwright who took up this form was Śrī Harṣa who produced two Nāṭikās. His Nāgānanda has been already noticed. We will discuss here the technique of his two Nāṭikās—Ratnāvalī and Priyadarśikā. His Nāṭikās especially the Ratnāvalī, fixed practically the form of this type. There are serious deviations in the Pratijñāyaugandharāyaṇa which do not allow us to call it a Nāṭikā in its true sense. But Ratnāvalī follows the model suggested by Bharata most faithfully and it is this play that serves as a model to the later formulators. The definition of this form as is found in the Daśarūpaka clearly shows that Dhanañjaya had before him Ratnāvalī as the model. The popularity of Ratnāvalī among the formulators seems to have rested on Harṣa's following the Śāstra faithfully. In fact, Harṣa's Nāṭikās clearly show his deep and extensive knowledge of the dramatic principles. Though he follows the rules very faithfully yet his Nāṭikās are creations of great artistic excellence. The reason is not far to seek. Harṣa knew his own limits and so never went beyond his depth. With his limited power he treated his themes according to the lines suggested by the Nāṭyaśāstra. No wonder, therefore, that Harṣa's Nāṭikās have always had a tremendous stage-success and appreciation from the readers. The success which he attained in his first specimen urged him on to the composition of the other. Yet the fact is that there is a striking resemblance between the two Nāṭikās. Harṣa is the first dramaturgist who produced the typical Nāṭikā in Sanskrit.

The Vastu

In his conception and execution, Harṣa proves a faithful follower of the Śāstra. His themes in both the pieces are Invented, and both the pieces abound in female characters. The plots are associated with ladies and are highly romantic in nature. The heroes are of the Dhīra-lalita type. Acts are also four in number in each, according as the Śāstra demands.

The themes of both the plays are the love affair of king Udayana. The Ratnāvalī depicts the love of the king for Ratnāvalī, the princess of Ceylon and the Priyadarśikā, love for another princess of the same name. The playwright presents both the plays almost in the same manner. In both, the queen Vāsavadattā proves at first to be a formidable barrier on the way of the king's union with the second beloved but in both, she turns favourable in the end and herself solemnises the king's wedding with the new lady of his heart, coming to know that the girl is her sister. In both the plays, the princesses in question are placed under the queen's charge under fictitious names and are included in the group of attendants in the harem. The king, in both, suddenly espies them and falls in love. He fears the wrath of the queen and so plans with the Vidūṣaka to meet his new lady-loves secretly. However, the queen comes to know everything and out of her jealousy puts to prison the wretched girls and the Vidūṣaka. By the help of a magician in the Ratnāvalī, and by administering poison in the Priyadarśikā, the union is executed in the presence of the Kañcukin and others coming from the respective courts of the fathers of the princesses, who recognise and identify the imprisoned girls as their princesses. In both the plays, the wrongly treated girls turn to be cousin-sisters of the queen and they are reported to have been offered to king Udayana as brides. In both, the queen magnanimously offers the princesses to the ashamed but pleased king.

The tenor of both the plays is thus almost identical. Even the situations and dialogue resemble each other in many places. Excepting two devices and a few names of the dramatic characters, the two are indeed the echoes of each other. The first device is to be seen in the Ratnāvalī where Yaugandharāyaṇa is the agent in bringing the princess and handing her over to the queen with the avowed aim of executing the union of her with the king. The minister has believed in an augury that the king, who will marry Ratnāvalī, will be the Rājacakravartin or the King of kings and so has asked the king of Ceylon to marry his daughter to Udayana. But the Ceylonese king has rejected the proposal as Udayana is already married to Vāsavadattā. The crafty minister has then circulated the canard of the death of Vāsavadattā in fire and has again sent his proposal to the king of Ceylon who has agreed to it and sent the princess to the capital of Udayana under the escort of his Kañcukin and others. On the way they have been separated from one another after a shipwreck, and the minister has found the princess and handed her over to Vāsavadattā, hoping that some day or other the marriage will take place.

The second device is employed in the Priyadarśikā. It is a charming one and perhaps served as a model for Bhavabhūti. The playwright puts a miniature play in the third Act. Vāsavadattā wishes to see the enactment of a play that depicts the wooing of Vāsavadattā by Udayana. The play is arranged in the harem and Priyadarśikā, known as Āraṇyakā plays the role of Vāsavadattā and her friend Manoramā plays that of the king. She, out of her love for Priyadarśikā, plans with the Vidūṣaka and gives her role to the king himself. Thus the king gets a grand chance of meeting his beloved before the very eyes of the queen. However, the plan becomes known to the queen in the end and she puts both the

Vidūṣaka and Priyadarśikā to prison. The device is well executed and speaks of the skill of the playwright. Excepting these two, there is nothing remarkable in the two plays, which can give a characteristic distinction to each. We will discuss both the plays simultaneously Act by Act.

The Prastāvanā

The Prastāvanā of both the plays are brief and serve the purpose well. The playwright names the play, playwright and the occasion and introduces Yaugandharāyaṇa in the Ratnāvalī, and the Kañcukin of Dṛḍhavarman in the Priyadarśikā. The praise of the play, playwright and the actors is the same in both the plays. The same verse is seen with a slight change in Nāgānanda as well. This praise is called the *prarocanā* by the theorists. The Prastāvanā of the Ratnāvalī is of the *kathodghāta* type as Yaugandharāyaṇa enters uttering the words of the Sūtradhāra. The other one falls under the category of *prayogātiṣaya* where the character is introduced by a direct reference to him like—'Here comes such and such'.

The Viṣkambhakas

In both the plays, the first Act is preceded by Viṣkambhakas. By these, the playwright supplies the preliminary information. In the Ratnāvalī, Yaugandharāyaṇa speaks how his plan stands. He makes it known that while the princess was on her way, her ship sank but fortunately she reached the shore. Yaugandharāyaṇa however, managed to contact her and to bring her to the capital and then hand her over to the queen. He further states that the courtiers escorting the princess have also survived and started along with commander Rumaṇvat to fight the Kośalas. In the Priyadarśikā, the Kañcukin of Dṛḍhavarman is presented who reports that the king Dṛḍhavarman is attacked by the king of Kaliṅga for the former's decision to marry his daughter to Udayana inspite of Kaliṅga's prayer to the contrary, and that unluckily while he (Kañcukin) was escorting the princess to the capital of Udayana secretly, he halted at the palace of king Vindhyaketu, where he lost the princess and came to know that Vindhyaketu had also been killed by some unknown men. The disheartened Kañcukin decides to return to his own lord who lies imprisoned and sorely wounded.

The first Act then presents the king Udayana and his Vidūṣaka, Vasantaka by name, in both the plays. In the Ratnāvalī, the king is presented as observing the Festival of Love (*Madanamahotsava*) along with queen Vāsavadattā. The heroine, Ratnāvalī alias Sāgarikā, is also shown, who sees the king secretly and recognises him to be the person to whom her father has betrothed her.

The first Act in the Priyadarśikā brings in the king who hears from Vijayasena the report of his victory over king Vindhyaketu and comes to know that Vijayasena has found a girl there, who is perhaps the daughter of the dead king. Udayana immediately asks the attendant to send her to Vāsavadattā. The king also orders for her training in all the arts. The Act ends with the decision of the king to send Vijayasena for the conquest of Kaliṅga.

A Praveśaka

The second Act of Ratnāvalī is preceded by a Praveśaka. The Praveśaka, having two female characters, reports that the king has obtained a magic power from a sage by which he can produce flowers in any tree at any time and that his power has been applied and found successful. A female attendant goes to report it to eth queen. The other goes to meet Sāgarikā who is reported to be resting in the plantain-orchard after leaving the pet parrot to the attendant's charge.

Then the playwright presents Sāgarikā in a state of intense love. She weeps and curses the God of Love and at last draws a picture of her beloved, the king Udayana. The female attendant, Susaṅgatā by name, enters with her cage and sees everything unperceived. When they meet, the shy lady wishes to hide the picture but her friend discovers it and sympathises with her. She then narrates the whole story of her love to Susaṅgatā who also humorously draws the picture of Sāgarikā by the side of the king. The extreme love-lorn condition of the heroine is depicted on conventional lines. Suddenly they hear the announcement from behind the curtain that a monkey has broken its chains and fled from the palace. this freed monkey is then reported to have opened the cage door and freed the parrot. This frightens the pair as they fear that the trained parrot will divulge all their secrets and so they begin to pursue it. The king, who is also out in the garden with the Vidūṣaka to see the flowering of the tree by his own magic, learns everything from the bird who repeats everything it has heard. The reporting of what the bird says by the Vidūṣaka is executed by the playwright in a humorous manner. He listens to it looking up and goes on reporting. The Vidūṣaka, then, finds the picture and hands it over to the king. In the meantime, Sāgarikā and her companion come there to fetch the picture and thus the first meeting of the two lovers takes place. But the meeting is interrupted by the approach of the queen. Sāgarikā hides herself behind the trees and the Vidūṣaka conceals the picture under his cloak. Unfortunately he begins to dance in joy on hearing the queen's admitting the king's magic powers, and the picture falls. The king is taken aback at this discovery and the foolish Vidūṣaka makes the situation worse by trying to shield the king. The queen shakes with anger and leaves the place in a frenzy. The king also makes haste to placate the queen by vouchsafing his deep love to her.

Priyadarśikā

The second Act of the Priyadarśikā has got no Viṣkambhaka before it. The Act depicts the meeting of Priyadarśikā alias Āraṇyakā and Udayana in the garden where Āraṇyakā has come to collect flowers. The king is captivated by her beauty and by way of rescuing her from the attack of the bees, a device suggested by Kālidāsa (Abhijñāna-Śākuntala), embraces her. The girl also coming to know from the Vidūṣaka that her rescuer is none other than the king Udayana himself, mutters to herself, like Ratnāvalī, that the rescuer is the man to whom she is betrothed. The second Act ends with this first meeting.

A Praveśaka

In the third Act of the Ratnāvalī, the playwright furnishes by means of a Praveśaka the information that there is going on a plan to unite the lovers in the bower. Kāñcanamāla, the confidant of the queen says to another that she has overheard the talks of the Vidūṣaka and Susaṅgatā and come to know that Sāgarikā and Susaṅgatā are to meet the king that very evening. In the disguise of Vāsavadattā and Kāñcanamāla respectively. She hurries then to report the matter to the queen.

Then the playwright brings in the love-lorn king and the Vidūṣaka. They go to the proper place and the king waits while the Vidūṣaka goes in search of the two damsels. The queen also, accompanied by Kāñcanamāla is brought in, whom the foolish Vidūṣaka takes to be Sāgarikā and Susaṅgatā and leads them to the king. The king also under the fit of strong passion accosts her as Sāgarikā and makes loud protestations of his love. The Vidūṣaka becomes as bold as to condemn Vāsavadattā as 'harsh'. This comedy of errors continues until the queen, no longer able to swallow the eulogies of the king, opens her veil and the king gets dumb-founded at the order of things. The queen then goes out along with her attendant in an extreme anguish, neglecting the repentant king who has fallen on her feet. Sāgarikā also in the guise of Vāsavadattā appears, who is greatly troubled by the recent discovery of her attachment to the king. She decides to hang herself from the nearby *aśoka* tree and is, however, noticed by the Vidūṣaka who cries aloud for help. The king quickly comes and removes the noose from her neck and he comes to realise by her voice that she is not the queen. When the king is thus engaged with his new love, the queen comes again repenting for her rudeness to the king. What she sees is too much for her to bear and she condmens the king and orders imprisonment for Sāgarikā and the Vidūṣaka.

Priyadarśikā

The third Act of the Priyadarśikā brings about the meeting of the king and Āraṇyakā by means of a trick. A staging of a play takes place at the order of the queen, the subject-matter of which is the winning of Vāsavadattā by Udayana. Āraṇyakā and her friend, Manoramā, are entrusted with the roles of Vāsavadattā and Udayana respectively. According to a plan between the Vidūṣaka and Manoramā, the king himself enters the stage and Manoramā keeps aloof. The queen scents mischief and her suspicion ripens when she sees the Vidūṣaka lying near the door of the green-room. She finds out Manoramā as well. In her fury she orders Manoramā to put the Vidūṣaka under chains. The same treatment is meted out to Āraṇyakā. The king tries in vain to placate the angry queen. The miniature play thus ends. In the conception and execution of this scene Harṣa shows commendable dramatic talent. Humour, fine dialogue and a series of interesting actions—these have rendered the scene a success.

A Praveśaka

The fourth Act in both the plays brings about the happy union of the lovers. In the Ratnāvalī, it is reported by Susaṅgatā that the queen has sent Sāgarikā to an unknown place at midnight and that she has handed to her a necklace of gems to be offered to some Brāhmaṇa. The weeping Susaṅgatā finds the Vidūṣaka in front of her. The Vidūṣaka is very happy at his sudden release by the queen. Susaṅgatā presents the necklace to him. Hearing the fate of Sāgarikā, the sorrowful Vidūṣaka weeps but accepts the necklace to give solace to the king. Both of them express their astonishment as to how such a valuable ornament came to Sāgarikā.

The rest of the Act shows the king deeply rueing for Sāgarikā, the presentation of the necklace to the king by the Vidūṣaka who puts it on at the request of the king, the advent of one, Vijayavarman who reports of the victory of the royal force in the battle with Kośala and the coming of a magician from Ujjayinī who shows magic feats to the king and the queen. When they are absorbed in seeing the magic, the king is informed that the chief minister of Ceylon along with Vasubhūti, the Kañcukin, has come. The queen is eager to hear the news of her maternal uncle, the king of Ceylon, and dismisses the magician. The minister and the Kañcukin are then called in. They come and relate their story of how they lost the princess who was given in marriage to Udayana at the request of Yaugandharāyaṇa. The queen is grieved at the news and weeps for her sister. At this time, the announcement from behind the curtain reports that there is a great fire in the harem. The anxious queen asks the king to go post haste to save Sāgarikā who is chained therein. The king, careless of the entreaties of all, rushes into the burning palace and meets the chained Sāgarikā. He rescues her and almost immediately sees in wonder that there is no trace of fire. Then the recognition of Sāgarikā by Vasubhūti and the Kañcukin as the lost princess, makes the queen blush at her rudeness to her. At her request the king removes Sāgarikā's chains. Yaugandharāyaṇa is then presented, who apologises to the king for his actions and accounts for them. The queen herself presents the hands of Sāgarikā to the king and the play terminates.

Priyadarśikā

The end of the Priyadarśikā is brought about almost in the self-same fashion. The fire scene is excluded here. Here also in the Praveśaka, Manoramā reports that Āraṇyakā is still under chains and that her agony is so keen that she has attempted to commit suicide but has somehow been dissuaded by her. Manoramā wants to convey this to the king through the Vidūṣaka. Then appears Kāñcanamāla, the confidant of the queen, who tells Manoramā that she is out to fetch Sāṅkṛtyāyanī to the queen. In the course of the conversation, she says that the queen has received a letter from the wife of Dṛḍhavarman entreating her to ask Udayana to arrange for the freedom of Dṛḍhavarman. Dṛḍhavarman being the maternal uncle, Vāsavadattā is too much perturbed at this news and wishes to have a talk with Sāṅkṛtyāyanī.

Then the playwright presents the queen and Sāṅkṛtyāyanī who consoles the queen and assures her that Udayana will difinitely take steps to free Dṛḍhavarman. The queen takes this with a grain of salt since she thinks that the king does no more love her. The king then comes and, knowing the reason of the queen's sorrow, says that he has already taken steps to crush the king of Kaliṅga. This statement gladdens the queen and immediately afterwards the arrival of Vijayasena, the commander, and the Kañcukin of Dṛḍhavarman is conveyed to the king. They come and narrate how Kaliṅga has been defeated and Dṛḍhavarman reinstated on his throne. This news pleases all and the queen wishes to see Āraṇyakā. Sāṅkṛtyāyanī goes herself to bring her. In the meantime, the Kañcukin narrates the story how the princess Priyadarśikā bound for Udayana's place was lost. Manoramā, now, brings the news that Āraṇyakā has taken poison and is about to die. All are alarmed. The queen asks to bring her before the king who can cure her. Āraṇyakā is brought in and the king cures her. The Kañcukin recognises her to be the lost princess, and the queen clasps her in affectionate embrace as her sister. In the end, the Vidūṣaka humorously says to the queen that the physician should be awarded a prize. The queen smilingly nods and presents Āraṇyakā to the king.

The technique of Harṣa

So far as the dramatisation is concerned, Harṣa is undoubtedly a skilful artist. His mastery over and appropriate use of the different *Saṁdhyaṅgas* have won all round appreciation from the theorists. The scheme of the Junctures and Elements of the Plot are so markedly observed in the plays of Harṣa, especially in these two Nāṭikās, that illustrations of these are generally supplied from these two. The success of Harṣa proves undoubtedly that the Saṃdhyaṅgas (64 in number) were conceived by a master mind whose dramatic sense was very deep. Even if the plot of a play is weak and a mere shadow of another, as is the case with Priyadarśikā, the proper use of these Saṃdhyaṅgas assures the success of the play. Harṣa's success depends not so much upon his power of invention or imagination as upon his practical sense and wonderful alchemy of making a creative use of the rules laid down in the Śāstras.

His diction is, in addition, very charming and suitable for the drama. He is never verbose or pedantic. In certain places his dialogue is so effective that one cannot but appreciate it. The sense of humour exhibited in his plays is also commendable and in a few cases (e.g., the sayings of the Vidūṣaka in the end of both the Nāṭikās) the humour is of a very high standard. Though his Vidūṣakas are not as dignified as that of Śūdraka, they are very naturally and charmingly drawn.

Conclusion

The influence of Harṣa on the later writers of Nāṭikā was immense and none could outsoar his all pervasive influence. To them Harṣa became the model for slavish imitation and so all the later plays become void of originality. The form and content of all the later Nāṭikās, in general, tended to be mechanical and so no development is noticable.

Rājaśekhara

In the field of Nāṭikā, Rājaśekhara has only one to his credit—the Viddhaśālabhañjikā. As his Nāṭakas manifest the signs of decadence so does his solitary Nāṭikā, inspite of his pride as a great scholar of so many branches of learning. It is sure that he is well informed about the treatises on dramaturgy, but his plays show that he had little dramatic sense. His poetic skill and mastery of language and the conceit therefor, do not allow him to remain satisfied with a mere adherence to and following of the rules as is done by his predecessor, Harṣa. His imaginative faculty languishes into mere declamation, and consequently in his Nāṭikā we get a series of verses, many of which are superfluous from the view point af the theme.

The Vastu

The theme is the usual love-intrigue of the king. The king Vidyādharamalla dreams of a beautiful maiden one night, who presents him her necklace. The necklace is not 'such stuff as dreams are made on'. He keeps it and falls headlong in love with the maiden of his dream. The effusions of this new feeling of love are so explicit that the queen turns jealous. The king ignores it and goes on describing his love to the Vidūṣaka. He sees the picture and a statuette of that very girl in the picture-gallery. The king gets more and more eager to see her in flesh and blood but inspite of his attempts she remains unseen. At last he comes to meet her and the queen herself is caught in her own toils and marries her to the king. The maiden turns out to be the cousin of the queen. By and by it is discovered that behind the dream and all other magical incidents, occuring in the course of the king's frantic search for his beloved, there is the plan of Bhāgurāyaṇa, the minister. He, like Yaugandharāyaṇa of the Ratnāvalī, believing in the augury that the daughter of king Candravarman will make her husband the king of kings, brings the only daughter of that king to the palace of his own king. Candravarman having no son announced publicly that the baby was his son and accordingly brought her up like a young boy. The secret was known to Bhāgurāyaṇa but the queen did not know it. She knew her to be a boy and so she was least worried about her. In her attempt to play a trick on the king she arranges a marriage of the king with the maiden masquerading as a boy for fun, but unfortunately to the queen, the secret becomes out and the king wins the palms of his beloved.

Though the story is modelled upon the Nāṭikās of Harṣa, Rājaśekhara shows considerable novelty in its presentation. The presentation of a girl in the guise of a boy is enough dramatic and dramatically does the queen turn a victim to her own plan of outwitting the king. Though the love-lorn condition of the king for the visionary beloved appears to be a bit over-wrought and his lamentations, at times, reach the point of tedium, the style in general is lucid and easy.

The Denouement of the play is brought about by two funny situations and these speak of Rājaśekhara's skill and dramatic sense. The Vidūṣaka is, as usual, the object of ridicule and merry-making to the retinue of the queen. He is made the object of merriment by Mekhalā, the foster-sister of the queen, which hurts the friend of the king most. The Vidūṣaka is called forth to marry a girl who turns out to be a servant of the royal household. The situation definitely gives rise to laughter but the sense of humour here is not of a high order. The disgusted Vidūṣaka plans for a retaliation and is successful in making her kneel down before him. At this, Mekhalā again is enraged and at the instance of the queen plans a similar trick to be played on the king himself. In this also, the queen and her patry are out-witted as the facts regarding the son of Candravarman becomes out and another maid who was thought of by the queen to be married to Mṛgāṅkavarman, the disguised daughter of Candravarman, is also offered to the king in marriage.

It is strange and unreasonable that the king himself is kept in darkness about the truth of his marriage. He plays almost a fool in agreeing to marry in deference to the queen's wishes. The secret is known only to the Vidūṣaka and the wise minister. The playwright manages admirably to make the end remarkably dramatic. The confused queen and the no less confused king, though with pleasure, provide us with a highly interesting and hilarious scene. A messenger is also presented in the end, who conveys that a son has been born to Candravarman who wishes to give his daughter, in the disguise of a boy, in marriage to a fit person. Thus the play ends in a happy union.

The Prastāvanā

The Prastāvanā is most prosaic but admirably brief. Rājaśekhara, though one of the greatest self-conceited writers in Sanskrit literature, dwells not much upon his own poetic powers and attainments. By the help of a song from behind the curtain and *ākāśa-bhāṣita*, the

Sūtradhāra announces the wish of the poet's patron to play the Nāṭikā and after a reference to the author and his powers in only two verses, goes out to reappear in the role of Haradāsa, a disciple of the minister, Bhāgurāyaṇa.

The first Viṣkambhaka

There are, in all, four Explanatory Devices of which three are Praveśakas and one is a Viṣkambhaka. The Viṣkambhaka in the beginning reports the fact of Candravarman's announcement of his desire to let his daughter pass for a son. Further it adds that the minister of king Vidyādharamalla has very judiciously brought that girl to the palace of the king to effect her marriage with him.

The first Act is taken up with the king's dream and his reactions thereto. The reactions are contained in what the king says to the Vidūṣaka.

A Praveśaka

A Praveśaka is then employed, in which it is reported that the queen is going to effect the marriage of the so-called son of Candravarman to Kuvalayamālā, a refugee princess, in order to make the king desist from paying amorous attentions to the said princess. She is also intending to play a practical joke upon the Vidūṣaka.

In the second Act we find the Vidūṣaka in a state of anger at being befooled, who runs to the king in the garden. The king is already there, lost in the enjoyment of melodious love-song, sung off the stage.

A Praveśaka

Another Praveśaka introduces two female attendants of whom one discloses the plan of the minister, and how at the order of the minister she showed the maiden, Mṛgāṅkāvalī to the king one day early in the morning, and placed the necklace on the hands of the king. She makes it clear how Mṛgāṅkāvalī has become elusive to the king. The other then reports that she has assisted the revengeful Vidūṣaka to outwit Mekhalā, the foster-sister of the queen by telling her in a weird voice that she will die within seven days if she does not bow down to a Brāhmaṇa and crawl underneath his feet.

The Act presents the submissive Mekhala and the queen before the king and the Vidūṣaka, and the frightened Mekhālā undergoes the humiliation of bowing down to the Vidūṣaka. The Vidūṣaka's laugh lets the cat out of the bag. Mekhalā and the queen both get angry and retire in a huff. The king then goes to the garden where he meets the girl of his desire. The information that the queen is approaching separates the lovers and the Actends.

A Praveśaka

By the last Praveśaka, the playwright discloses the intention of the queen to make the king an object of ridicule in the fashion of the Vidūṣaka. This is revealed by the wife of the Vidūṣaka in a dream. The queen, it becomes clear, has arranged for the real marriage of Mṛgāṅkalekhā, whom she knows to be a boy, with Kuvalayamālā and has wished to play the trick on the king on that very occasion. Hearing this the Vidūṣaka, naturally, laughs in his own mind as he foresees the discomfiture of the mistaken queen. He then goes to the king but does not let him know the secret.

The king, however, agrees to the proposal of the queen out of the sense of pleasing her but he still goes on doting on his favourite maiden, Mṛgāṅkalekhā. The Vidūṣaka humorously asks the king about his feelings regarding his once-favourite, Kuvalayamālā. The king replies that as she is going to be the wife of another, he should not think of her. Humorously does the Vidūṣaka refer to the saying of the villagers that 'the wife of one's brother-in-law is as good as one's own wife.' The statement is significant in the light of later happenings.

The marriage time approaches. The king and the Vidūṣaka find the queen, the bride Kuvalayamālā, Mekhalā and a host of attendants at the venue of the marriage. The queen laughingly comments to Kuvalayamālā aside on the wedding dress of her husband and the joke cruelly recoils upon her. The marriage ceremony ends and a messenger from Candravarman is immediately introduced. He conveys the happy news that a son to his lord is born and so there is no need to keep the princess in the guise of a man and further, she should be given in marriage to a suitable bridegroom. The minister, who also has accompained the messenger, and the Vidūṣaka both are pleased to see their respective plans succeed. The queen is upset to see her failure but she saves her face by assuming a very liberal attitude. The Vidūṣaka then proposes the marriage of Kuvalayamālā, as well, with the king and his proposal is supported by the minister. The queen, to keep up her dignity, again comes forward and offers the palm of Kuvalayamālā to the king herself. The Vidūṣaka again reminds the king of the common saying about the wife of the brother-in-law. The comedy thus ends with the smile on everybody's lips.

Conclusion

Rājaśekhara's diction in the Nāṭikā, is on the whole simple. Barring a few instances, where he uses long compounds, the dialogue in the play is brisk and simple. There is a plethora of redundant verses in this drama, and

Rājaśekhara makes his heroine use profuse Sanskrit and Prakrit verses in the protestations of her love. The Vidūṣaka also speaks out a good number of verses. This novelty introduced by Rājaśekhara fails to add any charm to the play though his method is imitated by his followers freely. The heroines in the later plays, wax eloquent to express their feelings, the only result of which is that we get a good number of Prakrit verses composed in the metres of Sanskrit.

In fine, Rājaśekhara did not possess the dramatic bent. To him drama was a handmaid for a display of his learning and skill in composing verses both in Sanskrit and Prakrit. To his influence is to be ascribed the fondness of the later dramatists to put Prakrit verses in profusion in the mouths of their heroines. It is thus clear that the creative contribution of Rājaśekhara in the field of drama is almost negligible.

Bilhaṇa

Bilhaṇa, the Kashmirian poet, 'who belonged to the second half of the 11th century' composed a Nāṭikā, Karṇasundarī by name, 'as a compliment to the Cālukya Karṇadeva Trailokyamalla of Anhilvad (1064-94)'. He celebrates in the play the marriage of the king to a princess within the framework of a romantic story. The story is also an imitation of the Ratnāvalī and the Viddhaśālabhañjikā.

In his matter and manner, Bilhaṇa fails to show any originality. In this four-Act comedy the story of the king's love for a maiden first dreamt in a dream and then seen in a picture, the jealousy of the queen to see the two meet in a secluded corner, her attempt at marrying the king to a boy disguised as the heroine, and her failure by the clever intervention of the wise minister, are depicted in the same manner as of his predecessor. The passion of love is expressed by means of verses both in Sanskrit and Prakrit, by the heroine and her companion.

The play abounds in the expressions of usual love pangs of the hero, the poetic effusions of the Vidūṣaka and of the heroine. The style throughout is simple and lucid. The versification also is commendable.

Conclusion

The only interest in and distinction of Karṇasundarī is its having a contemporary king as the hero. But, unfortunately this could not save the play from being conventional as regards manner and matter. This is the reason why Sanskrit drama, as a whole, could not flourish as it should have flourished even with such an effective technique. The art gradually degenerated into a slavish and mechanical imitation of the past models.

Madana

Another Nāṭikā demands special attention not for any novelty in its technique or subject-matter, which is but conventional, but for the interesting manner in which it has been preserved. The Nāṭikā is named Pārijātamañjarī or Vijayaśrī composed by Madana, surnamed Bālasarasvatī who was the preceptor of the Paramar king Arjunavarman of Dhāra and belonged to the first quarter of the 13th century. The play, composed in or about 1213 A. D., has been recovered in an incomplete form. The first two Acts have been found engraved on a slab of black stone at Dhāra in Central India.

That the play is a Nāṭikā is evident from the Prastāvanā and it is also known that this play also, like Karṇasundarī, was composed as a compliment to the king Arjunavarman and it celebrates the marriage of the king to the beautiful Pārijātamañjarī which is historical.

The play is obviously an imitation of the Ratnāvalī. The king is honoured by the gods with a garland of the *pārijāta* flowers at his victory over his enemy. The garland is metamorphosed into a beautiful maiden with whom the king falls in deep love. He keeps her sheltered under the care of the royal gardener and his wife, fearing the jealousy of the queen. The first Act, like that of the Ratnāvalī, shows the king and his party observing the festival of the love-God and in the course of it, the queen asks the king to witness the marriage of two garden creepers. The second Act brings about the union of the creepers after which the heroine is brought to light. The playwright uses a clever device to make the secret love of the king known to the queen. He makes the heroine's face reflected on the ear-ring of the queen. The king marks this and becomes absorbed in the contemplation of his beloved's face. The queen suspects his loyalty to her and goes out in anger. The king then proceeds to where the heroine lives. The king meets her and enjoys her company, but unluckily there comes Kanakalekhā, the confidant of the queen, who presents the queen's ear-rings to the king and conveys the sarcastic comment of the queen that it has been sent by her to alleviate the pain of the king's heart caused by the separation from the queen.

The tenor and treatment of this Nāṭikā, thus, are a close imitation of the same of the earlier plays of this type. The only point to be appreicated is that the treatment is soothing and the style is fair.

Conclusion

The account of the Nāṭikā variety thus comes to a close. It is clear from the extant Nāṭikās that the scope for the development of the technique of this variety was very limited. The first successful exponent created certain grooves into which all the later creations moved, lacking originality both in matter and manner.

In point of popularity, the Nāṭikā stands next to the Nāṭaka and the practice of composing Nāṭikā continued down upto the 18th century. But the want of real dramatic genius made the form degenerate into mere imitation. Nobody carved out a new way and consequently the variety lost its life-force and became staler and staler day by day.

SECTION—4 : BHĀṆA & PRAHASANA

Nāṭaka, Prakaraṇa and Nāṭikā are the three principal varieties that attracted the attention of most of the dramaturgists. Among these also, Nāṭaka and Nāṭikā were of greater importance to them as is evident from the rich crop of these two varieties. Leaving these three, or more properly two, the other eight types suffer more or less from a dearth of representative works. Excepting the Bhāṇa, the Prahasana and the Vyāyoga varieties, the rest viz. Īhāmṛga, Ḍima, Samavakāra, Vīthī and Utsṛṣṭikāṅka have hardly any representative specimen. As regards the absence of these latter five varieties, it cannot be held that these have been lost due to the ravages of time. It seems that most of the dramaturgists employed themselves in the composition of the Nāṭaka or the Nāṭikā which became very easy and mechanical to compose and also led a quick way to the plaudits of the people. The other five varieties demanded a variety of theme, treatment and Sentiment. Along with this, there was a greater difficulty in the shape of absence of good models, which might be imitated. Naturally these varieties were treated with scant respect.

The treatises on dramaturgy give an indication of the neglect shown to these varieties. All the treatises define the types elaborately but the definitions are more or less imitative of one another. Thus the definitions of Nāṭyadarpaṇa and of the Sāhityadarpaṇa are totally based upon those of the Daśarūpaka. Excepting Viśvanātha none cites any illustrations of these. So far as the Samavakāra, Īhāmṛga and Ḍima varieties are concerned, both the Daśarūpaka and the Sāhityadarpaṇa mention the names of the plays referred to by Bharata himself. The same is the case with all the other varieties excepting the Bhāṇa, Prahasana and Vyāyoga which have been represented by more than one specimens.

Bhāṇa and Prahasana are, to a great extent, allied to each other in having a ludicrous character. Structurally also both the types are similar. Both are one-Act plays, though the later Prahasanas came to be divided into two Acts.

This affinity, however, does not mean any sameness of the two. Bharata's definition makes Bhāṇa a monologue in which a clever Viṭa (rake) goes on describing his experiences by means of *ākāśa-bhāṣita*. The general trend is obviously romantic and is related with the courtesans and rogues. This type has only two Junctures—the Opening (*mukha*) and the Conclusion (nirvahaṇa), both to be shown in one Act. The experiences of oneself or of many being the subject-matter to be depicted, the Bhāṇa has got a peculiar appeal of its own.

The Prahasana, on the contrary is conceived to evoke laughter by the caricature of a Bhagavat, a Śrotriya (Vedic priest) or a Vipra or the like. According to Bharata, the Prahasana is of two kinds. The Śuddha or the Pure one is that in which the afore-mentioned characters are employed and the Saṃkīrṇa or Mixed one is that where a courtesan, the Viṭa and the rogues are introduced. This type is also limited to one Act with two Junctures—the Opening and the Conclusion.

The difference of Bharata with the later theorists regarding the Prahasana lies in the fact that the later exponents allow the Prahasana to go to two Acts and a few of them (viz : Dhanañjaya and Viśvanātha) speak of another kind, the Vikṛta one, which, however, can very easily be included in the Saṃkīrṇa kind.

Thus in the conception of these two types, there are many such points that can distinguish the two varieties. Vulgarity to some extent, it may be said, is allowed in the Bhāṇa as this type is the exposition of the experiences of a seasoned Rake, regarding the world of the courtesans. But this should not be understood to mean that vulgarity is the only point of interest in this type. That it is not so will be clear from the account of the following Bhāṇas. The Prahasana, on the contrary, has apparently nothing to do with vulgarity though unfortunately, it becomes grossly vulgar in the hands of the later playwrights.

A. The Bhāṇa

The history of the Bhāṇa is singular. The earliest Bhāṇas that have survived to this day are four in number and are jointly called the Caturbhāṇī. These four Bhāṇas are—(1) Padmaprābhṛtaka of Śūdraka ; (2) Dhūrta-viṭa-saṃvāda of Īśvaradatta ; (3) Ubhayābhisārikā of Vararuci and (4) Pādatāḍitaka of Śyāmilaka. In point of chronology, Vararuci is the earliest, Śūdraka comes after him, Īśvara-datta is the third and Śyāmilaka is the last. These four authors thus represent the Bhāṇa type from the beginning upto circa 1000 A. D.

All the four Bhāṇas exhibit novelty and variety of their own and speak eloquently of the great dramatic genius of their authors. The art of composing a Bhāṇa is, it is obvious, very difficult. A single character is to be employed and he is to go on describing his own experiences unaided. There is hardly any action and the main charm lies in the matter narrated and in the manner of narration. There is every chance of a Bhāṇa becoming monotonous and insipid. But the four specimens named above are exceptionally bright showing the Bhāṇa variety in its climax of perfection.

Vararuci

Vararuci's Ubhayābhisārikā is the oldest and the shortest Bhāṇa among the four. The Prastāvanā, which is very short, introduces a sorrowful Viṭa, just in the fashion of Bhāsa's plays. The very sentences—'*evem āryamiśrān vijñāpayāmi. Aye kinnu khalu mayı vijñāpanavyagre śabda iva śrūyate. Aṅgā paśyāmi*'—remind one of the Prastāvanās of the Bhāsa plays. The method also speaks of its great antiquity.

The Viṭa, Bhāvavaiśika by name, the only character of the play appears with a verse on the Spring season and announces that his friend, Kuveradatta has displeased his beloved courtesan, Nārāyaṇadattā by praising one of her rivals in the festival of Madana. He is now repenting for his misdeed and has asked him (Viṭa) to play the part of a mediator so that the lovers may meet that very night With this commission, he proceeds through the streets of the capital, Kusumapura. On his way he goes on talking with many imaginary persons of both the sexes all of whom are either courtesans or their messengers or their lovers. The Viṭa, is well-known to all of them and they respect him as an experienced and learned Viṭa.

Thus, in such one-Act monologue-plays the plot is remarkably slight and action is conspicuous by its absence. Still the playwright presents as much variety as he can within this limited scope. The Bhāṇas, in general, deal with the world of the courtesans and naturally some amount of coarseness is always there. From the Viṭa's conversation with the imaginary persons many interesting things are brought to light. By way of social satire, it points out that all types of human being are accustomed to visit the quarters of the courtesans. The greed for money of the courtesans is painted side by side with their sincere love.

Interesting glimpses of the revelry that goes on in these quarters and wherein assemble all sorts of men, high and low, can be had in these plays. The way in which these are depicted shows that merry-making with the courtesans was not considered immoral though it was shameful. The motive of the playwright in composing such plays must have been to expose the reality of this world where greed for money plays an upper hand over love. In addition, the Bhāṇa shows that the genteel society of ancient India did not dislike or ban the presentation of such plays as have for their theme the world of the courtesans and the convivialism associated with it.

However that may be, the playwright with the help of the technique of *ākāśa-bhāṣita* makes his chief character go on describing the various peculiarities of this world, finally putting him in front of the house of Nārāyaṇadattā. There he comes to know from the maid-servant that her mistress has herself left for the abode of Kuveradatta, forgetting her annoyance due to the bewitching influence of the Spring season and that the lovers have crossed each other's path. Both the lovers then have been given shelter by a friend of Kuveradatta. This news pleases the Viṭa and in order to meet the happy pair he retires with the Bharatavākya.

Conclusion

The style is very lucid and the prose used by the playwright is remarkably clear. The playwright is conscious of the fact that where only one man speaks, the language should be as simple as possible. In the depiction of the different situations also, the playwright shows great skill. The men and women referred to by the Viṭa are in no way abstractions but, thanks to the masterly descriptive power, these unseen characters become imbued with a life of their own.

Śūdraka

Śūdraka's Bhāṇa is named Padmaprābhṛtaka or a Gift of lotus as we find in it the Viṭa bringing a lotus as a token of love from the courtesan, Devasenā for his friend, the hero.

With the usual Prastāvanā which describes the beauty of the Spring season, the play begins. The Viṭa enters. He reveals that he is bound for the house of Devadattā, the beloved of his friend Karṇīputra. From him we come to know that Karṇīputra is blindly in love with Devasenā, the sister of Devadattā and that he has been requested by Karṇīputra to meet her and know her heart secretly. With this commission, he starts for the house of the courtesan, wending his way through the streets of the imperial city of Ujjayinī.

The Viṭa thus proceeds to the house of Devadattā and the main story ends with the simple incident of his meeting the maid-servant of Devasenā, from whom he comes to know that Devadattā has already left for the house of Karṇīputra and that Devasenā is alone in the house. The Viṭa thus gets the chance freely to talk to the heroine and settles the future union of the lovers. He then asks for a lotus from the hand of the courtesan as a token of her consent, gets it and retires. Devasenā and the maid-servant, as usual, are not shown on the stage.

The playwright makes the Viṭa give a vivid description of the capital, particulary the portions where the courtesans live. This description also includes interesting side-lights of the life led by the courtesans. We find a poet, a disappointed lover, the terrifying grammarian, Dattakalasi, the son of a judge who moves about stealthily, and so many other persons in the courtesans' quarters. The Viṭa's description, thus, gives a correct and at the same time mock-heroic outline of the iife of a particular section of people. The description is rich in variety and variegation.

Conclusion

Herein also the characterisation is remarkable. The poet, the pedantic grammarian Dattakalasi and the other frequenters of the hetaera's quarters are all objectively reported in so masterly a manner that they appear lifelike. In point of diction also the play proves itself to belong to the vintage years of the dramatic art.

Īśvaradatta

The third Bhāṇa is named Dhūrta-viṭa-saṃvāda (the dialogue between a rogue and a rake), written by Īśvaradatta.

This play presents a new variety in the theme and treatment. In it we find the Viṭa as the hero and he is not entrusted with any duty by any of his friends as in the other plays. The brief Prastāvanā describes the time which is the rainy seasan, and introduces the Viṭa. The

Viṭa, sick of the indoor indolence, wishes to enjoy the time in pleasureable pursuits. Between dicing and drinking he chooses none and settles to rove along the street where the courtesans live. The scene is laid in the city of Kusumapura. The Viṭa goes on talking with many persons who are supposed to cross his path and at last reaches the house where the roguish couple, Viśvalaka and Sunandā live. There he passes the day in discussing some of the knotty problems of erotics posed by Viśvalaka. The discussion is very interesting and the portion can very easily be treated as a companion volume to the Kuṭṭanīmata of Dāmodaragupta. His statements are 'an epitome of aesthetic and erotic laws which govern the life of a rake'. All the questions deal with the various aspects of the amorous life of the man about town and the courtesan, and the answers tally exactly with the Kāmasūtra and such other treatises on erotics.

The supposed encounter of the Viṭa with many courtesans and rakes is also interestingly presented. The character of the libert ne Kṛṣṇīlaka, the son of a rich merchant is beautifully drawn. The wretch does not wish to marry as proposed by his father and the Viṭa commends his decision and condemns all fathers in general. The comment is pithy and laugh-provoking. The Viṭa, bidding him adieu, proceeds towards the quarters of the courtesans where he meets Varuṇikā, Bandhumatikā, Ratisenā and a few other courtesans with all of whom he converses. Then he reaches the house of the roguish couple of whom Viśvalaka is very ably described. Viśvalaka is reduced to a pauper on account of his previous fast life and his mate Sunandā also has lost her youth and so both of them have formed a suitable couple. The Viṭa decides to meet them. He thus passes his day in amusement in the company of this couple, discussing racy problems of erotics.

Conclusion

The diction is neat and clean, and the versification easy and unlaboured. Though the descriptions of the courtesans and a few answers of the Viṭa may appear to be coarse, the interest is maintained throughout by the witty nature of the subject-matter.

Śyāmilaka

That the last of the four Bhāṇas, the Pādatāḍitaka of Śyāmilaka, is the latest Bhāṇa, is known clearly from its Prastāvanā. The Prastāvanā of this play is comparatively elaborate and furthermore, in it the names of the play and the playwright are given. The mention of the name of the playwright points out its comparative modernity.

But inspite of its being posterior to the other three Bhāṇas, it definitely falls within the first period of Bhāṇa-writing. Śyāmilaka's kinship with the other playwrights in the conception and execution of the play is evident. Though his subject-matter is coarser than those of the earlier three plays, his dramatic genius is unquestionable. His theme is highly interesting though indecent to the polished taste.

The Viṭa sets out to attend the assembly of the rogues and rakes who have met to consider the question of expiation, referred to them by one Tauṇḍikoki Viṣṇunāga, the son of a Mahāmātra and also an officer of the government, for the insult he has suffered by allowing a Saurāṣṭra courtesan, Madanasenikā by name, to kick on such a sacred place as his head. Viṣṇunāga had first requested the Brāhmaṇas to find out the suitable expiation for such a misdeed but they failed to find out any from the established treatises on Dharmaśāstra and then they asked him to go to the rogues and rakes to have the prescription. The Viṭa is very much amused at the foolishness of the nominal hero, Viṣṇunāga and wends his way towards the streets where the hetaeras live. He goes on enjoying the scene and asks the Viṭas occasionally to come to attend the conference. After walking for a long time, in course of which he supplies many glimpses of the notorious place, he reaches at last the venue of the meeting. The rogues assembled weigh the question put to them and suggest different expiations. One says that Viṣṇunāga should have his dishonoured head shaved; 'some think that it is not Viṣṇunāga but the girl herself who should expiate for setting her foot upon such a beast; others suggest that Viṣṇunāga should rub and shampoo her dishonoured feet; another proposes that he should bathe his head with the water with which she washes her feet and drink the same; but in the end, it is agreed, on the proposal of the presiding rake that Madanasenikā should put more sense into her lover by setting her foot on the President's own head in the sight of Viṣṇunāga.'

The playwright has a very keen power of satire. The picture of the foolish rogue, Viṣṇunāga is itself a grand example. His deep concern at suffering such an indignity and his eagerness to expiate are rendered highly ludicrous. The other pictures of the courtesan's quarters are none the less interesting and novel, though a few are nauseatingly vulgar. The picture of Bhaṭṭimaghavarman is indeed coarse. The author dislikes most the men of Lāṭa countries. He showers many abusive epithets on them. The fat Śivasvāmin who whiled away the night talking nonsense with the courtesan and made his fatness responsible for his discomfiture, is amusingly described. In relating the scandals of the cosmopolitan city, the playwright does not spare even the royal personalities. Perhaps this is the reason why he does not mention the name of the city where the scene is laid but calls it only the *sārvabhauma* city somewhere in the northern India.

Conclusion

In the style also, the playwright introduces a new thing. There is no use of Prakrit in the other three Bhāṇas of the group but in it Prakrit is also used. The language is simple and suits well with the theme. The verses in general are well composed and a few (e.g., 9, 13, 63, 68 120 & 121) are simply admirable.

All the four early Bhāṇas thus present a considerable number of interesting characters, all of whom are presented as distinct individuals. We meet, in them, to name only a few, 'Sārasvatabhadra, the sky-gazing poet with a verse on the Spring recorded on the wall, Dattakalaśi, the pedantic Pāṇinian with his sesquipedalian affectation and war on the Kātantrikas, Saṃdhilaka, the Śākya-bhikṣu who consoles the hetaera, Saṃghadāsikā with words of the Buddha......the penniless impotent Nagna Śramaṇaka, Viśvalaka and his dried up mistress, Sunandā' and such others, who are admirably presented and an altogether different world which these creatures of different stations of life live in. The main character is the Viṭa who is not the proper hero but is the only man who appears on the stage in his true colours, a position which the Viṭa loses in the subsequent Bhāṇas.

The tradition of the Bhāṇa is difficult to trace. After the Caturbhāṇī, we have to come down to the middle of the 13th century to find the next specimen of the variety, the Karpūracarita of Vatsarāja of Kālañjara (end of the 12th and beginning of the 13th century). After an interval of another century we get the Śṛṅgārabhūṣaṇa of Vāmana Bhaṭṭa Bāṇa (14th & 15th century) which contains clear signs of the decadence already taken deep root. Thus within the period in question (1200 A. D.) the Karpūra-carita is the last Bhāṇa.

Vatsarāja

Vatsarāja of Kālañjara was a versatile writer, who wrote six plays, most probably in order to illustrate the rarer types of the drama viz: a Vyāyoga, a Bhāṇa, an Īhāmṛga, a Ḍima, a Prahasana and a Samavakāra. It is obvious that for the composition of the Īhāmṛga, Ḍima and the Samavakāra, he had no model before him but only the treatises on dramaturgy and so these three are, more or less, artificial in form. However, his experiment with the other three comparatively popular varieties is remarkable and especially his Bhāṇa shows his dramatic genius at its best. Though he deviates from the accepted tradition by making the Viṭa practically the hero, he is nearer to the earlier writers of the Bhāṇa in his manner of handling the theme. 'The monotonous sameness of theme, sentiment, incidents, objects and characters' which is a marked feature of all the later Bhāṇas is absent in it and so this Bhāṇa should be treated as a representative specimen of the form.

The Prastāvanā of the play, after mentioning the names of the royal patron of the poet, the poet and the play, introduces Karpūraka, the rogue. He goes on describing his love, gambling and revelry with the courtesans to an imaginary friend by means of *ākāśa-bhāṣita*. He narrates to his friend how wittily he has deceived and put his rivals to trouble. At the end he comes to know from a new-comer who reports the success of all his plans. The satisfied Viṭa utters the Bharata-vākya.

Conclusion

This short play is remarkable for the impressive presentation of the Viṭa, the fascinating conversational tone and the absence of coarse vulgarity. Though this Bhāṇa is decidedly inferior to the earlier ones, it still does more than maintain the living tradition of the art.

The later Bhāṇas suffer most from coarse vulgarity and in them the incidents and conversations are both monotonous. They pull down the Bhāṇa to mere descriptions of the courtesans and the noisy crowds surrounding them. In these Bhāṇas, though the street of the hetaera is still the scene of action, the scene gives no evidence of novelty and variety. Coarse vulgarity takes the place of keen satire and thus the spirit of the Bhāṇa dies an ignominious death.

B. PRAHASANA

Closely allied to Bhāṇa but having a greater scope for comedy and satire, is the Prahasana. This is also a one-Act variety and is generally designed to cause laughter at the cost of worthless persons. The earliest Prahasana, that has come down to us, is the Mattavilāsa of Mahendravikrama Varman, a contemporary of Harṣa, and as the prologue testifies, a king of the Pallava dynasty, and the son of king Siṃhavarman. This play shows the Prahasana variety of drama at its best.

The play is a farcical sketch in one Act. It depicts with considerable liveliness 'the drunken revelry of a Śaiva mendicant bearing a human skull in lieu of alms-bowl and accordingly calling himself a Kapālin, his wandering with his wench through the purlieus of Kāñcī on his way to a tavern, his scuffle with a hypocritical Buddhist monk whom he accuses of the theft of the precious bowl which he has lost, his appeal to a degenerate Pāśupata to settle the dispute, and the final recovery of the bowl from a mad man who had retrieved it from a stray dog.' The story is presented very skilfully and the playwright succeeds in portraying the characters in an amusing manner. The satire is sharply pointed and enjoyable. The style is simple and elegant and there is nothing repulsive to the taste.

Mahendravikrama seems to have been a Śaiva and inspite of his attack on the Śaiva mendicants, the main object of satire is the Buddhist monk. The satirical comments are pungent but not in the least coarse. Not only for the reason of its being the first of the Prahasanas but on account of the skill shown by the playwright in the presentation, it deserves our appreciation.

Bodhāyana

The second Prahasana, in point of time, is the Bhagavadajjukīya of Bodhāyana Kavi. This Prahasana is the best of all the Prahasanas in Sanskrit literature. The playwright shows his genious in creating the comic situation by making the very plot ludicrous. It is not merely the foolery of the characters that causes laughter but it is caused as well by the very situation.

The play is significantly called the "Saint and the Courtesan". The saint is a true ascetic and learned teacher, well versed in Yoga, while his pupil is the typical Vidūṣaka of the Nāṭakas. The teacher and the pupil are introduced by the Prastāvanā which does not mention the name of the author. The teacher is seen teaching the pupil who is unwilling to study and is materialistic in outlook. The conversation of these two is amusing. Both of them go to a park where they sit down and the teacher goes on teaching the unmindful and scoffing pupil. There comes a courtesan along with her maid-servant and sits down under a tree to wait for her beloved. The pupil's attention immediately is diverted to her inspite of the teacher's protest. Suddenly there comes the messenger of Yama who, as a snake, bites the courtesan and takes her soul to the abode of Yama. At this sudden death, the pupil is too much shocked and rushes towards the courtesan. The maid-servent hastens to convey the news to the mother of the courtesan leaving the dead body under the care of the pupil. The teacher suddenly decides to convince his scoffing pupil of the potency of the Yogic powers by entering into the dead body of the courtesan. As a result, the courtesan gets up and begins to talk to the pupil like the teacher. The pupil is astonished to see the courtesan talking like his teacher. The mother and the lover reach by this time along with a curer of snake-bites, whom the courtesan puts to shame, making him turn away. Then the messenger of the Yama reappears and reports that he took the soul of the courtesan amiss. He now wants to replace the soul in the body but finding it already occupied puts it in the body of the saint. Now the case gets worse. The saint begins to talk and behave like the courtesan. All the onlookers are confused to see this strange happening. The problem is finally solved by the intervention of a second messenger from Yama, and thus the previous error is rectified. The exchange of souls thus ends the trouble and the play ends.

Conclusion

The play is thus replete with genuine humour. In plot as well as in characterisation the play is remarkable. The long dialogue between the teacher and his pupil is not void of comic relief and though there is a courtesan yet there is no vulgarity. The style is elegant and simple. The debate between the saint in the form of the courtesan and the curer of snake-bites is highly enjoyable. The dramatist is slightly satirical in his references to the Buddhistic ways. The playwright does not depend entirely upon satire to tickle his audience. He succeeds in creating humour of the true variety.

Vatsarāja

Unfortunately, the healthy tradition established by these Prahasanas lost its vitality within a short time. Like the Bhāṇa, the later Prahasana also suffers from crude vulgarity and 'becomes more a caricature with plenty of horse play, than a picture of real life with true comedy'. Fortunately the Prahasana of Vatsarāja, entitled Hāsya-cūḍāmaṇi, is an exception and it retains, to a great extent, the freshness of the best Prahasanas.

The Prahasana is divided into two Acts, though the division is nominal and might have been avoided. This division into two Acts is responsible for the formulation in the Sāhityadarpaṇa that the Saṃkīrṇa type of the Prahasana which abounds in a great number of rogues may have occasionally two Acts.[35]

The first Act of the Prahasana presents a hypocritical mendicant, Jñānarāśi by name, who is attended by a disciple, Kauṇḍinya. The disciple mispronounces

35. Vide SD. VI, 267.

Nārāyaṇa as *Nārījana*. A courtesan arrives at the Āśrama to know the name of the thief who has stolen away everything from her house. The mendicant with the help of the disciple poses to detect the theft by means of astrological calculation and at last gives the name of the thief to be Kapaṭakeli, the very courtesan herself. He, however, rectifies the mistake and then names the two servants of the house as thieves and the courtesan departs satisfied. The mendicant then goes to a secluded corner to practice *japa* for the success of one, Kalākaraṇḍaka in dice.

The second Act of the play brings in the mendicant practising *japa* with the disciple by his side. At the request of the disciple, the teacher adjourns his *japa* and suddenly they happen to see the beautiful courtesan, Madanasundarī, the daughter of Kapaṭakeli, who is out to meet her beloved Kalākaraṇḍaka. The sight of her gives birth to erotic feelings in both the onlookers but the teacher tries to hide his feelings from his disciple. The mendicant, then, being too much allured by her beauty writes a *mantra* to bring her under his control and asks the disciple to smear it with sandal paste. The disciple scents some mischief and sees the name which he changes and puts instead, the name of the mother, the old courtesan Kapaṭakeli. Due to the magical charm of the *mantra* Kapaṭakeli comes to the mendicant. The mendicant, however, rejects her advances and then there appear the two servants whose names he gave to the courtesan as thieves. They are about to drown the hypocrite in the nearby pond. They also find out Kauṇḍinya who has been seeing everything from the top of a tree. Suddenly coming to know the power of the mendicant in finding out the places of hidden treasure, the two ask him for the favour. The relieved mendicant smears the eyes of all including the old courtesan with a collyrium which renders all of them blind. The cunning servants of the courtesan then rub their own eyes forcefully with those of the teacher and his disciple and they also turn blind. Thus all of them scream aloud in pain, when there appear Kalākaraṇḍaka and his beloved Madanasundarī who cleanse the eyes of all with the water of the pond. The mendicant blesses the saviour and explains that by mistake he did apply a wrong salve whence the difficulty arose. Kalākaraṇḍaka pays his respects to the mendicant for having got success in dice, and the play ends.

Conclusion

This play is the last Prahasana which exhibits real power of presenting the comic farce in a charming manner. Inspite of the presence of two courtesans, the playwright does not resort to mean vulgarity like his followers. The characterisation is good and the picture of the hypocrite mendicant is amusing as well as life-like. Perfect comic spirit unalloyed with mean vulgarity is the chief merit of this Prahasana.

The later Prahasanas, like the Bhāṇas, suffer from monotonous themes and treatment. All of these are generally divided into two Acts and exhibit little literary taste and value. The Laṭaka-melaka of Śaṅkhadhara for instance, shows vulgarity in its extreme. The talks and actions of the different characters are too coarse and repulsive to any taste. There is nothing charming but unmitigated vulgarity centering round the courtesans.

About these decadent plays the verdict of the historian is more than justified—'The whole atmosphere is low and depressing. We have neither thoroughly alive rascals nor charmingly entertaining fools, for they are all thrown into fixed moulds without much regard for actualities. The characters are low, not in social position, but as unredeemingly base and carnal; and there being no credit for any other quality, they are hardly human...... Even if refinement is out of place in a farce, detailed and puerile coarseness is redundant and ineffective.'[36]

———

36. HSL. p. 500.

SECTION—5 : THE OTHER VARIETIES

The rest of the ten forms viz: Vyāyoga, Samavakāra, Ḍima, Vīthī, Aṅka and Īhāmṛga suffered a great neglect, excepting only the Vyāyoga form. Though all the treatises on dramaturgy define these forms as usual, illustrations of these are rarely found. From Bharata upto Viśvanātha, we find the following titles as representing these varieties.

Dhanañjaya, Rāmacandra & Guṇacandra and Viśvanātha speak of two Vyāyogas—the Jāmadagnyajaya and the Saugandhikāharaṇa. Of these the first is mentioned by Dhanañjaya and Rāmacandra while the second is only spoken of by Viśvanātha. The former is lost but the second is extant.

Of the Samavakāra type, Bharata assigns the authorship of one Amṛtamathana to Brāhmaṇa. Dhanañjaya perhaps refers to the same as Ambhodhimathana. Viśvanātha speaks of Samudramathana which is most probably the play of Vatsarāja.

Tripuradāha is the only Ḍima which is referred to by Dhanañjaya and Viśvanātha. This play also is mentioned in the Nāṭyaśāstra, which was enacted for the delectation of Śiva.

Rāmacandra names a Vīthī, entitled Indulekhā which is lost. Viśvanātha also speaks of another Vīthī—the Mālavikā.

Śarmiṣṭhā-Yayāti is the only Aṅka referred to in the Sāhityadarpaṇa, and of the Īhāmṛga type, it mentions the name of Kusumaśekharavijaya.

The scanty number of illustrations proves that these forms became antiquated even at the time of Dhanañjaya himself (c. 980 A.D.). Only the Vyāyoga variety found comparatively great favour with the later playwrights. These plays also were written in an age when decadence became manifest in the entire field of dramaturgic composition.

Vyāyoga

The earliest and the best vyāyoga that has come down to us is the Madhyama-vyāyoga of Bhāsa. Another play, the Dūtaghaṭotkaca, of the same author is also a specimen of the same variety. These two Vyāyogas, notably the Madhyama, show this form at its best. Both the themes are invented though the germinal idea comes from the Mahābhārata. The dramatic quality of the theme of the Madhyama is excellent and in this one-Act play, Bhāsa shows his great workmanship. The revelation of the identity of Bhīma is exquisitely dramatic. The other play, though of the same variety, is not at all an imitation of the former. It has entirely a new plot invented by the playwright. The success of the playwright lies in his free and elegant style, the exhibition of the heroic sentiment and characterisation which go to make all the characters alive.

The Vyāyoga being expressive of the Heroic sentiment, the later playwrights attempted to compose many Vyāyogas. Apart from the Vyāyogas mentioned in the treatises, a number of others are available to this day. But the freshness and charm seen in the early plays are absent in these. The living tradition of Vyāyoga ended, it seems, with Bhāsa. Coming to the beginning of the 13th century, we get again a few Vyāyogas which exhibit no dramatic genius. In these plays the rules are followed even to a fault and so these totally lack the spirit and vigour of an original creation. Needless it is to say that such plays as have only the code to guide them and not the living tradition of drama, are bound to suffer from want of life and interest.

The plays, for instance, the Kirātārjunīyavijaya of Vatsarāja and Dhanañjayavijaya of Kāñcanācārya are good so far as the faithfulness to the code is concerned. But as true dramas, they have almost nothing in them. Consequently, the Vyāyogas of the 13th century and onwards suffer most, though the versification at times is definitely commendable. Peculiarly the later playwrights began to think, it appears from their plays, that only the use of high sounding words and long compounds renders a theme heroic. The general signs of degeneration, as a result is to be seen in this field as well.

Samavakāra

The Samavakāra variety also shares the same fate. Herein also the play of Bhāsa entitled Pañcarātra, is the best specimen. In plot-construction, characterisation, varieties of emotions and situation, this Mahābhāratan play is simply charming. According as the laws of the Nāṭyaśāstra, the play is divided into three Acts and there are eleven protagonists. Bhāsa does not follow the code in a servile manner and so we find that as regards the length of the Acts, he violates the rules of the Śāstra.

According to Bharata the duration of the successive Acts should be in the proportion of 12: 4: 2. But Bhāsa's second and third Acts are almost equal in length.

The next playwright who attempted at this variety was Vatsarāja. His chief aim was to present specimens of these varieties which had died long ago. By the middle of the 13th century he composed a Samavakāra, named Samudramathana and in his composition, he had only the treatises to guide him. His play follows the rules strictly but fails to impress on account of its artificiality. The number of the heroes, the length of the Acts and all other details of composition given in the treatises are adhered to by the zealous playwright but inspite of everything the play lacks in life.

Ḍima & Īhāmṛga

The very same Vatsarāja of Kālañjara gave us a Ḍima, Tripuradāha by name, and an Īhāmṛga entitled Rukmiṇīpariṇaya. Both the plays follow the Śāstra steadily and hence in these plays the technique is wooden and does not merit any discussion.

Aṅka

The Aṅka also belongs to the rarest varieties. Bhāsa is the first and the best composer of this type so far our information goes. The Ūrubhaṅga is decidedly an Utsṛṣṭikāṅka and best illustrates the type. Karuṇa or pathetic is the Sentiment exhibited in it and Bhāsa does not deviate from the Śāstra in its composition. It is the solitary play of the type. We come to know, from Viśvanātha of another play—the Śarmiṣṭhāyayāti which is of a very later date.

Vīthī

Of the Vīthī variety, we have got two specimens from the pen of Bhāsa—the Dūtavākya and the Karṇabhāra. The Vīthī is defined by Bharata to be a play having only one or two characters and displaying all the Sentiments. These two one-Act plays supply us with good illustrations of the type without any deviation from

Bharata. In both the plays the main characters are only two and in both, heroic is the chief Sentiment.

The revival of Vīthī took place long after Bhāsa and the plays—Indulekhā and Mālavikā—mentioned in the Nāṭyadarpaṇa and Sāhityadarpaṇa respectively, are lost.

Conclusion

The discussion on the ten varieties of the drama thus concludes. We have seen that the Nāṭaka, Prakaraṇa and Nāṭikā varieties appealed most to the playwrights whereas all the other forms were more or less neglected. The scrutiny of the method of treatment of the dramatic theme shows that so long the dramaturgists possessed originality in the formation and execution of their plots, truly meritorious plays were composed. A living contact with the stage, in addition to the dramatic genius, gave birth to the best specimens of Sanskrit drama—the plays of Bhāsa, Kālidāsa, Śūdraka, Bhaṭṭanārāyaṇa, Bhavabhūti, Śrī Harṣa and a few others. With the gradual separation of the dramatists from the stage and the want of original outlook, Sanskrit drama began to degenerate. The characteristic features of this decadent period have already been enumerated.[37]

It is remarkable that the first specimens of all the varieties are the best of their type and all the later artists fail miserably to carve out a new path of their own and so their works are mere recasts of the earlier models and hence life-less.

The structure of the drama and the various technical devices that are conceived by Bharata, are greatly useful and practical and speak of the great insight of the

37. Vide p. 292 above.

first codifier. The technique of the Sanskrit drama is so rich and helpful that a mere adherence to it can very easily give any theme a dramatic form. But inspite of this richness and usefulness of the technique, the later playwrights fail to impress on account of their regrettable ignorance of the correct dramatic sense Technique, it has been already observed, can give everything to a dramatic theme but not its *soul* which is the outcome of the dramatic genius.

—•—

SECTION—6 : THE ADDITIONAL VARIETIES :

From the Prastāvanā of the Bhagavadajjukīya, we come to have a list of ten forms of drama which, it asserts, spring from the Nāṭaka and the Prakaraṇa (*nāṭaka-prakaraṇodbhavāsu vāra-īhāmṛga-ḍima-samavakāra-vyāyoga-bhāṇa-sallāpa-vīthī-utsṛṣṭikāṅka-prahasana-ādiṣu*, etc., pp. 4-5) and thus the total number of the forms become twelve. Vāra and Sallāpa are the two new forms spoken of here. The mention of these two new forms by such an old dramatist naturally suggests that there must have been more varieties of the dramatic composition than were accepted by Bharata. But though the commentator of the Daśarūpaka speaks of a few varieties in addition to the ten[38] Dhanañjaya himself says nothing about any of them.

Another new form is presented by Rājaśekhara. It is the Karpūramañjarī, called a Saṭṭaka. Verses from this play have been cited by the commentator of the Daśarūpaka but the author is silent about this variety.

The first Codifier to include these additional types are the authors of the Nāṭyadarpaṇa. They belonged to the period circa 1100 to 1175 A. D. They mention in the fourth *viveka* thirteen new varieties.[39] These are—Saṭṭaka, Śrīgadita, Durmilita, Prasthāna, Goṣṭhī, Hallīsaka, Nartanaka, Prekṣaṇaka, Rāsaka, Nāṭyarāsaka, Kāvya, Bhāṇaka and Bhāṇikā. A very sketchy description of these is also given. Of these newer types, we have to this day, a few Saṭṭakas and Prekṣaṇakas or Preṅkhaṇakas.

---

38. Vide DR. I, 8.
39. Vide ND. IV. pp. 213-14.

Viśvanātha in the Sāhityadarpaṇa adds more varieties to the number and makes the total number eighteen.[40] He adds—Troṭaka, Ullāpya, Saṃlāpaka, Śilpaka, Vilāsikā, Prakaraṇī and Nāṭikā (which is included by Bharata himself in the ten major forms). Viśvanātha does not mention the names of Nartanaka and Bhāṇaka and includes in this list the Prakaraṇī which the authors of Nāṭyadarpaṇa include in the general list of the major forms along with the Nāṭikā. There is hardly any specimen of these forms and so it is impossible to ascertain the nature of the technique in these varieties.

The few plays of irregular type that have come down to this day are—Karpūramañjarī, the Saṭṭaka of Rājaśekhara; Unmattarāghava, a Prekṣaṇaka of Bhāskara of the 14th century and the Saugandhikāharaṇa of Viśvanātha (about 1291–1322), also a Prekṣaṇaka.

Rājaśekhara's Saṭṭaka

The Saṭṭaka of Rājaśekhara has nothing remarkable in it excepting the language. Saṭṭaka is exactly the same as the Nāṭikā as regards theme and treatment. The only variation of the one from the other is that the Saṭṭaka is composed entirely in Prakrit and in it neither the Viṣkambhaka nor the Praveśaka is used and the Acts in it are called Jabanikāntaras. The definition found in the Sāhityadarpaṇa is clearly based on the Karpūramañjarī. The play has, just like the Nāṭikā, an abundance of the erotic sentiment in the story of the king's love with a new-found girl behind the eyes of his queen, depicted in four scenes named Jabanikāntaras. Having Karpūramañjarī as the model, a few more Saṭṭakas were written at a later date.

---

40. Vide SD. VI. 269–312.

The Prekṣaṇakas are one-Act plays and are almost similar to a Vyāyoga or a Vīthī. The two plays mentioned already furnish the specimens of the varieties. The Unmattarāghava 'describes Rāma's search and maddened soliloquies (obviously after Purūravas of Kālidāsa) on Sītā's transformation into a gazelle by the curse of the ever irascible sage Durvāsās and her recovery with the help of Agastya.' The pathetic sentiment depicted in the play suits the Vīthī variety well.

The other, the Saugandhikāharaṇa is called a Prekṣaṇaka by the playwright in the Prastāvanā while Viśvanātha mentions it as a Vyāyoga in the Sāhityadarpaṇa obviously considering the similarity of theme and treatment of it with the Vyāyoga variety.

Some of these additional varieties or the Upa-rūpakas might have been very old but those which have reached down to us are of later origin and are perhaps creations of the enthusiasts on the line suggested by the treatises. Even the Sāhityadarpaṇa which gives the most elaborate account of these, cannot cite illustrations of all of these varieties. We have to wait until more plays are recovered in order to form an adequate idea of these varieties.

CHAPTER VIII
THE GREEK AND SANSKRIT

Great value has been hitherto assigned to the comparative method of study. In fact, by a properly directed comparative enquiry many new points of interest come to light and this method has enormously benefited particularly the study of the Vedas. Unfortunately in the realm of Classical literature, this method has rarely been properly applied. In so far as this method has been applied, most of the scholars have done it in a lop-sided manner, either to give vent to conceit or express submissive acceptance. In comparing, for example, the literary tenets of Sanskrit and Greek, the tendency of scholars generally is somehow to defend the Sanskrit by observing that Sanskrit possessed much before the qualities spoken of by the Greek theorists. In such observations, the scholars overlook the particularity of both the languages, which is dangerous. It should never be lost sight of that Greek is Greek and Sanskrit is Sanskrit, and in a proper enquiry into the literary merit of these, one should the more engage himself in finding out the specialities rather than the common elements. The aim of comparative study should not be to prove one or the other superior or inferior. It should chiefly concern itself with a liberal as well as critical study of both and to find out the special features of the two. The judgment as to which one is superior to the other can thus be very easily given.

This much introduction, we think, is necessary before entering into a comparative study of the Greek and Sanskrit dramas from the standpoint of technique. So far as the presentation of the play on the stage is concerned, many different devices have developed in both the countries according as their different conditions. The line on which the present comparative study is to run will necessarily be confined to the techniques of dramatic creation as obtained in these two ancient lands.

At the very outset, two facts should be taken into consideration. One is that the Greek method of dramatisation is based upon entirely a different basis from that of the Sanskrit method. The dramatic literatures of these two ancient countries have had their peculiar and unique circumstances which conditioned their development. The stage itself was greatly responsible for the very many peculiarities of the dramatic output of both the lands. The other fact is that the dramas of both the countries were successful in their missions, inspite of the technical differences or the differences in merit. That is, one cannot judge the merit of either by means of applying the same literary standard. These two facts, if remembered, will save the enthusiasts from much banal criticism. The dramas of both the Sanskrit and Greek languages served the purpose of pleasing the audience in their own capacity inspite of their limitations.

Keeping these observations in mind, our aim is to take up two dramas—one Greek and the other Sanskrit—and compare them on the point of technique. The line of enquiry will be the same in both and thus the discussion may well be divided into the following heads—(1) the Prastāvanā or the Beginning; (2) the Pātra-praveśa or the Presentation of character (3) the Arthopakṣepakas or the Explanatory Devices, (4) the division into Acts, (5) Nirvahaṇa or the Conclusion, (6) Characterisation and dialogue and (7) the total effect of the piece or the Rasa.

In a comparison, another formidable obstacle is the type of the plays. Greek drama excels in tragedy but on the contrary, Sanskrit scrupulously avoids it. In order to find a common basis we have selected the only tragic play in Sanskrit, the Ūrubhaṅga of Bhāsa as representing Sanskrit drama and Oedipus the King, of Sophocles as representing the Greek tragedy. We have picked up Sophocles, the second of the great Greek trio, due to the consideration that Aeschylus being the first, the next in point of time must have been in a better position to display the dramatic art in its full bloom. In his Poetics, Aristotle also speaks of Sophocles as the truly representative Greek tragedian. Consequently, Sophocles has here been accepted as the representative of the Greek spirit.

Oedipus the King

The theme of Oedipus's tragic recognition of his identity was a very favourite one with almost all the tragedians. "The story of Oedipus, according to our present knowledge was dramatised more often than any other legend. Some thirteen different authors including Aeschylus, Sophocles and Euripides are known to have written plays on this subject."[1]

The story of Oedipus and his sons form the central part of the Theban cycle of legends and it was widely known throughout the Hellenic world. Sophocles, accordingly, was judicious to have chosen this story for dramatisation and in the absence of Aeschylus's play, we may safely accept the view of Aristotle that this play is the best of its kind. "In the Poetics, the Oedipus is cited more

1. Vide 'A Handbook of Classical Drama' Harsh, P. W., p. 113.

frequently and praised more highly than any other play." The play is acclaimed by Aristotle as having a complexity of plot, neatness, sudden reversal of fortune and fine execution.

The story of Oedipus has been taken to illustrate the Greek conception of life. It has been rightly stated by Harsh[2]—'The basic theme of the Oedipus is the irony of fate. No mortal man, however powerful and wealthy can be pronounced happy until after he is dead; for no man, however wise, knows what the morrow will bring. This is the burden of the last complete choral song and of the last lines of the play. This was a basic conception in Greek popular thought...' Thus irony of fate is the key-note of the theme and Sophocles stands in singular grandeur in his mastery in dramatising the theme.

The Ūrubhaṅga

The Sanskrit play, Ūrubhaṅga of Bhāsa, likewise, is based upon the Mahābhārata. In this play, the incidents of the duel fight of Bhīma and Duryodhana and the repercussions of it are dramatised and the playwright, singular in his attempt and success throughout the vast dramatic literature of Sanskrit, successfully depicts the character of Duryodhana as a real tragic hero. Bhāsa's canception of a tragic hero, it is interesting to note, is a perfect one, even according to the Elizabethan conception, particularly that of Shakespeare. The character of Duryodhana attains in this short play a rare tragic grandeur and the reversal of fortune is brought about in such a masterly manner that it never fails to arouse the deepest sense of sorrow or 'the sense of waste' which is typical of the Shakespearean tragedy.

2. Vide A. Handbook of Classical Drama, p. 118.

The Hero—Oedipus

The hero of Sophocles's play is Oedipus. He is depicted as a man of strong will and as a generous ruler. His sincerity has been displayed in his earnestness to redress the wrong, supposed to be the cause of the plague on the land. Though he is brave and heroic, he faces the catastrophe for which we find no adequate reason to hold him responsible. It is entirely Fate which conspires against him and brings about his downfall. So, in this play human life is too much belittled, a mere plaything as it is in the hands of all-powerful Fate.

Ūrubhaṅga

The conception of the hero of the Sanskrit playwright is different. Even though Fate is a great factor here as well, *man* is not belittled. Even in his dying condition Duryodhana retains the grandeur of an indomitable warrior, never failing to rise to the full stature of his fame. At the dying moment he revaluates his own life in a new light but finds no reason to blame his Fate. He looks at things in a new perspective and realises, though too late, that his was a wrong way. The death of Duryodhana is not so much a proof of the vanity of human life as how unrighteous designs lead to ruin. Thus the pessimistic note which we find in Oedipus (e.g. the last choral song) is entirely absent in Ūrubhaṅga.

The Beginning—The Greek way

All the Greek dramas begin, as a rule, with a monologue or a dialogue which is called the *prologos*. Etymologically *prologos* means an introductory speech and *prologos* in a Greek play is nothing but an introduction to the play. Three persons speak in the *prologos*—Oedipus,

Priest, and Creon and it is Oedipus who speaks first. Oedipus opens the play with a speech addressed to the people of Thebes, and in it he lets the audience know all the necessary information regarding his own name and position, the condition Thebes is in at the time, etc. The Priest likewise makes it clear how the plague is devastating the land and he implores Oedipus to find out a way of riddance, as he is considered the Saviour of the country by the people. As an ideal ruler, Oedipus responds to it and says that he has already sent his kinsman and prince Creon to the Delphic shrine of Phoebus to get divine assistance. With the arrival and report of Creon the *prologos* ends and the action gathers more momentum.

The Indian way

The Prastāvanā of a Sanskrit play, on the contrary, has an entirely different form. No principal characters are introduced in it. The Sūtradhāra or the Stage-manager is the only character who calls his associate and while conversing with him refers to the main action, or the hero. Generally the Sūtradhāra prays to God and then announces the names of the play and the playwright and last of all he creates the just situation for the entrance of the hero, and exits. In Ūrubhaṅga we find no announcement of the names of the play and playwright by the Sūtradhāra. Bhāsa, seems to have been very modest as regards giving out his personal identity. In none of his plays the playwright is mentioned and this is why there is a great problem, known as the Bhāsa-problem, in the history of Sanskrit literature.

In the Ūrubhaṅga, the Sūtradhāra after reciting his benedictory verse is about to announce something. But he is interrupted by a sound coming from behind the curtain. He then divines the meaning of the sound and finds before him his associate who enquires of him the whereabouts of a few persons who are approaching. The Sūtradhāra explains that these are the soldiers of the great Kuru war and that the duel fight between Duryodhana and Bhīma has begun, it being the last contest in the Kuru-Pāṇḍava war. After this announcement he retires. Here ends the Prastāvanā.

Conclusion

From the above account it is easy to judge the merit of thr two methods. So far as the introduction is concerned, both the ways serve their purpose. But the way in which the Greek playwright introduces his characters is definitely less dramatic than the Indian. The Self announcement—'I am Oedipus' or the like is completely prosaic and void of all charms. This problem of revealing the identity of the characters has been solved by the Indian theorists by resorting to so many devices. One such device is the Prastāvanā. In those days there were no printing machines nor there was any printed programme. So it would have become entirely impossible without the Sūtradhāra's help, to know the names of the play and playwright. The technique of using a Prastāvanā saves the characters from giving a very prosaic self-announcement. The Sūtradhāra is very fittingly given the character of a mediator who being an outsider happens to know all the preliminary information regarding the play. He takes a position, as if on the border of the actual drama and he does nothing more than supply the link (literally, Sūtra), with the help of which the audience easily grasps the unforeseen events of the play. Thus the Sanskrit play is not cumbered with long speeches aiming at disclosing the identity of the characters on the stage. The Prastāvanā being only a useful means, the merit of a playwright may also be judged by a careful study of this. The master artists never indulge in long Prastāvanās. One may ask, Who is to acquaint the Sūtradhāra to the audience ? No one else is required for the purpose. As a common Brāhmaṇa, announcing the beginning of a play, the Sūtradhāra requires no introduction at all. This character, moreover, is a typical one and hence requires no recommendation.

Another difficulty with the *prologos* of the Greek plays is its irregularity. If all the plays, as a rule, begin with the hero, the audience may easily come to know him. But there are plays in which the character first to arrive is not the chief one and as such, it causes confusion. This difficulty is the more felt by a foreigner who is unacquainted with the Greek practice. The Sanskrit plays on the contrary, can very easily be appreciated by any set of people provided they understand the language. This limitation is also felt in the technique of the Greek chorus. A Sanskrit play is directly approachable whereas a Greek play demands a fore-knowledge of the dramatic theory.

Pātra-praveśa—th Greek way

Pātra-praveśa or the presentation of the characters on the stage in a drama is a problematic factor. The dramatist has to provide for an adequate explanation for bringing in any character. And that explanation is the more dfficult as it is to come from the drama itself. The theorists have pointed out—*Nāsucitasya pātrasya praveśaḥ* i. e. there is no room for such a character in a play as is not properly introduced. This rule gives the piece a dramatic unity and saves the drama from being a mere collection of dialogues.

The Greek and Sanskrit both have invented their own methods of introducing the characters. The Prastāvanā is already discussed. It is also a method of introducing the chief characters. There are other methods too practised in both the countries. The Greek ways of introduction are, in addition to the *prologos*, the Chorus, the messengers and the Supernatural. The last one has a double function. At times it hints at the future progress of the dramatic action and sometimes supplies the solution at the end. Strictly speaking, the Supernatural does not usher in new characters but as this helps to bring about the next change in the dramatic action, this is also included in the list.

The Chorus serves too many ends in the Greek drama. One of the chief functions of it is to introduce a character entering the stage for the first time. The Chorus is supposed to know everything. Though the Chorus represents the common Athenian people, it utters great truths and gives a moral colour to the play. It functions as the spokesman for the playwright. The Chorus has the same monotone everywhere, the sole interest being the speech. With their typical dress and mask the members of the Chorus are seen in all the scenes. The Choral songs have poetic effects as well and thus these bring in a dramatic relief in an atmosphere of overcharged emotions. Poetic skill is also felt in the different choruses of different playwrights and in their function of modulating the tone of the play, these attain rare poetic perfection in the hands of Aeschylus, Sophocles and other great artists.

Sophocles introduces the Chorus very skilfully. The command of Oedipus in the *prologos*—'Summon hither the Theban folk'—prepares the proper background for the entrance of the Chorus of Theban elders. The Chorus is loyal to the king. It gives voice to the suffering and woes of Thebes. It describes in feeling phrases the condition of the city which is 'a city perishing!' They invoke the aid of all the gods—Zeus, Apollo, Artemis and Dionysus, so that the God of death may be driven out of the city. The Choral song, the critics observe, may be considered as furnishing the emotional exposition of the play.

The Chorus, here works, it should be observed, as an Explanatory Device (*Arthopakṣepaka*) of the Sanskrit plays. It is just like a Viṣkambhaka revealing the condition of the city and introducing the dramatic characters. Here also, Sophocles makes the blind prophet, Teiresias, enter the scene as announced by the Chorus. The Chorus, likewise, introduces the king and the queen, Jocasta in the second *episode* (lines 531, 631–33). It is the Chorus, which acquaints the messenger from Corinth with the royal palace and the queen in the third *episode* (lines 927–28). The Chorus recognises the herdsman who saved the child, Oedipus in the fourth *episode* (lines 1117–18). The Chorus announces the coming of Creon in the fifth *episode* (lines 1416–18). The messenger is also used for the selfsame purpose once in the play. He introduces the afflicted Oedipus in the fifth *episode* (lines 1294–95). These are the ways in which Sophocles introduces his characters.

The Indian way

In Sanskrit drama, the main character is generally introduced by the Sūtradhāra. But at times, the hero is introduced after an Explanatory Scene. This is done where a particular situation is to be shown and the hero to be presented as the centre of that situation. The subject matter of the first choral song in the Oedipus the King would have been placed first through an Explanatory Scene (Viṣkambhaka) were the play composed by a Sanskrit dramaturgist and the hero would appear as trying to solve the problem. Whether the hero is to be presented first or his entrance should be preceded by a Viṣkambhaka is left to the playwright's discretion by the Indian theorists. The deciding factor of putting a Viṣkambhaka first is the necessity of acquainting the audience with the condition in which the hero is presented.

The intimation of the entrance of new characters is given by the characters present on the stage. No group of men, like the Greek Chorus, is seen in any Sanskrit play. At times, the Pratihārī (female door-keeper) also introduces a character. An entirely new method is also seen in the Sanskrit drama. It is the Nepathyokti or a speech from behind the curtain. This technique is of a great help to the playwright particularly in those situations where none is present to introduce a new character.

The Pātra-praveśa in the Ūrubhaṅga is done by the Sūtradhāra and other characters. The Sūtradhāra introduces here a group of soldiers who participated in the great Kuru war. These soldiers introduce Baladeva who announces the entrance of Duryodhana as he hears Duryodhana speak behind the curtain. Dhṛtarāṣṭra, Gāndhārī, Durjaya, the son of Duryodhana and the wives of Duryodhana are all introduced by Baladeva. Aśvatthāman enters reciting a verse and Baladeva recognises him. Thus in this play all the characters are introduced by one or the other dramatic characters themselves.

Conclusion

So far as the technique of introducing new characters is concerned, it must be accepted that the Greek process suffers from limitations more than the Sanskrit one. The introduction of characters by the Chorus is bound to be stale and mechanical whereas the introduction of others by the characters in the drama itself is more natural and charming. The introduction of all the new characters by the same Chorus is a handicap which could not be surmounted fully by the Greek geniuses. The monotony, however, of this technique did not escape the notice of later dramatists and the function of the Chorus consequently grew more limited. As in the *prologos* so in this technique, Sanskrit method is definitely more effective and natural than and therefore, superior to the Greek method.

The Explanatory Devices

A comparison of the two techniques of reporting the past events and critical situations will be of great value. The entire subject-matter of a drama is divided by the Indian theorists into two-one is *rañjaka* or *sarasa* and the other is *arañjaka* or *virasa*. The *sarasa vastu,* as it is called, is given a full display through the Acts and the *virasa* but necessary *vastu* is reported through the Explanatory Devices (*arthopakṣepakas*) placed before the Acts. These are specially required for the reporting of those events which are prohibited to be shown on the stage. The non-presentable events are enumerated elaborately in the treatises. Though these are proscribed, these may, if necessary, be reported by short scenes known as Arthopakṣepakas.

The Greek way

There is nothing known to the Greek theorists as the Explanatory Devices. But the problem of reporting the non-presentable was ever present before the Greek playwrights and they have solved it in various ways. We shall discuss a few of these here and compare those with the Sanskrit ways.

In the play, Oedipus the King, Sophocles narrates such incidents through (1) the Chorus, (2) the Messenger, and at times (3) through the talks of the characters themselves.

The Chorus has been discussed already as a means of introducing new characters. In addition to that the Chorus is also the chief means of reporting such events as do not take place on the stage. Accordingly, we find the Chorus explaining to the audience the woes and sufferings of the City. Practically speaking, the reference to the plague in the City in the saying of the priest requires an elaboration and the playwright supplies a fuller description of the disastrous change of fortune through the first choral song. Without this, it is difficult to realise the reason of Oedipus's eagerness to do something immediately. Not only by the choral songs but by the conversation with the Chorus also much information is furnished. The Chorus is given the status of a regular character and it is always present on the stage. The Chorus speaks with both the hero and the villain and everywhere its attitude is impartial. Though the Chorus represents on the stage the common men of the City, it does not voice the common men's ideas. On the contrary, the Chorus is used as the spokesman for the playwright, expressing the very thoughts and philosophic moralisings of the dramatist himself. The Chorus remains present throughout the play after its entrance before the first *episode*. Through songs and conversations, the Chorus reveals the happenings off the stage and points out the significance of the actions and their consequences.

Sophocles presents his Chorus as a group of strong supporters of king Oedipus. The Chorus begins with the praise of the king and, at times, suggests the right path for the latter. Even when the king is accused by the blind prophet, the Chorus-singers do not support it. Though they have a strong admiration for the king yet they are more devoted to the gods and as a result, they alienate themselves from the king when they find him disbelieving the divine oracles. Whenever there is a quarrel, the Chorus tries to pacify the parties with reasonable arguments.

The Chorus and the messenger report the events that take place after the fatal self-identity has been revealed to king Oedipus. Violent scenes are, like the Sanskrit plays, proscribed in the Greek plays. They are therefore merely reported. The fifth *episode* of the play begins with a conversation between a messenger and the Chorus. The messenger reports the manner in which the wretched mother-wife, Jocasta has hanged herself and how the cursed Oedipus has blinded himself by the Golden clasp of of his queen's robe. After this reporting, the playwright presents Oedipus on the stage in the described form. This scene is just like the Viṣkambhaka of a Sanskrit play.

The use of messenger is also found in the play for the purpose of such reporting. The messenger already mentioned is an example. Another example is the presentation of the messenger from the Corinth. It is he who reveals the startling truth that Oedipus is no kin of Polybus, the supposed father of Oedipus and the king of Corinth. In the course of his conversation he reveals the manner how Oedipus reached the royal house of Corinth and was brought up there as the son of Polybus. (3rd Episode, lines 1010-1050)

The third means by which the playwright reveals the past happenings is the conversation of the chief characters. The conversation between Oedipus and Jocasta that follows the quarrel of Oedipus and Creon, brings to light the exact manner and place of the murder of the former king, Laius. The account of the murder given by Jocasta speaks of a host that killed the king in a place where three paths met. This startles Oedipus as he remembers himself committing such a murder at such a place. He becomes apprehensive as to the prophecy of Tieresias, the blind prophet. He finds a single ray of hope and wishes to ascertain the veracity of the account by summoning the only surviving eye-witness of the murder. The account says that the king was murdered by a host but Oedipus knows that he killed his victim all alone. So he says—

"If the same number still
He shall report, it was not I who slew him
One man is not mistaken for a host
But let him speak of one sole traveller
That turns the scale; plainly the deed was mine."
(2nd Episode, lines 771-860)

The Indian way

In contradistinction with the Greek way, Sanskrit theorists have conceived the Arthopakṣepakas of five kinds to serve the aforementioned purpose. We find, accordingly a Viṣkambhaka in the beginning of the play, Ūrubhaṅga. The Sūtradhāra introduces the soldiers and retires. These soldiers converse with one another and unfold the exact situation of the battle. The fight being unpresentable, these characters give a vivid description how the fight goes on between Duryodhana and Bhīma. They look at the wing and visualise the duel fight of the two heroes and acquaint the audience with it. These three soldiers supply us with the following pieces of information—the war has reached its final stage and all around the battle field the corpses of the warrriors are strewn; the entire battle field appears to be a deadly place; a great annihilation is to be seen all around; a duel fight between Duryodhana and Bhīma has begun in the presence of the few survivors of both the parties—Vyāsa the sage, Baladeva, Kṛṣṇa, Vidura, etc. In this duel, Bhīma proves weaker than Duryodhana and is about to be defeated and Kṛṣṇa, apprehensive of the defeat of the Pāṇḍavas, suggests something to Bhīma by striking at his own thighs. Consequently Bhīma rises up and strikes the king on his thighs violating the rules of the fight. At this attack, Duryodhana falls down with his thighs broken. At this treachery of Bhīma, Baladeva, the preceptor of Duryodhana, gets enraged and leaves the place boiling with anger. The soldiers disperse at seeing Baladeva coming towards them. The Viṣkambhaka thus ends introducing the angry Baladeva.

Conclusion

Having discussed both the methods, it is now easy to judge the merit of the two. So far as the reporting is concerned both the methods serve their purpose. It is in the manner of reporting that we are to find out merits and limitations. The reporting through the Chorus is more or less prosaic, sometimes tending to dullness. The Chorus-songs take the crude form of mere narration, when the Chorus soliloquises. Their impersonal and indifferent attitude also appears to be undramatic. With the very appearance of the Chorus the audience turns ready to listen to some philosophising or exposition of the dramatic theme. As a result, the sense of 'surprise and shock, that is considered to be the key-note of the dramatic event, gets impaired. Mere narration can be quite permissible and justified if the piece is a fiction or a tale. In a drama, narration should also come through some exhibitory means. Aristotle has rightly objected to the narrative element in the drama but we find plain narration in the speeches of the Chorus. The peculiar omniscient character of the Chorus also is an impediment which hampers the free development of the play. Though the Chorus is always present before the audience, the members of it are supposed to know everything taking place off the stage. The poetic element of the choral songs has been highly spoken of. Admitting this view unreservedly, one must hold that the role of the Chorus is undramatic.

The technique of reporting past events by the chief characters also suffers from great limitations. Such reports make the speech unnecessarily lengthy and thereby hamper the quick progress of the action. The report how and why Oedipus fled from Corinth and killed Laius covers 62 lines (2nd Episode, lines 770–833). Lengthy speeches are never considered as a merit of any drama.

In short, the Chorus is a very weak technique of expressing past events and it is the more awkward in such cases where the playwright unfolds the significance or the moral of the play through it. For example, the last speech of the Chorus in Oedipus the King, is void of all dramatic qualities. The didactic tales like those of the Hitopadeśa or the Aesop's Fables may have such moral teaching as their aim but in perfect literary creations such didactic teachings cannot be welcomed. The relation between Ethics and Aesthetics is a highly disputed topic, still all the literary critics are unanimous on the point that in Aesthetic creations, Ethics should be subservient to the former. No statement is required to prove the fact that the end of life proves its fruition and the playwright should have depended solely upon his dramatisation to instil the truth of what he explicitly says through the Chorus.

In comparison, the Sanskrit method is much more charming and full of novelties. The Viṣkambhaka used in the Ūrubhaṅga is remarkably brief and by introducing only three soldiers, the playwright gives a very vivid description of the desolate battle field and the fight between the two heroes. The clever hint of Kṛṣṇa and the wrath of Baladeva are also brought to light by this short Viṣkambhaka.

There are other methods too. These are elaborately discussed in the Chapter on the Arthopakṣepakas.[3] That the Sanskrit theorists on dramaturgy were keenly conscious of the sense of dramatic unity and charm, is evident from another technique—that of reporting things that are happening simultaneously, known as *ākāśabhāṣita*. This technique is used when something is to be reported to the audience by a single character. This character looks at the sky and talks in such a manner to an imaginary person that the audience becomes aware of the facts. This technique is adopted to suit stage-conveniences.

The chief merit of all these Explanatory Devices is their brevity. No chief characters are used in such scenes

3. See above, p. 42.

and through the conversation of such common characters as are closely connected with the chief characters, these necessary pieces of information are supplied. This technique, as it is proved, is definitely superior in charm and facility to the Greek one.

The division into Acts—The Indian way

All the Sanskrit plays are divided into Acts. The division is based upon the various Stages of Action. A full dramatic action consists of five stage—the Beginning, Efforts, Prospect of Success, Conditional Success and Attainment of the Result. These five stages, it should be observed, are present in every activity. It is the observation of the practical life that has led the Sanskrit theorists to recognise the five Stages of the Action and as the development of the full dramatic action depends upon these five stages they thought of five Acts in a drama.

The Greek way

As a remarkable contrast there is nothing as an Act in the Greek drama. The different stages are marked, it may be said, by the choral songs called *stasimons*. These *stasimons* separate one *episode* from the other and thus divides the entire play into many sections. Oedipus the King of Sophocles has got five *stasimons* and thus the play is divided into six sections. All the sections are related to one another and are interdependent in nature.

The six sections of Oedipus the King

In the Oedipus, the first section i. e. the *prologos*, bares before the audience the situation of Thebes and the deep concern with which the hero wishes to find out a way of solution. Creon, sent by Oedipus to the Delphian shrine, returns with the message of the God that the murder of the former king must be avenged and the criminal banished. This section marks the beginning of the action.

The second section, introduced by the Chorus, shows the action in its second stage, the Effort, according to the Sanskrit theorists. This first *episode* presents the hero in a state of mental restlessness eager to find out the murderer. He asks all, and then calls for the blind prophet, Teiresias who, peculiarly enough, wishes to avoid the answer first but being enkindled by the taunting remarks of Oedipus, gives out at last that Oedipus himself is responsible for the woes of the city—"Thou art unclean; for thee we are accursed" (lines 350-51). This news renders Oedipus the more restless and he begins to suspect a foul conspiracy against him with Creon at its head.

The third section, that is the second *episode*, shows the quarrel between Oedipus and Creon. Oedipus is fully confident as to his innocence, and denounces Creon strongly. Just at the time when their quarrel reaches its height, Jocasta the queen appears and appeases Oedipus who as a result, leaves Creon in peace. Coming to know the cause of the strife, Jocasta tries to prove the falsity of the prophecies by recounting the story of Laius's death. This story strikes hard at the self-confidence of Oedipus as he remembers to have killed one exactly at the place where Laius is said to have been murdered. In a frenzy he relates his own life and entreats his queen to send for the only surviving eye-witness of the murder. This section thus shows the action at its climax.

The same heightened emotional condition continues in the fourth section i.e. the third *episode*. Herein, we find a messenger from Corinth, who brings the news of the death of the Corinthian king. This news gladdens Jocasta as the death proves false the prophecy that Oedipus will kill his own father, the king of Corinth. She calls Oedipus who, hearing the story of the death of his father from the messenger, is no doubt pleased but denies to go to Corinth according to the prayer of the messenger, fearing the other prophecy that he will marry his own mother. The messenger then reveals the most fatal truth that Oedipus is no kin to the Corinthian king and queen, and that he was carried to the royal house by the messenger himself. The manner in which he received the baby Oedipus being related, Jocasta leaves the place and asks Oedipus not to delve any more into the matter. But Oedipus, though embarassed at all these revelations, determines to have the whole truth and waits for the arrival of the shepherd, the only eye-witness.

The fifth section i e. the fourth *episode* brings about the catastrophe. The old servant comes and at the repeated request of Oedipus narrates the story of Oedipus's childhood and how he was carried away by him and handed over to the Corinthian messenger. This revelation upsets Oedipus completely and he retires with the fatal realisation—

"Out and alas ! so all at last comes true !
Here let me look my last upon the Sun,
That sees father'd, mother'd, wived amiss,
And, whom I should not, sees that I have slain."
(lines 1182-85)

The sixth section i. e. the *exodos* reveals the tragic suicide of Jocasta and it brings before the audience the blood stained Oedipus who has rendered himself blind.

On the pathetic disaster that has befallen Oedipus, the Chorus philosophises and expresses the moral that a man can be judged as really happy who is allowed by the Fate to end his life in peace. The action of the drama, stirred by the cruel Fate against Oedipus, reaches its consummation here and fittingly the play ends. Thus in the Greek drama, the action is depicted in a graded scheme of development though the Acts are absent.

The Ūrubhaṅga

The Ūrubhaṅga is a one-Act play, so no question of Acts arises. But the Stages of Action are fully depicted. As has been said already, the action of the play starts with the entry of Baladeva, The king Duryodhana is next presented in his wounded condition. His thighs are broken by Bhīma in violation of the rules and regulations of the battle. Though Duryodhana never cared in his life for any such consideration as to whether his own attacks on the Pāṇḍavas were righteous or not, he accuses Bhīma for his unrighteous blow on his thighs. The lonely Duryodhana, completely subdued, now realises the truth that he is to reap the fruits of his own misdeeds. He can think no more of fighting. The final defeat works in his life a tragic reversal and he wishes, at this stage, the prosperity of the Pāṇḍavas. The first phase of his attitude towards the Pāṇḍavas is shown clearly in his conversation with Baladeva. Baladeva wishes to avenge the wrong done to Duryodhana but it is Duryodhana, the avowed enemy of the Pāṇḍavas, who pacifies him. This attitude indicates the thorough change in the outlook of Duryodhana.

The second incident is the meeting of Duryodhana with his parents. In the short conversation that follows, Duryodhana receives their blessings and expresses the desire to be born again as their worthy son. His pathetic attempt to prove himself right and victorious even at the point of death is really tragic.

The third thing, which reveals how he is affected by the final defeat at the hands of Bhīma, is the consolation which he gives to his two wives. He consoles them by pointing out the glory of a Kṣatriya's death. As a dignified and honourable warrior he has never taken to his heels and he wishes that his wives should recognise that and cease to mourn for him,

The next phase of his life is more pathetic than the former one. He accosts his child, Durjaya and advises him to follow the Pāṇḍavas as affectionately as Durjaya did his father. (*Aham iva Pāṇḍavāḥ śuśrūṣayitavyāḥ*) His advice to follow and revere his greatest enemies is a clear denunciation of his own past. He finds none other save Yudhiṣṭhira who may give shelter to his dear son.

The meeting with Aśvatthāman completes the picture of his tragic change. Aśvatthāman was ever a close associate of Duryodhana and when he meets the king he is greatly moved to see him in that plight. At the question of Aśvatthāman—'*Bhoḥ Kururāja ! Kim idam ?*' (O king of the Kurus ! What is this ?), the answer of Duryodhana is remarkable. He says—"Guruputra ! *Phalam aparitoṣasya*" (O Son of the preceptor ! it is the result of my discontent). In this statement Duryodhana admits the complete futility of his former activities. The changed Duryodhana appears clean in his attempt to dissuade Aśvatthāman from his proposed ambition of killing all the Pāṇḍavas. Duryodhana has, it seems suddenly changed to be a very considerate and righteous man who wishes to forget and forgive and to desist from all violence. Not only this, but at the taunting remark of Aśvatthāman that Duryodhana has lost simultaneously his thighs and his pride, he weighs impartially all the wrongs done to the Pāṇḍavas by him and says that the wrongs done by them are far less in comparison. Aśvatthāman is not pacified at these consoling remarks of Duryodhana. He pledges to kill all the Pāṇḍavas in a 'night-war' (*niśā-samara*) and blesses Durjaya, the son of Duryodhana, as the next king of the Kurus. This announcement, however, pleases the dying king and he feels the approach of death and succumbs to it.

Conclusion

The absence of Acts in the Greek drama imposes a few limitations. The first thing is the presence of the Chorus which has already been discussed. The other difficulty is based on the *unity of time*. The Acts in the Sanskrit plays present such incidents as happen in a single day. Thus the number of the Acts tallies with the number of the days required for the dramatic incidents. The passage of time is indicated by the Explanatory Devices. Thus the time-factor in a Sanskrit drama never reaches the point of incredulity. But in the Greek drama the constant presence of the same Chorus throughout the play gives rise to a sense of discrepancy. Even when two Episodes occur in different times and places, the presence of the Chorus impairs the *unity of time and place*. Such a discrepancy can never occur in a Sanskrit play. Moreover, true soliloquies are not possible in a Greek drama due to the constant presence of the Chorus. So many functions entrusted to the Chorus render it undramatic and highly mechanical.

The Nirvahaṇa

The Nirvahaṇa of a Sanskrit play is characteristically different from that of a Greek drama. In the play Oedipus, the Nirvahaṇa or the Conclusion depends not upon the hero so much as upon the Chorus. It is the Chorus which voices the Conclusion in Oedipus. Whereas the Conclusion in a Sanskrit play is brought in by the main agent of the action. It is Duryodhana who realises the end of his life and makes a revaluation, arousing thereby the sympathy of the audience.

The Characterisation and Dialogue

The characterisation and dialogue of these two plays are exceptionally wonderful. Admitting all the limitations mentioned above, the Greek playwright, Sophocles successfully presents the character of his hero in very bright colours. As we find no such serious deficiency in Oedipus for which his tragic reversal of fortune and utter ruin may be justified, the play has been classed as a tragedy of Fate. The greatest proof of Sophocles's success is the fact that Oedipus the king is still now hailed as the best specimen of the type.

Duryodhana also is presented as a great tragic character, who having lost everything near and dear to him, realises the truth that his selfish ways were all wrong and misdirected. His calm but dignified submission to his fate makes his character impressive for all times.

The Rasa

Herein, in the attitude towards life, the Greek and Sanskrit dramatists are keenly contrasted. A sense of completion may be said to be the key-note of all the Indian plays. Whether the hero is romantic and despotic and intolerant in nature, his life is presented in its entirety. Though there is downfall in the life of Duryodhana, he has to blame none but himself. The intrinsic worth of human life is accepted and Fate is not made responsible for the catastrophe that the hero meets with. Thus the pathos has become the Karuṇa Rasa and not merely a cause of grief.

But in the Oedipus the king, we find human power to be meaningless against the onslaughts of Fate. As a just and valiant ruler, Oedipus has nothing in him repulsive that may be responsible for the dire consequences that he has to face. He is not an immoral man and he, like a just ruler, is keenly alive to the question of the welfare of his subjects. Still he faces downfall and he finds none to blame but the designs of the gods. This submission to the Fate has got in it the elements of hopelessness and helplessness of man. The presentation of man as a mere plaything in the hands of cruel Fate can never fully satisfy human beings.

Conclusion

Thus it can be said, that the Sanskrit plays are superior to the Greek in point of technique, realism and in the fulness of their appeal. So far as the questions of depth and sublimity are concerned, both are remarkable in their own spheres.

APPENDIX 'A'

Tamil and Sanskrit Drama

The sub-continent of India can broadly be divided into two main linguistic divisions. Without going into the intricacies of the subtle linguistic divisions, we may say that two language groups dominate the entire Indian peninsula. One is the Aryan group or the Sanskrit which rules over the entire Northern India including some parts of South India as well and the other is the Dravidian group which rules over almost entire Southern part of the country. In other words, Sanskrit has got a strong rival in the languages of the South. Of all the languages of the Dravidian group, Tamil is the oldest and as such it will be enormously interesting to note the interaction of these two languages in the field of literature, particularly in drama. The object here is to study the art of dramaturgy prevalent in the Tamil literature and discuss the nature and structure of drama in that language in a comparative light.

The antiquity of Tamil literature dates back much beyond the beginning of the Christian era. According to Tamil literary tradition there were three Sangams or literary Academies, the last of which synchronised with the beginning of the Christian era. About the exact date of the first, nothing can be said definitely in the absence of regular historical data. Still the learned editor of the Śilappadikāram has examined the point in question elaborately and has assigned to all the Sangams approximate dates. He says—'Roughly speaking the Sangam epoch may be assigned to a period commencing with the fifth century B. C. and ending with the fourth century A. D.'[1]

1. V.R.R. Dikshitar, Śilappadikāram, Introduction, p. 8.

The Sangam, as the name itself suggests, was an assemblage of the scholars, the chief function of which was to judge the literary output of the time. Under the patronage of the Southern kings (Pāṇḍya, Cela, Cora), these Academies flourished and passed critical judgments on the works of about five thousand poets.[2] As a result of so many deluges that swept over the vast Tamil country, few of these works have survived to this day, though references to these are found in almost all the post-Sangam works.

"Tamil literature falls into three great divisions: Iyal (poetry), Isai (music) and Nāṭakam (drama). The second and third sections have no representative works extant after the two great deluges, though their names have survived them. Isai Nurukkam, Perunarai, Perum kuruku, Indra-kaliyam, Pancha-marapu, etc. were on Isai. While Muruval, Sayantham, Seyittyam, Gunanool, Mathivanam, etc. treat of Nāṭakam." This is the general account furnished by M. S. Puranalingam Pillai.[3] Unfortunately, no specimen of the Nāṭakam is extant and hence to form an adequate idea regarding the conception, construction and varieties of this type of literature is difficult and one has to rely upon the references to these found in books like Śilappadikāram, Ṭholkappiyam and the commentaries thereon.

Ṭholkappiyam is the oldest treatise that has survived the ravages of time. 'It is the oldest extant Tamil Grammar', the name signifying ancient book or the preserver of ancient institutions. The object of this treatise is to treat of the first variety of Tamil literature, namely

2. Vide Tamil Literature, M. S. Puranalingam Pillai.

3. Vide Ibid. p. 2.

Iyal or natural Tamil. The three sections of this book deal with systematically and successively the three important topics of Orthography, Etymology and Matter (Eluthu, Sol and Poruḷ).

Though this treatise of the first century A. D. has got no direct bearing upon the drama as such yet in its treatment of matter or the subject for literary compositions, there are indications which prove the existence of a number of dramatic works as well.

From this it can safely be said that the forms and definitions of drama must have crystallised by the second or third century A. D., if not earlier. This view is held by V. G. Suryanarayana Shastri.

The ancient Tamil classics viz: Śilappadikāram (2nd century), Manimekalai, etc. also abound in many references to drama. Śilappadikāram a Sangam Mahākāvya of great fame and antiquity speaks of the existence of drama. There is a description of the stage whereon dances used to take place.[4] These and such other references lead us unmistakably to form the idea that there was a well-developed branch of dramatic literature.

On the ground of these scattered references, Suryanarayana Shastri has given a survey of the Nāṭakam branch of literature in his treatise on dramaturgy, the Naṭakaviyāl. A great authority as he is, his views may be taken into account for our purpose.

According to him, the drama must have originated from the singing and dancing performed by the artists on the occasion of religious festivals. In the epic, Manimekalai (the poet of which was a contemporary of Ilango

4. Vide, Śilappadikāram, p. 101-2.

Adigal, the poet of Śilappadikāram), there are found casual references to two types of dramatic literature—one meant for the royal court and the other for the commoners. Again, Adyar Kunallar, the commentator of Śilappadikāram mentions a number of Nāṭakas and works on Nāṭaka. The names, Muruval, Sayantham, Seyittyam are mentioned as dramas. These must have been known to the commentator who belonged to circa 11th century A. D. The same commentator further mentions a number of other treatises which, though have got no direct bearing upon the drama, have some connection with it. The authors of these treatises belonged, according to the commentator, to the time of the second Sangam (circa 100 B. C. to 100 A. D.).

The commentaries on Śilappadikāram are very important to form an idea of the condition of drama in the Tamil language. The commentary on the Poruḷ Adhikaram of Ṭholkappiyam by Nacchinarkinyyar is also of great importance.[5]

The gradual development of the Tamil drama was impeded by the Jaina and Bauddha influence. The age of Buddhists and Jains had its beginning near about the first Christian era and it assumed more and more importance in a quick measure. So much so that this age marked the extinction of drama in Tamil and ushered in the dark age particularly for drama, which lasted upto the 18th century A. D.

Due to paucity of materials the typically native Tamil drama cannot be found. The modern form is a product of a resurgence which began in the 18th century.

---

5. Vide, Nāṭakaviyāl, Introduction, V.G. Suryanarayan Shāstri.

This new form is so greatly influenced by the Sanskrit and also Western dramaturgy that it does not help us in forming an idea about the technique of original Tamil drama.

In the absence of sufficient material, it is hard to determine how much influence Sanskrit exercised over the Tamil conception of drama and dramaturgy. But one fact is significant. The three branches of literature in Tamil are known as Iyal, Isai and Nāṭakam. Of these the first two, Iyal and Isai mean respectively the Tamil lyric or literary Tamil and Music. The two words, Iyal and Isai are native and as such we can hold that the development of these two branches must have been from purely Tamil traditions. But the third branch is named Nāṭakam and the very name suggests that it was influenced by the Sanskrit from the very beginning. From this it does not seem unplausible that drama in Tamil originated and developed under the direct influence of Sanskrit dramaturgy.

The Sanskrit Prastāvanā

It has been severally observed in the main body of the thesis that the Prastāvanās of the Sanskrit plays bear clear indications whether the play belongs to the creative period of Sanskrit drama or to the decadent period. Prastāvanā, being a preamble to the main play, should be as brief as possible and should be devoted only to introduce the main action as artistically as can be done. With the setting in of degeneration in the field of drama, the Pratāvanās began to be treated as a means of introducing not the dramatic action but the dramatist in a self-laudatory manner, rendering the technique prosaic and meaningless. The later Prastāvanās, as a result, are unnecessarily lengthy, serving almost no purpose. The difference between the Prastāvanās of the two periods is shown below from three representative plays. The first two are of Bhāsa's and Kālidāsa's, showing the Prastāvanā in its brightest form and the last one is of Murāri, showing it at its worst.

A. Bhāsa : Svapnavāsavadatta

सूत्रधारः —उदयनवेन्दुसवर्णावासवदत्ताबलौ बलस्य त्वाम् ।
पद्मावतीर्णपूर्णौ वसन्तकम्रौ भुजौ पाताम् ॥

एवमार्यमिश्रान् विज्ञापयामि । अये, किं नु खलु मयि विज्ञापनव्यग्रे शब्द इव श्रूयते ? अङ्ग पश्यामि ।

(नेपथ्ये) उस्सरह उस्सरह अय्या उस्सरह ।

सूत्रधारः —भवतु विज्ञातम् ।

भृत्यैर्मगधराजस्य स्निग्धैः कन्यानुगामिभिः ।
धृष्टमुत्सार्यते सर्वस्तपोवनगतो जनः ॥ (निष्क्रान्तः)

B. Kālidāsa : Abhijñāna Śākuntala

सूत्रधारः —या सृष्टिः स्रष्टुराद्या वहति विधिहुतं या हविर्या च होत्री
ये द्वे कालं विधत्तः श्रुतिविषयगुणा या स्थिता व्याप्य विश्वम् ।
यामाहुः सर्वबीजप्रकृतिरिति यया प्राणिनः प्राणवन्तः
प्रत्यक्षाभिः प्रपन्नस्तनुभिरवतु वस्ताभिरष्टाभिरीशः ॥

अलमतिविस्तरेण । (नेपथ्याभिमुखमवलोक्य) आर्ये यदि नेपथ्यविधानमवसितं तदिहागम्यताम् ।

नटी —(प्रविश्य) अज्ज इअम्हि । आणवेदु अज्जो को णिओओ अणुचिट्ठीअदुत्ति ।

सूत्रधारः —आर्ये, इयं हि रसभावविशेषदीक्षागुरोर्विक्रमादित्यस्याभिरूपभूयिष्ठा परिषद्, अस्यां च कालिदासग्रथितवस्तुना नवेनाभिज्ञानशाकुन्तलनामधेयेन नाटकेनोपस्थातव्यमस्माभिः । तत्प्रतिपात्रमाधीयतां यत्नः ।

नटी —सुविहिदप्पओअदाए अज्जस्स ण किंपि परिहाइस्सदि ।

सूत्रधारः —(सस्मितम्) आर्ये, कथयामि ते भूतार्थम्—

आ परितोषाद् विदुषां साधु न मन्ये प्रयोगविज्ञानम् ।
बलवदपि शिक्षितानामात्मन्यप्रत्ययं चेतः ॥

नटी —(सविनयम्) एवं णेदम् । अणन्तरकरणिज्जं दाणीं अज्जो आणवेदु ।

सूत्रधारः —आर्ये, किमन्यदस्याः परिषदः श्रुतिप्रमोदहेतोर्गीतात् करणीयमस्ति ।

नटी —अध कदमं उण उदुं अधिकरिअ गाइस्सम् ।

सूत्रधारः —आर्ये, नन्विममेव तावदचिरप्रवृत्तमुपभोगक्षमं ग्रीष्मसमयमधिकृत्य गीयताम् । संप्रति हि—

सुभगसलिलावगाहाः पाटलसंसर्गसुरभिवनवाताः ।
प्रच्छायसुलभनिद्रा दिवसाः परिणामरमणीयाः ॥

नटी —तह । (इति गायति)—

ईसीसिचुम्बिआइं भमरेहिं सुउमारकेसरसिहाइं ।
ओदंसयन्ति दअमाणा पमदाओ सिरीसकुसुमाइं ॥

सूत्रधारः —आर्ये, साधु गीतम् । अहो रागापहृतचित्तवृत्तिरालिखित इव विभाति सर्वतो रङ्गः ! तदिदानीं कतमं प्रयोगमाश्रित्यैनमाराधयामः ?

नटी —णं पढमं ज्जेव अज्जेण आणत्तं अहिण्णाणसाउन्दलं णाम अपुब्बं णाडअं अहिणिअदुत्ति ।

सूत्रधारः —आर्ये, सम्यगनुबोधितोऽस्मि । अस्मिन् क्षणे खलु विस्मृतं मयैतत् । कुतः—

तवास्मि गीतरागेण हारिणा प्रसभं हृतः ।
एष राजेव दुष्यन्तः सारङ्गेणातिरंहसा ॥ (इति निष्क्रान्तौ)

———

C. Murāri : Anargharāghava

सूत्रधारः — निष्प्रत्यूहमुपास्महे भगवतः कौमोदकीलक्ष्मणः
कोकप्रीतिचकोरपारणपटुज्योतिष्मती लोचने ।
याभ्यामर्धविबोधमुग्धमधुरश्रीरर्धनिद्रायितो
नाभीपल्वलपुण्डरीकमुकुलः कम्बोः सपत्नीकृतः ॥

अपिच,

विरमति महाकल्पे नाभीपथैकनिकेतन-
स्त्रिभुवनपुरः शिल्पी यस्य प्रतिक्षणमात्मभूः ।
किमधिकरणा कीदृक् कस्य व्यवस्थितिरित्यसा-
वुदरमविशद् द्रष्टुं तस्मै जगन्निधये नमः ॥

अलमतिविस्तरेण । भो भो लवणोदवेलावनालीतमालतरुकन्दलस्य त्रिभुवनमौलिमण्डनमहानीलमणेः कमलाकुचकलसकेलिकस्तूरिकापत्राङ्कुरस्य भगवतः पुरुषोत्तमस्य यात्रायामुपस्थानीयाः सभासदः ! कुतश्चिद् द्वीपादागतेन कलहकन्दलनाम्ना कुशीलवेन रौद्रबीभत्सभयानकाद्भुतरसभूयिष्ठं कमपि प्रबन्धमभिनयता नित्यं किलायमुद्वेजितो लोकः । तत् कस्यचिदभिमतरसभावभाजः प्रेक्षणकस्य प्रयोगानुज्ञया नाट्यवेदोपाध्यायब्रह्मरूपान्तेवासी मध्यदेशीयः सुचरितो नाम भरतपुत्रोऽहमनुगृह्ये । यतः —

प्रीतिर्नाम सदस्यानां प्रिया रङ्गोपजीविनः ।
जित्वा तदपहर्तारमेष प्रत्याहरामि ताम् ॥

(आकाशे कर्णं दत्त्वा) किं ब्रूथ—'वैदेशिको भवानसमग्रपात्रः कथमीदृशो कर्मणि प्रगल्भते' इति ? (विहस्य सप्रश्रयमञ्जलिं बद्ध्वा) हन्त

भोः, किमेवमुदीर्यंते। भवद्विधानामाराधनी वृत्तिरेव मे पात्राणि समग्रयिष्यति। यतः—

यान्ति न्यायप्रवृत्तस्य तिर्यञ्चोऽपि सहायताम्।
अपन्थानं तु गच्छन्तं सोदरोऽपि विमुञ्चति॥

(पुनराकाशे कर्णं दत्त्वा) किं ब्रूथ? 'तर्हि प्रहितेयमस्माभिः पत्रिका' इति?

(प्रविश्य नटः पत्रिकां ददाति। सूत्रधारो गृहीत्वा वाचयति)

"यत्र सर्वंषुरुषार्थं रहस्यनिःस्यन्दिनि—

चेतःशुक्तिकया निपीय शतशः शास्त्रामृतानि क्रमाद्
वान्तैरक्षरमूर्तिभिः सुकविना मुक्ताफलैर्गुम्फिताः।
उन्मीलत्कमनीयनायकगुणग्रामोपसंवल्गन-
प्रौढाहङ्कृतयो लुठन्ति सुहृदां कण्ठेषु हारस्रजः॥
तस्मै वीराद्भुतारम्भगम्भीरोदात्तवस्तवे।
जगदानन्दकन्दाय संदर्भाय त्वरामहे॥"

(विमृश्य सहर्षस्मितम्) मारिष, रामायणमिति शृणोषि तत्रभवतः कवित्वावतारप्रथमतीर्थस्य वल्मीकजन्मनो मुनेः सरस्वतीनिर्यासो यशःशरीरमिक्ष्वाकूणाम्।

नटः—अथ किम्।

सूत्रधारः—तत्प्रतिबद्धप्रबन्धानुबन्धिनी परिषदाज्ञा।

नटः—(विहस्य) अहो सकलकविसार्थसाधारणी खल्वियं वाल्मीकीया सुभाषितनीवी।

सूत्रधारः—मारिष, किमुच्यते—

अपि कथमसौ रक्षोराजस्तताप जगत्त्रयी-
मपि कथमभूदिक्ष्वाकूणां कुले गरुडध्वजः।
अपि कथमृषौ दैव्यो वाचः स्वतः प्रचकाशिरे
सुचरितपरीपाकः सर्वः प्रबन्धकृतामयम्॥

तत्र तावन्निरूपयामि रूपकमभिरूपमीदृशम्। (मुहूर्तमिव स्थित्वा स्मरणमभिनीय सोल्लासम्) अस्ति मौद्गल्यगोत्रसंभवस्य महाकवेर्भट्टश्रीवर्धमानतनूजन्मनस्तन्तुमतीनन्दनस्य मुरारेः कृतिरभिनवमनर्घराघवं नाम नाटकम्। तत्प्रयुञ्जानाः सामाजिकानुपास्महे। (विचिन्त्य सहर्षम्) अहो रमणीया खल्वियं सामग्री परिषदाराधनस्य यतः—

मद्वर्ग्या रसपाठगीतिगतिषु प्रत्येकमुत्कर्षिणो
मौद्गल्यस्य कवेर्गभीरमधुरोद्गारा गिरां व्यूतयः ।
वीरोदात्तगुणोत्तरो रघुपतिः काव्यार्थबीजं मुनि-
र्वाल्मीकिः फलति स्म यस्य चरितस्तोत्राय दिव्या गिरः ॥

अयं तु प्राचेतसीयं कथावस्तु बहुभिः प्रणीतमपि प्रयुञ्जानो नापराध्यति श्रोत्रियपुत्रः । पश्य—

यदि क्षुण्णं पूर्वैरिति जहति रामस्य चरितं
गुणैरेतावद्भिर्जगति पुनरन्यो जयति कः ।
स्वमात्मानं तत्तद्गुणगरिमगम्भीरमधुर-
स्फुरद्वाग्ब्रह्माणः कथमुपकरिष्यन्ति कवयः ॥

उपक्रममाणश्च स कविः स्वनिर्भासशब्दब्रह्माणमाचार्यं प्राचेतसं गिरं च देवतामेवमुपश्लोकितवान्—

तमृषिं मनुष्यलोकप्रवेशविश्रामशाखिनं वाचाम् ।
सुरलोकादवतारप्रान्तरखेदच्छिदं वन्दे ॥
धातुश्चतुर्मुखीकण्ठशृङ्गाटकविहारिणीम् ।
नित्यं प्रगल्भवाचालामुपतिष्ठे सरस्वतीम् ॥

नटः —(सहर्षम्) भाव, तत्प्रस्तूयताम् । अस्य हि मौद्गल्यानां ब्रह्मर्षीणामन्वयमूर्धन्यस्य मुरारिनामधेयस्य बालवाल्मीकेर्वाङ्मयममृतबिन्दुनिष्यन्दि कन्दलयति कौतुकं मे ।

सूत्रधारः —मारिष, स्थाने भवतः कुतूहलम् । ईदृशमेवैतत् । तथाहि—

तत्तादृगुज्ज्वलककुत्स्थकुलप्रशस्तिसौरम्यनिर्भरगभीरमनोहराणि ।
वाल्मीकिवागमृतकूपनिपानलक्ष्मीमेतानि बिभ्रति मुरारिकवेर्वचांसि ॥

(नेपथ्ये गीयते)

दिणअरकिरणुक्केरो पिआअरो कोऽवि जीअलोअस्स ।
कमलमउलकवालीकिअमहुअरकढ्ढणबिअड्ढो ॥

सूत्रधारः —(आकर्ण्य) कथमुपक्रान्तमेव नर्तकैः, यदियं दशरथोत्सङ्गाद्रामभद्राकर्षिणो विश्वामित्रस्य प्रावेशिकी ध्रुवा । अये, कथमत्रैव तत्रभवतः कमलयोनिजन्मनो मुनेरायतनात् प्रतिनिवृत्तेन ऋत्विजा वामदेवेन किमपि तद्वात्निकमभिधोयमानो महाराजो दशरथस्तिष्ठति । तदेहि, न द्वयोस्तृतीयेन भवितव्यमित्यावामप्यनन्तरकरणीयाय सज्जीभवावः । (इति निष्क्रान्तौ)

—

ENGLISH EQUIVALENTS

अङ्क	Act
अङ्कास्य	Anticipatory Scene
अङ्कावतार	Continuation Scene
अद्भुत	Marvellous
अनुबन्ध	Secondary Juncture
अनुभाव	Consequents
अनुसंधि	Subjuncture
अपवारित	Confidence
अभ्यूह्य	Inferential
अर्थप्रकृति	Elements of the Plot
अर्थोपक्षेपक	Explanatory Device
अवतगित	Transference
आकाशवचन, भाषित	Speaking to the Sky
आधिकारिकवृत्त	Principal Subject
आरम्भ	Beginning
आलम्बन (विभाव)	Fundamental
इतिवृत्त	Theme, Plot
उत्पाद्य (वृत्त)	Invented
उत्साह	Energy
उद्घात्यक	Accidental Interpretation
उद्दीपन (विभाव)	Excitant
उपेक्ष्य	Negligible
करुण	Pathetic
कथोद्घात	Opening of the Story
कार्य	Denouement
कार्य-अवस्था	Stage of the Action
क्रोध	Anger
गर्भ (संधि)	Development
चूलिका	Intimating Speech
जनान्तिक	Personal Address
जुगुप्सा	Disgust
दृश्य-श्रव्य (वृत्त)	Presentable
धीरललित	Light-hearted
धीरशान्त	Calm
धीरोदात्त	Exalted
धीरोद्धत	Vehement
नाट्यधर्मी	Conventional Practice
नान्दी	Benediction
नायक	Hero
नियताप्ति	Conditional Success
निर्वहण	Conclusion
निर्वेद, शम	Renunciation
पताका	Episode
पताकास्थानक	Episode-Indication
प्रकरी	Episodical Incident
प्रख्यात (वृत्त)	Legendary
प्रतिमुख (संधि)	Progression
प्रयत्न	Effort
प्रयोगातिशय	Particular Presentation
प्रवृत्तक, प्रवर्तक	Entrance of a character

प्रवेशक	Introductory Scene	विमर्श	Pause
प्रस्तावना	Introduction	विष्कम्भक	Explanatory Scene
प्राप्त्याशा	Prospect of Success	विस्मय	Astonishment
प्रासङ्गिक वृत्त	Incidental Subject	वीर	Heroic
पूर्वरङ्ग	Preliminaries	वृत्त	Plot, Subject
फलागम	Attainment of the Result	वृत्ति	Style of Procedure
		शान्त	Quietistic
बिन्दु	Prominent Point	शोक	Sorrow
बीज	Germ	शृङ्गार	Erotic
बीभत्स	Odious	संधि	Juncture
भय	Terror	संध्यन्तर	Special Juncture
भयानक	Terrible	सात्त्विक भाव	Temperamental State
मिश्र (वृत्त)	Mixed		
मुख (संधि)	Opening	सूच्य (वृत्त)	Indicatory
रस	Sentiment, Rasa	सूत्रधार	Stage-manager
रति	Love	स्थापक	Introducer
रौद्र	Furious	स्थायिभाव	Dominant Emotions
लोकधर्मी	Realistic Practice	स्वगत	Soliloquy
वस्तु	Theme, Plot	हास	Mirth
विभाव	Determinant	हास्य	Comic

GENERAL INDEX

L

M

N

O

P